Intellectual Property Regime Evolution in China and India

Social Sciences in Asia

Edited by

Vineeta Sinha
Syed Farid Alatas
Chan Kwok-bun

VOLUME 27

Intellectual Property Regime Evolution in China and India

Technological, Political and Social Drivers of Change

By

Paul C. Irwin Crookes

BRILL

LEIDEN • BOSTON
2010

This book is printed on acid-free paper.

Library of Congress Cataloging-in-Publication Data

Crookes, Paul Charles Irwin.
Intellectual property regime evolution in China and India : technological, political and social drivers of change / By Paul Charles Irwin Crookes.
p. cm.
Includes bibliographical references and index.
ISBN 978-90-04-17975-2 (pbk. : alk. paper)
1. Intellectual property—China. 2. Intellectual property—India. I. Title.

KNC370.C76 2010
346.5104'8—dc22

2009046270

ISSN 1567-2794
ISBN 978 90 04 17975 2

PRINTED IN THE NETHERLANDS

CONTENTS

ACKNOWLEDGEMENTS

I would like to thank John Forsyth at the Centre of International Studies, University of Cambridge, for his encouragement and guidance throughout the research process required to create a work of this kind. I am also very grateful to all of those who gave me their time and perspectives during my research.

Finally and most importantly, I would like to thank my wife, Haiyan, for her unstinting support, enthusiasm and warm good humour throughout an endeavour that can at times take its toll on normal family life. I dedicate this work to her.

LIST OF ABBREVIATIONS

BCS	British Computer Society
BPO	Business Process Outsourcing
BSA	Business Software Alliance
BSD	Berkeley Software Distribution
c. i. f.	Carriage, insurance and freight (trade valuation)
CASS	Chinese Academy of Social Sciences
CBI	Central Bureau of Investigation (India)
CCP	Chinese Communist Party
CEAC	Copyright Enforcement Advisory Council (India)
CII	Confederation of Indian Industry
CIS	Computer and Information Services Trade
CMM	Capability Maturity Model
CSI	Computer Society of India
CSIA	China Software Industry Association
DMCA	Digital Millennium Copyright Act (US)
EC	European Communities (especially within the WTO)
EPC	European Patent Convention
EPO	European Patent Office
ERM	Enterprise Resource Management
EU	European Union
f. a. s.	Freight alongside (trade valuation excluding loading costs etc.)
f. o. b.	Freight on board (trade valuation including loading costs etc.)
FDI	Foreign Direct Investment
FTA	Free Trade Agreement
GATS	General Agreement on Trade in Services
GATT	General Agreement on Tariffs and Trade
GPA	Government Procurement Agreement of the WTO
GPL	General Public License
ICANN	Internet Corporation for Assigned Names and Numbers
ICT	Information and Communication Technologies
IDC	International Data Group
IDMA	Indian Drug Manufacturers Association

IIPA	International Intellectual Property Alliance
IoD	Institute of Directors (UK)
IPA	Indian Pharmaceutical Alliance
ISI	Import Substitution Industrialisation
ISP	Internet Service Provider
ITA	Information Technology Agreement (of the WTO)
ITES	Information Technology Enabled Services
JPO	Japanese Patent Office
KMT	Kuomintang
KPO	Korean Patent Office
MFN	Most Favoured Nation trading status
MOST	Ministry of Science and Technology (China)
NASSCOM	National Association of Software Service Companies (India)
NCAC	National Copyright Administration of China
OECD	Organisation for Economic Cooperation and Development
OPPI	Organisation of Pharmaceutical Producers of India
OSDL	Open Software Development Labs
P. R. China	People's Republic of China
PCT	Patent Cooperation Treaty
PLT	Patent Law Treaty
RDBMS	Relational Database Management System
RMB	Renminbi (lit. People's Money—Chinese currency)
RoK	Republic of Korea (South Korea)
SAIC	State Administration for Industry and Commerce (China)
SCP	Standing Committee on the Law of Patents (WIPO)
SEZ	Special Economic Zone
SIPO	State Intellectual Property Office (China)
SME	Small and Medium Sized Enterprise
SPLT	Substantive Patent Law Treaty
STP	Software Technology Parks
TBR	Trade Barriers Regulation (EU)
TMO	Trade Mark Office (China)
TRIPS	Trade Related Aspects of Intellectual Property
UK	United Kingdom of Great Britain and Northern Ireland
UNCTAD	United Nations Conference on Trade and Development
UPOV	Union for the Protection of New Varieties of Plants

US	United States of America
USPTO	United States Patent and Trademark Office
USTR	United States Trade Representative
W3C	World Wide Web Consortium
WCT	WIPO Copyright Treaty
WFOE	Wholly Foreign Owned Enterprise (China)
WIPO	World Intellectual Property Organisation
WITSA	World Information Technology and Services Alliance
WPPT	WIPO Performances and Phonograms Treaty
WTO	World Trade Organisation
Y2K	Year 2000

CHAPTER ONE

INTRODUCTION

1.1 *Overview*

The economic and technological transformation of India and China provides a topic of interest for researchers across the world. The pace of change over recent years in both countries has been remarkable, propelling once little known company names such as China's Huawei Corporation and India's Wipro Technologies on to the global stage as multi-billion dollar businesses and creating heartlands of innovation in formally rustic outskirts of the cities of Suzhou, Hangzhou and Shenzhen in mainland China and Bangalore, Pune and Hyderabad on the Indian subcontinent.

It will be argued that these transformations are part of a multi-faceted dynamic that connects the economic objectives of a developing country's government actors with the commercial imperatives of its domestic knowledge industry innovators, both of which will be shown to have converged on the issue area of intellectual property (IP) as a function of achieving their objectives. It will be further argued that this convergence is a complex trajectory that demands closer analysis in order to better understand two important research areas: first, the evolution of a country's national IP policy in concert with the development of systemic norms; and second, the increasing visibility of private sector actors in bringing about progress in IP regime development outcomes at national and transnational levels.

Evidence will be presented that highlights not only the motivations that can persist within developing countries to stimulate local high technology sectors through the creation of sympathetic protection regulations, but also the critical shifts in policy attitudes towards IP principles that take place during that country's switch from an import substitution industrialisation model to an export-led growth strategy.

Explanations will also be sought to enable a detailed discussion of how movement along this pathway to embrace trade by once closed economies influences decision-making about IP regime development in both domestic and overseas markets, using the experience of China and India as illustrative of such a progression. It will be shown that distinctive phases of regulatory evolution appear evident, with attitudes towards IP by both state and non-state actors in these countries changing as technological development takes place within each stage.

This progression is shown to move from conditions of conflict with trading partners caused by an early-stage lackadaisical approach to IP enforcement, through a period where domestic enterprises in knowledge sectors begin to recognise the value of enhanced IP as they move up production value chains. They begin to bring influence to bear to promote policy shifts within each sector, towards a later stage where an embrace of IP regulatory characteristics more in synergy with industrialised economies would appear to take place, characterised by an enthusiastic engagement with international regime norm setting, and prompted by innovation oriented business models within increasingly sophisticated national knowledge sectors.

It can be argued that a very important message emerges from such a scrutiny: attitudes towards IP by actors in an export-driven developing country should be seen as not just an outcome of national economic ideology or domestic corporate strategy, but also a product of pressure brought to bear through the diplomatic, legal and commercial leverage exercised by state and non-state actors of that nation's new trading partners.

1.2 *The Research Question*

This research has sought answers to three important questions: first, what are the drivers that have moved China and India towards a closer embrace of international intellectual property norms; second, how have domestic and systemic influences shaped the character of this engagement; and third, how do state and non-state actors interact within the international system to promote legal transformation of the kind required to ensure a successful domestic IP regime.

Finding answers to these questions will provide a better understanding of the efforts involved in promoting technological growth within these two countries. It will also cast new light on how non-state actors have come to directly affect IP regime evolution in both international as well as domestic domains. In this context, this work makes important clarifications on how increased market opening and greater international trade links, combined with the defensive strategies of overseas

IP owners, may have critically effected the development of different knowledge sectors in both China and India.

1.3 *Structure and Chapter Outline*

The remainder of this introductory chapter reviews the academic debates concerning connections between IP and technological development and relates these to arguments about the nature and future of intellectual property regimes and the role of state and non-state actors in regime formation.

In chapter two, *IP in the Context of International Trade*, different types of intellectual property are located within the international trading system. A more detailed evaluation of the drivers prompting advanced developing countries such as China and India to adopt a more rigorous approach to IP regulation are explored. In this context, an analysis is made of increasingly closer interconnections between states, commercial entities and multilateral organisations. Chapter three, *Software as a Knowledge Industry*, charts the evolution and growing significance of the software industry as a key knowledge sector within the international economy. It explains how trade in software outputs captures a number of emerging tensions in dealing with knowledge-based and service-oriented products at a transnational level and how current trends in IP regime development may impact upon the industry's growth opportunities. Chapter four, *IP Regime Adoption in Asia*, outlines the development trajectories of leading South and East Asian economies and uses evidence of their respective knowledge industry evolution, and the concomitant growth in sophistication of their domestic IP regimes, to argue that trends observable in China and India are not a unique phenomenon but instead are part of a wider set of deliberate policy objectives.

Chapter five, *State Sponsored Initiatives in China*, shows how leadership elites in the country have spearheaded drives to prioritise knowledge sector expansion and embrace international IP norms. Tensions within the country between actors having different IP interests are explored in detail and it will be shown that in China an IP system has been built from scratch as part of wider market opening strategies. In chapter six, *Market Driven Development in India*, similarities and differences with development dimensions in China are presented that show how India's inherited IP regime was first adapted to support import substitution strategies and subsequently remodelled as the country reopened to trade. Tensions within its pharmaceutical industry and the contrasting unity of the software sector will be put in the context of IP regime norms that have changed under the influence of a market opening strategy and which has provided both economic incentives for local knowledge sector expansion and legal leverage for overseas private sector interests.

Chapter seven, *A Central Role for IP in the Global Domain*, presents evidence of how a global IP regime may be developing, based on widening actor participation and deepening subject area prescriptions that unite different knowledge sectors in both developed and developing countries. Finally, the concluding chapter reiterates the findings that have been drawn out and presents some areas for possible further research.

1.4 *The Global and Functional Evolution of the IP Regime*

There has been much discussion amongst scholars on the role of the state in an IP context as it operates a domestic policy agenda in concert with systemic tendencies towards global regulatory norms and harmonised standards setting.

The functional approach has a long history examining integration and intersection of interests between actors beyond the nation-state. David Mitrany (1975) pioneered the functional perspective and predicated a transition over policy outcomes from national to international control within a self-determining technical organisation. This approach may have had particular appeal during the period immediately after the end of the Second World War, and especially in the context of European integration and regeneration. However, a number of critics have pointed to its overtly rationalist assumption of behaviour by individuals and governments that would be required for such power shifts to take place and have questioned the dismissal of the state from competitive market dynamics (Rosamond, 2000).

In terms of the development of international institutions in trade policy management, a neo-functionalist interpretation would determine international trends as part of a functional compromise between "the expansion of the global market and a predictable social response to that expansion" (Wolfe, 1999) but where consensus in the governance model is more important than actual rules (Ibid.:153). Many scholars point to regimes being appropriate vehicles for this consensus building, characterised by a collection of actors whose ideas have converged on an agreed issue to achieve efficiencies in determining outcomes and achieving results (Rittberger, 1993). Intellectual property regulation can be seen as a functional regime to the extent that actor participation focuses on increasingly converging global issues and that the role of the state is not absolute in defining characteristics or outcomes (Evans, 2000).

However, the role of private sector actors in regime building does not seem to have been fully explored, nor have some of the unique characteristics of this engagement yet been fully recognised or explained. Whilst a number of scholars have pointed to the important contribution of private entity interests in drafting international trade agreements, there appears to be less discussion about the increasing interconnections between private sector corporations and lobby groups that take place internationally but that are independent of state actors. This research shows that these private enterprises regularly communicate across national boundaries in increasingly complex industry alliances as part of shared objectives to achieve unified and reliable outcomes for new IP norms in order to further their business objectives.

The linkages between the international intellectual property regime, national technological development and investment driven growth within developing countries have also generated considerable debate and controversy over recent years.

1.5 *Intellectual Property and Technological Development*

Scholars have long pointed out that economic development is a function of multiple influences and that the success or failure of nations is based on a complex interplay of different factors. Porter's "diamond of determinates" highlights the interconnection between each of a number of factors and it is important to see a nation's IP regime as part of this interplay that governs competitive advantage (Porter, 1998).

In different ways, scholars have highlighted that economic progress has led to fundamental changes in national attitudes towards policy areas such as export promotion, tariff protection, foreign investment and intellectual property. Wade, for example, charts the move from import substitution to export-oriented expansion in Taiwan and Japan, and explains how market opening can be combined with government intervention and sectoral support to facilitate export-led growth and that Taiwan in particular has used export incentives to stimulate market expansion (Wade, 2004). Chang presents similar arguments in the context of the Republic of Korea's government-nurtured economic development model that rejected the neo-liberal approach in favour of government selected sectoral support, but also argues that both China and India are successes because of strategic levels of economic planning based on a "nationalistic vision" (Chang, 2007). Neither, however, fully acknowledges the important role that independent commercial enterprises and industry groups operating in developing countries' knowledge sectors can potentially play in fostering innovation and in promoting government's policy shifts as state actors respond to market needs and changing commercial priorities.

In an IP context, Heeks (1996) has highlighted increased actor interest in adopting higher levels of IP protection as part of market stimulating policy liberalisations to help support the growth of the Indian software industry, but that these higher protective levels emerged only after overcoming earlier preferences for weak regimes that facilitated royalty free technology dissemination.

Heeks (1996:332) also points to the role taken by some foreign software firms in exerting pressure on the Indian government to secure further market access liberalisation in the IT sector through the use of "trade reciprocity" and "their willingness to assist exports *from* [sic] India as a lever to allow more exports *to* India of their own products". This is all part of a direct response to the country's export promoting strategy for domestic high technology enterprises. Ó Riain (2004:7) develops this theme further by maintaining that India and Taiwan are both examples of a "Developmental Network state", each of which "has undergone liberalisation, to the point where they are 'open' to the global economy", with development strategies that "have emerged from within the dynamics of the global information economy". Moreover, Yang (2003) introduces the concept that participation in open-market world trade can exert an influence on the national IP protection policies of developing countries, enhancing cooperation with the industrialised world to facilitate improved access to the ideas and products that encapsulate the latest technology.

However, these arguments fail to capture the connections between the role of intellectual property as an economic engine, the shift in its significance as international trade grows and the increasing proactive role of private sector enterprises in policy formation leverage as they seek commercial advantage by moving upwards in the value chain of IP outputs. Without such recognition, it is difficult to explain how key influences are brought to bear on domestic technology policy development during different stages of a country's economic development. This is especially the case given the distinctive character of the power held by commercial actor interests as they defend their IP assets. This power only arises as a function of greater market engagement between different producer-oriented economies. Evidence to support these intersections underpins the central arguments of this research.

However, it should be recognised that a number of scholars are deeply suspicious of the international intellectual property system as a whole and its efficacy in promoting developing country growth. Those holding a negative perspective, such as Bhagwati, Chang and Stiglitz, focus on a number of dimensions. First, they (Bhagwati, 2004; Chang, 2007:17) point to the relationship between states at the international level, which has disadvantaged emerging powers by coercing the adoption of developed country standards of IP protection when not necessarily appropriate, accusing the industrialised economies of "kicking away the ladder" having already reached the top.

Second, they (Chang and Grabel, 2004:19; Stiglitz and Charlton, 2005) are concerned with increasing firm level tendencies towards the assetising of IP in the context of private sector rights, where concepts such as "social profit" and "social welfare" are left out of the equation, to the overall detriment of the public commons. Stiglitz (2006), in particular, appears to reject the entire notion of intellectual property regulation as an inefficient and unsatisfactory monopoly power, especially in industries such as pharmaceuticals, suggesting that instead, prize reward funds should be established by governments, perhaps linked to peer recognition within industries, both of which should take the place of patents in most instances.

Dutfield (2003:1–20) acknowledges this salience of IP in current academic thinking by asserting that "[i]ntellectual property rights have never been so economically and politically important" but casts serious doubts on whether the IP regime as evolved in its current form is in the interests of the poor. He (2005) maintains that this is encapsulated by growing rent transfers from poor to rich countries in the light of increased licensing activity over recent years. Particular criticism has been levelled at leading nations that have achieved success in knowledge goods production using specific IP policies that suited themselves but who now, once having achieved higher levels of development, are attempting to infuse the international regime with norms geared only to the interests of technological leaders.

The Commission on Intellectual Property Rights in the United Kingdom (UK) supports this perspective by questioning the redistributive impact of IP rights and by making an assessment that stronger regimes would be more likely to favour developed economies, with the United States (US) being the main beneficiary with additional license inflows amounting to billions of dollars (Commission on Intellectual Property Rights, 2002). This draws, in particular, upon assessments made by World Bank researchers on an economic postulation of increases in license flow volumes in the light of enhancements to the IP legal systems of many developing countries that have taken place since 1995 (World Bank, 2002).[1] However, some caution on this point may be necessary as a World Bank 2000 study that examined growth in IP related international transactions asserted that much of the volume of licensing receipts into the US were in fact inter-firm transfers (Primo Braga, Fink, and Paz Sepulveda, 2000).

Whilst it is highly likely that domestic transfers from developing countries would have increased in line with their absorption of multilaterally agreed IP rules, the significant presence of US multinationals around the world cannot be ignored when assessing licensing revenue models. Moreover, as the US is also the main owner of IP-rich assets and has been seeking redress from piracy in a number of regions over the last decade or more, developments of this kind may not be so surprising and could also show the extent of violations that have occurred in the past and may lend some legitimacy to American aims that seek to rebalance the producer/consumer equation as part of knowledge transfer agreements.

A number of scholars have highlighted positive correlations between the strengthening of patent laws and market driven technology flows across countries. Maskus and Reichman (2005:13) make the point that "the evolving system of stronger private rights in new technologies could lead to global gains in innovation and additional market mediated information transfers to developing countries" but they advise assessing the full benefits of a strengthened IP regime. The argument is

[1] The Commission references work done in 2001 but the World Bank updated its research for 2002 indicating likely positive transfers to the US to be in the sum of US19.08 billion. See (World Bank 2002) especially pp. 129–150 and Table 5.1 on page 133.

developed that, even as trade tensions have to some extent been "liberated" through multilateral agreements, there has been a "concomitant re-regulation" of knowledge goods, leading to external constraints on firm level competition that could harm follower firms' capabilities to exploit technology (ibid.:20–21). Maskus (2008:84–85) does acknowledge an important role, however, for different kinds of IP regulation in certain sectors of economic activity, pointing to the usefulness of patents in pharmaceutical endeavours and the value of copyright protection in software and internet commerce initiatives, but goes on to assert that there exists "an inherent tension…between countries at different levels of economic development in their perceived interests in the global and national systems of protection."

In this context, it is important to understand that there is a considerable diversity in views and economic structure across different developing countries and it may be useful to bear in mind that "the developing world does not and cannot speak with one voice" (Dutfield, 2003:18). This perspective is amplified by Barton (2003:60–1),[2] who asserts that IP regulatory strategies are likely to be different for advanced developing nations, for whom the regulatory system "may encourage domestic innovations and for the larger ones…may even encourage outside innovation". Correa (2003:209–17)[3] continues this theme by contending that the role of IP regulations will "vary significantly in accordance with productive structures and levels of development" and that the main challenge facing these economically emerging nations is to find ways to integrate their development policies with their IP policies.

The technological evolution of China and India is therefore telling, as they present examples of growing economies with increasing firm level strategies in moving up the value chain of IP product development, which has been coincident with an expansion in their own domestic innovative capabilities. This can be seen especially in the fields of advanced electronics research, software development and software services, where enterprises in these countries appear to be adopting positions on IP regulation that has an increasing similarity with that being proposed by industrialised country corporations.

[2] Note that Prof. Barton was Chair of the UK Commission on Intellectual Property Rights.
[3] Note that Prof. Correa was also a member of the UK Commission on Intellectual Property Rights.

Drahos (2005), however, continues to view these current tends towards regime expansion pessimistically and has characterised the growing internationalisation of IP rights as an erosion of state sovereignty. These trends, he (2005:46–64) says, are illustrative of the way that US interests predominate to the exclusion of third countries, whereby hegemonic power is used in combination with "the carrot" of multilateral bargaining together with "the stick" of bilateral trade sanctions to achieve objectives. He (2005:6–8) maintains that, since the end of the Second World War, "the US has been the most influential actor in the globalisation of regulation". Supporting Drahos' view, Keohane (2005:65–8) points to multilateral forums in which power "is distributed in a highly asymmetrical fashion" and that negotiating positions are dominated by the distributional priorities of a corporate inspired agenda,[4] drawing influence from a combination of US, European and Japanese interests rather than one that seeks to achieve optimal creativity.

Nevertheless, Keohane (2005) points out that international institutions can promote effectiveness through the creation of agreed new norms, although rule on non-compliance and bargaining are commonplace in the global arena in the absence of an authoritative government. There is also the consideration that the evolving spectrum of international IP treaties can generate restraints as well as restrictions on all state actors participating within them (Keohane, 2005), which would indicate that there are more complex interplays between states at this level than simply pure power politics. It can be argued that it is as important for the United States to have as wide a participation as possible in agreeing to the rules of a stronger regime as it is for less powerful nations to have the American presence within the fold of multilateral constraint. In this context, observations of a rise in the use of bilateral trade accords by the US may present a more worrying trend for smaller nations than might a stronger multilateral framework.

In respect to firm level interaction with IP regulations, a number of scholars have asserted the view that the IP regime should not be bound into benefiting individuals but that account should be taken

[4] For more on US corporate concerns over IP piracy and subsequent government reaction, see Peter Drahos with John Braithwaite, *Information Feudalism: Who Owns the Knowledge Economy* (Earthscan Publications London 2002). See especially pp. 89–93.

of the original public interest bargain for which IP rights evolved in the first place (Correa, 2005; Sterkx, 2005). This argument rejects the "consequentialist economic justification" that is implied by innovation incentives in contemporary IP norms (Sterkx, 2005:193). Although acknowledging the significance of wealth bound to national innovation and the positive relationship between foreign direct investment (FDI) and IP rights in developing countries, patents in particular are characterised as limiting the use of inventions by others rather than promoting knowledge disclosure under the umbrella of patent protection.

This negative positioning is, however, far from being a universal perspective. Pugatch (2004) reiterates the significant salience that IP protection has in the international pharmaceutical industry and explains the critical contribution that data exclusivity under patent disclosure protection makes in safeguarding expensive investment in the pre-marketing stages of a new drug's development. Nor is this just in respect to patents, as pharmaceuticals are also dependent upon trade secret enforcement during submission phases of manufacture as well as trademark assertion that can stimulate brand loyalty and maintain consumer safeguards in respect of quality and reliability for out-of-patent drugs (Pugatch, 2004).

Granstrand (1999) maintains that the current characteristics of the international economy have moved commercial attitudes into a pro-patent era, displacing the socialised principles of monopolistic protection with privatised grants of control to achieve commercial success. Goods that are rich in IP have had an increasing significance in world trade and domestic industrial expansion over recent years, which is symptomatic of a "relative shifting of material (physical) [sic] to immaterial (non-physical) sources of economic growth" (ibid.:3).

Continuing this theme, Alikhan (2000:1) describes the intellectual property system as "one of the cornerstones of modern economic policy at the national level and a catalyst for development" and emphasises that it is important to see IP regulations as part of a developing nation's wider socio-economic development and not just of technological growth. In this way, the Indian software industry can be seen to have evolved to the benefit of the whole national economy (ibid.). Nor is this phenomenon confined to large multinationals: protecting investment in R&D through the protection of inventions and generating subsequent revenues through the control of licensing is particularly important to smaller and medium sized enterprises as they seek to compete in international markets. In the software heartlands of California's Silicon Valley—the offshore development hubs of India's Bangalore and Mumbai and the innovation clusters of China's Hangzhou—copyright protection and patent applications provide a stimulus for creativity and an asset basis from which to develop markets and seek further investor funding for expansion.[5] A natural corollary of such initiatives is that, as Kamil Idris (2003:8) maintains, alliances between companies are formed "to obtain mutually beneficial competitive advantages through cross-licensing".

Kamperman Sanders (2001:44) points out that mutual interest in a stronger IP system can actually act as "a bridge between different cultural and industrial mores... so as to provide a common regime for the information industries to operate in" and points to close cooperation between Europe and America in evolving suitable policies for the management and protection of electronic databases. This perspective could also be applied to what has been happening in a wider sense since the turn of the millennium, whereby the interests of major industrialised nations in IP regime evolution may have now begun to intersect at both a national and corporate level with those of leading developing nations, such as China and India, each of whom has nurtured their high technology industries to the extent that domestic enterprises that now exist have embraced innovation and have engaged in trade based on their high value outputs. An improved IP regime, at both national and international levels, could now be interpreted to be in the policy interests of important groups in these countries, in order to facilitate the pursuit of gains from bringing knowledge-based products into domestic and overseas markets.

Andersen and Kanzelmann (2006) further develop this view by putting forward a concept of increasingly unified perspectives between industries, governments and international agencies on the importance of strong IP regulation and enforcement in securing competitive advantage and increasing national welfare. By focusing on the reality that cooperation in IP system development does not have to mean a sharing of all interests, actor groups can, instead, see different values in the norms of the regime and can retain varied opinions on exactly

---

[5] Ibid. See also growth rates in use of WIPO's Patent Cooperation Treaty by developing countries at http://www.wipo.int/pct/en/index.html last referenced 16th February 2007.

what might comprise an ideal legal and institutional implementation (ibid.). During the process of negotiation in regime development, they will also recognise, out of national self interest, that an effective regime is sufficiently important to warrant cooperation (ibid.). Moreover, Watt (2000:16) takes this argument to its logical conclusion by maintaining that "regulatory mechanisms to protect property rights [have] the effect of creating markets in which these rights can be transacted", showing the connection between regime evolution and market evolution.

Pascal Lamy (2004) projects a combination of optimism and caution in his view of IP's efficacy to promote development that may reflect the realisation that there continues to be marked sensitivities to this topic by protagonists at multilateral forums. Whilst on the one hand describing how "skills, knowledge and technology have become the decisive assets in the global economy" (ibid.:923) and that strengthening IP regimes operate as a response to a social need to encourage innovation and creativity, on the other, he cautions that IP regulations "could become hypertrophic, acting as a barrier (and not a spur) to further innovation" (ibid.:924) and that "collective understanding of the role of IP in the development process is incomplete" (ibid.:932).

This divergence of opinion amongst experts concerning the potential benefits and risks of IP regulations in regard to fostering and sustaining technological development in developing countries may stem from new complexities in analysing incentives that influence the way that these countries react to, absorb and exploit IP norms.

It would seem to be clear that the current literature does not fully recognise the fundamental shift in strategic outlook that is taking place in countries like China and India as they engage with the international trading system through their embrace of export-led strategies that bring with them responsibilities to act in line with systemic norms rather than pursuing individualistic attitudes under their old ideological preferences. Whilst countries such as India have continued to exploit TRIPS flexibilities in their pursuit of wider strategic policy objectives in the context of the Doha Development Round, even after creating TRIPS-compliant patent regulations (Basheer, 2005),[6] and China has

---

[6] The work of IP legal specialist Shamnad Basheer has been extensive in this area. See, for example, Shamnad Basheer, 'India's Tryst with TRIPS: The Patents (Amendment) Act, 2005', *The Indian Journal of Law and Technology*, Vol. 1, 2005, and Shamnad Basheer and Preshan Reddy, 'The "Efficacy" of Indian Patent Law: Ironing Out the Creases in Section 3(d)', *Scripted*, Vol. 5 Issue 2, August 2008. On issues of

continued to have arguments with developed governments such as the United States about the legal implementation of its intellectual property regime,[7] the important point is that such activities have been conducted within the framework of internationally agreed norms and procedures, and on the basis of mutual recognition of each county's adherence to these principles. These developments are relatively new and the drivers behind them need to be uncovered and explored in more detail, which is the principal objective of this research work.

There also appears to be a weakness in some research in that it fails to recognise that not all developing countries are the same and that significant variations now exist in national economic and technological sophistication amongst them. Analyses that attempt to draw too generalised a projection of the implications and merits of IP regime evolution *vis-à-vis* the developing world may not now be convincing without first distinguishing between the different dimensions observable in the first tier of this group of nations. In this sense, the traditional perspective of a North/South divide that has characterised much of the debate is shown as no longer being a useful analytical framework (Narlikar, 2003).[8]

Instead of focusing on whether IP regimes are good or bad for developing countries *per se*, it is better to acknowledge these differences and highlight shared characteristics amongst nations that are leading the engagement with the technology-driven international economy. In this way, an examination may be conducted with a view to evaluating both their propensity to adopt IP rules and their underlying cultural, economic and technological framework that might allow those rules to be absorbed.

These points make a more detailed study of China and India particularly compelling as the two nations exemplify the policy shifts and the pace of change evident within fast-developing countries. They have

---

broader TRIPS compliance by India, see Shamnad Basheer and Mrinalini Kochupillai, 'Exhausting' Patent Rights in India: Parallel Imports and TRIPS Compliance', *Journal of Intellectual Property Rights*, Vol. 13, September 2008, pp. 486–497.

[7] See WTO details of the dispute between United States and China within the Dispute Settlement Understanding on China's criminal regulatory implementation of TRIPS at <http://www.wto.org/english/tratop_e/dispu_e/cases_e/ds362_e.htm> accessed 15th January 2009.

[8] For an interesting discussion of how these developments may have impacted international diplomacy and alliance building at GATT, especially in relation to services. See especially pp. 83–104.

embraced international IP norms as part of a strategy of export promotion and technological development that has been focused on specific areas of comparative advantage, which has led to a rapid expansion of key high-technology industrial sectors. This has brought both nations to a point where there has been a noticeable convergence amongst state and non-state actors on policies to upgrade levels of IP protection, all of which introduce important new dimensions to old debates about policy options as a stimulus for economic transformation in developing countries.

CHAPTER TWO

IP IN THE CONTEXT OF INTERNATIONAL TRADE

This chapter will trace the history and emergence of IP regimes both nationally and internationally and will look to explain some of the reasons for their development. It will also introduce the debates that surround the implementation of intellectual property in different jurisdictions and the way that these issues affect relationships between states. It will locate the importance of the rise in products that have a high IP content[1] within world trade in general, and for the key developing nations of China and India in particular.

It will be argued that it is time to re-evaluate some of the long-standing differences that have existed between first and third world nations in respect to IP regulations and their motivations. It will be emphasised that complex connections can now be identified between a country's embrace of export-led growth strategies, its technological development and the increase in worldwide IP related trade with the strength and effectiveness of local regulatory regimes. The stages under which IP regime evolution has been driven within China and India will be introduced and discussed within the context of the potential for greater global convergence in norm development.

This chapter will show that there are increasing trends for private sector organisations to play a greater role in determining the shape of IP regime developments as well as in influencing the outcomes of international negotiations. The chapter will conclude with an overview of recent initiatives in IP centric communities, including the rise of patent exchanges between companies as a sequitur from a more defensive IP strategy, the influence of key corporations in principal economic sectors and pioneering trends towards innovative IP-centred business models.

---

[1] Hereinafter referred to as "IP-rich goods".

2.1 *History and Emergence of Different Types of Intellectual Property*

It is useful to review the origin and incentives for intellectual property regulation. In political economy terms, IP regimes are a state's response to the potential for market failure in the provision of public goods to a consuming community. Public goods possess two key attributes (Deardorff, 2006:222): they are non-rival, such that their "consumption by one user does not reduce the amount of the good available for consumption by others" and they are non-excludable whereby, once having been made available for consumption by one individual it is not usually possible to exclude others from an equal consumption without specialist intervention. The knowledge and information generated during the process of innovation and technology development may be seen as examples of the "public good" problem, as, without intervention of some kind, their provision to the community may be suboptimal.

Intellectual property rights attempt to respond with legislative restrictions that construct an artificial exclusion on these goods to control their consumption and thus defend their exploitation by their inventors or authors whilst ensuring that these creations are still made available for the benefit of the wider community in the first place. It is especially important that a reliable framework exists to defend creators' interests when dealing with intangible products such as computer software, motion pictures and e-books, where the highly distributed and geographically diverse markets that have developed under the growth of international trade often combine with collections of anonymous buyers that have arisen with the advent of internet driven business sales models. The cost of each sales transaction would quickly become prohibitive in the absence of dependable regulatory mechanisms that at least try and protect owner interests and it can clearly be seen that in this situation "property rights reduce the transaction costs of dealing with a group of widely dispersed buyers" (Merges, 1996:282).

There are a number of different kinds of protection that fall into the category of "intellectual property right". They include the "patent" for protecting inventions and designs, "copyright" controls on authorship and software development, "trademark" registration that governs brand recognition, product quality indicators and provides for consumer protection, as well as less obvious rules that govern the handling of trade secrets within and between organisations and the enforcement of specialised contractual terms that may include additional provisions outside publicly available legal minimums.[2] Taken together, an effective IP regime "displaces the dependency on traditional tangible fixed assets as a means for commercial success" (Granstrand, 1999:10).[3]

The most widely recognised intellectual property right in economic terms is the patent. Protection applies to the manifestation of an idea through a design or an invention and has to be actively sought by the inventor.[4] The granting of patent protection is, effectively, the bestowing, through state recognition, of a temporary monopoly reward for an invention for a certain length of time.[5] Patents thus introduce an element of exclusion. This is a particularly important concept, in that permission to use a patented idea must be explicitly granted by the owner and can be withheld to maximise the economic benefits of the monopoly, although the state may reserve to itself the right to demand that permission is given compulsorily in special circumstances, where, for example, public health or security is at risk.[6] If the patent owner grants permission to use the patent, a license fee is typically charged for the inclusion of the protected idea into any new or modified technological development.

The impact of this exclusory power of patents is often explained from a wholly negative perspective, sometimes put forward by public interest pressure groups and NGOs, which are frequently active participants in the process to exert pressure for change that better accommodates their perspectives.[7] However, there is, in fact, sharp disagreement over

---

[2] Unlike other IP regulations, contract specifications are typically not extended to include obligations on any third party and are designed only restrict the behaviour of those bound by the terms of the contract itself.

[3] Until relatively recently each component of an IP regime was only loosely interrelated so their history does not form a coherent whole and it required the convergence of trade incentives through the expansion and importance of knowledge goods in modern international commerce with the creation of international forums that sought to scope key IP principles and legal minimums to make possible the contemporary interconnection of different intellectual property elements.

[4] This is like trademark registration but unlike copyright which is deemed, under current norms, to subsist automatically on a work's creation.

[5] Under international treaty, a 20 year minimum is now in force for all WTO members through the TRIPS agreement.

[6] For example, the Compulsory License Provisions of the TRIPS agreement granting the enforceable consumption and distribution of patented products without permission from the patent owner for public health emergencies.

[7] For example, see Oxfam's recent criticisms of strengthened patent rights agreed in the US/ Andean Free Trade Agreement. It has been also argued by some observers that NGO's played an important part in shaping elements of India's patent reform policies, in particular influencing the crafting of a section that restricts incremental

the extent of exclusion, and a number of scholars have highlighted that patents represent largely "input monopolies" (Granstrand, 1999:48) rather than conferring power over specific outputs. In this way, and especially with complex products, it is often possible to substitute one factor for another to generate the same output effect, and that, indeed, by a process of creativity to work around the patent, substitute factors may become available. There are also some industries that depend on monopoly exploitation in order to secure a viable economic return on investments in R&D, such as with pharmaceuticals. These principles of public utility coupled to private protection were a natural development from the previous tendency of inventors to keep secret the arts and ways of new creations through highly protective guilds of craftsmen (ibid.:55–106).[8]

Patents provide a number of advantages to the state: first, they could be granted at virtually no cost to the public purse, save for general administrative bills, many of which could be passed back on to the patent applicant; second, they publicly promote invention for the benefit of the wider community; third, they offer a reliable form of state sponsored protection for inventors within their territory. Patents also ensure that the details of ideas being protected reached the wider community in a coherent and structured form, as a natural corollary of the patenting procedure was disclosure of the idea and its operation, thus creating an economic bargain between the patentee and the national authorities.[9]

---

patent applications on existing products (a practice known as known as ever-greening). See later sections on India's patent law in this book for further discussion of this topic.

[8] Ibid. Granstrand provides an excellent historical account of early IP initiatives and their growing significance in economics (pp. 55–106). The existence of early patents can be traced as far back as ancient Greece around 500 BC where a one year monopoly was introduced in the colony of Sybaris to protect the recipes and preparation secrets of chefs from being unlawfully duplicated. From these early beginnings there developed the links between recognition, reward and protection that was first encapsulated in a codified patent system by Venetian authorities in 1474. The first English codifications took place in 1623 which sought to bring together and rationalise the traditions that had begun centuries earlier. The first American patent law emerged on to their statute book in 1790 along with the granting of its first patent, although protection for a citizen's "exclusive right to their respective writings and discoveries" had been empowered to Congress and enshrined in the US Constitution by the founding fathers of the country. See Article 1, Section 8, Clause 8 of the United States Constitution (sometimes referred to as the "intellectual property clause"), United States Archives.

[9] Indeed, disclosure was such an important part of this bargain that when a major fire at the US Patent Office in 1836 destroyed thousands of models and original docu-

A more recent addition to the patenting approach is the "utility model" or "petty patent", granted to innovators by some jurisdictions for ideas whose inventive step is considerably lower than that required for full patent recognition, and sometimes, in this case, the award of protection may even be granted without examination.[10] Their origin can be traced back to the 18th Century where some countries made grants on innovations related to simple, stepwise refinements of manufacturing processes or for "improvements in the functional design or operational utility of an industrial product" (van Lam and Wattanapruttipaisan, 2005:123). They are typically granted faster than inventive product patents and have an exclusive period which is normally not more than 10 years, and is generally much less than the time granted to full patent awards, although precise details of regulations for utility models vary by jurisdiction.[11]

Utility model patenting systems are available in only a selection of jurisdictions: for example, mainland China, Japan and the Republic of Korea offer such facilities, in common with most of the continental European nations, whilst the United States, the United Kingdom and India do not.[12]

Copyright, in contrast to a patent, protects the expression of an idea rather than the idea itself and is typically used to control the distribution, reproduction and reward payment for the written word, pictures, works of artistic performance and, in the modern era, films and software programs. In concert with other IP regulations, a bargain exists to balance public benefit and reward between the parties asserting and acknowledging copyright. A typical implementation gives a finite

ments pertaining to granted patents at the time, it caused over 7,000 existing patents to be cancelled by the US authorities for want of design evidence and led to America mandating the publication of drawings and design descriptions as part of the patent application process and initiating more sophisticated off-site storage of patent records, in case such a fire happened again. See commemoration of the 165th anniversary of the fire, United States Patent and Trademark Office, <http://www.uspto.gov/web/offices/com/speeches/01-60.htm>, accessed October 2006.

[10] For an overview of petty patents see United Kingdom Patent Office.

[11] A concise summary of utility model filing issues may be read at the website of specialist UK Patent Attorney's (Page Hargreave).

[12] The European Union (EU) recently conducted consultations on the possibility of the Commission issuing a Directive for a pan-Union utility model award that would apply in all EU Member States, although negotiations were subsequently suspended following the failure to bring about a Community-wide full patent. The Community Patent will be further explored in later sections.

period of protection[13] combined with a set of exemptions of fair use for the works which enable legitimate copies or extracts to be made for various purposes, such as for the work of academic research and private study. However, unlike the exclusory potential of patents, the main power granted under copyright is to control reproduction and unauthorised copying through the payment of royalty fees or to take counter-measures granted by national law against piracy (copying) of the copyrightable item.

The emergence of copyright can be traced to the creation of the printing press by Johann Gutenberg in 1450, due to the fact that the newly created ease with which printed matter could now be copied necessitated a review of ways to protect authors' interests in their creations and publishers' interests in printing and distribution.[14]

These new regulatory structures created new powers for the owners of works and concomitant obligations for consumers. At the same time, they significantly increased the amount of material in circulation whilst also widening the public audience for this knowledge through new ways in which such information could thus be disseminated. Moreover, technological progress has continued to be an important driver in the regulatory development of copyright norms. The latest controversies centre on the availability of copyright material on the internet, especially with music, where the most recent cases of copyright infringements and illegal distribution have indicated weaknesses in the current protection regimes of some jurisdictions, requiring new legal interpretations and active state intervention to rebalance the regulatory bargain.[15]

Copyright systems typically distinguish between different forms of expression, such as the creation of a book or software program versus sound recordings and broadcasts of performances, and a number of

---

[13] Under the TRIPS treaty the minimum requirement for copyright is for life plus 50 years in the case of the works of natural persons and 50 years from creation in the case of legal persons.

[14] Prior to this, the cost of reproduction of works was extremely high and involved almost as much effort as would have the creation of the original, whilst channels for the distribution and the dissemination of knowledge were highly regulated by the Church across Europe. It was not until the technology of the press threatened the enforcement capability of the existing regime did there become a need to consider new ideas such as copyright principles.

[15] For example, see the discussion on US Supreme Court judgment on the so-called 'Grotkster' case, named after one of the firms cited in the trial, in (Economist Print Edition 2005c).

jurisdictions have assigned terms of protection that differ based on this distinction in the subject matter of the copyright. For example, the United Kingdom (UK), in keeping with its commitments under European Council Directive 93/98/EEC of October 1993,[16] provides protection for the life of the author plus 70 years in the case of literary works, and life of the last survivor amongst the director, music composer or screenplay author plus 70 years in the case of films, irrespective of when the work is made available to the public. Whereas copyright in broadcasts subsists for only 50 years, either from the date of its creation or from the date of its first release.[17]

The United States, on the other hand, chose to adopt a different approach with their copyright legislation, categorising all works based on their date of creation and/or publication, and generally providing protection of either life plus 70 years where the personal authors are concerned or 95 years from the date of publication in the case of corporate copyright ownership, what the US terms as "works made for hire" (United States Copyright Office, Overview of Copyright). The definition of copyrightable items under US law covers all "original works of authorship" that include literary works, motion pictures and sound recordings that were created after 1st January 1978. American law further protects works that were already in circulation before this date for a total of 95 years from the date of their original creation or publication (ibid.).[18]

The time period granted to rights-holders for protection of copyright has public benefit implications: the longer is the time during which unauthorised reproduction remains prohibited the lower is the public benefit available from the free dissemination of the value encapsulated in the copyrightable item. The public benefit argument achieved particular salience during the American Congressional debates surrounding the passage of the Sonny Bono Copyright Term Extension Act 1998 which increased the protective time period under US law to the current levels by adding a further 20 years to the date when applicable works would come out of copyright (United States Copyright

[16] Most recently, Directive 2006/116/EC of the European Council and Parliament of 12th December 2006 codified a number of harmonisations made to copyright protection across Member States and actually repealed Directive 93/98/EEC. See (EUR-Lex 2006).

[17] See United Kingdom Copyright Service.

[18] Note that US Copyright Law has a number of additional regulations pertaining to works formally created but neither registered nor published as at 1st January 1978.

Office, Copyright Law), covering, amongst other things, many popular motion pictures from the inter-war era that were about to enter free circulation under the previous rules.

Proponents of the Act argued that an increased term was justified by greater human life expectancy in the modern world that needed to be recognised in a longer period of protection. Congressional supporters also asserted that US law needed to be harmonised with the regulatory changes that had already been made by EU Member states under Directive 93/98/EEC, which mandated that copyright protection for works that originated in countries outside the Community would be the lesser of either EU protection levels or those applicable in the originating country's laws—the so-called "rule of the shorter term".[19] It was therefore argued that the previous levels applicable under US law would have disadvantaged American right-holders seeking protection abroad and that commercial trading interests were at stake. The politicians argued that change was thus required "[i]n order to safeguard the Nation's economic interests and those of America's creators in the protection of copyrighted terms abroad" (United States Congress, 1996:5).

Opponents of the Act asserted that the changes represented a move that would "harm academicians, historians, students, musicians, writers, and other creators who are inspired by the great creative works of the past" (ibid.:29–36)[20] by prolonging the time before the public would have unfettered access to those works and granting significant advantage to copyright holders such as film studios. Such a move would also, it was alleged, provide "a contractual windfall at the expense of the public" (ibid.). This position failed to find support and the Bill was passed into American copyright law in 1998.

Trademarks are very different from both patent and copyright protection as they are not time limited and provide safeguards to a product's consumers as well as producers. They signal an identity for the creator and at the same time provide a very distinctive indicator of safety for the consumer by transmitting key elements of information to potential purchasers, such as the expected quality, anticipated cost and likely origin of a product.[21]

---

[19] See Article 7, op. cit. Directive 2006/116/EC, adopting the *Rule of the Shorter Term*.

[20] Minority Views of Mr. Hank Brown.

[21] This indication may be in the form of a particular combination of colours, a distinctive logo or one or more keywords in a particular order with a special font and

One of the particular characteristics of trademarks versus other types of IP is that a mark, once registered, can be maintained permanently within a jurisdiction, although it is possible for a mark's registration to be cancelled if a period of time elapses before it is used within a territory.[22] This feature is particularly important in respect to the usefulness of trademarks as their economic value may accumulate over time. This is especially unlike the typical value curves associated with patents, where both technological progress, leading to obsolescence, and further inventiveness leading to alternatives, effect a gradual decline in the license income stream, which becomes more marked as the patent nears its expiration (Granstrand, 1999:74).[23] For example, analysts have estimated that the value of the world's top brand, Coca-Cola, to be in excess of US$60 billion and growing (BusinessWeek Online Edition, 2005).[24]

The different types of intellectual property protection thus try to strike a balance between adequate incentives to develop new technologies, to reward investment in the design and product management of high quality goods, to bring ideas and cultural expressions into fruition, and to protect both producers and consumers within the economy (Maskus, 2000).

2.2 *Creation of an International Regime for IP Protection*

Intellectual property rights comprise a set of regulations that have traditionally been territorially based and this characteristic "has long been a problem to rights holders whose works, inventions, and brands are the subject of transnational trade" (Bentley, 2004:5). By the second half of the 19th Century, tensions had begun to emerge amongst nations whose IP regime differed in terms of strength and application.

such arrangements have a long history. Early trademarks on ancient pottery identifying their creator have been found to exist as far back in the past as 3,200 BC, whilst by Roman times trademarks were used on an "everyday basis" to identify, categorise and value different products. See op. cit. Granstrand, page 28.

[22] For example, TRIPS standards mandate a three year period during which a mark may remain un-used but still registered within the jurisdiction of WTO members. Op. cit. (World Trade Organisation) See Art. 15 (3).

[23] See especially his view of time and innovation links in patent valuation at page 74.

[24] Further protection exists for special brands under provisions to safeguard abuse of "well known marks" and related geographic indicators such as "scotch whisky" and "champagne".

Inventions, written material and marks owned by foreigners were typically treated less favourably than those of nationals and, sometimes, were not protected at all.

This introduced particular complexities in terms of international trade. IP rich goods are "distinctive in terms of international comparative advantage" (Maskus, 2000:73) and represent effort and expenditure in their production. Moreover, flows of technology meant that publication under patent in one country for national protection invariably meant revealing the invention to those with technical know-how in another country. Exporters of IP-rich products were also looking to move beyond collections of bilateral agreements to more inclusive multilateral arrangements that better reflected the growth of international trade that was developing with particular intensity during the second half of the 19th Century.

The motivating event for tackling these difficulties was the failure of Austria-Hungary to attract sufficient number of inventors to an international technology exhibition in 1873 as their existing legislation did not provide sufficient protection for foreign inventors. The authorities in Vienna decided to create a special ordinance that provided appropriate protection for the purposes of conference attendance, and the resulting success of this initiative spurred action at an international level. A subsequent political conference, also held in Vienna, led to a consolidation of aims and objectives that became enshrined in the Paris Convention for the Protection of Industrial Property of 1883 that laid foundation in the modern era for patent protection. Complementary motivations in the field of copyright at the same time led to the creation of the Berne Convention in 1886.

These two treaties had a small joint administrative staff operating as an International Bureaux originally based in Berne but which subsequently moved to Geneva in 1960 in order to be closer to the United Nations and to lead an internationally focused framework for promoting intellectual property issues across the world. In 1970 a treaty came into force that established the World Intellectual Property Organisation (WIPO), which then subsequently became a specialized agency of the United Nations.[25]

---

[25] It should be noted that, in contrast to the General Agreement on Tariffs and Trade and the subsequent World Trade Organisation, WIPO is strictly limited to states rather than customs areas. This means that, for example, China continues to

The Paris Convention introduced distinct improvements in regulating patents internationally and created norms of behaviour that bound states as they became contracting parties[26] and brought into being two fundamental requirements for an effective regime. First, National Treatment mandated that, for the purposes of patent application, management and enforcement, contracting states had to treat foreign nationals of other contracting states no less favourably that they did their own nationals. Second, the Right of Priority was introduced and agreed, under which nationals of contracting parties are given a grace period[27] to make multi-country patent applications, whereby the date of application for such third country patents would be deemed to have been backdated to the original time of the first patent filing. This ensured that inventors did not have their ideas stolen as part of the disclosure arrangements of an application.[28]

The increasing integration of international transactions and national economies along with a growth in transnational corporations[29] during the latter part of the 20th Century led to the consequent need to seek patent protection for inventions traded across more than one jurisdiction.[30] In response, contracting parties to the Paris Convention agreed on a process of streamlining and integrating the patent application process that became encapsulated in the WIPO-administered Patent

represent both of its special administrative regions through its mainland representatives and Taiwan is excluded from membership and from its treaties.

[26] The Convention enshrined the protection of works being exhibited at international exhibitions across contracting states in a manner similar to that first used in Vienna, whilst also introducing trademark controls that attempted to regularise the registration and use of marks across states, especially in the case that a mark is registered but then cancelled within a jurisdiction due to alleged non-use.

[27] This period is typically one year.

[28] Note that although Taiwan is not a member of the Paris Convention it has sought to negotiate bilateral reciprocity on this issue under special arrangements, most notably with the United States under a Memorandum of Understanding from April 1996. For a concise and practical explanation of this dilemma, see the website of Ladas & Parry Patent Attorneys See also the originating letter bringing into force this reciprocity by United States Department of Commerce.

[29] The United Nations Conference on Trade and Development (UNCTAD) provides a useful working definition of the characteristics of a transnational corporation: "an enterprise comprising entities in more than one country which operate under a system of decision-making that permits coherent policies and a common strategy".

[30] Those seeking patent protection in more than one country had an increasingly complex task to regularise and ensure compliance with many different patent application systems, contrasting timetables and different national laws.

Cooperation Treaty (PCT) negotiated in 1970 and entered into force in January 1978.

The PCT does not by itself create an "international patent" but instead streamlines the way in which an individual or organisation is able to make patent applications in any number of Contracting States by providing for a two-part process. First, an initial "international search" procedure takes place in one of a number of designated patent offices[31] to verify citations and deduce prior art and determine commercial inventiveness, the result of which is to produce a non-binding report on the likely success of subsequent national level applications. Second, a 30-month filing window is then provided for making a bundle of local applications through the standard required procedures of desired jurisdictions. In particular, applications may usually be lodged electronically in the patent office of the state in which the applicant is resident or may be served at WIPO's offices in Geneva. The benefits of efficiency and timeliness accrue to both applicant and to local patent offices.[32]

The Berne Convention attempted to achieve similar regularisation for Copyright as had the Paris Convention for patents. Prior to its endeavours, copyright had developed through bilateral negotiations as a means of protecting foreign authors and artists in a third country. One of the most important improvements achieved by Berne was to enshrine the principle of National Treatment into the handling of copyright on the international stage, as well as dealing with the minimum length such protection from unauthorised copying should be allowed.[33] A distinctive feature introduced by Berne was the principle of "automatic protection" for works once created without the need for a mandatory notice period or registration process.[34]

---

[31] WIPO: especially footnote 1 listing the current 'International Searching Authorities' for PCT applications, <http://www.wipo.int/treaties/en/registration/pct/summary_pct.html>, accessed 22nd November 2006.

[32] Note that Taiwan is not a party to the Patent Cooperation Treaty as it is not a member of WIPO. This means that a territorial level patent filing must be therefore made through the Taipei Intellectual Property Office. For an example of a software program supporting patent applications, see <http://www.patanalyst.com/>, accessed 20th March 2007. This program was designed through a partnership between a French and German consortium.

[33] This was set at 50 years after the author's death if the owner is an individual or 50 years after first put into public circulation if ownership is corporate.

[34] There is some evidence to suggest that such requirements have presented some countries with a particular challenge. For example, the United States was not able to

However, despite this progress, there continued to be discord and differences across the international system in respect to regime strength and effectiveness of national enforcement. These tensions led to a change of emphasis away from the WIPO-regulated conventions towards a greater focus on trade related implications of intellectual property regulation and shifted attention to GATT. These moves intensified after the failure of the advanced economic powers to secure reforms of the intellectual property conventions through negotiations at WIPO during the 1980's. Moreover, improvements in the technology available to pirates[35] had meant that, over time, the cost of copying high value goods had been falling relative to the cost of originally creating the product.[36]

2.3 *The Uruguay Round and IP in the World Trade Organisation*

The increase in capability amongst IP violators coincided with recognition of the importance of knowledge-based goods to the future success of a number of industrialised economies. IP violations had particular impact on enterprises that were the owners of IP-rich high technology exports in advanced countries, who brought pressure to bear on their national governments to use the trading system as a mechanism for linking access to their home markets for a concomitant improvement in respect for intellectual property rights for their goods in partner trading nations.[37] By the late 20th Century, IP had become "a highly

become a signatory to the Berne Convention until 1988 (effective 1st March 1989), in part because of the registration issues that were then part of US copyright law, even though it was recognised that in comparative terms, the American copyright regulations were both strong and effective. See United States Congress Office of Technology Assessment March 1990.

[35] Technological progress made during this time such as the arrival of sealed unit removal backup tape cartridges, higher storage floppy disks and the growth of use of both home PCs and departmental mini-computer systems (as opposed to corporate mainframes), all created the downside of facilitating easier software piracy, whilst also, of course providing many other benefits to commercial computer users.

[36] This is particularly resonant with the software industry as an important element in the high cost of production in this sector centres on the required salary levels of suitably skilled designers and programmers, whilst at the same time, many months of work may be copied illegally in a matter of seconds.

[37] Regular reports from producer organisations such as the International Intellectual Property Alliance (IIPA) and the Business Software Alliance (BSA) have consistently shown increases in piracy worldwide. Whilst methods of data collection have aroused

valued resource and the comparative advantage of technological leaders" (Sell, 2003:3) who had increasing incentives to move from "ad-hoc bilateral negotiations to binding global rules" (ibid.:4–5). It was in this context that the negotiations for the Uruguay Round of the GATT began in 1986.

A number of scholars (Trebilcock and Howse, 1999:320; Ostry, 1997:184) maintain that it was largely members of the United States delegation who "spearheaded the movement to have intellectual property rights included" in the Uruguay Round in the first place, whilst European Union (EU)[38] officials actually "required some prodding from high-technology industries and other domestic interests that stood to benefit from higher international standards for IP [sic] protection". The EU's initial "foot-dragging strategy" could perhaps be explained by their reluctance to engage in negotiations on agriculture given the internal political implications of its own Common Agricultural Policy (Ostry, 1997:184).

The inclusion of intellectual property into the multilateral trade negotiations generated considerable controversy—both at the time and subsequent to agreement being reached—and rested on fundamentally differing perspectives.

The US, along with the EU and Japan, saw the inclusion of IP as fundamental "to correct the basic asymmetry of the GATT" which focused largely on border issues and did not take account of what were increasingly being seen by IP exporting enterprises as barriers to market access that were behind the border "and not necessarily transparent" (ibid.:176), reflecting American corporate "resentment of structural differences in market systems" (ibid.:223). In this way (Adhikari and Athukorala, 2002:1; Ostry, 1997:185), these states sought to broaden the coverage of trade rules to include "virtually all economic activities relevant to economic interaction" that reflected an "ongoing trend to deeper integration, including the push to regulatory convergence and harmonization of legal systems in an increasingly legalistic

---

controversy, based on cost evaluations between potential and actual losses, broader overall trends over the two decades of statistical research cannot be ignored and would appear to have crystalised commercial concerns very effectively. See <http://www.iipa.com> and <http://www.bsa.org/country.aspx?sc_lang=en-GB>.

[38] Note that the European Union member states operate as a single block within the WTO for negotiating purpose under the name of "European Communities".

trade regime". IP was seen as one of the important new areas that required a more vigorous multilateral approach (Das, 2001).[39]

Developing countries took a different view (Ostry, 1997:189; Sell, 2003:13), seeing greater legal and institutional regulation of previously domestic concerns such as IP protection as an invasion of their sovereignty and a development which would represent "higher costs of technology acquisition" by establishing a regime that would favour "protection over diffusion (i.e. private rights over public goods) [sic]", which were a departure from GATT precedent. It was argued that such concepts were largely in the interests of developed countries, with many developing nations seeing little benefit to themselves in such commitments, preferring instead to concentrate on market access agreements in textile, clothing and agriculture (Michalopoulos, 2001). Some developing countries, particularly India, were concerned about the proposed broad nature of Trade Related Aspects of Intellectual Property Rights (TRIPS) and "sought to draw an important distinction between work on trade in counterfeit goods and IPRs [sic] more broadly defined" (Hoekman and Kostecki, 2001:283).

Negotiations on TRIPS reached agreement under what has been termed the "Grand Bargain" (Ostry, 2002a:285) of the Uruguay Round that led to the creation of the WTO under the GATT 1994 treaty.[40] This was encapsulated into the concept of a "Single Undertaking" for the whole of the treaty under an "all or nothing" arrangement (ibid.). It comprised "an implicit deal: the opening of OECD markets to agriculture and labor-intensive manufactured goods...for the inclusion into the trading system of trade in services (GATS), intellectual property (TRIPS) and investment (TRIMS) [sic]" (ibid.:287). In finally agreeing to the inclusion of TRIPS, the implied threat of US unilateral action against individual countries using American trade law sanctions may have been particularly salient in moving opinion, in that "given a choice between American sanctions or a negotiated multilateral arrangement, an agreement on TRIPS began to look better" (ibid.:286).

[39] Other new areas in the Uruguay Round besides intellectual property included trade in services (GATS) and trade related aspects of investment measures (TRIMS).

[40] The original GATT 1947 treaty was incorporated into the GATT 1994 treaty and the WTO replaced GATT as an international organisation. The TRIPS agreement is part of the accession protocol for membership to the WTO under Annex 1C and all such members are bound by its regulations.

Some scholars have also pointed out further motivators that may have been considerations. Developing countries (Michalopoulos, 2001:137; Abbott, 2002:313) may have felt that TRIPS "was of symbolic importance" and that "their adherence to international IPR norms would demonstrate to foreign investors that they were 'open for business' [sic]" and that, although final agreement was in part due to American pressure, there may also have been, to some extent, "a shift in the perceived value of IP protection to the developing countries".

There remains considerable disagreement as to the costs and benefits of the Round's outcomes, and in regard to TRIPS in particular, with some opinions maintaining that "TRIPS was heralded by many trade analysts as a triumph of the Uruguay Round" (Das, 2001:109). These largely developed country perspectives focus on the Agreement having introduced the principles of national treatment and MFN into the international trade of knowledge goods, along with the flexibilities of mutual recognition rather than direct legal harmonisation. This means that state regimes may differ from each other so long as they each adhere to the minimum standard mandated in TRIPS. Also of importance in this context is the provision to protect organisations subject to what the agreement terms "anti-competitive practices in contractual licenses" that might "have adverse effects on trade and may impede the transfer and dissemination of technology" (World Trade Organisation TRIPS Agreement, 1994: Art 40 Para 1).

Whilst some acknowledge that "[a] rules-based, rather than power-based, trading system is in the interests of developing countries" (Srinivasan, 2002:31), developing country arguments generally reflect the view that the outcome of the Round was "unbalanced" (ibid.:32), with smaller nations having to undertake costly commitments with few concrete benefits made in return by the industrialised economies. This "asymmetric" (Ostry, 2002a:290–91) perspective is especially sharp in regard to the TRIPS agreement and its associated implementation costs, particularly where advanced economies have seemingly failed to provide incentives to their enterprises for them to promote technology transfer to the least developed countries (LDCs) in the WTO.[41]

Indeed, some scholars (Bhagwati, 2004; Stiglitz and Charlton, 2005; Srinivasan, 2002:343) wholly reject the idea that IP should be part of a

---

[41] Article 66.2 of TRIPS stipulates that this should take place. See also. Michalopoulos, Developing Countries in the WTO, pp. 140–42.

trade agreement at all, maintaining that US lobbyists were focused on the collection of royalty payments on patents, operations that do not belong in the WTO, and consider that the inclusion of TRIPS was "a colossal mistake".

It has also been argued (Sell, 2003:2) that the successful implementation of TRIPS within a wider trade agreement "offered important lessons about the increasing role of private power in international politics", encapsulated in the Intellectual Property Committee (IPC)[42] that represented American corporate interests in software and pharmaceutical manufacturing in their dialogue with US trade policymakers. In this way, the GATT system, and the subsequent WTO, has been characterised by some analysts to be in large part "products of US entrepreneurship, persuasion, and pressure" that combines the influence of state and non-state actors in ways that are "made possible by the United States' hegemonic position in World politics" (Shaffer, 2005:130). In particular (ibid.:135), it is pointed out that "business and non-governmental groups in smaller countries…are unable to harness state power to advance their international priorities", sharpening perceived asymmetries already present in the system.

However, it is also acknowledged that power to influence outcomes in trading systems is linked to market dynamics and that the control leveraged over the WTO by both the US and the EU is because of the importance and size of their own markets (ibid.). In this context, evidence presented here of the significant growth of the trade in knowledge-based goods over recent years—originally centred from within the markets of Europe and North America—and the increasingly significant licensing-based global software industry within this trade cannot be ignored as a major driver for enhanced international regulation and as a stimulus for enterprises to promote the case for reliable minimums to exist in their trading partners. Moreover, the increased importance of technology in domestic knowledge sectors within key developing countries may have begun to change the perspectives of this argument. Market expansion and increased local company sophistication create incentives that may be converging with those of

[42] This powerful voice comprised representatives from 12 leading US knowledge industry corporations who co-ordinated argument and coalesced industry opinion during the shaping negotiations for the eventual TRIPS Agreement.

industrialised countries, at least for enterprises within economies such as China and India.[43]

Perhaps a balanced analysis of the overall Uruguay bargain might conclude that it was "not great, but not bad" (Ostry, 2002a:11), with the TRIPS element of the Single Undertaking continuing to be the focus of ongoing differences in perspective on the efficacy of the international intellectual property system.

In concert with the development of a global regime, regional integration of IP regulations in Europe has also been strengthening. In 1973, the European Patent Convention (EPC) was signed that established a European Patent Office (EPO) in Munich to provide "a single central office for the granting of bundles of national patents" (Bentley, 2004:25) whose remit was in fact wider than the European Union as it included both Switzerland and Turkey as signatories. Such national patents that are issued by the EPO must however be validated and litigated under the national court system of individual countries across the European continent and at present, a Europe-wide patent does not exist.[44]

Moreover, despite the harmonising tendencies promoted by agreements such as TRIPS that mandate minimum standards, distinctions still remain within national IP legal systems, even on fundamental issues. The United States, for example, maintains a "first to invent" patent system whilst the European Patent Office maintains "first to file" approach, along with much of the rest of the world; second, the US is unique in permitting widespread use of patents to cover software inventions. There is also some dissimilarity in copyright protection for software, particularly with jurisdictional differences in determining "fair use" to evaluate a computer program's operational functionality under "reverse engineering" approaches.[45]

---

[43] These issues are further explored in this and subsequent chapters.

[44] However, the importance of trade in knowledge goods between jurisdictions has in the past prompted some convergence of regulatory norms, at least between the EPO and the USPTO. For example, in the case of America's drive to harmonise its own copyright terms with those of the European Union during the copyright term extension debates.

[45] "Fair use" determines how the copyrightable work may be used by the licensee whether or not referenced in the stipulated license agreement, and are typically laid down in statute law as fair dealing exceptions. For example, the extent to which a computer program may be reverse engineered to facilitate interoperability of complementary programs is generally accepted in many countries. More problematic, however, is reverse engineering in order to obtain source code examples and data flow

2.4 *TRIPS and the Dispute Settlement Mechanism at the WTO*

The TRIPS Agreement is one of the central pillars of the current international intellectual property system.[46] In particular, TRIPS is subject to the Dispute Settlement Understanding (DSU) of the WTO, which sets it apart from previous international conventions in having a distinctive and defined dispute management mechanism for addressing IP concerns.[47] It can be argued that the inclusion of IP within an overall trade related agreement under GATT-based disciplines, rather than being hosted under WIPO, was particularly attractive to the industrialised economies in no small part because of the umbrella of dispute settlement mechanisms that the Single Undertaking made available.

Dispute management characteristics are important for a number of reasons. They reflect a continuing tension between dispute settlement mechanisms that are power-based, which may be likely to favour the interests of major developed member states such as the US and EU, and those that are rule-based, which could facilitate a more balanced approach. The transition towards the latter model in the DSU has been characterised as "incomplete" by a number of observers (Wilkinson, 2000:136). Some scholars further contrast the formalities of the system's legalism with more fluid "informal processes" that are used to frame operational rules, whereby developing countries "can find themselves ill-equipped to utilise this system to their advantage" (Narlikar, 2005:86).

---

handling logic for the purpose of creating a competitor (or clone) product, and where such actions are permitted or not will depend on the jurisdiction and the flexibilities of the copyright law in force. However, whilst international treaties have sought to create greater uniformity to national laws in copyright generally, this is a particular area where domestic distinctions still exist, and where legal argument and technical complexity continue to persist. For a very useful overview of these tensions, see Brian C. Beherens and Reuven R. Levary, 'Legal Aspects of Reverse Engineering', In *Reverse Engineering. An Industrial Perspective*, Springer, 2008. Eds. Vinesh Raja and Kiran J. Fernandes. Springer Series in Advanced Manufacturing.

[46] It comprises seven parts, of which four are particularly important. Part One outlines the codes of required behaviour and the set of principles inherited from existing WIPO conventions, such as national treatment. Part Two details the features of different types of IP regulation including patents, copyright and trademark protection. Part Three covers enforcement provisions required of member countries. Part Five covers dispute settlement, where the WTO Dispute Settlement Understanding procedures are used.

[47] See especially entries for 'Patents', 'Copyright' and 'Trademarks' in the index of disputes by type at the WTO's DSU online gateway.

Two particular weaknesses with the current system have been perceived. First, the cost and complexity of legal process of disputes has been highlighted (Shaffer, 2005:137). Commentators point out that defending or prosecuting cases within the DSU requires expertise and access to financial litigation resources that can undermine the ability of poorer countries to play a full and active part in asserting their positions. In an attempt to address this imbalance, the Advisory Centre on WTO Law was established to redress some of this imbalance in accessing legal resources by providing legal opinion and advice "to developing country and economy in transition [sic] Members of the Centre and all least developed countries free of charge up to a maximum of hours to be determined by the Management Board".[48]

The second weakness in the WTO's dispute system that has been highlighted by some reflects the concern that retaliation within DSU proceedings is based on trade rather than on financial compensation (Narlikar, 2005:96–7). It is also argued (Busch and Reinhardt, 2002:475; Shaffer, 2005:159) that cases are ultimately solved through diplomatic negotiations, even within the context of panel judgements and appellate body decision-making, wherein there may even be a tendency towards conciliatory behaviour towards powerful states "to minimise the risks of institutionally damaging noncompliance", all of which give the major developed economies an advantage within this framework, under what is termed a "second order institutional power".

Some scholars point to further changes that could assist poorer countries in this respect. In particular (Chaisse and Chakraborty, 2006; Narlikar, 2005), the introduction of group retaliation, as a complement to the existing ability to cross-retaliate across different trade sectors when implementing successful judgements[49] coupled with the introduction of DSU dialogue being able to be located locally rather than always having to be based in Geneva, which may assist smaller countries with staff resource and budget constraints.

Nevertheless, (Adhikari, 2002:8; Chaisse, 2006:528; ibid.:508) despite many believing that "there is ample scope for betterment of the current

[48] See Advisory Centre on WTO Law at <http://www.acwl.ch/e/legal/legal_e.aspx>.

[49] In this way, for example, Ecuador was able to suspend TRIPS obligations to the EU in its dispute with the European Union over banana imports into Europe. See Dispute Number DS27 'Regime for Importation, Sale and Distribution of Bananas' at <http://www.wto.org/english/tratop_e/dispu_e/cases_e/ds27_e.htm>.

system", it is also important to recognise that a number of observers do regard the DSU "as a major balancing tool in the system", and point out that it does provide an element of "security and predictability to the multilateral trading system" which has led to the leading developing countries making use of the mechanisms in their own interests, "bringing cases against developed and developing country members".[50]

Whilst some argue (Davis, 2006:219) that "less developed countries are at a disadvantage when negotiating with more powerful counterparts", it may be more useful to reflect on whether they would be at a greater disadvantage if the WTO and the DSU did not exist and they were having to engage in bilateral negotiations outside of the multilateral framework (ibid.).[51] In this context (ibid.:210; ibid.:254), it can be argued that "the WTO dispute settlement procedures provide developing country members with a distributive tactic that helps them to negotiate the reduction of trade barriers against their products" and that, at the very least, the DSU's existence "adds to the tactical toolkit available to a developing country".

It may be that this inherent flexibility is now persuading some developed economies to move "offline" with trade issues, especially in respect to TRIPS. In particular, the United States appears to be

[50] For example, India has challenged the EC on its tariff preferences granted to some developing countries and secured a partial victory after ruling by the Appellate Body in April 2004 that led to changes in EU law that took effect in July 2005. See WTO, Dispute No. 246, <http://www.wto.org/english/tratop_e/dispu_e/cases_e/ds246_e.htm>, accessed 22nd February 2007. Also, Brazil challenged the US on its safeguard rules for imported steel and also secured a favourable outcome whereby the American government terminated all of the measures that were subject to dispute at the end of 2003. See Dispute No. 259, <http://www.wto.org/english/tratop_e/dispu_e/cases_e/ds259_e.htm>, accessed 22nd February 2007. At the end of 2006, 24 TRIPS specific complaints had been filed over the previous decade, mostly by industrialised countries, except for one case brought against the United States by Brazil, who were seeking consultations about US Patent Code provisions. Four of these disputes have focused on IP enforcement deficiencies in different nations, three have centred on copyright disputes between jurisdictions and eleven have involved disagreements over patent laws in member states. See also Dispute No. 224, <http://www.wto.org/english/tratop_e/dispu_e/cases_e/ds224_e.htm>, accessed 28th February 2007.

[51] Davis contrasts two cases—see pp225–40. First, the Peru / EC dispute over labelling of sardine exports, DS231-Trade Description of Sardines, at <http://www.wto.org/english/tratop_e/dispu_e/cases_e/ds231_e.htm>, in March 2001. Peru was successful by using "legal bandwagoning" after Canada and the US became third parties to the case. Second, in July 2000, the unsuccessful attempt by Vietnam, not a WTO member, to negotiate with the US over America's attitude towards imported Catfish, based on a bilateral treaty between the two countries.

increasingly ready to embark on bilateral dialogue as an expression of frustration in multilateral progress. Some observers see a growing tendency for American negotiators to seek solutions to problems outside of the formal multilateral negotiating venues, with the US now trying to achieve its IP regime goals through regional and country specific free trade agreements (FTAs) and related enforcement linkages rather than within the multilateral context.[52]

Ongoing tensions within the international IP system, both in a multilateral and a bilateral context, continue to be focused on those perceived to be enjoying the benefits of trade in IP goods without the associated cost of creating those goods—the free-riders—through the piracy of copyrighted materials and products under patent and the counterfeiting of trademark protected goods.

Different countries are often involved in different types of IP dispute, based on the priorities of their own domestic industrial base. For example, a great deal of the conflict between the EU and China rests on trademark disputes, especially those involving "well-known" marks in high-value apparel such as Versace and famous marks of origin such as French "Champagne" and Scottish "Single Malt Whisky". In a recent report by the European Chamber of Commerce in China, three out of the top five concerns on IP trends (including the top two issues) focused on weaknesses in Chinese trademark administrative procedures and enforcement (E.U. Chamber of Commerce I.P.R. Working Group, 2007–07). In contrast, many of the IP conflicts that exercise the US administration with China typically involve the very high piracy rates on copyright products such as software and audiovisual entertainment DVDs.[53]

However, it may now be too simplistic to see this as a conflict between the first and third world or just between industrialised and developing nations. In recent yeas, a number of developments can be observed to have taken place in the relationship between those nations traditionally seen as IP producers and those typically categorised as IP consumers. This may change the dynamic of future disputes.

[52] Interview with an official of the Indian Mission to the WTO, Geneva, July 2005. See also the FTA with Singapore for further examples of this trend.

[53] Note that one particularly notable exception to the US focus on copyright was the trademark disputes between Starbucks Coffee and various Chinese imitators that had attempted to exploit the American corporation's signage, either in its colour and layout or by using similar sounding Chinese character equivalents. For an overview of the case see (Managing Intellectual Property Online Edition 2006a).

2.5 *Introducing the Drivers for IP Regime Evolution in China and India*

The strengthening of IP regulations and enforcement characteristics within a national economy can be seen as being subject to a number of endogenous and exogenous influences. These changes would appear to take place within distinct phases of a country's economic development, with the interplay of diverse groups of actors, including the ideas of inspirational national leaders, the policy objectives of the national government, the strategies of domestic and international market enterprises and the principles espoused by the outcomes of collaboration within international norm-setting institutions. Each of these elements can have different levels of influence that they bring to bear at different times in each phase of this transition.[54]

The development over recent years of China and India as export-oriented centres with an increasingly innovation-based knowledge economy would seem to provide a useful illustration of these trends, acting as a reprise of development policies and IP regime trajectories evident in the economic models of other Asian nations such as Japan and the Republic of Korea in previous decades. It also introduces distinctive characteristics related to the political and economic conditions that persist in each country and that acts as a framework to regime building.

Empirical evidence suggests that attitudes towards IP regulations for IP-rich products change fundamentally when a country's growth strategy shifts from traditional import substitution industrialisation (ISI) towards one focused on export-led expansion.

Under ISI conditions, local industrial and technological capacity is accumulated as quickly and cheaply as possible and is accompanied by typically scant regard for the intellectual property interests of either domestic or overseas rights holders as products are copied and technology is mimicked from all possible sources as an industrial framework

[54] For a particularly interesting discussion of these levels of growth in software industries within developing country perspectives, see John McManus, China and India: Opportunities and Threats for the Global Software Industry. See especially pp. 6–7. Writing from a strategic management perspective and focusing on corporate strategy, they highlight multiple levels wherein IPR has a different salience at each stage, ranging from times of high piracy, through initial concerns of domestic produces, to a progressive clampdown and a growing acceptance of international norms, stimulated by a combination of domestic enterprise growth and multinational market penetration.

is established. Whilst IP violations can be recognised by outsiders as occurring, their impact on overseas rights holders could be interpreted as being less significant at this point as the domestic markets of countries adopting ISI are largely closed to overseas penetration, with pirate goods mainly aimed towards local consumption. In this sense, piracy is perceived as a problem but is confined to operations within national boundaries and has not yet become an international issue.

By contrast, under export-led strategies, there would appear to be a narrower focus on specific sectors in the economy, introducing the necessity that these industries need to be brought closer to the leading edge of technological development in order to compete effectively in the international market. It therefore follows that there would have to be different technological requirements in an export-led strategy versus one linked to import substitution, as industrial imperatives of competition in international markets increase the significance of innovation and specialisation.

Under these conditions, evidence would suggest that domestic actors in these countries, at both a government level and within knowledge-based industries themselves, begin to consider policies and behaviour norms that focus more on accumulating and defending their own stock of IP in order to expand their penetration beyond protected domestic sales and enter export markets with products suitable for more discerning consumers rather than expropriating and imitating the IP of others. Over time, local companies seek ways to move up the value chain of products that retain high IP, as they expand both the size and sophistication of their enterprises, making them more concerned with ways to legitimise both their own IP and that which they have absorbed from foreign companies through partnerships and knowledge spillovers, often domestically promoted by local government in clustered technological development areas.

However, the evidence from both China and India would also suggest that these changes in approach take place across distinctive periods in the regulatory evolution of a country's IP system, and, indeed, timelines may often vary across industry sectors even within the knowledge economy. It is important, therefore, to recognise that an increased propensity for respecting IP within an economy need not be coincident with an embrace of export-oriented growth and wider market opening strategies, but that it should instead be seen as the essential starting point from which later stages of IP regime development are based.

It can be argued that each of these discrete phases can be characterised by different levels of actor involvement and different kinds of pressure in respect to the emerging national IP regime. It may therefore be useful to provide a brief overview of each stage, highlighting the underlying drivers within each one and summarising the distinctive character of their effect in both China and India.

In the first phase of this shift, the state typically seems to take the lead in decision-making, perhaps initiated by inspirational national leaders such as India's Rajiv Ghandi and China's Deng Xiaoping,[55] with policy initiatives focusing on nurturing and promoting domestic knowledge-based industries as an economic priority and as the basis for a successful export-oriented strategy. Market entry by domestic enterprises is encouraged with a broad range of sector specific stimulus and these early stage companies use the export-oriented environment to gain essential cross-sector based market intelligence on potential trading partners and overseas customers.

Most importantly in respect to IP, this phase would appear to be typically characterised by a lackadaisical approach to IP protection. Such an attitude uses a lax regulatory environment as a vehicle for sharing much needed technical know-how across firms active in knowledge sectors. This understanding can be accumulated by exploiting knowledge from new trading partners who may have been attracted into the market by at least bare minimums of protection or it can be facilitated by a deliberately lax IP regime that favours deliberate IP appropriation.

These features can help to explain both China and India's early period of technological development. In China, the commercial potential of the market size attracted much interest in technological engagement by overseas corporations as the national leadership began to open different economic sectors to export orientation in special development zones, in which both legitimate and illegitimate knowledge exchange with local firms took place. In India, even after broad national policies had embraced an export driven growth model, market opening was accompanied by the maintenance of a weak patenting regime to

[55] Chinese family names are traditionally listed in front of first names. However, some Chinese also adopt western first names in addition to their own natural given name, whereupon they typically reformat their name to be firstname-surname, perhaps also giving their real Chinese name in surname-firstname format in brackets, often in Chinese characters.

promote further growth in India's pharmaceutical industry and weak copyright regulations that assisted the early stage of India's software industry evolution.

In particular, it is during this phase that specific tensions can arise between local and international firms active in the knowledge industry, whereby national protection regulations start to become an international issue as foreign IP owners exploit market opening opportunities to penetrate local communities with their own products. This strategy typically brings overseas enterprises into direct conflict with pre-existing centres of local counterfeit production, in terms of both the circulation of pirate commodities within the domestic market and in the export of these goods to third countries. Collisions in markets between the genuine article and its imitations cause anxieties amongst these IP owners over lost sales and reduced profits, all of which increase their propensity to lobby for intervention by state actors of their home country to force greater respect for their IP rights abroad.

In China, as foreign firms sought to enter and exploit the potential of China's large domestic consumer base with their own products, disputes over IP violations in various provinces arose to provide a basis for tension and conflict between China and its trading partners. The United States became especially vexed over copyright violations, promoting what they regarded as an ongoing attitude to piracy that brought the two countries to the brink of a trade war during the mid 1990's.

In India, such tensions were distinctly visible in pharmaceutical manufacturing with particular international concern centred on the growth of exports of products that included drugs still under patent protection outside India but legally developed within the country under different patent rules by local pharmaceutical firms.[56] Within the IT industry, issues arose over the use of advanced software reverse engineering techniques and selective program module piracy by the country's pioneer technology companies as a complement to their low-IP intensive, labour-exporting, early growth model.[57]

---

[56] Despite the very real disputes that this engendered between Indian and international drug manufacturers, much of these exports were in fact based on formulations that were already out-of-patent. These issues will be explored in further detail later in a later chapter.

[57] For a more detailed discussion of reverse engineering in an Indian legal context, see the section in this book entitled "Knowledge Acquisition in India's Technology Growth" in the chapter entitled "Market Driven Development in India".

Early stage activities in China and India therefore led to defensive policies by IP owners in overseas markets. This caused conflict from the entry point of both countries into export engagement, especially with the US, as firms and commercial interest groups lobbied government actors for the country's inclusion in Presidential trade reports as a foundation for seeking redress through trade sanctions.

The increased trading interdependencies that accrue between countries when their predominant policy is export-oriented can also empower non-state actors to influence tensions and regime evolution in ways that are also separate from state-to-state negotiations. Using the independence and power of judicial mechanisms in nations governed by rule-of-law systems, private sector actors possess the capability to seek judgements that can have a direct effect on the exporting possibilities of trading partners, either by seeking to block IP infringing imports through customs seizures, or by imposing legal obligations on politicians and states that can have consequential impact across the broader scope of trade negotiations.[58]

For example, the US International Trade Commission is empowered by American law to investigate potential IP violations within imported products and can prevent their circulation into the US if violations of US interests are found. These so-called "Section 337" investigations (from the 1930 Tariff Act) may be initiated by individuals and enterprises, as well as government agencies. According to a 2006 US government report, use of such IP protection powers were "up more

[58] The long-running dispute between Canada and the US on softwood lumber subsidies presents an important example of this power as national courts and private companies had considerable salience throughout the dispute in concert with governments and multilateral forums. For an overview of the legal framework of the Softwood Lumber Dispute see PINR Internet News Portal <http://www.pinr.com/report.php?ac=view_report&report_id=361&language_id=1> and also see Mike Moffat: *Softwood Lumber Dispute Resource Center* at online economics discussion website http://economics.about.com/cs/agriculture/a/softwooddispute.htm. All accessed 22nd February 2007. For details about the US Trade Commission, which acts in a quasi-judicial capacity to adjudicate outcomes in trade disputes. See the Commission's website at <http://www.usitc.gov/ext_relations/about_itc/index.htm> accessed 22nd February 2007. There is now an agreement in place that resolves these subsidy issues until 2013. In 1986, US commercial lumber producers successfully petitioned the Federal Department of Commerce to take action under the terms of America's domestic Countervailing Duty Law. In response, Canadian interests also made recourse to US domestic legal institutions in order to try and resolve the dispute, independent of the dialogue between the two governments at an inter-state level on the matter in dispute settlement forums offered by both the North American Free Trade Agreement (NAFTA) and the WTO. See (Foese 2006). See also (Grimmett 30th January 2007).

than 80% over the last five years" (United States Trade Representative, 2006b:16). This shows the potential power of individual firms to disrupt international trade using available domestic legislative routes.

Despite the inevitable challenges, this first stage is, however, extremely important in the evolution of a country's IP system and was a necessary starting point for both China and India's subsequent regime evolution. During this phase, an essential grounding in market knowledge for enterprises in both countries was generated, enabling them to gain important insights into overseas industrial sectors whilst providing a platform for their own domestic expansion.

The progression into the second phase of IP regime evolution typically takes place in different ways within different sectors of the knowledge economy, based on the extent to which legal systems relevant to each industry are modified and the effects that different characteristics of cultures within society can have on commercial behaviour. In particular, India's less regulated software industry appears to have embraced more conservative trends towards IP regulation at an earlier stage than the more protected pharmaceutical industry, given the different historical legal regime in place governing patents versus that which controls copyright. Moreover, in China, a propensity towards East Asian familial culture in business development and a concentration on earlier Asia specific technology and software services exports may perhaps explain how Chinese attitudes towards IP in technology seem to have evolved at a different pace to those of India.

The key transition to recognise is that during this second phase of regulatory evolution, shifts in influence begin to take place amongst different actors as enterprises within a particular knowledge sector take on greater visibility in their influence of the rulemaking process. This is based on new interests that businesses have during this time to move up the IP value chain by exploiting the generalised knowledge accumulated previously and transforming it into more specialised vertical market understanding that has far higher returns in business transactions within different market sectors.

Developments of this kind can involve the establishment of stronger international partnerships and full joint ventures at a commercial level and the creation of industrial hubs and high technology clusters to promote legitimate spillovers at a policy level. International norms and the institutions promoting them begin to gain greater visibility as higher value products and services require higher levels of domestic protection, as both industry and government look to acceptable standards of behaviour that can promote greater levels of technological growth into the future. Messages to this effect may be transmitted to government through different channels based on the cultural character of the country concerned, perhaps directly through corporate communication channels, more generally via stronger industry specific pressure groups or by ideas and attitudes put forward by commentators and national politicians.

In China, the characteristics of this phase appear to have been typically hierarchical in the transmission of messages between firms and government, in a way that prioritised the attitudes of the national leadership, those of academic thinkers and specific enterprise managers in sectors of high IP output, whose connections with the political system appeared to give them special access to decision making elites.

In this way, Chinese attitude in some sectors towards piracy can be seen to have altered during this stage to better recognise the value of IP-rich exports in electronics and technology hardware, along with the potential value of software skills and off-shored services to both Asian and international clients, all of which were seen as being important to sustain the country's economic growth. This may help to explain the shifted positions of both senior policy leaders and innovative commercial entrepreneurs in their respect for absorbing IP norms that have taken place in the country over the last decade, and also why some other sectors, such as apparel, did not change attitude in the same way.[59]

In India, a more pluralist dimension shaped the emergence of more conservative IP attitudes, with powerful industry groups taking corporate concerns directly into agenda-setting meetings of the political leadership. Such levels of pluralism may even be counter-productive when combined with attitude differences within a particular sector, most usefully illustrated by pharmaceuticals, which has strong industry cleavages centred around differing attitudes towards innovation-based export growth.

In respect to some pharmaceutical companies, the initial embrace of export-oriented growth strategies led some of them to look with interest at proactive overseas engagement and a greater willingness to

[59] Author interview with an official attached to the Permanent Mission of the People's Republic of China to the WTO, Geneva, May 2005. See also a presentation on changing attitudes to IP within China's film and music industries, given at a conference at Cambridge University to discuss economic and social transformations in China (Montgomery 2007).

invest in more innovatory research. These companies looked to a lobby group that could promote their calls for stronger IP rules and changes in patent laws. Other industry corporations, however, whilst enjoying benefits of revenue growth from the export of generics, had less interest in patent law changes and formed a lobby group that promoted their own attitudes at government levels. Such domestic tensions may explain the longer timescales and policy disagreements involved in strengthening domestic IP policy in respect to drug patents and why the strictures of international norms and treaty obligations may have had a particularly high level of salience in India's pharmaceutical policy development, as the government sought to find an appropriate and responsible pathway through conflicting interests.[60]

This can be contrasted to attitudes prevalent in the Indian software industry, where the second phase of IP evolution was based on incentives derived from rising revenues and from increasingly high value international contracts. In this case, the issue of stronger IP regulations to support industry expansion found agreement across enterprises and government and led to high levels of uniformity in attitude to new IP measures, combined with lower levels of conflict with trading partners.[61] The industry-sympathetic content and smooth legislative passage of the Copyright Amendment Acts of 1994 and 1999 and the IT Act of 2000 may present a useful illustration of increasing corporate influence and uniformity of attitude within the IT industry that was absent from pharmaceuticals during the promulgation of the Patent Amendment Acts of 1999, 2002 and 2005.

Movement into the third phase of IP regime evolution within a country can be characterised by an embrace of innovation as a central feature of national knowledge industry development strategies. Different industries in different countries will move to an innovation based strategy at different points in time and as a corollary of higher value

---

[60] Op. cit. author interview, Indian Mission to WTO, Geneva, July 2005.

[61] Author's interview with a NASSCOM vice president, held at the organisation's Annual Conference in Mumbai, February 2006. NASSCOM is an extremely effective and well-organised industry association, with respected links into the Indian government ministries, and recognition internationally as a credible source of industry trends and statistical background. For example, when seeking an replacement Chairman for troubled outsourcing supplier Satyam, after its accounting and reporting problems became public in early 2009, it was to a former NASSCOM head, Kiran Karnik, that the Indian government turned. See Reuters News Agency, 6th February 2009, available online at <http://uk.reuters.com/article/euPrivateEquityNews/idUKTRE5151HV20090206>, accessed 9th April, 2009.

engagement with overseas markets. An accumulated level of industry abilities enable individual firms to provide products and services that are at the leading edge of their respective industries. The need to secure stronger and more effective protection for their own innovation-driven IP-rich outputs in both domestic and international markets provides the framework for an increasingly proactive stance by these companies.

In this phase, enterprises and industry specialist groups not only connect with national political leaders as part of their operations but also seek to take their regulatory goals directly into dialogue with complementary organisations in other countries and within international forums, operating beyond national borders, bringing influence to bear on IP regime development at multiple levels.

In the context of China and India, perhaps only the Indian software industry has really reached this level of sophisticated engagement in IP system building, mirroring the complex levels found in developed economies such as the United States and United Kingdom. In India, the software industry's special position is evident from the strong relationship its industry association continues to have with national government and with domestic anti-piracy policies, as well as its increasing involvement with a wider collection of international specialised interest groups seeking to raise levels of IP protection through the adoption of stronger global norms.

Within the Indian pharmaceuticals sector, innovation oriented attitudes are emerging from leading domestic corporations who have been amongst the first to exploit new legal protections for inventive patents and who had already developed significant international market penetration through having adopted a whole-hearted drive to exploit export-oriented growth strategies. However, the current fragmented model of the Indian drugs industry, still representing a range of markedly different attitudes to IP amongst their key corporations, make it more difficult to emulate the strength of purpose and the sophisticated use of communication channels, both domestic and international, that is exhibited by the country's software industry.

In China, innovation strategies can be seen in some enterprises within high-value, network electronics hardware and related communications software, as well as within some sectors of the software services industry, as they have moved into international markets beyond their East Asian base and have tackled advanced software development for customers in western computer technology firms (sometimes in direct competition with Indian enterprises). A proactive national leadership can be seen to be operating in lieu of industry lobby groups, where political leaders liaise directly with overseas commercial IP owners seeking to resolve conflicts in tandem with inter-state level dialogue and increased Chinese visibility in multilateral regime building institutions such as WIPO and the WTO.

In this context, Chinese President Hu Jintao's meeting with Microsoft's Bill Gates at the latter's home at the start of his official visit to the United States in April 2006 may well also be a pointed example of such a condition. There was considerable industry speculation at the time that one of the items under discussion included recent moves by the Chinese government to ensure that only legitimate licensed software would be installed on Chinese produced computer hardware. In particular, the Chinese President may have been considering the export implications to his own domestic producers of computer hardware if Microsoft had sought legal redress in US courts to prevent imports with unlicensed software entering the American market (Microsoft Corporation, 18th April 2006).[62] This may have also been one of the motivations behind Lenovo's agreement with Microsoft to guarantee that their hardware would only embed legitimate Windows versions (Noto, Shah and Harrop, 1999).

These moves imply that political and commercial elites must take into account the sensitivities that may be present in their target overseas markets when expanding export-oriented growth strategies with major trading partners such as the United States (National Bureau of Statistics of China, 2006).[63] This can be seen as part of trends towards widening actor participation in IP regime evolution that connects explicitly with observable increases in cross-border enterprise and lobby group activity, in terms of both horizontal communications amongst

---

[62] See also (Microsoft Corporation 17th April 2006).

[63] For 2005, official Chinese statistics put Chinese exports to the US at 21.4% of total exports by value (US$162 billion for 2005), making the United States China's most important export market. See Table 18–8, pp. 740–43. Note the US import figures from China for that year, at US$243 billion, are markedly higher. This can be traced to ongoing disputes between the US and China on statistical recording and aggregations in this area, which may help explain the difference, allegedly in particular respect to "third country" trade. See also (Fung, Lau, and Xiong 2006).

these entities and upward pressure towards influencing national and international political institutions.[64]

Moreover, the evolution of consumption preferences towards more sophisticated products by elements in the domestic constituency of developing countries can help to adjust local production priorities, with a rising middle-class having become more evident in China and India over recent years (McKinsey & Co 2006.; Economist Print Edition, 2005a). This can also help to explain the growing change in attitude about IP infringement within these two countries, emphasising an apparent shift in the balance between those that see the benefits of piracy and those who are now coming to appreciate the potential gains to be made by concentrating on legitimate IP-rich product development.

In this way, the IP regimes of China and India can be seen to have developed subject to multi-faceted influences operating within distinctive phases of regulatory evolution, inherent in drives to move up the value chain of technological production in order to satisfy sophisticated consumption requirements in both overseas and home markets.

It can therefore be argued that these first-rank developing nations may now have more to gain through adherence to regulatory IP principles than to continuing counterfeit production. It can also be argued that they are beginning to achieve intersection with the preferences and priorities of their partner nations in the industrialised world.

In an IP context, therefore, the implementation of more effective regulatory and enforcement strategies within their jurisdictions may be based upon the increasing importance of the knowledge goods trade to themselves and within the international system, and of the associated benefits that can be derived from market entry as a producer. It is therefore useful to explore this rise in the IP content of world trade to better understand how these trends have evolved, both internationally and their impact on China and India specifically.

[64] These observations and the supporting evidence for such trends are covered in much more detail later in this research: see the section entitled: 'A Central Role for IP in the Global Domain'.

2.6 *Value of Knowledge Sectors in the Trading System*

The world trading system is geared towards recording trade in merchandise goods and traditional services and recording mechanisms have not yet adjusted to changes in structure that illustrate the importance of more advanced services such as IT, software and business process services and especially in the increased propensity towards the outsourcing of the supply of such domestic service activity to foreign domiciled companies. The WTO has tackled this with two reports over the last two years that attempt to quantify some of these trends whilst the overall picture of trading activity across the world is updated over time to take better account of these developments (World Trade Reports, 2005; 2006).

There have been ongoing challenges to capturing the growth in trade in such transactions. First, only a limited number of economies report balance of trade statistics data in computer and information services to organisations such as the IMF and WTO. Survey data of the kind typically used by government statistical organisations to report national economic growth can have inbuilt weaknesses, where some sectors are not properly represented in aggregate analysis, especially in respect to smaller enterprises and service-based industries such as companies in IT and software. Perhaps the most marked example of this kind of problem occurred at the end of 2005 when the Chinese National Bureau of Statistics had to re-evaluate China's GDP figures upwards by several billion dollars in order to recognise the contribution made to national wealth by small and medium sized service industries in major towns and cities (People's Republic of China Government Statement, 2005).[65]

Second, there are difficulties in how to categorise IP-rich activities across the standard transaction classifications of the reporting tables, with many Balance of Payment (BOP) statistics on measures that are either too small or too large to catch the precise breakdowns required (World Trade Report, 2005).

Third, there can be import/export discrepancies between bilateral trade in IT services even between two reporting economies with close trading relationships. For example, India and the United States exhibit

[65] This re-evaluation included non-IT sectors such as small-scale hairdressing salons and family-run restaurants, as well as other kinds of service supplier, and it shows the potential weaknesses of assumptions that can be made in national survey data collections.

reporting discrepancies in bilateral trade in computing and information services amounting to some US$4.8 billion for 2003 (ibid.).[66] WTO research has speculated that this may be caused by a distinction in how Indian nationals working under H1-B visas in America have their contribution classified. The implication is that India may be claiming these nationals as their own in terms of wages paid and benefits accrued whilst the US authorities regards them as being local residents and thus not accounted for as import costs (ibid.).

Moreover, the actual tradable unit element itself is often just a license or permission to exploit and not a physical unit of transferred ownership and the value reported of such activities "might be affected by tax considerations and not always reflect the market value accurately" (World Trade Report, 2006:22). Indeed, even with the sector's growing importance and recognising that data collected by the International Monetary Fund (IMF) highlights license fee transactions, "[a] detailed breakdown of royalty and license fee payments by type is not available" (ibid.).

Given some of these difficulties, it may be most appropriate to isolate broad-based activities and highlight ongoing trends within a set of classifications. Based on official figures from the WTO gathered under estimations of this kind, there is evidence that within world trading activity over the first years of the new millennium, the value of advanced and complex IP-rich computer and information services has been increasing significantly. For the year 2003, the value of exports for all business services has been estimated by the WTO using BOP statistics at US$494 billion,[67] of which the significant subsection of "Computer and Information Services" (CIS) accounted for US$75.1 billion,[68] growing from US$51.7 billion in 2000, with India having the second highest figure (at US$11.2 billion) for CIS exports in 2003, just behind Ireland. Thus, the growth rate of the specific technology-driven CIS category of services for the three years from 2000 to 2003 was 45%, which is greater than the growth in more general business

[66] Such problems represent an area that will likely need to be clarified in the future as IT trade between these two countries continues to have greater salience in world figures.

[67] See Table 1: 'Global IT markets, trade and off-shored IT services'. The total figure includes accountancy, call centres, R&D activities, auditing and bookkeeping as well as IT and information services (which includes a range from software development to satellite news feeds).

[68] See Table 2: 'The major traders in computer and business services, 2000 and 2003. Section A: Computer and Information Services'.

services (including CIS), estimated to have been 31% for the same period[69] and also greater than growth estimates for the wider category of general commercial services, which was put at 21% over this same time.[70] It is also greater than the growth in merchandise trade, put at 16% for those years (World Trade Report, 2005).

Further developments can be observed in respect to the two most significant developing countries, India and China, both of which stand out as high achievers within the broad category of General Commercial Services exports, according to the WTO report, increasing the value of their general services exports significantly over recent years. In this category, these two countries achieved, for the period 2000 to 2005, an average annual growth rate of 33% for India, reaching US$68 billion by 2005, and 22% for China, reaching US$81 billion for that year. These rates of services export growth were higher than that achieved by any of the other named countries or regions (including the United States) over the same period in the WTO's report (ibid.).[71] Whilst it is difficult to determine the precise extent of IP content in all of these commercial services exports, due to aforementioned reasons, these figures do help to illustrate the growing contribution made in non-merchandise goods by both India and China to the international trading system.

Commercial reports and industry surveys, even despite their shortcomings, provide further evidence of significant expansion for technology-based services, software development and IT product consumption. The European Information Observatory, for example, issued findings in their latest report for 2006 that indicates growth in the IT market within countries outside the US, EU and Japan—what it terms as "the Rest of the World", wherein East Asia and South Asia dominate—has far outpaced that in developed nations, achieving a rise of 9.3% for 2005 and predicting rises of 8.6% during 2006 and 8.8% for 2007 (European Information Observatory, 2006). Given this rate of expansion in the IT markets within the leading developing nations, it is perhaps not surprising that these trends have occurred in concert

---

[69] See the section: "Major traders in global IT services trade 2000–2003".

[70] Note that on page 275 of this report, total commercial services exports were estimated at US$1,800 billion for 2003 whilst total world GDP for 2003 was reported as US$36,000 billion.

[71] "World Trade 2005. Prospects for 2006": Appendix Table 2: 'World Trade of commercial services by region and selected country, 2005'.

with changes in the characteristics of the intellectual property protection system.

2.7 *Current Trends in Regulatory Regimes*

There has been a marked development in intellectual property regime complexity over the last few years indicating that the regulatory landscape has not remained a static phenomenon and that the TRIPS Agreement should be seen as part of a series of wide ranging measures to deal with transnational[72] issues of intellectual property. This can be seen as part of a continuum, whereby the Great Conventions[73] of the 19th Century introduced the behavioural norms and treaty principles upon which trade in knowledge goods could reliably take place and were then followed by the minimum-standard setting trends introduced by the TRIPS policies of behind the border lawmaking. What is now clear is that an expansion of the scope and a deepening of the intensity in international IP regulation is taking place and that this process has highlighted an increasing visibility of the role taken by the private sector in the development of the international system of property rights protection.

This has manifested itself in a number of ways. First, the workings of the regulatory system have become more interconnected over the last few years as the importance of asserting IP ownership in different regions has become more important in achieving commercial success in international markets. A particular example of this trend has been the expansion in use of the PCT enacted through WIPO and now having membership of 133 Contracting States with international applications having risen by an annual average of 16% from 1990 to 2005 (WIPO Patent Bulletin, 2006).

Whilst the ease of electronic filing and the costs management reductions of initial multi-country assessments make the PCT attractive for smaller and medium sized commercial enterprises, the mechanism is especially suitable for large multinationals seeking protection across the globe as it provides a single point of input and a 30-month delay

---

[72] In terms of international relations, "transnational issues" implies inter-actor communication rather than the inter-state dialogue of "international" issues.

[73] A group term applied to the Paris and Berne Conventions.

on desired national filings, during which time products are protected from local imitation. These types of organisations can more than cover the costs[74] of multinational patent filings and it is perhaps not surprising that over 135,000 filings were made under the PCT in 2005 (a rise of over 10% from the previous year) and that Philips, Matsushita, Siemens, Nokia and Intel feature as principal participants within the top ten users of the system (Economist Print Edition 2005d; WIPO 2006a, Patent Report, 2006).[75]

Second, global patenting activity has increased steadily over the last few years, and especially in the ten years between 1995 and the end of 2004 for which current WIPO analysis exists, during which time a sharper increase in non-resident cross-country patenting became detectable in WIPO reports (excluding PCT processes which are handled separately for statistical gathering purposes). These non-resident filings rose at 7.4% per year compared with the 4.75% growth exhibited by patenting activity overall for the same period (WIPO Patent Report, 2006). Centres exhibiting a particularly high growth in all patenting applications include China and India, amongst others, as well as continued growth in the more expected locations of the United States and the European Patent Office and it is particularly interesting to note that in the top five patenting locations for 2004, three are from East Asia (Japan, China and Republic of Korea)[76] with Japan actually tops the list having received almost 450,000 patent filing applications in 2004 (WIPO Patent report, 2006). According to WIPO, at the end of 2004, there were 5.4 million active patents across the world with an upward trend projected into the future and a dominance amongst the first world multinationals with IBM heading the list as the organisation which filed the most patents in 2004 with 3,248 (ibid.).

---

[74] Commercial estimates put the cost of preparing and filing a single patent with the US Patent and Trademark Office at approximately US$35,000 with a timescale of around two to three years.

[75] See also World Intellectual Property Organisation, 'Top 500 PCT Applicants', <http://www.wipo.int/ipstats/en/statistics/pct/applicants_ranking.html>, accessed 20th October 2006.

[76] Note that reports from different sources describing "Korea" using the nomenclature Republic of Korea, RoK or South Korea interchangeably. Similarly, "China" refers to the mainland provinces of the People's Republic of China and does not include its Special Administrative Regions of Hong Kong and Macau and also not the disputed territory of the Republic of China on Taiwan, the latter being variously referred to as RoC, Taiwan or Chinese Taipei.

This not only shows the trend towards greater worldwide patent visibility amongst international business but also that the Asian markets and especially East Asia, have markedly increased their importance over recent years to organisations that seek to protect their inventions and realise returns form their R&D. In particular, China's rate of growth in the number of patent applications made by residents in the decade to the end of 2004 was a remarkable 557% (ibid.) although this also shows the highly disadvantageous position in which the country emerged from its years of isolation under an ideologically driven communist party leadership. Huawei leads China's high technology firms in patenting activity and it has become more pronounced in this in recent times as the company has moved out from its previous domestic focus into international export markets thereby needing to better protect its assets from multinational competition.

On the other hand, India features less markedly in such activity as its dominant technology driven industry has long been software services and it has only recently realigned its commercial strategy towards the creation of packaged software outputs.[77] Moreover, in tandem with new patent legislation for pharmaceutical products introduced in January 2005, and also in response to TRIPS obligations, innovations by Indian research firms may lead to greater activity in this respect in future (Economist Print Edition, 2005b).[78]

The third feature that is prominent in recent developments to the international IP protection regime is the strengthening that has taken place in key areas of copyright control in respect to technology driven knowledge goods. Copyright trends are less measurable than those that relate to patents. This is because, in most jurisdictions, there is no requirement to register a right in order to secure legal protection: a work's creation is sufficient for it to have copyright protection. Instead, it is often necessary to examine initiatives in IP protection that affect the underlying copyright based industries themselves to gain a better understanding of their growing importance. This is illustrated by the so-called "internet treaties" introduced under the auspices of WIPO:

---

[77] Some companies, such as Wipro, have been pioneering service oriented business methods, which, whilst not yet capable of being patented *per se*, are increasingly the subject of considerable corporate and government debate. See media article by Noronha.

[78] Some companies, such as Ranbaxy, Biocon and Dr Reddy's, having already begun to expand sales and to develop what have been described as "daring patent strategies" to challenge western firms.

the Performances and Phonograms Treaty (WPPT) and, particularly, the Copyright Treaty (WCT).

These measures were first presented in 1996 just after TRIPS had been introduced on the creation of the WTO but in fact neither came into force until 2002, due in no small part of the controversial nature of key measures included in these agreements, illustrated by the significantly smaller number of contracting parties (58 and 60 respectively as at the end of 2006).

Leading nations such as the United States and the United Kingdom, along with most of the member states of the European Union (Brown), have now brought into force domestic legislation that implements these measures, although not without considerable controversy in some instances. The United States introduced regulations contained in its wide-ranging Digital Millennium Copyright Act (DMCA), whilst the EU issued an Information Society Directive[79] and an IP Rights Enforcement[80] Directive.[81] In France, the new law implementing tighter internet copyright controls led to considerable national debate and even faced a constitutional challenge in July 2006 after it had been passed by the National Assembly the previous month, and it was not until August 2006 that the law finally came into force.[82]

Although there are differences in emphasis between the European and American interpretations, in terms of the substantive protections mandated by the treaties to facilitate internet-based transmissions and create frameworks for controlling countermeasures, there is broad similarity between the legislation of both parties. Those differences that remain reflect the wider public controversies about "fair use" exceptions (termed "fair dealing" in the United Kingdom). These are manifested in what has become known as the "three-step test", originally introduced by the Berne Convention,[83] to determine whether an exemption for "fair use" should apply, with evaluation typically being

[79] European Union Directive 2001/29/EC.

[80] European Union Directive 2004/48/EC.

[81] For a considered discussion on these issues, see (Sideri 2005)

[82] For discussion on the controversies surrounding French implementation of Directive 2001/29/EC, see (Cook and Rambaud) Pages 18–20. See also commentary by international law firm Bird & Bird last referenced 28th February 2007 at http://www.twobirds.com/english/publications/articles/Long_complex_French_implementation_information_society_copyright_Directive.cfm.

[83] See Article 9 (2) Berne Convention 'Right of reproduction' at WIPO website accessed 28th February 2007 http://www.wipo.int/treaties/en/ip/berne/trtdocs_wo001.html#P140_25350. These three steps are: i) Exemptions should be for special and spe-

made during subsequent legal proceedings that involve copyright exemptions.[84]

Whilst a number of countries have not signed either of these treaties, some major emerging nations are either considering such a move or maintain that their existing legislation provides adequate coverage for internet-based activity. For example (Wang, 2006:21–23), in July 2006, China brought into effect laws that have been characterised by some commentators as implementing the principles of the WCT, whilst other Chinese legal experts have maintained that their law has for some time been subject to relevant judicial interpretation within the spirit of the Treaty's obligations.[85] India has also been looking at making legal changes to its copyright legislation to introduce digital rights management controls to better protect IP owners in internet domains.[86]

The two internet treaties have together established a significantly stronger set of controls that are notably applicable to the use of the internet in the distribution, sharing and resale of musical, literary and software works between the residents of contracting parties. Among the most controversial and significant of these policies are measures that have outlawed the sale, use, dissemination and support of anti-encryption techniques that break the protection that controls the electronic use and distribution of a copyrightable work. This is particularly relevant for music and video downloads: the computer file containing the audiovisual sound recording is protected by a digital key that will

---

cific cases. ii) They should not conflict with normal exploitation of the work. iii) They do not unreasonably prejudice the interests of rights holders.

[84] An example of using the test multilaterally involved a WTO Dispute Panel that considered the three-step test as implemented under TRIPS Article 13 in its findings against the United States in a dispute brought by the EU over business exemption clauses of the US Copyright Act. The panel ruled that some exemptions granted by the US Copyright Act did not meet Article 13 requirements. See Dispute No. 160 last referenced 28th February 2007 at <http://www.wto.org/english/tratop_e/dispu_e/cases_e/ds160_e.htm>.

[85] See legal interpretation by Jiang Zhipei of the Chinese Supreme People's Court: 'Judicial Protection for Copyright in Internet Environment by the People's Court' which discusses the changes made to copyright protection in China in the light of internet complexities and introduced in December 2003. See <http://www.chinaipr-law.com/english/forum/forum50.htm> last referenced 31st October 2006.

[86] See government amendments and explanations at <http://www.copyright.gov.in/View%20Comments.pdf>. See also Frederick Noronha: 'Copyright Debate Heats up', *Intellectual Property Watch* <http://www.ip-watch.org/weblog/index.php?p=391&res=1024&print=0> for independent discussion, accessed 31st October 2006.

only provide access to the file's content when either a special code is used when opening the file or special hardware (such as an iPod) is used to store the file. The so-called "circumvention technologies" bypass these copyright enforcement restrictions to facilitate royalty free access to the content.

This area has most recently become the subject of a number of legal disputes between competing commercial enterprises in respect to the legitimacy and ease with which copyright material of all kinds can be allegedly infringed using internet technology. In their landmark decision against Grokster Limited in June 2005,[87] the United States Supreme Court admonished the company for its encouragement of music piracy through the firm's aggressive marketing of the available technology.

In other actions, Apple Corporation has been seeking to retain control over the secrecy and effectiveness of their iPod musical encryption methods and have been active in pursuing those which the company believes are transgressing new legal principles.[88] For example, a Norwegian technology specialist, who had successfully broken the internal code that governs how such iPod restrictions work,[89] was brought to court in Norway's jurisdiction. However, under different interpretations of what is considered "fair use" of copyright materials between legal systems,[90] he was acquitted.[91]

---

[87] US Supreme Court: *MGM Studios Inc. et al. versus Grokster Limited et al.*, 27th June 2005.

[88] Developments announced in April 2007 may indicate a change of approach by Apple in this context as they have formed an alliance with EMI to offer an alternative download option of non-DRM controlled music from their iTunes music webstore, but at a higher price (news item broadcast by BBC News 24 on 9th April 2007 at 00:30 BST). This action would be consistent with public concerns about DRM technology already expressed by Apple's CEO, Steve Jobs, earlier in the year. It remains to be seen what impact this may have on DRM legal development. For background, see Adrian Larkin, *BBC Music Online*, <http://www.bbc.co.uk/6music/news/20070402_apple.shtml> accessed 11th April 2007.

[89] This would, in this example, enable anyone with access to the anti-encryption code to copy musical and other items made available from Apple's website on to computer devices other than Apple's own iPod.

[90] Critically in this case, the music DVDs which formed the basis of the original legal case had been bought by the accused quite legally and both the first level and Appeal Court found that no violation of Norway's IP protection laws had thus taken place. The American DCMA places a far greater test on what is "fair use" in line with the WCT and WPPT although disagreements with the EU on this point remain.

[91] It is particularly significant that Norway is not a signatory to either the WCT or the WPPT and many commentators believe that the results under US jurisdiction

The introduction of these legal measures, the litigation activities that have resulted and the strengthening of such controls internationally can be interpreted as representing the growing strength of the IT, film, television and international publishing industries in their capacity to set the agendas of national, and, through exerting pressure on to state actors, international priorities in respect to IP regulation and enforcement. A noticeable symbiosis would seem to have developed between states and commercial IP holders, with the latter exhibiting a growing tendency to assetise private rights in order to defend their business interests in an emerging corporate landscape that is increasingly recognising IP as a valuable tool with which to protect their knowledge-based products.[92]

These organisations have sought, and have secured, government support for their endeavours at forums where, traditionally, the corporate sector has had no direct rights of audience, such as in the WTO and TRIPS Councils and at WIPO Assemblies, save as observers through national non-government organisations and as expert contributors in dispute settlement cases.[93] This has been especially apparent within the United States, which has a singularly powerful collection of lobby groups and trade bodies with long-standing avenues of direct dialogue to senior Administration officials and members of Congress, illustrating the "emergence of a transnational civil society in which powerful private entities with the ability to coerce action are also demanding a voice in global lawmaking" (Evans, 2000:12–13).

A number of scholars, however, see these trends as a very counter-productive development. It is maintained that "the persisting drift

would have been different. See Robert Levine: 'Geek Breaks iPod Code', *Sunday Times Business Section* 29th October 2006, page 17.

[92] The influence of private sector media organisations may be behind the long running negotiations at WIPO on improved protection and an expansion of rights for cable companies and television broadcasters in the digital age under the proposed WIPO Broadcasting Treaty. See briefing paper 'Standing Committee on Copyright and Related Rights Fifteenth Session' dated 19th July 2006 available online at <http://www.wipo.int/edocs/mdocs/mdocs/en/sccr_15/sccr_15_14.pdf> last referenced 2nd November 2006. See also William New: 'WIPO Broadcasting Treaty Advanced Past Disagreements' *Intellectual Property Watch* 14th September 2006 <http://www.ip-watch.org/weblog/index.php?p=395&res=1024&print=0> accessed 2nd November 2006. This treaty moves into the WIPO Assembly for further debate during 2007.

[93] See WIPO observer rules at <http://www.wipo.int/members/en/organizations.jsp?type=NGO_NAT> and at the WTO <http://www.wto.org/english/thewto_e/whatis_e/tif_e/disp1_e.htm> on the role of experts and advisors within the Dispute Settlement Understanding, both last accessed 31st October 2006.

of institutional change towards stronger, more extensive and globally harmonized system of intellectual property protections during the past two decades has dangerously altered the balance between private rights and the public domain in data and information" (David, 2005:82).

It is further argued that such moves represent a "second enclosure movement" that mirrors the division of land during the industrialisation of Britain in previous centuries and which will have profoundly negative effects on the distribution and exploitation of knowledge by raising the transaction costs associated with its acquisition through the payment of license fees and other associated controls (Boyle, 2003). Some maintain that even the notions of theft and piracy make "little sense" in an international context in respect to intellectual ownership and show an ongoing tension between a rights-based and a utilitarian approach to regulation (Bhagwati, 2004:183).

These regulatory initiatives have been interpreted as representing an increasing disconnection between IP owners who look towards government to secure for them more wide ranging and stronger protection and IP consumers whose priorities are concerned with access to and transfer of information resources in the public space. In particular, IP protection measures such as TRIPS mandated 20-year patents are, "from the viewpoint of worldwide efficiency, suboptimal" (Bagwati, 2002:75).

Initiatives such as the WCT and the WPPT (Correa, 2005:227–56), coupled to increased patenting intensity, both at a national level through domestic patent and trademark offices and internationally through the PCT, are all used as evidence to point to a "high-protectionist paradigm" that is emerging within contemporary regulatory norms. In this, there is opposition to what is characterised as a US-inspired attitude to "fair trade", based on equality of opportunity over equal outcomes, where "fairness rather than justice is the defining moral principle" (Bhagwati, 2002:52).

The argument continues that this increased activity undermines the original bargain upon which the philosophy behind IP protection was based. It has prioritised the interests of powerful business groups in first world economies at the expense of maintaining knowledge and intellectual outputs within the public domain, whilst hindering the emergence of developing countries as true competitors.

These characteristics can, however, be interpreted in a more positive light, wherein the first world could better be seen as now having to compete more aggressively with a rising competitive threat from the more advanced developing nations. In this way, the stock of IP held by commercial organisations becomes an important indicator of potential future growth. The financial contribution of first mover advantage possessed by an innovating enterprise with a new invention within the sales cycle has been reduced, in relation to its competitors, by the pace of change in both innovation and product development processes, as change can now be built on change very rapidly. This trend is observable across knowledge-based industries, but in particular it is present within the software sector. It can therefore be argued that it is no surprise that there has been increased significance for IP at both domestic and international levels, as government actors have sought to work in unison with corporate IP owners in their local commercial sectors to promote mutual interests and industry success.

The changing role of the emerging economies in this dimension can be seen in a number of ways. First, top-tier developing countries are becoming initiators of innovative activity. This is happening not just in the advanced manufacturing of electronic goods in which East Asia has been traditionally strong, but also in other more recent areas of pioneering activity. For example, in the area of biotechnology research, China has created a highly successful centre for stem cell analysis that attracts international as well as domestic patients each year (BusinessWeek Print Edition, 10th January 2005:20).[94] In a related discipline, South Korea has made considerable advances in embryo research although recent controversies about fabricated evidence have undermined some of the progress (Science Magazine Online Edition, 10th January 2006). In software and enabled services business models, India leads others through using innovation by smaller enterprises as well as within multinational organisations.[95] It is not clear that developments have been inhibited by increased protective norms for international IP regulation. Indeed, in contradiction, each of these nations has been concertedly strengthening their own intellectual property regime in concert with their economic and technological progress and their engagement with international partners.

---

[94] See also a recent report by the UK government's Department of Health on the success of China's initiatives at <http://www.advisorybodies.doh.gov.uk/uksci/global/china.htm> accessed 31st October 2006.

[95] See India National Association of Software Service Companies, 'Innovation Forum' *NASSCOM* <http://www.nasscom.in/Nasscom/templates/LandingPage.aspx?id=572>1 accessed 31st October 2006.

Second, the globalisation of trading patterns and the relative ease with which research, development and production can be located to best exploit a particular market's needs, independent of distribution localities for finished products, has created forms of horizontal convergence within like industries and between very different countries. This has tended to break down the traditional understanding that divided perspectives on intellectual property between nations, whereby the industrialised nations saw the concept as a form of comparative advantage for knowledge-based countries whilst key developing economies saw IP as "no more than the common heritage of mankind".[96] Whilst it is true that such a philosophical position is still maintained by some commentators, the technology driven era of the modern international economy is softening such cleavages that were once so apparent.

2.8 *Explaining the Current Depth and Strength of IP Regimes*

Expansions in regulatory breadth and strength have been brought into sharp relief by distinctly different interpretations by commentators and scholars. It is, therefore, clearly important to try and seek an explanation as to why they are taking place at this time and whether their impact is both as negative and unreasonable as some have suggested.

First, given the increasing value of IP goods within the international trading system, commercial organisations have been seeking to protect their interests and achieve material reciprocity for their IP development investments in relation to their competitors. This has led to a number of initiatives, which, whilst certainly not being sympathetic to the underlying concepts of the knowledge commons, should perhaps be seen as more an understandable response to the growing incentives that now exist in a pro-patent business environment than as a specific attack on the principles of an intellectual public domain *per se*.[97] These initiatives include new business methods such as defensive patenting and patent exchanges.

[96] For a useful introduction to this concept in an international domain, see Joyner January 1986.

[97] In this sense, it can be argued that "business" is about making profit and returning value to shareholders to whom directors of public companies have a legal responsibility.

A defensive patenting strategy is one that seeks to build a strong portfolio of patented technology that can be used primarily to defend against potentially hostile legal attacks from competitors in a climate that has become increasingly more litigious in respect to intellectual property protection. It is a concept that has found particular resonance in the United States where many now consider it a rational response to new commercial mores.[98] It is especially relevant when dealing with technologies that involve incremental and inter-linked progress, such as in the cases of the software development industry and microprocessor hardware manufacturing. In some cases, evidence suggests that the trends towards defensive patenting may have changed corporate behaviour significantly.[99]

A patent exchange is simply a natural progression from an accumulation of defensive patents in that it can be used as a form of IP trade between two companies in dispute and as an alternative to formal litigation. It effectively formalises the idea of cross-licensing that emerged under partnership models of business activity and has grown in its importance to the revenue models of technology companies over the recent years. One of the most striking examples of a patent exchange (Economist, 2005d:12; Day, 2006) can be seen from the business strategy of the Seattle-based innovation company 'Intellectual Ventures',[100] which has variously been described as an organisation akin to a "patent troll" or a "patent supermarket".

It is particularly interesting that practises of this kind have become so popular in America, which has had a long tradition of corporate litigation rather than adopting any spirit of arbitration. In East Asia, by contrast, the cultural traditions of conciliation and informal dispute

---

[98] For an introduction to defensive patenting strategies see review of business sector implications by the United States Federal Trade Commission *US FTC* <http://www.ftc.gov/os/2003/10/innovationrpt.pdf>. See also (Chiou Grenoble Applied Economic Laboratory April 2005)

[99] For example, Hewlett Packard (HP) has a team of over 50 specialists in its in-house legal division that concentrate exclusively on intellectual property issues, having only been created just a few years ago in 2002. The company now derives over US$200 million annually from licensing revenues. Economist Print Edition, Report on Patents, page 8.

[100] Its objective is to fund patentable innovation which it will then sell under license to consuming companies, merging the activities of a venture capital fund, a research and development hub and a law firm. The company has credibility through the reputation of its founder, Nathan Myhrvold, who was formerly the Chief Technologist at Microsoft and it illustrates trends in viewing patents as part of an economic war-chest for corporations. See Intellectual Ventures (Corporate Website).

settlement are giving way to an increasingly aggressive recourse to civil suits in court. Companies in Japan and the Republic of Korea in particular have had a number of legal disputes that illustrate this trend and show that in IP areas at least, an analysis based on past stereotypes may no longer be accurate.

In the United Kingdom as well, the importance of patent portfolios that provide the foundations of expansionist business models has become increasingly apparent. The founder of Cambridge-based Smart Holograms Limited recently emphasised how important it had been to the company's initial value propositions to venture capitalist investors of having already registered upwards of 40 patents prior to funding rounds and that an IP focus was a critical first step in the company's move from its pure-research incubation within the University's Institute of Biotechnology.[101]

Indeed, recognising this symbiosis between innovation, IP protection and market reward, the University of Cambridge has itself recently changed its own rules on IP exploitation for researchers and academic staff who wish to exploit the fruits of their inventions. Previously, such work would largely have been rested within their own IP ownership and control, but now, such registrations as patents and trademarks are required to be granted to the University itself which then shares eventual rewards and success with the original commercialising academic (University of Cambridge, Intellectual Property Policy).[102] Such moves by Cambridge have been described by some legal commentators as "more benign than in many universities in the United Kingdom" (Poore, 2006) but, nevertheless, the new emphasis still marks a sea-change in the commercialisation of rights within an academic framework and mirrors international developments in the salience of IP in business transactions.

A second explanation to the deepening and strengthening of IP protection is the sheer cost of R&D for technology products. Required expenditure for some knowledge-rich outputs is now so great that the exploitation of domestic markets, even within the United States, provides insufficient returns on investment and must be met with overseas export expansion to recoup profits, which of itself requires the

[101] Director of Institute of Biotechnology, University of Cambridge, (Lowe 2006).

[102] Interestingly, the policy refrains from exerting controls over non-registration IP outputs such as copyright items like software programs.

security and safety of asset protection (Govaere and Demaret, 2001). According to industry reports, the costs of bringing a new pharmaceutical "molecular entity" to market have now reached almost US$1.5 billion, having risen from a little over US$250 million twenty years ago (McKinnon et al., 2004). The pharmaceutical market worldwide is estimated to reach US$700 billion by 2008 (Economist Print Edition, 2005b).

This burgeoning of cost bases is not seen as just a factor of increased timescales through more rigorous regulatory procedures and the increasing cost of human resources, but, instead, has been caused more by "a failure to increase productivity sufficiently to compensate for a reduction in operating margins" (McKinnon et al., 2004:4).[103] In this way, cost increases that centred on heavy investment in marketing, both to the medical profession and to domestic consumers, have been coincident with charging pressures wherein "pharmaceutical price inflation has fallen by 2%–3% relative to other goods over the past two years [from November 2004]" (ibid.; Economist, 2005b: 3–5).

In these circumstances, intellectual property has come to be seen by corporate leaders of innovating drug companies as an essential part of their organisation's ability to operate as a viable commercial entity. It should not perhaps be surprising, therefore, that a highly protective international IP regime for pharmaceutical goods has emerged over recent years. Commentators point to research which has maintained that between 60% and 65% of pharmaceutical products would either not have been developed at all or would have failed to have been introduced into the market without patents, in contrast to 8% as an average for other industries (Mansfield, 1986; Schacht, 2006).

There have been long-standing contrary views to these perspectives (see for example, the writings of Bhagwati, Stiglitz, and Chang, as well as the opinions put forward by the interest group the "Adelphi Charter").[104] However, the cost structures and competitive nature of knowledge sectors in modern economies cannot be ignored, and it can be argued that the incentives offered by patents to commercial

---

[103] Op. cit. Mckinnon, Marakon Research Report, page 4.

[104] The Adelphi Charter is an online community of commentators and academics that exchange perspectives and put forward viewpoints on some of the latest thinking in intellectual property regime development. The Charter emerged from a research project that sought to analyse best practice in intellectual policy formulation, and members include leading academics, legal specialists and policy makers. See <http://www.adelphicharter.org/>.

enterprises that invest in commercialising inventions—whether that be for a market in pharmaceuticals, internet servers or software—may make them the least worst option for securing public benefits in the long term, by facilitating a finite monopoly that enables a material reward for commercial risk-taking.

Arguments that reject market-mediated rewards in favour, for example, of government sponsored prizes and associated peer recognition for successful product development in knowledge sectors, particularly in pharmaceuticals, do not seem to be a convincing alternative as it is difficult to see how a reward-issuing evaluation committee, even when comprised of peer professionals, could replace market decisions by foreseeing the potential value of radical new commercial products (Stiglitz, 2006). A generalised version of such an approach was in fact tried in Maoist China during the 1950's, but subsequently fell into disuse and has not been repeated.

It is not just pharmaceuticals where this principle holds. The underlying technology for the internet and the core invention of hypertext transfer were products of publicly funded research, respectively at the US Defense Department in the 1970's and at CERN in the early 1990's, establishing what could be considered the basic chemistry of a network system. However, many who have used the internet since its earliest days can recall its mechanisms at that time as somewhat cumbersome[105] and it can be argued that it was not until major investment in commercial software code by Netscape in the mid 1990's, using sophisticated software innovations to create a commercial web server that usefully exploited the hypertext transfer protocol (http), did the internet's potential for general popular use begin to be recognised.[106] Since then, further commercial endeavours, some successful and some not, have harnessed this technology in ways that have transformed everyday life.

Nor is it simply patents that are important as a stimulus to certain kinds of commercial activity. Trademarks are especially important for pharmaceutical industry as they help to foster and maintain brand identity and loyalty amongst both professionals and patients at a time

[105] The author has been a user of the internet in its different forms since 1984.

[106] Note that software in the United States may be patented under certain conditions and note also that the Netscape "browser" was of secondary importance in this innovation and was thus given away free to private users.

when there is an increasing trend towards moving prescription drugs into the over-the-counter market (Economist, 2005b).[107]

Trademarks are also important in other new technology product markets, such as consumer electronics and software based business solutions. Some of these products have an increasingly short shelf life[108] as the pace of development and innovation creates rapidly changing new streams of technology so that sustainable revenue generation and the promotion of the company's identity through trademark assertion are as important towards maintaining market presence and future success as are the innovations in the first place. This is especially the case for smaller and medium sized organisations that may seek to manage their business-exit strategy through sale to a company rather than through an Initial Public Offering (IPO). In the case of a trade sale to a competitor or partner organisation, the store of trademarks possessed by the company markedly enhance the exit value by raising the internal store of goodwill that they can offer as part of an acquisition.

Trademarks and trade secrets are less visible but still important parts of the panoply of intellectual property protection that can help to drive commercial success and leverage business opportunity. In this context, international regime developments are discussed extensively in later sections of this book, not least to illustrate how such norms have had an impact on domestic legal judgements in both China and India.

2.9 *Conclusion*

The evolution of the international regulation of intellectual property rights is an issue of central importance to both states and private sector organisations and clear trends have become visible in recent years,

[107] In this context, it is important to differentiate between two very different types of goods when looking at salience of intellectual property regulations and a company's propensity for defensive strategies. The first is "experience" goods such, as pharmaceuticals and software where producer reputation is an essential ingredient in the buying mindset in terms of expected reliability and safety versus "search" goods like foodstuffs that may be compared and inspected for obvious qualitative characteristics before purchase.

[108] Within five years a business software applications solution is likely to have undergone such enhancement and modification that it can bear no relationship in content from the original version save for its trading name and it is often this that retains the ongoing value proposition for the company. In terms of hardware electronics, the timescales are even shorter: two years can be an eternity.

marking a move towards strengthening and widening the scope of those controls. Whilst still a national issue in legislative terms, with contrasts even amongst first world nations in the extent and scope of regulations, especially in respect to patent filing rules and utility model implementations, IP has become a significant subject of debate, both within WIPO as the original home of the Great Conventions, and at the WTO where trade linkages exhibit special pressures on the relationship between developed and developing countries.

It is now too simplistic to see IP protection as just a first world priority. Clear propensities towards patenting activity in top-tier developing countries like China, and to a lesser extent India, can be observed and these can be attributed to an increased visibility in world trade for IP-rich outputs from these nations. Moreover, IP regulatory development is no longer just the preserve of states operating as strategic leaders in normative rule setting and there is growing evidence that the increasing importance of knowledge-based sectors within national economies have placed commercial organisations into a new partnership with governmental bodies. Through pressure groups, within industry organisations and in representations to multilateral bodies, corporations are increasingly interacting with state actors at multiple levels. The value of these markets is simply too important to ignore the priorities and requirements of major corporate actors when determining the next steps in regime development.

One market that is particularly prominent in this evolution is the international software industry, as products and services from this sector illustrate a number of the ongoing tensions and regulatory trends that have been introduced in this chapter.

CHAPTER THREE

SOFTWARE AS A KNOWLEDGE INDUSTRY

This chapter will put the international software industry into broader context. First, its characteristics and contribution within the international economy will be explored and a breakdown of its constituent parts will be provided, setting out the increasingly blurred relationship between software as a product and software enabled services.

Second, the industry's salience within international IP regimes will be discussed, with particular reference to the way that software as a high value unit crosses a number of boundaries within existing systems, in terms of different trade policies between products and services and in terms of different IP regulations such as copyright and patent controls. These distinctions will be shown to have introduced both tensions within the international trading system for software products, and uncertainties for commercial actors seeking to exploit their own IP-rich goods in multiple overseas markets.

Third, the dominant position of the United States within the international software industry will be assessed through the lens of first-tier developing countries such as India and China, both of which have ambitions towards greater significance in their roles as consumers of software outputs and producers of software inventions. Finally, the importance of different types of commercial software license will be presented to indicate how national IP policies interact with contractually regulated commercial transactions in the software market, and special mention will be made of the growing trend towards open source arrangements and distinctive IP initiatives such as patent pooling.

3.1 *The Software Sector within the International Technology Industry*

The value of knowledge in the international software industry is vested in a set of instructions that make computers work in different ways and which enable them to perform a variety of functions to service different human needs. These operations range in scale and complexity from simple routines familiar to all users across both commercial and domestic sectors, such as sending an email or painting a web image into a browser screen, to highly complex industry specific operations such as assessing an individual's credit risk as part of a mortgage application or reconciling financial transactions from a stock exchange trading day.

These instructions are rendered in two main ways: human readable source code and computer executable object code.[1] Software is the instruction set that makes computer hardware function. But it should also be seen as the underlying set of routines which help to make other software function, with different software programs and networking technologies interacting to provide ever more complex solutions to business needs and personal entertainment demands.

There are various ways in which the global market for information and communications technology (ICT) products may be quantified, including assessments for installed bases for hardware units, software implementations and software service utilisations. There are considerable differences in sector values depending on the extent to which the "communications" part of the wider ICT market is considered, which includes telecoms, electronics, microprocessors and ancillary equipment. Communications technologies are also an important illustration of the national priority for infrastructure investment by a country in its technological capability, rather than just an indication of its individual or corporate spending preferences.[2]

According to the OECD, the global revenues of the top 250 ICT firms (including well-known names such as Nokia, Sony, IBM, HP, China Telecom, Tata, Infosys and Microsoft) totalled over US$3,000

---

[1] In the case of source code, the logic, processing sequence and operational flow of data through the program can be viewed and understood relatively straightforwardly by someone familiar with the constructs of the programming language that has been used to solve the problem. There are many different programming languages that specialists can choose to use but the principal ones in commercial use today are based on the Roman alphabet and use decimal numbering principles. In the case of object code, the source script is then processed within the computer itself and effectively translated into machine-readable object code (a process called compiling) that can then run against the hardware of the computer, whilst also making use of other existing programs, such as printer drivers, as necessary in order to complete the requested function.

[2] The telecoms element in particular introduces both the issues of communications penetration, either through fixed line or mobile, and domestic and corporate internet use and its type (broadband or telephone dial-up), which governs viable access to new types of internet delivered services, either as an individual or corporate consumer.

billion by the end of 2005 with 46% of this revenue accounted for by US registered corporations (Organisation for Economic Co-operation and Development, 2006). Interestingly, however, this level of American dominance was actually a reduction on assessments from previous years and is seen as an indication of the rise and growing visibility of emerging Asian companies from South Korea, India and China. It is especially noteworthy that China overtook the United States as the world's largest exporter of ICT goods in 2004 with US$180 billion, largely within the field of electronic components and related computer equipment (ibid.).

Revenue growth across the world was strongest amongst software and services companies, which averaged 8% per year between 2000 and 2005, although, with annual income averaging respectively US$6.4 billion and US$5.6 billion, organisationally, these are typically smaller firms than component and telecom giants. This growth was in concert with the software industry's leadership position in R&D intensity between 2000 and 2005 (ibid.),[3] which, whilst significant in its own right, also illustrates the commitment and investment required for successful software product development and helps to explain the importance attached to protecting such investment through effective IP regulations. In order to gain a more detailed understanding of the computer related and software enabled elements of the wider market, it is important to further dissect the trends of the global commercial ICT operations which will reveal detail about the role and growth of different types of software products and the growing visibility of software services for organisations of all sizes in many different countries.

Removing the "communications" element of the industry and focusing instead on the traditional staples of computer equipment hardware, software and services (the "IT" elements of the wider "ICT" market), it becomes clear that around half the overall ICT market is comprised of these sub-sectors (ibid.). In attempting to quantify just this "information technology" part of the wider market, one of the more reliable methods of analysis is to observe actual spending levels on different IT elements across economies as these may then be related against declared revenues for different companies and previous growth predictions for market sectors. This method is particularly popular among some of the leading market forecasters, including the

[3] The software industry devotes on average a 14.5% share of its revenues to R&D.

research company IDC, part of the International Data Group of companies, whose market intelligence has been presented through analysis reports for over 42 years.

The IT industry itself is broken into a number of different units, each of which has been influenced in different ways by the tendency towards globalisation of trade and manufacturing along with increased use of outsourcing business models for designing, building and delivering IT solutions. The highest level breakdown of the overall IT market separates hardware from software and it is within the software element of this market that some of the most significant changes have taken place in recent years.

According to recent market estimates made by IDC in concert with the India's National Association of Software Service Companies (NASSCOM, 2006),[4] the worldwide IT industry represents a market with spending of just over US$1,470 billion for 2005,[5] and this includes computer hardware sales, software product revenues and income from software services of both programming and consulting types as well as business process outsourcing operations.

Interestingly, the hardware sector is now very much a minority part of the global market, with spending across the world amounting to little over US$400 billion for the year and a growth rate of less than 5% year-on-year. The reduced significance of the hardware sector reflects changes in the economics of the industry, whereby the balance between the hardware and software cost elements of a computerised solution have shifted as the manufacturing costs of producing and distributing ever more powerful hardware have fallen across the world. This trend has accelerated over recent years through increasing use of off-shore manufacturing centres in developing countries as well as improvements in efficiencies during the production process. Hardware has thus become a shrinking percentage of a computerised solution's "total cost of ownership" (Barroso, 2005).[6] This contrasts sharply with the software side of the industry, where software products

---

[4] NASSCOM is India's national software industry organisation. It is important to note that NASSCOM collects software industry data on behalf of the Reserve Bank of India and has built a reputation for consistency and reliability in its assessments.

[5] This figure equates to around half of the wider ICT global market, which is consistent with the OECD estimates made both for the overall industry and the narrower assessments for the IT component.

[6] The computing profession's Association for Computing Machinery website is a useful starting point at http://www.acm.org for relevant articles on cost elements to

and IT software services elements comprised the substantial part of the 2005 overall figures, at US$206 billion and US$863 billion respectively, with growth rates for some service elements rising at over 9%. The worldwide software product sector is expected to grow by a compound annual growth rate of 7.7% between 2006 and 2010 (Heiman and Picardi, 2006).

The software sector breaks down at its top level into 'software products' and 'software services', and whilst such a division in reality is becoming more notional than absolute as products and services increasingly interact within the digital economy, it acts as a useful bifurcation with which to analyse the industry in overview.

The software products market subdivides into those that may best be described as 'packaged' or 'shrink-wrapped' software versus 'custom-built' or 'customisable' software, wherein the main difference is the degree to which the software solution purchased can be used immediately for deriving benefits or whether it needs to be oriented around a particular business' operating procedures through discrete additional coding. Examples of packaged solutions are myriad, and include some operating systems themselves, such as Microsoft Windows. Further examples of software packages are word processors and spreadsheet managers like Microsoft's Word and Excel, along with web interfaces, such as Microsoft's Internet Explorer or Mozilla's Firefox browser, and security utilities such as anti-virus modules, like Symantec's Norton suite. Installation sequences for these packaged products are typically straightforward requiring only minimum customisations.

The custom-built or customisable software sector, by contrast, involves products that require more than just simple configuration to enable their use within either a personal or corporate infrastructure, and often necessitate either substantial customisation or even additional coded design extensions prior to a solution's implementation. They predominate in the corporate sector and the business software solutions market presents many examples of this type of system, with the level of customisation being required acting as a typical indicator of both the price point and scale of commitment needed by customers in this area. Sales from this sector are the mainstay of many

solutions and how software has increased over time to comprise the greater element over hardware today.

medium and large software products enterprises in Europe and the United States.

For example, at one end of the customisable scale might be a small company's contracts and correspondence repository, made available to internal users with a relatively simple tool which, whilst not being shrink-wrapped, requires fairly simple levels of orientation and modification to work successfully. A more complex custom solution might include a business workflow system for a large insurance company that might require significant application customisation and new code design to derive maximum commercial benefit. At the top end of the scale of customisable software solutions are sophisticated enterprise resource planning (ERP) and Customer Relationship Management (CRM) products, targeted especially at public companies and multinationals, that handle a panoply of activities, ranging from sales cycle, accounting, through to business management cost modelling and financial transaction recording.

Use of more advanced software solutions by corporations has risen in recent years, driven by a number of factors, including the importance of maintaining effective customer relationships in the enterprise-software sector, as well as from the influence of new legal requirements for external scrutiny by regulators and shareholders, such as the increased burdens imposed by the Sarbanes-Oxley Act.[7] Indeed, such software implementations can require so much ongoing consulting involvement from the vendor that they often create an intersection with the IT services element of the software sector, and were amongst the first business operations to be outsourced as part of offshoring tendencies that have particularly taken hold in this industry over the last five years, and from which countries like India has benefited in particular.[8]

The software services market subdivides into on the one hand, 'IT Services' and, on the other, IT *Enabled* Services (ITES), that includes Business Process Outsourcing (BPO), as well as more recent sector

[7] Its full title is the Public Company Accounting Reform and Investor Protection Act 2002 No. 107–204, 116 Stat. 745. For further detail, see search page at American Center for Audit Quality, <http://thecaq.aicpa.org/Resources/Sarbanes+Oxley>, accessed 18th November 2006.

[8] The author's own experience as a technology consultant over the last 20 years confirms this observation.

specific initiatives such as Knowledge Process Outsourcing and Legal Process Outsourcing (LPO).[9]

IT Services are those operations that relate primarily to information technology specific activities such as consulting, design, programming and maintenance functions for delivering technology products, where knowledge of both programming languages and the vertical business market is typically important. This part comprised US$440 billion worth of revenues for 2005 (NASSCOM, 2006) and is the area wherein most interest in intellectual property regulations, copyright laws and patentability of software resides. This sub-sector can be usefully contrasted with ITES-BPO, which covers many different kinds of corporate operations, across different types of businesses and generated around US$395 billion of income for 2005,[10] wherein pertinent interest focuses especially on legal instruments such as data protection and privacy laws, including cross-border regulations on the exchange of personal information about customers by suppliers and their subcontractors.

The use of offshore IT services in general, and ITES-BPO services in particular, can be best explained as "a process of digital migration facilitated by the technology that allows for the cross-border supply from remote locations of a range of services, often in real time" (Chandrasekhar, 2005). The ITES-BPO sub-sector has seen some of the greatest expansions in business activity over the recent past, with India's achieving an estimated year-on-year growth of 37% for the financial year 2005/06.[11] Moreover, business related process outsourcing from high-cost regions to low-cost suppliers has now become an important part of broader corporate strategy, resulting in economic

---

[9] Unfortunately, the industry has not formally agreed on what exactly comprises either of these sector descriptions but the author has used terms most familiar to the current debates that dominate the potential growth and direction of the services market.

[10] Activities in the BPO sector include call centre management for telecom companies, medical records document processing for the government health departments, such as the UK's National Health Service, and human resources and accounting functions such as payroll and expense management.

[11] See National Association of Software Service Companies (NASSCOM India), 'Business Sector Summary', <http://www.nasscom.in/Nasscom/templates/NormalPage.aspx?id=11043>, accessed 10th November 2006.

stimulus for countries as diverse as Mexico, Egypt, Czech Republic and China, as well as India.[12]

In terms of the economic geography of the IT industry, it mirrors the wider ICT marketplace, with the American continent, and in particular the United States, continuing to have a significant dominance. At the end of 2005, over 44% of the global IT spending was based in the US alone, with Western Europe and Asia Pacific taking 28% and 17% respectively. The US, in particular, dominates in software products and services income (NASSCOM, 2006). For example, for the financial year 2006, Microsoft alone accounted for nearly US$45 billion of global software revenue across all of its operating divisions, which was substantially more for the same period than the entire Indian hardware and software market for both export and domestic revenues put together (Microsoft Corporation, 2006c).[13]

3.2 *Technological Development in India and China*

China has been recently expanding its technological capability across all of its provinces in a state-led drive towards enabling greater IT access for its population. Chinese sources now put the internet user community across the country at 123 million, of which 77 million are of the "broadband user" category (China Internet Network Information Center, July 2006),[14] and with over 410 million mobile phone subscribers at the end of 2005, the potential for mobile internet content

---

[12] See in particular a report that reviews the range of locations and vendors: 'The Black Book of Outsourcing', available originally only in book form but now with updates and surveys published online at <http://www.theblackbookofoutsourcing.com/2008-results-menu.aspx>, accessed 7th April 2009. The IT software product and services sectors of both India and China are also explored in further depth in later chapters of this research, along with the implications of this sector growth on both countries' evolving intellectual property legal system.

[13] This shows revenues of US$44.2 billion. For comparison, see NASSCOM estimates for India showing total market revenues of US$36.3 billion at <http://www.nasscom.in/Nasscom/templates/NormalPage.aspx?id=28485>, accessed 10th November 2006.

[14] Note that there is not a one-to-one correlation between an internet *subscriber* and an internet *user*: in terms of Chinese fee-paying internet subscribers, the OECD estimates that there were 73.2 million across the country recorded at the end of 2005, of which 37.5 held broadband subscriptions. See http://www.cnnic.net.cn/en/index/0O/index.htm accessed 21st November 2006.

is also significant (OECD, 2006).[15] Moreover, growing wealth across parts of the population has enabled more discretionary spending after the staples of food, accommodation and education have been satisfied, and official figures show that computer ownership per 100 urban households has reached up to 89 in some cities like Beijing, and is even over 50 in relatively poorer urban areas of central provinces like Anhui. However, rural areas, by contrast, struggle to reach even 10% ownership of technology products like computers and digital video (VCD) players, indicating the skewed patterns of development and illustrating China's ongoing challenge to widen participation in economic prosperity.

Although the Chinese broadband speed ratings are generally slower than those available in Western countries, and the network as a whole suffers from a high degree of monitoring that can also degrade the interactive experience, the growth in higher-speed internet access across the country is significant as platforms such as these are key to enabling a more sophisticated retail and commercial interaction with web delivered services. Within Beijing, for example, it is now quite possible for new, professional class apartments to offer tenants the combined services of cable TV (although Chinese only unless specifically approved for foreign broadcasts under the regulations), broadband internet from an approved ISP and digital telephone connections, all as a matter of routine.[16]

Although the only Chinese corporation to rank officially within the world's top 250 firms by revenue is China Telecom, the OECD makes the specific point that considerable change is taking place across the IT industry in China in respect to the potential for expansion and rapid growth of key companies (OECD, 2006). This supports commercial research findings that there are at least some technology companies in China, such as Huawei, that have "strong globalization potential" (Beebe et al., 2006:3–5). These reports, by IBM and the OECD, both emphasise the importance of prioritising increased innovation and effective brand management as critical success factors to tackle global expansion by Chinese organisations, indicating linkages with the role that IP regulations may have in the country's future through their direct

[15] The figures for mobile phones covers only *subscribers*, as a number of middle class Chinese have more then one phone and switch SIM cards.

[16] The author has personally seen many such apartments across the city and spent the second part of 2003 and much of 2004/05 living in just such an example.

effect on commercial trademark protection, the patenting of telecom inventions and the safeguarding of software through copyright.

In terms of global demand for ICT products and services, the domestic Chinese marketplace "is the sixth largest... and about two-and-a-half times that of India" (OECD, 2006:17), although, in comparative terms to OECD leading economies, China's market "was still only about one tenth that of the United States in 2005" (ibid.). However, these quoted internet usage figures still represent only a modest percentage of the overall Chinese population (around 8%), indicating the potential growth opportunities and perhaps illustrating the surge in interest by software and communications multinationals to establish proprietary footholds in the domestic market.[17]

The OECD report also highlights trends within the Chinese commercial sector, referencing as yet preliminary survey data from China's National Bureau of Statistics, that show a significant proportion of Chinese firms are already using the internet in many industrial sectors, at least for either email communication and information referencing purposes. For example, up to three quarters of companies surveyed in sectors such as financial intermediation use the internet regularly in this way. Some very progressive organisations in retail and manufacturing are even using the internet for direct e-commerce ordering and delivery transactions, although to a much lesser extent than in OECD nations. For example, 18% of manufacturers receive orders via online sources and 31% provide some form of customer service function using the internet (OECD, 2006).[18] This includes real-time communication and messaging channels such as Microsoft's messaging network MSN, which is often used by export-focused software and service firms to overcome spoken language shortfalls of programming staff by relying instead on cross-time zone written communications with western client companies.[19]

Local analysts point to a number of other catalysts that underpin the potential for future growth of web-centric transactions in China: a growing tendency to provide high-speed net cafes and kiosks in major

[17] For example, software companies Google, Oracle and Microsoft together with broadcaster News International are all seeking to make further penetration in the domestic sector within business, media and entertainment areas.

[18] See Table 4.A1.3: 'Preliminary Chinese ICT Usage Indicators', page 181. From Chinese National Bureau of Statistics, May 2006.

[19] Author's interview with co-founder and vice president of a mid-sized Chinese software development outsourcing services firm. Beijing, January 2005.

urban areas for internet gaming and discussion group participation; a developing sophistication by domestic banking systems to accept online financial transactions, either through Chinese only debit card clearing systems or through the progressive introduction of western style credit card operations; and a growing middle class with a greater propensity to spend on luxury and high technology products.[20] For example, in the year to December 2005, internet spending on Chinese "visa" credit cards rose from almost nothing to represent over 17% of all visa card transactions across the country—a rise of some 96% in 12 months for internet "visa" use (VISA Asia, 2005).[21]

Interestingly, China's own Internet Information Center [sic] highlighted that two of the main inhibitors to increased use of the internet for purchasing goods by the Chinese were, first, the problem of guaranteeing product quality of the delivered item and, second, the reliability of the overall purchase process itself (CNNIC Statistical Report, 2006:17). These concerns show the importance to both domestic and international firms of investment in brand development, trademark protection and supply logistics networks in order to be able to fully exploit the emerging Chinese e-commerce market, and illustrate why IP enforcement continues to have such visibility across different business sectors.

In this way, China is seeking to become a more active participant in the technologically driven international economy, both as a consumer and now, increasingly as a producer of high value goods and services.

India's infrastructure investment continues to be a challenge for its highly successful software companies and stands in marked contrast to its East Asian neighbour, with commercial analysts reporting that the country spent only US$24 billion across the range of infrastructure development projects, including electricity supply, transport and telecom, whereas China spent over US$150 billion in the same areas for 2003 alone (Ahya and Sheth, 2005).

---

[20] Author's interviews with a Chinese technology consultant. In Beijing, March & August 2005 and in Cambridge, February 2006.

[21] Whilst it is certainly true that culturally, the Chinese retain a considerable loyalty towards, and reliance on, cash based transactions for many things in everyday life, the signs of change are visible within at least the urban professional classes of the Eastern provinces, within which the use of credit cards and bank loans are concentrated.

Telephone density across the Indian subcontinent is still very low at just over 11 per hundred of the population, and even this level is only achieved if fixed and mobile figures are combined, giving a total of just over 125 million units as a national installed base, with a sub total of only 47.7 million fixed lines and 78 million mobiles respectively, to the end of 2005. Broadband penetration grew significantly over the 12 months to November 2005 from 0.49 *lakh* (approximately 50,000 users) to 7.50 *lakh* (approximately 750,000 users), but still far below Chinese levels[22] (Indian Budget Office, 2006). Given these base points, it is actually surprising that over 35 million internet users were recorded by the OECD for 2004, although it is likely to be based on the high concentration of telephony use within urban households, the growth of urban internet cafes and the dominant user profile of the professional class elites who are most likely to have both the need and the interest to procure internet access (OECD, 2006).

In terms of telephony penetration, direct comparisons with China are more difficult as the Chinese Bureau of Statistics records its social development indicators based on a division between urban and rural households, rather than individuals. However, by way of a broad indication of the contrasts, the Chinese government records national averages for fixed line phones (mobiles are recorded separately) per 100 households of 94 for urban residents (National Bureau of Statistics of China, 2006) and 58 per 100 rural households (ibid.), illustrating tangible results for the differences in overall infrastructure investment between the two countries.

The most interesting characteristic of the Indian dimension is the disconnection between overall telecom sophistication for the country at large versus the technology-dependent market leading strategies of the country's outsourcing and software service providers. These major organisations, such as Infosys, Wipro and Tata, have the resources and incentive to create separate technology parks to promote clustered knowledge spillovers, distinct and reliable electricity supplies for their operations and internet enabled working environments for their staff. Even these companies, however, have faced challenges in raising the profile of infrastructure deficiencies with local authorities in some of the major hubs of the country's IT industry, with Bangalore being a

[22] For conversion of Indian *Lakh* and *Crore* to decimal, see <http://www.kshitij.com/utilities/LnCtoMnB.shtml>, accessed 22nd November 2006.

particularly relevant example of a city where clear evidence exists of significant shortfalls in services to meet current demands, in terms of roads, airport facilities, electricity and telecommunications (Economist Print Edition, 2006).

In both India and China, the software industry within the wider technology sector has had increasing salience over recent years, although for diametrically different reasons. In India, software is significant because of its internationally renowned central place as a generator of billions of dollars worth of export earnings, predominantly in enabling specialist offshore services to be provided to international clients.

In China, its software sector is still evolving with a relatively small share of its earnings accounting for exports. But the software sector has also had national prominence, with the national leadership promoting the industry as a major target of future growth, both through increased domestic consumption of local software industry outputs and through the industry's growing presence in the export markets, especially for off-shore development projects, particularly to Japan. China and India have been enhancing their intellectual property regimes over recent years, both in response to the strategic importance of the industry domestically and the incentives that this generates and the prominence that IP issues in general have had within the international trading community.

The regulation of software as a high value knowledge product holds particular complexities due to special characteristics of the industry itself. It is therefore useful to explore these in more detail to gain insights into their nature and how technologically driven economies have addressed them.

3.3 *Special Characteristics of Software in International IP Regimes*

Software presents particular difficulties in defining its precise location within current intellectual property regimes as it is actually capable of encapsulating all of the principal types of IP: copyright; patents; trademarks and trade secrets. Software industry outputs are also now increasingly blurring the distinction between the definition of goods and services in respect of international commercial transactions and cross-border trade which has recently introduced tension into multilateral negotiating forums such as the WTO. It is, therefore, perhaps not surprising that there exists much disagreement amongst states concerning an appropriate legal treatment for software products in both domestic and international jurisdictions.

These differences and disagreements in how to treat software related products and services internationally introduce uncertainties and complexities to the growth strategies of companies that seek to expand through multiple market penetration and online product delivery. Tensions of this kind may help to explain why there has been increased activity within norm-setting institutions at the international level to find avenues of convergence in IP regulations as both state and non-state actors recognise the twin significance of the IP industries to national economic development and the framing of an agreed set of uniform regulatory structures to future industry expansion.

In a report published in 1998, the OECD maintained that it saw the internet as having an important role in "helping to create a single global market for software by cutting through many of the distribution and marketing barriers that can prevent firms from gaining access to foreign markets" (Organisation for Economic Co-operation and Development Directorate for Science Technology and Industry, 1998:18). However, whilst there were even then clear trends towards an "increasing globalisation of the software market", the OECD pointed out that the "crucial issue for international trade in on-line activities is...to eliminate international barriers to market access". In the context of IP regulatory convergence, the report concluded that, in addition to securing agreement on tax issues and tariff controls for software, a global framework for IP was "essential", and represented "an issue of particular relevance for digitised products, since firms cannot appropriate much of the benefit of product innovation without some form of legal protection" (ibid.:19–25).

These findings are still highly relevant to contemporary market development in the international trade of software goods. Whilst some progress has been made in harmonising copyright controls for software and other digitised transactions, problems still persist in a number of areas. These include conflicting jurisdictional treatment in respect to patents, variations in enforcement reliability of national IP laws, and a failure to resolve intersections between product and service delivery elements of software industry outputs in multilateral treaties.

These complexities in determining appropriate software regulations, coupled to the increasingly global nature of the industry and its growing economic significance, may help to explain the raised profile of corporations during the process of setting and agreeing new regulatory norms that impact the industry. Nor is this just a feature of corporations in industrialised countries such as in the United States and the European Union member states. It is also a characteristic of countries where the industry has significance in economic growth, regardless of whether that country is considered advanced in other sectors. The importance of software to Indian export growth, for example, gives its industry and associated business lobby group very special significance in its dealings with the Indian government, in ways that the most recent research has indicated are quite unlike any other business sector in that country.[23] The international software industry therefore provides a distinctive illustration of trends within the wider international system to include corporate interests as part of a multi-level dialogue between state and non-state actors across national boundaries.

The modern software industry emerged from the decision by hardware manufacturers, like IBM in 1969, to "unbundle" the software element from the hardware that traditionally supported it, in order to create new discrete revenue streams and to find ways to recover some of the costs of inventing and marketing the software in the first place.[24] IBM's historic decision in 1981 to cede distribution rights over the operating system software of its new microcomputer range to a then relatively unknown software company called Microsoft acted as a springboard for the home PC market and the standardisation around MS-DOS, and subsequently, Microsoft Windows.[25]

---

[23] See research by Amrita Narlikar on India and its relationship to the international trading system. Comments about the special position of India's software industry were made by Dr. Narlikar in a presentation to the Centre of International Studies, University of Cambridge, 14th February 2007.

[24] For an excellent economic history of the software industry and an introduction to legal issues surrounding these tensions, see (Galler 1995) In a further move at that time, IBM's introduction of their System 370 range of computers also boosted the nascent software industry as it marked a seismic shift within IT, in that it created, for the first time, an entire hardware family of corporate-level machines which had been introduced with the capability to run the same operating system across each one of them. This enabled an ease of migration within the power range of the hardware family and thus stimulated the incentive to build additional software that could be licensed and used across the whole of the hardware range.

[25] By the end of 1981 Microsoft was certainly no longer a backroom start-up but had already become a successful medium sized company with over 120 employees, and posted revenues of US$16 million for that year. The deal with IBM, and the development of MS-DOS as a common operating system, help to initiate the Microsoft phenomenon. It is interesting to note that, at that time, Microsoft also wrote software for Apple Computer Corp. as well.

Companies evolved business strategies that depended specifically on income from software revenues and the issue of IP protection for that revenue stream thus became one of commercial significance as the software industry itself was born and rapidly grew to maturity. The emergence of PC-based mass-market public consumption of software during the 1980's further influenced the dynamics of business risks by rendering the purchasing process completely anonymous, leading to highly standardised terms-of-use that depended fundamentally on the effectiveness of copyright enforcement within a jurisdiction as a realistic means of distributed transaction control. In the traditions of the American political system, lobby groups such as the American-based Business Software Alliance (BSA) emerged to represent the interests of these growing companies and sought to move the concerns of IP owners into the federal legislative domain.

These debates took place within legal, commercial and political communities simultaneously in different economic regions of the world and centred on how best to locate software within the panoply of available IP protection mechanisms. Differences in the extent and type of protection to be afforded to software are illustrative of a divergence in dealing with industrial change and technological development, and help to explain why tensions still prevail even between the most advanced communities, such as North America and Western Europe. These conditions also put into context some of the challenges faced by nations that are still developing but that have also begun innovating, such as India and China, as they strive to consolidate their own protective regimes whilst seeking to internalise appropriate international norms when, in fact, complete uniformity in this area is absent.

There has evolved, however, noticeable consensus amongst different states in at least two areas of protection when dealing with software's legal status: copyright and trademarks. First and foremost, software has been widely recognised as the expression of an idea that is created by the programmer in human readable form and it has long been argued that as a work of authorship its natural form of legal protection should rest with copyright. Over the last thirty years or so, the domestic legislation of both the leading producer and consumer nations have converged towards agreed policies that are broadly consistent with international norms set by the Berne Convention and reiterated through the *minimum* legislative requirements of the TRIPS Agreement. These grant to software the protection of copyright for the lifetime of the author or authors plus at least a period of 50 years afterwards.[26]

In terms of recognising software copyright, for example, the United States introduced a Software Amendment in 1980 to cover a product's explicit protection under registration with the US Copyright Office,[27] whilst the European Commission issued a Software Directive in 1991 which mandated similar recognition across the member states of the then Community (now Union). China first recognised software as copyrightable material under Special Regulations promulgated in 1991 whilst India adopted a similar tactic in 1984 with its Software Copyright Regulations.

Second, software companies have traditionally made use of trademark protection for both their products and their corporate identity, both in the traditional realms of paper-based transactions and physical signage, and now increasingly in respect of website domain name and internet presence. The principles of consumer protection and qualitative product delivery to software customers share common ground with many other industries, whilst a registered trademark can also help to nurture goodwill in domestic and overseas markets that can provide tangible returns on a company's eventual value at its time of sale or flotation.[28]

However, whilst there may be agreements of broad principle in respect to software's copyright protection and a company's power of trademark registration, the position in regards to the patenting of all or part of a software module is distinctly more diverse. The principal challenge for legislators and subsequent litigators to understand is that software is capable of combining the expression of copyright with the functional utility of a patentable idea. It has been in the United States' legal jurisdiction that the most significant developments on software

[26] For example, the United States extended protection beyond the baseline "life plus 50 years" in 1998, with the controversial Copyright Term Extension Act, settling on "life plus 70 years" for human authors, 120 years from creation for corporate authorship and 95 years from publication date for works created before 1st January 1970. The European Parliament recently voted in favour of extending musical copyright protection to "life plus 70 years", matching current EU levels for authors.

[27] For much of the 1980's, and in contrast to many other nations, the US actually required registration with the Copyright Office before protection could be asserted. This ceased once the US became a Contracting Party to the Berne Convention.

[28] Author's interview with CEO of a London based software company who registered the mark of his company's software product as part of the firm's IP value protection. London, March 2005.

patenting have taken place and where software has come to be seen as something which has of itself a distinctive construction, wherein its value as a product is derived not only from the literal nature of the source code but also from the nature of the tasks that the program performs when interacting with a computer.

The landmark decision that effectively confirmed software as a patentable entity in its own right within the US took place at the country's Supreme Court in 1981 in *Diamond v Diehr*[29] and concerned the use of a software program to manipulate recorded timings made during the process of manufacturing synthetic rubber seals (O'Rourke, 2006).[30]

Scholars have emphasised that, whilst relatively narrow in its original judgement, this case is particularly important as it changed the behaviour of the US Patent and Trademark Office (USPTO) in its attitude to subsequent patent requests, whilst also setting a legal precedent for others to follow, such that, since then, "the lower courts have interpreted Diehr in a way that favors [sic] including software itself as patentable subject matter" (ibid.:195). Moreover, this change was coincident with the significant rise in the software industry's importance and its expansion as a separate business sector, fuelled by rising revenues through the growth of mid-range and micro-computers during the years after the decision. In this way, patents became increasingly seen by vendors as a more effective protection for their software IP, replacing their previous dependence on trade secrets between known parties in more confined contracted partnerships.

The industry had entered into an era of two new dimensions that crystallised the importance of patents: first, multiple development companies began to proliferate across the United States, as distinct software clusters emerged driven by venture capital funding and University-inspired invention, whereby an effective patent portfolio made

[29] *Diamond v Diehr* 450 US 175 (1981).

[30] A chemical engineer working for the Federal Mogul Group, James Diehr, found that by making adjustments to critical event timings based on the histories stored on the computer, significant improvements could be made to the overall sealing process which gave the company a competitive edge in their market. An attempt by the company to patent the computer program that manipulated the timings was initially rejected by the US Commissioner for Patents and Trademarks, Sydney Diamond, under the then operating norm that computer software was not patentable. However, in a majority verdict on appeal, the Supreme Court held that the grant of patent should be allowed and that algorithms which provided a useful application could enjoy patent protection.

for a more attractive presentation to potential financial backers.[31] Second, within these new companies, some initiated what were often overlapping product development strategies that could sometimes involve the deliberate analysis of the behaviour of a rival's software product, whereby the process-oriented protection offered by patents for software was seen as having far stronger legal standing than even the maximum extent offered by copyright law if a dispute as to ownership of a resulting program's logic flows reached the courts. Software patents thus evolved to perform a dual role as both an arsenal for an effective legal defence and an asset for increased market valuation.

Within the US, these trends have led to marked increases in patenting activity by software companies over the years, since, to such an extent that there is now much debate about the inventive quality of newly granted software patents. Despite hiring software specialists into the USPTO as early as 1994 in order to improve its ability to determine obviousness, inventive steps and related prior art in software patent applications (Galler, 1995:36), controversy persists about the quality and appropriateness of some of its more recent decisions. Perhaps one of the most controversial of recent times has been Amazon's patenting of its "one-click" ordering method which was first granted US protection in September 1999,[32] and which, although subsequently withdrawn and replaced by two later more restrictive patents, still essentially protects against unlicensed use what is effectively just the operation of a single mouse-click to achieve an arithmetically summarised sales delivery order.

Some commentators have emphasised further concerns. They point out that because the US does not support utility models within its patenting system, which could grant protection for a shorter time based on simpler assessments, the patents awarded within America's "Utility" category (under which software is classified within the application process) produces a full 20-year grant of protection for the invention. It has been argued that this could be most restrictive in terms of industry progress if the creation of direct implementations of the "basic

[31] Author's interview with the CEO of a UK based high tech start-up, who, during the mid 1990's, worked as a technical consultant in Silicon Valley, California, at a time when the power of patents was becoming fully apparent.

[32] See US Patent No. 5,960,411: 'Method and System for Placing a Purchase Order via a Communications Network', granted 28 Sep. 1999.

truths" of computing logic were to become closed due to patent protection and license restrictions (O'Rourke, 2006:198).

Others have highlighted two factors that challenge this overtly pessimistic perspective to patenting. First, the USPTO has maintained that it considers use of the term *software patents* to be a "misnomer" and that, moreover, it has never permitted the patenting of underlying mathematical algorithms, but that, instead, it grants protection for computer hosted processes that the software carries out, on the same basis as it does for conventional industrial procedures (United States Congress Office of Technology Assessment, 1990:2). Second, technology specialists maintain that any protective timescale beyond just a few years for a program module becomes increasingly meaningless when the industry moves with the speed of innovative change that is typical in software development, where the return on investment of software projects and the lifetime value of software inventions approximate to around five years.[33]

Outside the United States, there has been even sharper debate and more polarised disagreement about the extent to which software can be classed as an "invention" for the purposes of enjoying patent protection. Whilst the laws of many jurisdictions might specifically exclude software *per se*, and mathematical algorithms in particular, from inventive protection, court decisions in different countries that could reinforce the message through statutory interpretation have been much more mixed.

Within Europe, the role of the EPO may even add to confusion in this regard. The EPO grants a set of separate patents for each of the different countries within the Convention for which an application has been made which are then asserted at national level. It has earned a reputation for looking sympathetically on requests for patent protection for algorithms and software methods. One source has estimated that the Office has already issued "30,000 patents relating to computer-implemented inventions" (Guibault and van Daaten, 2006:131) since its creation. The British Computer Society (BCS) has gone as far as to maintain that under the issuing norms of the EPO, "a computer program is patentable if the program when running on a

---

[33] Author's interviews with the Finance Director of a London-based mid-sized software company, May/June 2005. The author's own experience also confirms these perspectives.

computer...brings about...a technical effect which goes beyond the 'normal' physical interaction between the program (software) and the computer (hardware) on which it is run" (British Computer Society, 2000:12). However, the United Kingdom courts, for example, have a reputation for looking "less charitably" on attempts to assert patent protection for software utilities within British jurisdiction (ibid.).

Most recently, there have been attempts in Europe to create a new approach by combining a "Community Patent" grant with policies that would also formally recognise the establishment of a patent for computer implemented software processes (in terms that would have been broadly consistent with, even if not identical to, those in force in the United States). However, these measures failed to gain support in the European Parliament and proponents of these moves were unable to secure a majority vote in favour of a Second Reading for the Bill when it came before legislators on 6th July 2005 (European Parliament Observatory, 2002).[34] Some analysts believe that it was a mistake to combine two complex and controversial measures together and that the business implications and potential benefits for software patenting in particular required further clarity and understanding which had become clouded by multiple amendments to the final text of the Bill (Sherriff, 2005).

3.4 *Software and Ecommerce Services in the International System*

Nor is it just the domestic and regional tensions over software's IP categorisation that has captured the industry's attention in recent years. In the multilateral forum of the WTO, there continues to be dispute over the treatment of software-enabled electronic commerce (ecommerce) transactions in respect to their regulation. Ecommerce has been defined by the WTO General Council as "the production, distribution, marketing, sale or delivery of goods and services by electronic means" (Wunsch-Vincent, 2005:1–2). This covers a wide range of activities and in order to better understand the points of greatest tension, some scholars have found it useful to examine how the WTO

[34] See also BBC News reporting the defeat by 648 votes against versus 14 in favour of a second reading last accessed 15th November 2006 at http://news.bbc.co.uk/1/hi/technology/4655955.stm.

treats IT products by dividing them into a number of product "baskets" (ibid.).

Four product baskets have been suggested which effectively define a separation for technology goods and their treatment. First, a category comprising the physical IT goods that facilitate basic access to any type of information technology, such as computers, memory boards and microchips. Second, the internet infrastructure services such as telecoms and network connections that enable a platform for web-based transactions. Third, electronically traded services such as audio-video streams, financial and travel services. The fourth basket is of particular concern to software companies in that it comprises the core of ecommerce digital content products of which the principal example is software itself, although it can also include digitised books and games.

One of the more significant characteristics of these "Basket Four" products is that their mode of delivery has now increasingly become wholly electronic across the internet. In the recent past, even if ordered electronically online, these products would have typically been subject to a traditional trading arrangement, whereby there would have been cross-border delivery in the context of a physical medium, such as a CD with paper manuals, or as a physical book sent through the post. It was, in fact, this physical medium that classified them as goods for the purpose of trade. It is the character of this wholly digitised environment that is now generating disagreement between WTO members.

In terms of horizontal agreements underpinning these baskets, trade in IT products, particularly software, crosses four interlocking frameworks within the WTO: first, the WTO's work programme on ecommerce; second, the WTO's Information Technology Agreement (ITA) under its General Agreement on Tariff and Trade arrangements (GATT); third, the General Agreement on Trade in Services (GATS); and finally, the TRIPS agreement itself.

The WTO's work programme on electronic commerce was introduced in 1998 with the Ecommerce Declaration of the WTO's Ministerial Conference in May of that year. The most significant output from this Declaration was the confirmation that member states would continue the informal practice of not imposing customs duties on wholly digital ecommerce transactions under what became the "Duty Free Moratorium on Electronic Transmissions" (Wunsch-Vincent, 2005:129). This was seen by many in the industry as a useful stimulus to the generation of increased ecommerce trade but, despite this, a number of problems continue to persist with this memorandum, especially in respect to its current status: as a political declaration, it is not binding on WTO members and thus cannot be subject to a formal dispute process if one member decides to unilaterally impose duties.

Moreover, its validity is not permanent but instead is subject to re-declaration at ministerial conferences and it has thus been seen by some as a temporary measure to deal with the reality that trade rules for digital content were still evolving. When no mention of the policy was made at Cancun, its validity became especially uncertain, until a formal re-declaration took place at the Hong Kong ministerial meeting, confirming that the measures do still in fact subsist,[35] at least for the present.

The second part of the WTO's framework is the Information Technology Agreement (ITA) which was established in 1998 and is now incorporated into the framework of GATT. The ITA covers the broad spectrum of trade related regulations for IT goods, including software when carried in physical form, as part of general cross-border tariff liberalisations, with the aim of reducing tariff levels and eliminating other non-tariff measures such as unfair testing and localisation requirements for products.[36] The ITA is a plurilateral agreement in that its signatories are a subset of the wider WTO membership, and only they are subject to its provisions, whilst other non-signatory WTO members, largely confined to less technologically developed nations, still enjoy preferential terms as free-riders to the liberal regime under Most Favoured Nation (MFN) principles. However, as the ITA includes all of the most significant IT producing and consuming territories, including the US, the EU, China, India, Japan, South Korea and Taiwan, its characteristics and objectives are of importance to international software vendors.

The third part of the framework governing ecommerce transactions rests with GATS, which is the WTO's set of rules that covers international trade in services, covering a wide range of sectors from education, finance and healthcare through to communication and technology consulting services. Services are classified by the mode of delivery and consumption, with four distinctions being made: cross-border

[35] There have been a number of calls for the Memorandum to be made permanent. See WTO Ministerial Declaration 2005, paragraph 46 in which the further temporary nature of the agreement is reaffirmed.

[36] The ITA does not include consumer electronic goods like televisions and digital cameras etc.

delivery; consumption abroad; commercial presence; and movement of natural persons. In terms of ecommerce software consumption, the dilemma exists to agree whether such transactions should be classed as cross-border or consumption abroad. These distinctions matter because each mode has its own set of agreements, exemptions and applicable policies. The core objective of GATS is to reduce discriminatory regulations within member nations in order to promote further trade within each sector, but, having behind-the-border implications on a country's working practices impinges on cultural sensitivities that have made GATS more complex in negotiations and less liberal in its achievements. Scholars point to the fact that obligations under GATS are restricted to particular commitments rather than to broad principles and often have country specific exemptions that are far more extensive than anything permitted within the GATT (Wunsch-Vincent, 2006:52–55).

Software delivered through electronic commerce falls directly between the restrictive pull of domestic services constraints and the promoting push of cross-border trade liberations. Two key questions emerge in respect to ecommerce software transactions: are they an item of trade in a cross-border supply to be thus granted the benefits of the trade liberalising principles of GATT or, are they instead an element of a service, which would make them subject to the less liberal and less formulated rules encapsulated by the GATS? The answer to these questions would appear to differ significantly depending upon to whom the question is put: this divergence is at its most marked between the US and the EU, which are obviously two of the most significant actors within the multilateral negotiating forum, but which seem to have adopted markedly different positions.

The United States takes the view that ecommerce and trade in digital products should be subject to GATT provisions and controlled by agreement within the ITA membership. Indeed, the US passed its own Trade Act in 2002 that has been described as "a mandate for free trade in digital content" which puts forward ambitions for an aggressive negotiating position to achieve "the liberalisation of trade in telecommunications, computer and audio-visual entertainment and other electronically deliverable services" (ibid.:117–20).

The European Union, on the other hand, seeks to treat digitally delivered content (into which basket it includes wholly digital software purchases) in keeping with its own internal market rules, which regard such activity as services. Intra-member state relationships also play an important part in national level negotiating stances in that "trade agreements that affect cultural and audio-visual services are excluded from the EC's exclusive common commercial policy powers" (ibid.:130), which gives member states that wish to protect domestic sectors considerable rights to either operate independently or exercise vetoes on potential progress at an EU level. France, in particular, has a long-standing interest in maintaining its culturally distinct French language services.[37]

Finally, there is tension between some states in respect to the technological neutrality of TRIPS and whether, therefore, ecommerce related products require special and additional measures, over and above the full panoply of protections that can already be asserted and enforced under its conventional terms. This issue is of particular importance given the rapid growth of internet use around the world and in regard to the global nature of ecommerce transactions and the copyright and fair-use issues introduced by increased use of handheld devices and personal multimedia data stores. These issues have yet to be properly addressed and resolved which introduces some uncertainty into the future direction of the software industry in an integrated and networked international community.

One aspect of the debate in the international system that is especially noteworthy for countries such as India and China concerns the necessary steps that the WTO believes are required to be taken by developing country governments in order to fully participate and exploit ecommerce software transactions. Scholars and practitioners have focused on five broad themes that can influence ecommerce acquisition within a state.[38]

First, addressing trade regulations and behind-the-border measures to liberalise access to technology inputs such as hardware and operating system software, in tandem with ensuring infrastructure enhancements that make networked communications more widely available. Second, improving local skills in key areas to reduce the barriers to entry by national participants. For example, by raising the standard of English through specialist and targeted education programmes, both in language generally but also in technology specific vocabulary in

[37] France even went so far as to create new French words for all of the key aspects of technology, including "computer" as *l'ordinateur* and "software" as *le logiciel*.

[38] For a useful discussion of these and other aspects of developing country participation, see (Mann 2000) and (Panagariya 2000).

particular. Third, improving the restrictions placed on the movement of natural persons into the economy from overseas, in terms of both returning nationals who may now hold foreign citizenship, as well as natural born foreigners to help the general climate of technological skills acquisition and to help grow micro-sized businesses (of less than five people). Fourth, providing a stimulus for IT organisations by promoting government procurement for new technical solutions and helping support groups that provide channels of communication to policymakers by small and medium sized enterprises (SMEs). Finally, creating government-led policies that foster a technologically enabling approach by improving consumer protection through the enforcement of IP rights and data privacy rules whilst also enabling access to electronic signatures and network transactions.

By examining these points through the lens of current developments in India's and China's software industry, it is possible to see a direct connection between their attempts to address these issues and the improved visibility enjoyed by the software industry in these two countries. Within each of these areas, both China and India, as newly innovating nations, are seeking to make enhancements to their competitive position: through creating new policies on IP protection;[39] by stimulating new development areas for clustered software building;[40] by attracting members of the country's diaspora to return with their overseas acquired skills and working practices; and by promoting the use of new business methods that exploit ecommerce opportunities.[41]

Software companies operate both nationally and internationally and generate business through conventional and electronic transactions. Whilst multilateral debate continues about trading policies, service restrictions and taxation agreements, individual companies still need to conduct their business, generate revenue and create new products for sale within a climate that can safeguard their IP assets to the maximum extent possible.

---

[39] China has radically overhauled its IP regime in recent years and has appointed senior government ministers to tackle enforcement issues. India, meanwhile, has introduced ecommerce and digital signature recognition under its IT Act of 2000.

[40] Both India and China have extensive networks of software parks and general IT development clusters enjoying a variety of fiscal stimulus, including income tax breaks and export duty relief.

[41] Both governments have embarked on programmes to "e-enable" dialogue between citizen and government, with some noticeable progress taking place at the local level in India.

The mechanism by which trade in software and market penetration by firms is controlled from a corporate perspective, operates at three principal levels:[42] first, known violations of IP regulations can be pursued through recourse to national laws asserted directly through local courts and enforced as required by specific jurisdictions. Second, protection may be sought under international IP treaties such as TRIPS or through special arrangements such as with the International Arbitration Courts, with both industry lobby groups and major multinationals operating at the political level of their home state to make representations for action where commercial entities have no direct right of audience (such as at the WTO). Third, in terms of day-to-day operations, the primary means by which business is transacted is through software licensing agreements that complement general commercial contracts between supplying and consuming parties. It is, therefore, useful to summarise how licenses have developed and explore the current context of this evolution.

3.5 *The Evolution of Software Licensing Models*

The right to exploit the value of IP-rich technology products such as software solutions under modern IP regimes has traditionally rested within a business licensing agreement between supplier and consumer, structured in different ways dependent on the type of product or service being purchased. The role of the license agreement is to assert ownership and copyright protection over the software by the originator and to create a binding set of rules that will govern the way in which one party will use the software whilst a version of it resides within their control, including restrictions on reproduction and copying of the software, controlling the distribution to others and limiting the resale or modification of the software other than under the owner's specific instructions and approval. It is, therefore, a legal contract governing both parties in the relationship but placing particular emphasis on the obligations and duties of the consumer.

The license grants a right of use over a particular time frame to a third party rather than a transfer of ownership of the software itself.

[42] Much of this draws upon the author's own experience as a software company owner and technical developer over the last 20 years.

Indeed, selling the stock of IP held by a software company is a major strategic decision for the directors and shareholders of an enterprise and is typically only undertaken as part of the commercial acquisition of the company by another, or during an asset divestment operation or as part of some other similarly significant business event.

In the broadest terms, the determinants for calculating license charges in the software industry have been two-fold: first, an assessment is made as to the number of people who are likely to use and derive benefit from the solution, expressed either as a maximum concurrent number or as a total group of all possible users; second, account is made of the power of the hardware on which the software will be run, often expressed in terms of the number and type of CPUs in the machine's configuration, or perhaps the number of separate machines in an organisation's data centre. Moreover, there are a number of different types of commercial software license from which to choose and that are in use across the industry at this time, including the 'perpetual license', which has been the mainstay of the industry for many years, the 'subscription license' which has become attractive in an era of rapidly changing technology and internet delivered software service models, and the 'utility license' that extends a subscription's flexibility with a 'pay-on-use' approach.

The 'perpetual license' has long been the preferred approach within the industry (Software Information Industry Association, 2004:4–5). This type of license is used across all manner of different relationships, from single-user pricing prevalent in anonymous, individual sales from high street retailers, through to group and corporate level implementations. Indeed, it can also include schemes such as market sector discounts (as with, for example, academic and educational use) and differential pricing for high volume user communities. The approach has been particularly popular with mass-market, shrink-wrapped products, manifested by the pre-formatted legal agreement included in the box or with the download, that is both easy to understand and could be enforceable in a consumer's jurisdiction should either the need or opportunity ever arise. This helps vendors maintain a semblance of protection to their IP whilst also minimising the transaction costs of each sale to individuals.

The 'perpetual license' has many examples within the public domain and is likely to be very familiar to purchasers of utilities such as Microsoft Office through a commercial outlet, such as PC World, or from the web where a download page might require the acceptance of terms prior to concluding the sale transaction or trial download. Upgrades and support are typically not provided within the license and must be purchased through a separate exercise, but, equally, nor is maintenance and support schedule enforced by the supplier as part of the contract. A perpetual license typically has a number of different sections: it asserts copyright ownership of the software by the vendor; it reiterates restrictions in terms of copying, resale and technical deconstruction of its working methods (de-compilation); and it will specify remedies and related rights that could be the basis for piracy charges if license terms are thought to have been infringed.

A variant of the perpetual license is used by many large-scale vendors selling into the corporate sector, with the main difference over the retail version being more specific, with details concerning the client company's right to distribute the software over multiple machines. Also, such variants almost always include a chargeable amount for both technical support services, product upgrades and fault maintenance over the usage life of the software. This "support and maintenance" section is especially prevalent where vendors have designed their own customised or special purpose software for different clients and where, as a result, they have built strong relationships with customers which they wish to preserve into the future. Many software companies have designed their revenue models such that, whilst they primarily recognise the bulk of a sale's income at the start of the contract, they can include these future recurring revenue streams spread across subsequent years. Some very large international software companies have pursued acquisition strategies of smaller enterprises based almost entirely on expected future recurring revenues for support and maintenance within the target software product's customer base.

In this way, the standard perpetual license is tailored and combined with one or more years of support and maintenance fees, both of which are then charged annually as a percentage (usually 15–20%) of the original up-front license fee. In the first year, the additional charges are added to the base price of the software as part of the commencement contract. At least one year of support is usually mandated as part of the original license cost in order to provide some level of commercial 'lock-in', whereby a customer is financially and technologically tied to a supplier for at least that extent of time, enabling the supplier the potential to secure further follow-on sales within an ongoing relationship.

More recently, other alternatives to the traditional approach have begun to emerge, prompted in part by the facilitation of new technologies that have opened further revenue generating possibilities and in part by large scale user companies who have been seeking better returns for their annual IT spend (SIIA, 2004).

A 'subscription license' is an example of this new trend. In contrast to the perpetual alternative it emphasises that the customer is seeking to pay only for the services and software elements that are most useful for the time period that is most convenient. They are relatively new in the international software market and many industry commentators consider the trend towards their increased adoption to be linked more to the growth of internet-based delivery and service-oriented supply mechanisms under new business arrangements offered by emerging suppliers, than to any real drive or initiative by old traditional vendors to change the industry standard approach, many of whom continue to be "wedded to the perpetual licensing [model]" (Hicks, 2004).

The subscription approach to software licensing represents a new departure from previously used controls and may be connected to the rise in outsourcing of software-enabled services. An organisation may now purchase the operational functionality of a business department or division, such as document scanning and image management, financial accounting, human resources or even software programming itself, and receive the benefits of that service via technology delivered methods of consumption. A balance between what is maintained in-house and what is outsourced is also becoming usual, in order to restrict sensitive data or code from being included in the outsourced arrangement. Within this trend towards increased use of outsourcing, there have emerged a number of layers of complexity which sub-divide the service delivery model and the associated license and transaction relationships linked to it.

The most sophisticated parts of the outsourcing spectrum fall into the category of "tailored, bespoke technology services" (Economist Print Edition, 2004:11) offered by major organisations, both nationally and internationally, and usually involve complex contractual negotiations and the practical commitment of both sides to a long-term working relationship. Suppliers like America's Accenture and EDS and India's Wipro and Tata are leaders in this field. At the other end of the spectrum there exist operations that are now organised in such a way that their delivery has effectively become a commodity in terms of costs and transaction complexities. Outsourced software-enabled document scanning and filing bureaux management is an example of this tier, where licensing arrangements can be as simple as one-off consumption agreements in return for a set of CDs or may involve rolling annual levies based on pay-per-use arrangements and may include computer data-entry document indexing. Between these two ends of the spectrum there exist a large number of suppliers, each offering a range of services that may be more or less tailored to suit different company requirements.

Moreover, increased high speed networked infrastructure for even small and micro-sized companies (less than five people) has expanded the scope for all sizes of commercial enterprise to consider an outsourced approach to at least some of their business functions. It has also blurred the line between near-shore outsourcing to local service centres, whose charges often rivalled an in-house approach but which could still handle capacity expansion better than an internal department, and offshore outsourcing to international suppliers with a comparative advantage in low-cost but high-skilled labour, often in India or China. In this way, a greater range of company sizes and types has been able to explore the cost saving and capacity expansion capabilities offered by new business models and the licensing arrangements that support them (Institute of Directors, Outsourcing).

The number and range of service delivery organisations available to companies has also increased through the power of internet solution procurement, which enhances the ability to reassess value for money and service quality of suppliers on an ongoing basis and has further entrenched the growth of subscription and transaction-based licensing models. For consuming individuals and companies, the power of the internet has deepened the coverage of available suppliers within an industry to new organisations which would never before have been able to gain access to supplier shortlists but which have gained this visibility through search engines such as Google, using novel and cost effective advertising pricing methods such as Google's "keyword sponsored link",[43] instead of being constrained by the cost of the traditional

[43] In this approach, a company pays to appear in specially formatted search results when a single or combination of keywords are entered by the user into Google's search engine. The supplier is only charged for their appearance, however, if a user subsequently clicks through to the company's website, increasing the quality of leads generated by the advertising spend. The author was director of two software companies that used exactly this approach to gain visibility and capture new customers.

advertising and marketing spheres. Commentators have described this phenomenon as the internet's "long tail" (Anderson, 2004) which first rose to prominence in the retail markets of book sales and music downloads but has now become evident across business operations.

This growth and variety of choice in supplying organisation is especially attractive in making a subscription framework a powerful tool that thus avoids the "lock-in" associated with the previous generation of legal arrangements. A particularly sharp differentiator between old and new approaches to licensing has developed by way of "utility" based pricing and service consumption, anchored on the ability of customers to choose only those sub-elements of a software product or service that actually suits their business operation, rather than having the all-or-nothing option under older models.

This globalisation of business methods in software service models and the increasingly sophisticated technological capability of online infrastructure may help to explain why there has been growth in both the visibility and the number of international treaties and agreements that pertain to the high technology sector in recent years. It should be noted, however, that these moves have proceeded in tandem with continuing tensions in respect to the global governance of digital services and product delivery at a regulatory level. Whilst disagreements persist in GATS, especially in the treatment of software services, and whilst tensions remain in GATT, particularly in terms of taxation, it has been corporations and individual states that have sought responses to the commercial imperatives to facilitate trade in IP-rich products.

Some countries have interpreted this situation as an opportunity to differentiate their own regulatory advantages, often in response to requests by their own domestic industry interests, in order to help attract new business and foster technology driven growth. For example in 2000, India passed a wide-ranging set of measures encapsulated in the Information Technology Act that paved the way for acceptance under law of digital signatures and set out legal responses in cases of specialised copying of digital databases. Initiatives of this kind by India are illustrative of the general point that in the context of the international software and services industry, regulatory development has now evolved into a complex interconnection between the traditional actors of states and treaty organisations together with industry interest groups and major corporations.

In tandem with this revolution in licensing and delivery that has transformed international trade in software and related services, underlying product development itself has become increasingly more sophisticated and modularised so that functional units of a given software solution are now being separated and individually identified within the wider product. This impacts two areas: first, it enables much finer specificity in billing arrangements to be offered to commercial customers to better meet their precise needs; second, it facilitates the introduction of license enforcement technologies that enable suppliers to link actual consumption made with fees paid, and to electronically detect when violations are being attempted as opposed to relying solely on paper contracts and anti-piracy law. These licensing technologies could have a direct impact on the market penetration of legitimate software and associated royalty payments from high piracy communities such as China. Microsoft, for example, are to ensure that versions of its Windows operating system will implement tamper detection systems for a machine's license management controls and online violation protection mechanisms that would lead to the functional degradation for specific parts of the software if the controls detected an unlicensed software instance (Rooney, 2006; Thurrott, 2006; Microsoft Corporation, 2006d; 2006e).

However, some scholars and commentators maintain that the most striking challenge to conventional licensing business models comes not from illegal activity but from the legitimate and growing trend towards the adoption and use of open source software development and distribution.

3.6 *Open Source Licensing in the International Software Industry*

The open source software development community, by which is meant that the source code of the software is made available as well as the computer readable element, has had increasing visibility within the international software industry over the last few years and has been the subject of a number of controversies and some misunderstandings. These relate to its structure, the technical arrangements by which solutions are marketed and revenue generating business models are created, and its legal position in regards to IP regulations. It is therefore useful to explain the movement's origins, its current scope and likely future trends.

Open source initiatives provide an interesting intersection between competition and trade policy and illustrate how a convergence of interests can take place between state actors pursuing national industrial policies and non-state enterprises pursuing their own commercial objectives. Corporate level participants within open source ventures have sought to maintain maximum inter-operability for their software products, whilst also creating a deterrent to market domination by any one company in the industry, which, in the reality of the contemporary international software industry, means finding ways to combat the growing market share of Microsoft. In so doing, these corporations are taking measures that protect their positions should regulatory controls in competition policy at a state level fail to be effective, and their actions can thus be seen as complementing moves by state level actors, such as the United States and European Union, which have sought to constrain the perceived proprietary dominance of Microsoft in international software markets through anti-monopoly regulatory measures.

The structure of the open source communities has ranged over time from academic/industry collaborations through to multiple commercial partnerships that have provided both funding and personnel towards the costs of source code enhancement. A number of different examples of open source software have emerged over the last twenty years or so, starting with the Unix operating system[44] initiative under collaboration between AT&T and Berkeley University in the United States.[45]

The Unix-inspired Linux operating system is a more recent example of the open source initiative, having been originally created by Linus Torvalds in collaboration with a network of software developers around the world. From the small beginnings of individual software developers emailing each other with code updates and bug fixes, Linux has progressed to become one of the main challengers to the hegemony of Microsoft's Windows operating system within both server and desktop domains (BusinessWeek Print Edition, 31st January 2005). This has been accompanied by an increasing trend towards commercialising

---

[44] Unix (registered as a trademark as "UNIX") is a portable computer operating system originally developed by AT&T specialists at Bell Labs in the 1960's and 1970's. See <http://www.bell-labs.com/history/unix>, accessed 20th November 2006.

[45] In this example, the creation of the open source element came as a direct result of attempts by the commercial partner (AT&T) to restrict the free distribution of code by the academic partner (UC Berkeley). This led to the formation of the Berkeley Software Distribution (BSD) which underpinned many Unix implementations throughout the 1980's and into the 1990's.

the creation of the code itself under a not-for-profit organisation known as the Open Software Development Labs (OSDL), using funds provided by interested industry partners such as Intel, IBM and HP, which also provide members of their own paid staff resources to support the next stages of the operating system's development in concert with those at OSDL (including Linus Torvalds himself). These large scale vendors appear to have deliberately created business models that exploit the Linux product suite as a platform for their own revenue-based solutions but without the need for them to pay a third party for a proprietary operating system software license. It may also be helpful in the creation of a potential defensive position against market share domination by Microsoft.

Nor is it just in operating systems that open source software is to be found: in the web server domain, Apache leads Microsoft by two-thirds to one-third in terms of number of hosted websites across the world.[46] In web browsers, the open source Mozilla Firefox,[47] which emerged from the development of Netscape's "Communicator" browser technology, has gained popularity as an alternative to Microsoft's Internet Explorer, whilst in database management systems, the open source MySQL[48] has held a credible presence against closed-source operations such as Ingres, Oracle and Microsoft's SQL Server for at least the last eight years.[49]

The open source approach is one of "collaborative creation"[50] with often loosely connected individuals and groups designing, building and releasing software within a multi-layered community of specialists, each of whom may concentrate on only one aspect of the overall project, with perhaps only a handful of individuals coordinating and integrating the results.

---

[46] See Netcraft Web Statistics Review, <http://news.netcraft.com>, accessed 21st November 2006. It records that as of November 2006 there are 101 million websites hosted across the world, with 61% using Apache as the Web Server versus 31% using Microsoft.

[47] See 'Firefox', <http://www.mozilla.org/support/firefox/faq>, accessed 21st November 2006.

[48] See 'MySQL', <http://www.mysql.com>, accessed 21st November 2006 for further details.

[49] More recently, there has emerged what the IT industry terms the "LAMP" stack of open source service products: Linux, Apache, MySQL and Perl (a programming language for web applications), all of which enable an entire technology infrastructure to be built upon an open source architecture.

[50] Op. cit. Guibault, Unravelling the Myth around Open Source Licenses, page 1.

In its purest theoretical form, the open source approach seeks to exhibit a number of characteristics which sharply differentiate it from conventional software building models (van Wendel de Joode, De Bruijn, and van Eeten, 2003), the so-called "closed source" operations.[51] First, open source solutions have distributed ownership and control spread throughout those in the programming community, which become visible through their interest, enthusiasm and technical capability. Their competence to take leadership positions is judged by peer review, based on the perceived quality of their outputs rather than by any position that they may hold within an organisational hierarchy. In open source solutions, copyright is asserted by the individual responsible for writing a particular module or function but is then being freely donated to the community at large, whereby the source code of the results is not seen as a commercial asset to be hidden and protected as with conventional business models.

Second, it has been argued that there is less commercial lock-in for clients using open source software as the base of their computing architecture (Guibault and Van Daatten, 2006). The collaborative nature of its programming development engenders a unified approach to technology standards, handling routine tasks like printing, network interconnecting and providing support for inter-program communication interfaces are likely to be consistently dealt with across different versions and between different distributions of an open source solution. All of this inherently makes future client decisions to migrate all or part of the software infrastructure from one supplier to another or from one version to another far easier. Moreover, it may be that the proprietary software vendors, in seeking to provide value-added functionality to justify higher license fees, actually use such facilities to build client dependence across the infrastructure so as to significantly raise the transaction cost of switching away from the "closed" software solution.

Third, the source code of the open source solution is freely available and included as part of the delivered solution. It is perhaps in this area that confusion and misunderstanding arises most in respect to what exactly is "free" about open source software. There is confusion because

---

[51] Closed source is a description used by any in the open source community and refers to software whose source code is either kept completely secret or is only released through special legal licensing arrangements that prohibit free sharing with third parties.

the term "open source" has often been used interchangeably with the term "free software" and there is misunderstanding over exactly what is actually "free" about the software, and, if the code is free, how it is that commercial organisations can build successful revenue models within an open source environment.

The source code of any "open source" product is provided in full and at no cost to the consumer, and, indeed, is now typically available for download and install from an appropriate website.[52] This software, however, is unlikely to be useful for non-technical individuals or for corporations: it is likely to have no additional features such as graphical interfaces; it is likely to have minimum levels of installation and usage documentation; and, perhaps most critically of all, it is provided without technical support and consulting to enable the product to be used to solve business problems and generate value-added solutions for a company. It is these latter issues that impact the "total cost of ownership" for software solutions in commercial terms as much as the price of the underlying software license itself, such that removal of just the software license fees has only a marginal effect on the economics of systems management. It is these areas of "value added" services that provide the incentive and revenue basis for making open source attractive to commercial vendors: subscription fees may be levied for documentation and support whilst additional revenue generating software products built on the open source operating system may also be supplied as part of a "distribution bundle" provided by profit-seeking operations such as Red Hat within the Linux community (Redhat Linux Solutions, 2004).

There are a number of controversies and misunderstandings surrounding the licensing and intellectual property of what is contained within open source releases. This is exacerbated by the fact that there are a number of different types of open source licensing template. The first misunderstanding is based on whether licenses are actually of relevance to open source initiatives. In fact, a license agreement is a critical part of the approach and most emphatically exists for the consumption of an open source deliverable. Indeed, there are even different types of licensing arrangements that the industry categorises based

[52] For example, see <http://www.kernel.org>, accessed 21st November 2006, for the Linux operating system kernel source code. The "kernel" of an operating system comprises the essential modules that handle core functions such as writing to disks, reading from terminal screens and handling data safely whilst in computer memory.

on their empathy with underlying open software principles. These differences are typically based on the extent to which closed, proprietary code may be integrated with the open source kernel prior to building a distribution.

The BSD license, for example, permitted any number of non-open source modules to be integrated with the original code so long as the original code was always distributed with Berkeley copyright notifications. At the other end of the spectrum, the General Public License (GPL), which predominates in the Linux market, requires that any code directly integrated with the original kernel must of itself become open source (this is distinct from layered products built on top of the underlying operating system).[53] In the case of Linux and the GPL, such an approach is termed "viral" in design, as the license's "open" character effectively "infects" the new code that was introduced to enhance the original solution, ensuring that the complete code line then continues to be open in its licensing character.

A second misunderstanding of open source products is that intellectual property has no meaning or value for the community: on the contrary, scholars and commentators alike have pointed out that "far from rejecting the rules of copyright law, the open source movement relies on the application of these rules to set their own open terms of use" (Guibault: 89). Nor is it simply with copyright that open source touches international IP regimes: Linux itself, for example, is trademark protected, whilst commercial stakeholders including IBM are supporting OSDL's attempts to create a pool of software patent licenses granted into the community by multiple vendors for common benefit, to reduce the likelihood of patent infringement litigation against Linux distributors or users.

Red Hat actually maintains a stock of patents in its own right in order to use them as bargaining counters in potential disputes with non-participating commercial entities who challenge Linux code and also offers to indemnify customers against potential suits through its "Intellectual Property Warranty". This is likely to be put into sharp relief against moves by Microsoft to change the dynamics of open

[53] In keeping with the individualism of the Linux community, one man—Richard Stallman—is credited with being the pioneer behind the principles of the General Public License, although, most recently, there have been disagreements amongst open source advocates over the extent to which a new release of the GPL, with further restrictions, is actually merited in the market.

source revenue models through its attempts to charge fixed fees to distributors in return for promises not to pursue patent infringement law suits (Lawsky and Zawadzki, 2006).

3.7 *The growth potential of Open Source Solutions*

Open source solutions may be starting to change the dynamics of the operating system market as leading distributors and hardware vendors see advantages in furthering their own proprietary sales in conjunction with a generic hardware-independent software platform. However, in the context of current market penetration for server operating systems[54] (as opposed to desktop operating systems), proprietary Unix versions and Microsoft Windows would appear to still hold joint leadership, with sales of server machines running versions of MS Windows Server reaching just over US$17.7 billion for 2005, whilst sales of server computers running proprietary Unix versions together totalling US$17.5 billion for the same year (Shankland, 2006). By contrast, Linux, the leader in open source server solutions, achieved revenues worldwide of just over US$5 billion.[55]

In China, whilst acceptance of Linux as a viable alternative to Microsoft Windows has strengthened over the last three years, driven especially by government procurement processes and supportive publicity for the country's leading Linux distributor "Red Flag Linux" (Taft, 2005), business analysts report that behind the headlines, total revenues across the country for Linux in 2005 reached only US$11.8 million, and, although this represented a growth rate over the previous year of 27%, this was from a relatively low base point (IDC, 2006b). By contrast, Microsoft continues to dominate the Chinese desktop computer sector and is reported to have a market share of at least 50% across the country. (China Daily Online, 2006c). Most recently, the software leader has signed three agreements with leading Chinese PC manufacturers, including a US$1.3 billion distribution agreement with Lenovo as well as less valuable but equally significant contracts with Tsinghua Tongfang and TCL, to pre-install legitimate operating

---

[54] Servers are medium to large-scale computers that can host large numbers of user desktop conections.

[55] Ibid..

system software on to hardware prior to their distribution, as part of anti-piracy initiatives (Microsoft Corporation, 2006a).

In India, where server market sales have been steadily rising as information technology continues to penetrate the domestic business sector, of the 96,000 enterprise servers sold across the country in 2005, over 63% were pre-installed with the latest Microsoft Windows Server operating system.[56] There are, however, a number of industry figures who believe that there are significant opportunities for India to embrace open source approaches as a lever to expand both service collaboration and technology innovation, and point to rapidly increasing interest amongst Indian enterprises, in what is still a relatively new concept (Knowledge@Wharton, 2008).

Nevertheless, when the operating system elements of the market are removed from analysis, the dominance of proprietary software would appear to be clear. In business areas such as word processing and publishing (with, for example, Microsoft Word), enterprise databases (with Oracle's RDBMS), and resource management and accounting (with Germany's SAP product suite), the market is led by "closed", privately held and assetised software. For the present at least, it is likely that leadership of the IP-rich technology sector by corporations such as these will continue for some time into the future.

3.8 *Conclusion*

The chapter has shown that the software industry is undergoing considerable change within the international economy and that both intellectual property regulations and related market development policies are having to respond accordingly. Products are blending with technology driven services and ecommerce delivery models to introduce tension and disagreement into multilateral regulatory trading regimes. Responses to these difficulties can be seen to have developed within both state and enterprise domains, with increasing levels of intersection becoming visible between regulatory developments and commercial imperatives.

[56] See IDC web article, 'Server Revenues Surge More than 28% in 2005, India Poised to Become the Second Largest Market in [Asia-Pacific Japan]', *ICD Market Analysis*, <http://www.idc.com/getdoc.jsp?containerId=prIN20083206>, 7th March 2006, accessed 22nd November 2006.

These same trends have also facilitated a greater global presence of emerging suppliers of software-enabled services from nations in Asia and Eastern Europe, as commercial enterprises in these regions have increased their share of this international market whilst also initiating upward pressure on their governments' focus towards promulgating sympathetic and supportive regulatory regimes.

Some of the most striking manifestations of this change rest with the increased strength and visibility of the technology sectors and intellectual property protections exhibited by developments within China and India. Both countries, to a greater or lesser extent, have updated their legal and regulatory IP systems to support their own knowledge sectors and have simultaneously upgraded their capacity to exploit the products of the high technology sector. Through an increased internet and broadband-enabled participation in the online economy, linked to growing success within their own domestic software industries, both countries present compelling case studies of the way that technological development, economic growth and reliable knowledge-based product protection regimes are interconnected. Each demands further and more detailed investigation in the context of the global, regional and national characteristics that have promoted their recent development.

CHAPTER FOUR

IP REGIME ADOPTION IN ASIA

The emerging globalisation of IP rights and regulations has evolved within a system of relationships and incentives that have affected knowledge economy actors in different countries in different ways and at different times. The role of the nation-state and its institutions retains a key position in this dynamic but its power in respect to regime formation and regulatory adoption have increasingly been subject to restraints and interconnections within a network of non-state parties such as major corporations and political lobby groups, both within the domestic territory and directly between groups across national boundaries.

It will be shown that a three-level game has been developing that changes old presumptions about how states interrelate (Ataman, 2002; Lisowski, 2003). These interactions can be seen to have moved beyond the original idea that states operated at two levels of dialogue (Putnam, 1988), one vertically with their own domestic constituency and the other horizontally, in multilateral forums with other states. Now, evidence appears to be emerging of a significant new third group that have become involved in a more complex set of relationships: transnational corporations and industry lobby groups—with the latter representing both large and smaller-sized enterprises—would appear to be operating horizontally and vertically simultaneously, in networks and through dialogue with both state and non-state actors that cross national boundaries, whilst also maintaining connection with their own government as part of their strategy to further their commercial interests.

Progress of this kind appears to be especially visible within the high technology and IP-rich industries. This is likely to have been due to a number of interrelated factors: the increased salience of international transactions and growth of technology product trade in these industries, the particular significance of domestic knowledge sectors in a number of economies and the ease with which technological capability now facilitates communication channels such as the internet and video conferencing that are independent of national borders.

It will be argued that states now face multiple constraints in terms of domestic policy formation in an IP context. First, they can be subject to bilateral pressures from powerful state actors operating internationally. Second, states are becoming increasingly bound by obligations set through multilateral treaties such as TRIPS. Third, they are subject to influence from interconnected groups of business interests from the domestic constituencies of both their own and overseas knowledge industry sectors.

It will be further argued that economically significant nations within East and South Asia present a particularly useful illustrations of these trends in that, over recent years, they have emerged to co-exist with first world economies within the global IP regulatory landscape and have faced these competing pressures whilst adapting their priorities towards greater international market engagement and domestic technological development. Advances in India and China would appear to present a movement along a continuum of regime development and regulatory adoption that in many ways can be seen as a reprise of that which transformed the Republic of Korea and, in earlier decades, that of Japan. This would seem to show that there is an observable symbiosis between a country's level of expertise in the creation of knowledge goods, their incentive to protect the economic fruits of these domestic outputs and the propensity for their governments to willingly encourage and actively to introduce the elements of a robust IP regulatory system. Scholars have already observed these trends occurring across the region (Maskus, 2000:92).

It is, therefore, useful to make a review of regime trajectories across this region that take account of the factors that can influence such progress in some developing countries and the way in which these states and their sub-state entities have come to participate in the wider global regime.

In the context of domestic regulatory evolution of a state's IP regime, three key questions appear salient: first, what are the motivators to regulatory development that have impact on a state's IP adoption and from where do these factors originate; second, what other influences besides IP regulations might influence technology-based success; and third, how does the state interact with non-state stakeholders in regime development.

The traditional view of intellectual property regulations being imposed as a blueprint by first world economically and technologically advanced *have's* on to struggling and ill-equipped developing country *have nots* would seem to be far too simplistic an assessment of what appears to be a more complex combination of national motivators and actor interdependencies. First-tier developing nations such as India and China can be seen to have been actively implementing regimes for protecting IP within their borders with vigour and many leaders of both a political and corporate nature in those two nations view such developments as an issue of national advantage. Instead of being a subservient response to either systemic influences or bilateral pressures, IP adoption and the effective embedding of regime norms within an economy comes about through an intersection of endogenous and exogenous factors.

In this connection, power dynamics and global regime evolution certainly play an important part in the process, but a successful outcome is also linked to internal factors such as the technological level of development exhibited by leading domestic firms, their propensity to embrace export-led strategies at the expense of import substitution policies and the concomitant engagement with the international trading system, combined with the positive results of knowledge acquisition derived from the spillovers of that engagement.

4.1 *Bilateral and Multilateral Power as Agents of IP Regime Change*

Bilateral pressure, especially from the United States, cannot be ignored as a motivator for change across Asia. The driving dynamic for America in this respect is its ongoing belief in the need to vigorously protect its economic interests in relation to the domestic growth and export orientation of its IP-rich knowledge sectors, such as software, entertainment and pharmaceuticals. Asian nations operate as both consumers of these products and exporters of their own goods and services into the American domestic market which creates both a symbiosis and a tension which has been centred on perceived weaknesses by the US in respect to the IP regimes across Asian markets.

America has developed responses to these priorities at both legislative and corporate levels. First, there is considerable power vested in the scope of the retaliatory trade action available under the provisions of Section 301 of the US 1974 Trade Act (Amended, 1988), known as the "Special 301" procedures. These give executive powers to initiate trade sanctions to defend American corporate interests. Second, the US has more recently focused on using its market power through bilateral trade agreements that can include heavier burdens of intellectual property based legal obligations than those mandated by TRIPS (United States Trade Representative, 2004).[1] Third, institutional capabilities have been combined to good effect with lobbying efforts by US multinationals and IP industry groups, both of which have jointly commissioned many reports and country surveys that have sought to justify state action. These can be seen as "soft law"[2] drivers for determining action by congressional and administration leaders who have frequently cited their content as justifications for a target nation's inclusion in Watch Reports and its liability for trade sanctions.

A number of Asian countries have been subject to investigations under the Section 301 regulations, and India, China and Taiwan have all been regularly censored for inadequate IP regime implementation over many years. Similar circumstances pertain to IP's regime history in the Republic of Korea (Ramcharan, 2006).[3] Japan had also been long characterised as building an economy based on copying and had been criticised by many US commentators over its weak IP regime over a number of years between the 1950's and the 1980's (Maskus & Reichman, 2005).

Some of the motivations for American intervention in this way may be explained by development trajectories in many parts of Asia. In countries across this region, the economic models can be seen to have evolved from protective and isolated industrial development, focusing on import substitution strategies to ones that have fully embraced the opportunities of export-led growth and engagement with the

---

[1] This outlines the IP burdens mandated as part of Australia's FTA with the US. Also see Chapter 16 of the US FTA with Singapore in 2003 appeared to bring standards on some areas into close line with US domestic policy, moving beyond TRIPS. For Singapore's FTA see United States Trade Representative, <http://www.ustr.gov/assets/Trade_Agreements/Bilateral/Singapore_FTA/Final_Texts/asset_upload_file708_4036.pdf>, accessed 20th March 2007.

[2] A number of scholars distinguish between non-binding "soft law" encapsulated in resolutions, reports and pressure group surveys and binding "hard law" of treaties, statutes and legal obligations that bind states in their behaviour. See especially Maskus and Reichman, The Globalization of Private Knowledge Goods and the Privatization of Global Public Goods, pp. 3–45.

[3] In 1985, Korea was declared a "Special Watch" country under with that nation also being subject to direct lobbying by American interests over what they saw as a deliberate policy across Korean schools and universities of copyright infringement of academic books throughout the country. See also Drahos with Braithwaite, pp. 19–20. This may be seen as a little ironic given America's refusal to respect European book copyright during the 19th Century.

international trading system. In the process of opening their economies, however, developing nations like China and India will often face the problem that the extent of their domestic legal deficiencies in respect to IP protection become far greater concerns of both state and industry actors in other countries, as legitimate and pirate goods come into conflict within the trading system in ways could not occur under a closed market.

This can prompt IP owners located in these foreign industrialised countries—and supported by their political lobby groups—to make demands for action by their own state actors as they seek to defend what are seen as legitimate commercial interests, by preventing both the export and circulation of pirate products. This trajectory can help to explain tensions in the relationships between many of the Asian countries and the United States, whose own knowledge industries have significant political influence within the government administration, given the sector's importance in the US economy (Business Software Alliance, 2005).[4] The IP industries as a whole are estimated to contribute approximately 5% of US GDP (Comey, 2005), whilst the Business Software Alliance has estimated that the US generated revenues from software production alone of over US$98 billion in 2004,[5] giving an indication of why the country may be so focused on IP issues.

However, some scholars have pointed out that, as a contributor to a country's domestic action in the realignment of its legal system, such coercive tactics may not be all that useful (Sell, 2004). There is a distinct difference between simply effecting a change of law through the promulgation of statutes in a third country and fully establishing a new climate of behaviour within a state's borders. Indeed, the perspective that generating change through coercive means alone rarely engenders the required level of transformation would seem to be borne out by empirical evidence: in Korea throughout the 1980's and early 1990's piracy remained a problem despite the country having promulgated protective measures under a Copyright Act in 1987 (Drahos with Braithwaite, 2002). In China, throughout the 1990's, no discernable change in attitude could be detected in either piracy levels or in government enforcement attitudes even after the threat of

[4] See also report on Science and Engineering Indicators about the significance of US high technology and IP centred sectors accessed 28th February 2007 at http://www.nsf.gov/statistics/seind06/c6/c6h.htm.

[5] See joint study between BSA and IDC.

significant trade sanctions by US authorities and the signing of two Memorandums of Understanding on specifically IP related measures.

In parallel to bilateral pressures for change, Asian nations have also been subject to influence within a multilateral framework of organisations and processes. The international commitments contracted through treaties such as TRIPS have established amongst states a new set of norms in relation to many IP regulations and have provided for agreed legal minimums in respect to many aspects of substantive measures in a country's IP regime. However, the existence of international norms do not by themselves capture the way in which IP rules become embedded within the agenda priorities of national leaders, the corporate priorities of a country's knowledge sector industries and across a nation's wider community.

The structure of inter-firm relationships and the prevailing cultural conditions that can be in place during early periods of high-technology growth may have a role to play in understanding why bilateral pressure and systemic development may not have been as effective as might have been expected during the initial periods of technological evolution. The industrial structure of technology enterprises can make IP principles more or less attractive as a means to protect endeavours and gain reward at a particular point in time and, in this context, some parts of East Asia have some distinct characteristics.

It is important to acknowledge historic differences in the way that societies have chosen to regulate their industrial and technological development and a recognition that not every nation begins with a US model to regulatory protection and inter-firm independence.[6] It is equally useful to remember that not all developing countries are the same and that indeed, a spectrum of competence and regime sophistication has clearly been emerging in recent times that creates far more of a mosaic in terms of technological upgrading and innovation capacity development, within collections of developing countries, and not just between developed and less developed categorisations.[7] It is not

[6] The Anglo-Saxon emphasis on exclusive rights, a strong defence of ownership issues and the paramount position of privacy in business transactions is not the starting position that has necessarily been adopted worldwide.

[7] For further discussion on the needs to create a more sophisticated approach to country classification, see Shamnad Basheer and Annalisa Primi, 'The WIPO Development Agenda: Factoring in the "Technologically Proficient" Developing Countries' In *Implementing WIPO's Development Agenda*, Jeremy DeBeer, ed., Wilfred Laurier University Press, 2009. Available at SSRN: <http://ssrn.com/abstract=1289288>.

clear whether current institutions such as WIPO or WTO, nor even major economic actors such as the United States and the European Union, even fully appreciate the nature and range of heterogeneity that now exists. Misunderstandings of this nature can exacerbate tensions at an international level, and the significant changes in regime evolution underway in parts of Asia right now present evidence that should spur decision-makers to embrace the need for finer granularity in country classifications.

East Asia in particular has long-standing traditions of adopting what scholars have termed "group firm"[8] cultures in economic system building, whereby strong vertical linkages exist between commissioning and supplying organisations, exhibited in their most pronounced form by *chaebols* in the Republic of Korea and the *kieretsu* (Dedrick and Kraemar, 1998)[9] in Japan, whereby smaller enterprises are effectively locked into ongoing unitary relationships with more powerful partners. In China, networks of government and university contacts often combine with strong familial ties inside many companies: this arrangement especially characterised early private sector developments in high technology after the reforms that helped dismantle Maoist control took hold in knowledge industries during the 1980's, such as with Legend and Huawei.

Inter-firm connections of this kind can help to preserve secrets and restrict knowledge leakage outside of the protected relationship and also control the escalation of transaction costs of doing business with knowledge goods that might otherwise be subject to piracy and counterfeit.[10] During early periods of technologically driven economic growth, it can therefore be argued that the traditions of IP regulation

---

[8] Ibid., page 202.

[9] Note that some specialists maintain that small and medium sized Korean supplier within *chaebols* were even more tightly integrated that those of their Japanese neighbour.

[10] Piracy is generally accepted as being the illegal copying of goods subject to copyright controls or in violation of patent licenses whilst counterfeit is seen as the illegal production of goods subject to trademark protection. Software and other high technology knowledge goods are predominantly the subject of piracy, wherein the copies, whilst still being illegal, are actually that of legitimately produced originals by the manufacturer, which in this case renders the term "copy" somewhat differently to that of the counterfeit case. However, some regions of Asia, especially in China, have suffered from counterfeit production of popular software in local language, such as word processors and spreadsheet managers, with versions being "passed off" as original manufactured conversions.

may not have been as central to development strategies where this type of firm structure prevails. However, domestic industry's perspectives on IP and the structure of different sectors can change over time as greater international engagement takes place in the context of export strategies combined with higher value domestic innovation.

There certainly appear to have been transformations of the IP regimes across the Asian region in recent years. These changes have been both substantial and substantive, therefore mandating a review of both their actual extent and an analysis of how and why such change may have taken place.

4.2 *Characterising Asian Regime Transformation*

Japan and Korea are now widely acknowledged as major centres of innovation in their own right exhibiting IP regulatory norms that match, in substance, those in western societies. In fact, Japan introduced its own first proper patent law in 1885 under a "Patent Monopoly Act" (Japanese Patent Office)[11] after opening its local economy to European and American trade and its promulgation was seen as part of an international influence spreading across Japanese practices.

Since 2003, Japan's Patent Office (JPO) has co-operated closely with both its American and its European counterparts (respectively, the United States Patent and Trademark Office or USPTO and the European Patent Office of the European Patent Convention or EPO) as part of what is termed the "Trilateral Scheme". Co-operation between these offices takes place at multilateral organisations such as WIPO as well as through bilateral integration of patent filing and examination regimes through the "Patent Prosecution Highway" program (Dudas, 2006:1).

A further trilateral policy, led by Japan, connects the Korean Patent Office (KPO), the Chinese State Intellectual Property Office (SIPO) and the Japanese patent offices with the objective of furthering intra-Asian co-operation. This initiative has recently made progress on exchanging information about "common issues in the three offices [and] global

[11] Note that Japan attempted to create provisional measures for patent controls as early as 1871 but quickly suspended the law's operation as there was insufficient understanding of IP concepts in the population at that time.

issues in the field of intellectual property".[12] The KPO has also been working more closely with that of its Asian neighbours in similar ways to Japan and acted as host nation to the "Trilateral Policy Dialogue" meeting between JPO, SIPO and KPO in December 2005, whilst also operating as a centre for education about IP principles and procedures for potential applications (Korean Patent Office).

In terms of IP activity at an enterprise level, the changes over past events are equally noteworthy as applicants seeking IP protection have increasingly looked to legal registration and assertion of their rights. According to official statistics, Japan and Korea respectively have the top and the third most active patent offices in the world. Filing activity is also increasingly being carried out by domestic resident applicants in these countries showing both an incremental pace of local innovation and an increasing regard for the instruments of IP policy protection. Resident applicants from Korea in particular showed growth rates of 76% between 1995 and 2004 (World Intellectual Property Organisation, 2006a).

Corporate strategies amongst Japanese and Korean high technology enterprises have increasingly included active patent portfolio building in the jurisdictions of their principle partner economies, including the United States and China. Japan was the country of origin of the largest number of "non-resident" patent filings across the world in 2004, with Japanese companies filing almost twice the number of patents in China as compared to their American competitors in that same year, which some commentators have seen as a potential future danger for American enterprises in not taking seriously enough the rise in credibility of the Chinese protection system and its future importance in the IP portfolios of US corporations (Kasper, 2006).

Nor are these two Asian nations averse to using their rights to assert patent violations and seek redress in foreign courts. Some legal experts have noted in particular an increasingly litigious culture emerging from Japanese and Korean boardrooms, in contrast to a more conciliatory approach that had traditionally characterised Asian dispute handling philosophies (ibid.). This has included interconnected suits over similar patented technology (Tsigarides, 2005; Taplin, 2005), such as plasma

---

[12] See Japanese Patent Office web page, 'Intellectual Property Cooperation in the Asia Pacific Region', <http://www.jpo.go.jp/rireki_e/index.htm>, especially 'Cooperation Activities Provided by Country', accessed 1st February 2007.

display panels in flatscreen televisions, whereby Korean Samsung pursued Japanese Matsushita just subsequent to Matsushita launching suit against Korean firm LG. This patent and litigation dynamism is indicative of successful companies in both countries seeking to protect their hard-earned reputations as international innovators whilst operating within an increasingly integrated, highly globalised and competitive marketplace (Managing Intellectual Property Online Edition, 2004).

A similar trajectory has taken place in India which has had a history of conflict with American and European jurisdictions over its implementation of IP regulations, but which now has domestic knowledge sectors that are both innovative and respected and which are operating under internationally set IP norms. The country first appeared as a target under the US Special 301 trading rules in 1991,[13] just as the Indian government reforms under then finance minister Manmohan Singh were opening the economy and relaxing import substitution restrictions in a number of industrial sectors.

India's pharmaceutical industry had rapidly expanded their domestic operations and had begun to engage in exports of popular generic manufactured drugs of foreign branded equivalents, to consumer markets in the rest of Asia and other regions across the world where these brands had not been patented locally, or where compulsory licensing provisions prevailed. Although perfectly legal under India's 1970 Patent law in force at that time, the move to export these generics was bringing them into direct conflict, in an IP context, with international patent owners.[14] Throughout the decade after 1991, India was frequently characterised by American lobby groups, whether fairly or unfairly, as failing to provide for adequate protection of pharmaceutical product patents and for its slow implementation of its multilateral commitments under TRIPS.[15]

---

[13] India spent two years in the category of Priority Country in 1991 and 1992 and was then designated a Priority Watch target from 1993.

[14] Prior to 2005, when the new legal system for product patents came into force in India, there was considerable argument about where or not these medicament exports from India were in fact in violation of international patent principles, as exports *were* permissible under existing TRIPS flexibilities within "Medical Emergency" provisions. The key issue was that there was dispute between patent owners and Indian firms as to whether these exports were actually responses to genuine medical crises in destination countries.

[15] However, it can be argued that India was in fact just keeping strictly to the undertakings of its obligations as a developing country implementing TRIPS, in that countries such as India were given transition periods of up to 10 years under the TRIPS Agreement to implement full conformity with IP requirements.

Over time, however, tensions also began to develop within the Indian pharmaceutical industry between those companies that wanted to embrace innovation and exploit export-led growth and those who sought to continue with protected production of generic products, even in the face of impending legal system reforms that were required to recognise product patents in order to comply with TRIPS norms. Since 2005, when these new laws came into force within India's domestic jurisdiction, the country has seen an expansion in activity by domestic innovating drug manufacturing companies who are actively using their newly acquired legal rights to pursue product patent protection for their own pharmaceutical inventions (Sampath, 2006).

The Indian software and services industry, by contrast, has always been export-oriented, which may have helped to engender a different attitude towards IP principles amongst business leaders in this sector.[16] The country is now widely recognised as a leader in offshore software services and has begun to focus on domestic software product development and opportunities in its local markets, all of which have put the maintenance and support of effective IP protection in the forefront of the industry's strategic thinking.[17]

In an illustration of this move by India's IT enterprises, the country now has high value relationships with many leading British and American corporations which are outsourcing even their own high technology research and development functions to Indian services. Moreover, some of the very largest Indian technology service firms such as Wipro and Tata Consulting Services (TCS) are expanding their own presence beyond local shores, and becoming more globalised by exploiting their own cost advantages and creating new service innovations in business process and technology development outsourcing that mix overseas off-shoring[18] with localised near-shoring[19] and in-shoring (Trefler, 2005).[20]

---

[16] The software sector was also granted exemption from many of the domestic controls that burdened other industries in India.

[17] The development of India's pharmaceutical and software industries is covered in more detail in later chapters.

[18] Off-shoring in this context means the relocation of business operations without an appreciable loss of quality or reliability to a lower cost location which is typically located overseas and increasingly in Asia.

[19] Near-shoring is related in terms of benefits and motivators to off-shoring but the locations chosen are typically geographically closer to the customer's original base. They may even be in the same country.

[20] In-shoring is effectively the reverse of an offshore model: in this case it is the exporting of service skills in which the local domain continues to have a comparative advantage which can be in terms of quality, quality or value for money. In this way,

In particular, these approaches use a transnational delivery model to tackle different tasks of a solution in different places, with each location chosen for its appropriateness to secure the right outcome at the right price (Marsh, 2006). In this way, technology solutions that involve a mix of software development, hardware manufacturing and high skilled customer-facing consultancy can be provided using resources from distinct locations such as India, China and the United States, but all within the umbrella of a single point of contact and at a highly competitive cost base. Such innovative approaches in high technology solution building and service delivery can only function when there is consistency and reliability in knowledge protection laws across different regions, and helps to show how much international progress in this area may have positively influenced Asian business development, especially in emerging economies such as India and China.

The territory of Taiwan has exhibited a pathway to better IP protection that has been "filled with zigzags" as both political and business elites have sought to embrace the principles of IP protection as a stimulus to its own innovative industries (Sun, 1998:6–7). Interestingly, unlike other parts of the region, Taiwan's business culture has resisted the trends towards group firm dynamics exhibited elsewhere and has instead forged technology driven growth using smaller and more nimble organisations along with a focus on specialist hardware engineering, especially in laptops, rather than in software or services (Dedrick and Kraemer, 1998). One of the territory's best known companies, Acer, is a manufacturing giant having posted over US$11 billion of revenues for 2006.[21]

Throughout the previous two decades, Taiwan had been regularly criticised by US trade officials and has had ongoing appearances in Special 301 Priority Watch List reports, until a government action plan launched reforms of both legislation and attitudes in 2003 (Dernbach, 2005). Since that time, major progress has been reported with the US formally removing Taiwan from its violation listing in 2005 and acknowledging the progress made. Copyright Act revisions have been

---

the United States may continue to have a comparative advantage in high skills and software product innovation which would enable it to service the rest of the world accordingly.

[21] See Acer Global Website at http://global.acer.com/ last referenced 10th February 2007.

influenced by some of the American legal norms of its own DMCA but the territory's government has also made effort to change wider attitudes in both educational institutions and the general community by pointing out the cost consequences to local industrial success of IP infringements.

Taiwan's progress has some special characteristics as its territorial status precludes its participation in forums designed for nation-states, such as WIPO and its various IP conventions, but it has been able to join the WTO along with mainland China and Hong Kong as a separate Customs Territory. This distinctiveness and its relationship to the US in terms of both defence and trade links may give bilateralism a greater visibility in explaining regime evolution, but internal factors of "self awareness, self image and self interests" cannot be ignored in its domestic regulatory evolution, and it can be argued that Taiwan now has some of the strongest IP regime characteristics in Asia (Sun, 1998:6).

Within the technology industry in mainland China, attitude changes can also be detected that are mirroring legal system improvement. Recent years have been characterised by an upsurge in domestic patent applications and an increasing propensity of domestic companies to pursue and settle IP-related disputes within the official state mechanisms of administrative and civil court proceedings rather than always relying on traditional networks and informal conciliation.

This greater understanding within China's business and political classes of the importance of IP as an instrument with which to build a successful knowledge-based economy may well have been influenced by two interlocking factors. First, there has emerged in China a national leadership that sees technology driven innovation as a means to maintain required levels of growth to ensure both social cohesion and economic development. Second, this growth has presented opportunities for wealth generation that have attracted overseas resident Chinese to return after education and business experience abroad. They have brought with them not only an enthusiasm for entrepreneurial business building but also western-influenced attitudes and perspectives on how effective IP regulations can form an important element in the success of a true knowledge economy.

These members of the country's returning diaspora are supported by a growing community of leading domestic actors such as university academics and members of the judiciary which lend their weight to the argument that a strengthening IP regime is now in the national interest.[22] These developments can be seen as being part of what many have characterised as a fundamental commitment by China to adopt a "responsible attitude" in respect to its engagement with international trade and to building an effective domestic IP regime (People's Daily Online, 2005a). Whilst problems still remain in many parts of the mainland, and especially in terms of provincial level corruption in regard to inconsistencies of IP enforcement, it would be incomplete not to highlight that progress made in recent years has been driven as much by internal as external agents and has been seen to provide tangible benefits for local enterprises as much as for foreign multinationals.

It can be argued that this IP-focused activism now being exhibited in these countries is operating on linked dimensions: that of state institutional reform at one level and firm-level legal engagement at the other. It is also operating to different extents in different countries, often reflecting different priorities in technological development.

Trends such as these in IP regime evolution cannot be explained solely as a function of external motivators, such as bilateral actions by economically powerful hegemonic states or the conditioning of domestic policy by multilateral norm-setting institutions. Power dynamics alone do not appear to be a sufficiently compelling explanation for these transformations and, instead, it may be better to see IP regulatory absorption as a multi-faceted dynamic, whereby domestic conditions operate alongside, and have as important an influence as external ones.

4.3 *State and Non-State Interaction in Domestic Regime Evolution*

Change to an IP regime within a state can take place in two main ways: it can be imposed or induced. Imposition may originate from both internal and external sources. Internally, government actors will recognise the necessity for promoting greater IP controls to strengthen the innovative capacity of the country to attract foreign direct investment (FDI) and to promote skills acquisition during the nation's technological evolution. Externally, state actors respond to the changing landscape

[22] The contribution of academic and judicial actors to China IP regime evolution will be explored in greater depth in a subsequent chapter.

of regulatory norms and the power dynamics that link national policy objectives, bilateral relationships and multilateral engagement.

Changes can also be induced. Economic incentives can accrue as knowledge sector corporations seek to widen their productive activities beyond the safe havens of localised domestic relationships, both into new areas of the national territory and into overseas markets. These commercial enterprises may increasingly recognise that a strengthened IP regime can be a key means of achieving these objectives.

Regime evolution can thus be seen as a confluence of different dependencies in the relationship between state and non-state participants: the capacity and willingness of national institutions to make regulatory changes; the effectiveness of communication channels between different types of actors that can transmit the need for change; and the extent to which local technology enterprises have begun to recognise that strengthened IP rules would be in their interests.

The dynamism that a state exhibits in facilitating IP regime evolution and technological development can be influenced by a number of domestic factors. First, the personalities and strength of national leaders must be considered. In an historical context, individual leaders have played pivotal roles at different points in national technological development.

In China, Deng Xiaoping focused his single minded belief in dismantling the constraints of Maoist society into creating a more devolved system of government than had previously experienced. These moves made it easier for lower level politicians to experiment with reforms that promoted wealth creation and technology driven growth in different parts of the country, especially in provinces of the East and South, such as Zhejiang and Guangdong, where IT clusters and export promotion zones created a platform for both foreign engagement and domestic growth.

In India, Rajiv Ghandi assumed power in 1984, after having spent a number of years working as a commercial airline pilot, which may have given him a more global outlook into both the importance of, and potential for, high technology products and processes. He specifically prioritised supportive policies as a stimulus for India's economic growth that many believe laid the foundations for the emergence and success of the country's then nascent computer and software development industry.

Second, the policy objectives of a country's political elite must be taken into account. It can be argued that linkages evolve which connect leadership attitudes towards IP regime adoption with other policy areas.

This is particularly important in helping to explain how governments resolve domestic difficulties that can arise as the IP regime changes in strength and character. Regime strengthening often introduces tensions between innovators within a society and those elements of domestic industry that have profited to date by concentrating on the creation of counterfeit and pirated products under loose attitudes to IP protection. This can result in difficult domestic decisions by government institutions and may even, for a time, bring local and national state entities into conflict with each other as regime changes take place.

Elites within the state may try to address these conflicts by looking at a broader picture in respect of the national interest that is often only available to those at the top of the political hierarchy, drawing linkages between potentially unrelated areas of policy.

In an Indian context, for example, recent research has uncovered important shifts of interests within the elites of domestic constituencies that contributed as much to the country's changes in its patent policy as did external trade pressure and treaty commitments. The long-standing Indian support for "the common heritage framework" in opposition to patenting of genetic resources and pharmaceutical products appears to have begun to be replaced by a "private property view" that, to some extent at least, may have support from within the domestic leadership (Ramanna, 2005:151). This has manifested itself in altered political attitudes to state sovereignty concepts in the exploitation of natural resources and traditional knowledge under bio-diversity rules, as well in changed commercial priorities as innovating drug manufacturers recognised advantage in exploiting a new patent regime.

However, other scholars have also pointed out that "the ideology of common interests of developing countries is still important to India" and that within global governance forums India continues to project a leadership role (Humphrey and Messner DFID China Office, 2006:8). These disagreement within the Indian elite have yet to be resolved as the country's new patent policy was only introduced in 2005, but it can be argued that the growing significance of innovating service firms within its thriving IT sector, and the rise in the use of patent portfolios by drug companies may well strengthen the power of those who support this "private property" shift in national thinking.[23]

[23] Evolution of India's IP regime and associated interconnections within the country's pharmaceutical and software industries are examined in more detail in later chapters.

Nor should the role of pressure groups and NGOs be omitted from the panoply of influence in India as these important civil society actors operate through both public and private channels to reach elite decision-makers and project their perspectives and can exert considerable influence in shaping policy responses. Linked to pressure group activism in an international context are tensions over the future development of IP as a whole, voiced by many developing countries in forums such as the Doha Development round of talks at the WTO, and exercised through blogs and discussion forums across internet communities.[24]

In a vibrant democracy such as India, a mosaic of viewpoints from separate constituencies must be coalesced into coherent policy responses, and ongoing tensions can persist between domestic and systemic levers of change in issue-sensitive areas such as intellectual property law.

In China, disparate influences are more contained. Policy objectives need to be understood from interlocking perspectives that occupy the national leadership: foremost is the requirement to maintain political control and ensure social stability by encouraging high levels of domestic growth and by attempting to better balance the fruits of that growth across different parts of the country. Within this domestic focused dimension, therefore, IP regulations and the support that they provide for emerging innovative firms can be seen as just one part of a market stimulating process that better meets future needs for sustained and prolonged growth than would a continuing policy of tolerance towards the pirate economy.

During policy execution in China, national and provincial politics have at times clashed, as not all parts of the country have yet achieved the same levels of technological progress and some areas have become reliant on counterfeit production as drivers for the local economy. This can perhaps be traced back to the fact that China developed productive capacity in low technology manufacturing as a response to the needs of western enterprises seeking low cost suppliers. The capability to produce industrial-scale volumes of goods thus predated the development of locally produced innovations in many areas, which may explain why some provinces have a greater tendency to sustain pirate production than others.

---

[24] For an example of one such issue-specific blog, see <http://spicyipindia.blogspot.com>.

Even within those locations that do have significant innovative capacity (such as Zhejiang and Guangzhou), individual factories that have legitimate production schedules have been known to create additional output from product lines that are fed into local pirate transmission and distribution networks for the benefit of both factory managers and local politicians.[25] This "skimming" is far more difficult to determine, investigate and prevent, both for western business owners and Beijing-based Party cadres. The determination of the extent of the problem coupled with the need to ensure continuing stability and employment in these regions will thus be reflected in the way national response is formulated: attitude to IP infringement will thus be balanced by other factors.

Another dimension in China's policy priorities is the international perspective that reflects on how China is perceived by others and on how its leaders wish the country to be perceived. A number of observers now maintain that as China pursues its own self-interested agenda at the global level its political leaders will be met with "increasing pressures to exercise leadership responsibly" (Humphrey and Messner, 2006:8).[26]

Third, IP regime evolution can be influenced by the political regime in place within a country and its traditions of institutional leadership are important. These help to frame the character of state involvement and its ability to act in respect to national advantage. Similarities of the interventionist approach exist across East and South Asia in relation to the way that state levers are exercised to promote industrial progress, technological change and legal regime evolution. These characteristics seem to operate regardless of the type of political system in place within a particular nation's territory: the democratic government institutions of India actively promotes the expansion of its software sector with the same legislative rigour and industrial policy mix with which the national and local levels of the autocratic Chinese Communist Party are now seeking to nurture the growth of their own IT industries and to encourage domestic technological innovation.

---

[25] Author's conversation with a former Senior Consultant for a Beijing based legal firm at the Cambridge Technology Expo, November 2006.

[26] This behaviour will be particularly important as China's interests may increasingly intersect more with developed nations and less with developing nation agendas.

Fourth, the level of development and sophistication of a country's local knowledge sector industry will contribute critical determinants to the IP system. It will underpin both the nature and extent of the state's exclusivity in rule-setting as well as shaping the regulatory strength deemed most appropriate for the domestic IP landscape.

In the early stages of the evolution of a country's knowledge sector, state involvement is often characterised by greater pro-activity, with many national initiatives likely to originate directly from within relevant government departments, either from officials themselves or from those opinion formers who help shape government thinking, such as nationally renowned or politically trusted academics. Tax regulations, export subsidies and educational investment programmes all play a part in nurturing the nation's stock of knowledge and its propensity to expand its high technology sectors.

At this point of early stage growth, the state's attitude to IP regime strength is often at variance with international norms and it is typical for actors to support a regime that is weaker than those of more developed economies in order to diffuse new ideas as quickly as possible and to exploit as efficiently as possible any knowledge that can be gleaned from foreign sources. Indeed, a number of scholars have pointed to the advantages for developing countries of having such a lackadaisical attitude to IP enforcement by their state institutions during early stage knowledge industry growth, promoting the pirating of required know-how without the expense of procuring foreign licenses (Heeks, 1998; Bender, 2006).

These characteristics would seem to be clear from the empirical evidence of early knowledge sector development in countries such as Japan, Korea, China and India. Some national strategies have combined a mix of import substitution protection and public sector procurement preferences operating under an umbrella of weak IP regime characteristics, whilst others, such as the Indian software sector, have developed different types of policy stimulus, export incentives and skills promotion policies, all of which are very different to the old Anglo-Saxon liberal traditions of a "night watchman" role for national institutions (Hammarlund, 2005:50–55).

However, once a level of locally retained capability in knowledge sector product building has been achieved, a "cross-over point" can be reached as domestic growth combine with the attractions of export engagement (Bender, 2006:244). It may now be in the interests of local innovators to re-evaluate and strengthen the IP protection and enforcement rules. It is also at this transition point that domestic tensions may be most visible as industry groups with different interests may seek to either promote or constrain regime evolution.[27]

In tandem with domestic actors taking more of a lead in seeking to advance IP regime development themselves, the increasing interconnection between state institutions and commercial entities can engender a shift in emphasis as government responds to industry messages to strengthen the national regime. Two-way communication can develop between state actors and leading enterprises in order to determine the way that further progress should be made as enterprises seek to move up the value chain of IP product development. These consultations can take place either directly with major firms or through emerging industry lobby groups that typically arise to drive through new policy requirements. The norms of the global IP regime may also develop greater visibility at this point as they can act as templates for national regulatory evolution and as benchmarks by which to evaluate the transaction costs of engagement with other countries that may not yet conform to agreed standards.

Government action can also become increasingly concentrated on the promotion of knowledge sector industries and related policies required to achieve growth as the balance changes between the interests of the innovation sector and those of the pirate sectors within an economy. The strengthening of the country's IP regime as a policy priority is thus pursued in the national interest rather than as a defensive response to external events. China, for example, has been characterised by its own officials as "undergoing strategic economic restructuring" that is "promoting IT for national economic and social development" and that moves to strengthen its IP regime and put in place senior political advocates of rigorous enforcement norms should be seen in that light (Shi, 2001:59).

It can be argued that developments of this kind form part of moves towards a national innovation *system* (NIS) in both China and India, with state and non-state actors operating in concert to enhance quantitative inputs and qualitative outputs from the R&D process as a whole. In this way, investment in physical resource stock in terms of

[27] An example of this conflict may be seen in recent developments within India's pharmaceutical industry, where different lobby groups, representing innovators and generic producers, respectively put their competing positions on the country's IP regime evolution to state decision-makers.

science parks and funding for educational institutions feeds into the nurturing role that government can take, boosting human resources with the appropriate skills and clustered working environment to make progress at the frontiers of innovation research and increasing the visibility of both nations in terms of outputs such as research papers, patent applications and new product. In this way, both China and India can be seen to be in the early stages of moving up the value chain as they introduce strategic policy initiatives familiar to a number of leading OECD economies such as tax credits for R&D investment, incubator support programmes and the promotion of increasing links between universities and young innovating companies (Irwin Crookes, 2009).

As part of this strategy, growth often begets a more sophisticated approach to technology partnering and solution building. Corporations will begin to establish networks of communication with complementary commercial entities in other countries, independent of formal agreements and often facilitated by the ease with which voice, video and email messages may be exchanged across the world. Personal networks can be maintained through these technologies having been established in one or more of the business conferences that take place around the world such as the Software Leadership Forums in India and the Computer Technology Expos in Beijing and San Francisco. These interconnections can typically operate at both a personal and an enterprise level rather than through any explicit state intervention. All of these actions will create more complex relationships and incentives for IP regime evolution and stronger regulatory adoption than those that can be explained by a domestic agenda alone.

There are a number of examples of these kinds of dialogue. In particular, the sophisticated three-way relationship that now exists between the Indian software sector, its lobby groups and the national Indian government is complemented by the way that discussion also takes place between India's technology industry organisations and overseas equivalents. All of this can be usefully contrasted to the more simplistic, hierarchical pathways that currently shape interaction between the Chinese software sector and its respective state institutions. In this case, it may be less important that one country is democratic and the other is not but that, instead, the Chinese software sector has not yet evolved to the point where it has sufficient strength and cohesion to attempt the extent of engagement of its Indian counterparts.

However, it remains to be seen whether the interplay in China may ultimately be constrained by characteristics in national culture such as the distinctive leadership role of domestic state actors in China's top-down decision-making structure (Yuan, 2006). This may, in fact, continue, even despite the ongoing growth and sophistication of its high technology IT sectors. In this sense, therefore, China's domestic corporations may never mimic the more pluralist conditions that characterise the engagement of India's IT community with their own country's government.

These trends that promote change can best be seen as part of a continuum of development in evolving the sophistication of national knowledge industries and the IP regime that can best support them. During this process, adjustments can take place that alter national power dynamics such that industry corporations and lobby groups may begin to interact in partnership with state institutions to achieve specific objectives, in terms of both IP regime evolution and specific sector growth targets.

Such a transition illustrates some important points. First, engagement with the international trading system by knowledge sector enterprises in both advanced and emerging economies can promote a wider interest in the IP regulatory matrix, both in terms of domestic and overseas regulations. This interest becomes particularly visible as state level decision-makers in developing countries abandon import substitution strategies and embrace an export-oriented dynamic that coincides with knowledge industry promotion and development. It is important to note that this development also marks the point when the domestic knowledge protection regulations that pertain to a developing economy become of particular concern to IP owners in other countries, as these overseas enterprises seek out opportunities for their own market entry and potentially encounter goods that violate their own IP.

Second, a key element in the functional dimension of IP regime evolution is that the state does not act alone in setting agendas for change. There would appear to be strong evidence of the emergence of an increasingly important dialogue amongst individual enterprises often through peer-organised conferences or through industry groups, which can promote shared understanding and can facilitate converging actor interests on acceptable regulatory principles.

4.4 *IP Protection and Technology Market Engagement*

Firms in technology industries in different countries across the world and especially software-based product development and service enterprises display particular resonance with these behaviour characteristics. IP regulatory protection has special significance for the software industry as its outputs are products that encapsulate the challenges of regulating knowledge-based goods. They are relatively easy to copy once having been first produced but they involve a heavy investment in their development in terms of both the financial expenditure of employing a highly skilled labour force and the time it takes to bring functionally rich and suitably tested software solutions to market. This industry thus provides a useful litmus test for the way in which stronger IP regulations promote sector growth and act as a platform for a two-way engagement in both attracting foreign direct investment and in promoting international trade.

During the process of IP regime building, an intersection of interests takes place between three parties: commercial interests in developed economies; leadership elites in emerging economies; and domestic producers in these developing states that are active in knowledge sectors.

Major companies in the knowledge-based industries of developed economies want to be able to expand their sales overseas into nations with large potential home markets, such as India and China. However, they have strong preferences to conduct transactions of this kind in ways that will still safeguard their own stock of intellectual property. Meanwhile, leadership elites in emerging economies want to attract foreign direct investment that can increase productive capacity in local technology industries and promote learning spillovers to improve local skill sophistication and product building abilities. Coupled to the interests of their political leaders, enterprises within the emerging knowledge sector in these developing economies want to interact with first world firms to secure agreements for joint product development and also negotiate potentially two-way distribution contracts that can facilitate entry of their own innovations into the overseas markets of developed economies. All of these motivators can inevitably create the momentum for strengthening local IP regulatory and enforcement principles in the developing country concerned.

However, a problem exists for developing country policymakers: regulatory evolution in respect to local IP regime strength must balance the interests of local firms at different points in their growth lifecycle with the benefits of attracting high value overseas investment and skills exchange from foreign partnerships. Too strong a regime introduced too soon could stifle nascent local industries and enable foreign knowledge owners to dominate local markets to the exclusion of domestic development, whereas too lax a regime in place may inhibit international engagement to the detriment of the local industry's learning opportunities whilst also undermining the successful expansion of domestic producers by failing to curb IP violations and reducing the incentive to innovate. This can help to explain how regimes can alter over time and how countries such as China and India have modified the thrust of their regime commitments to reflect changing domestic circumstances and new economic incentives.

Added to this interpretation are other important factors that are particularly relevant to the Asian experience. Firm development and knowledge acquisition is a two-way process in successful trading relationships and that, in East Asia in particular, cultural concepts of trust and mutual cooperation are just as important in achieving successful outcomes as contract law and market dominance. It can be argued that trading relationships are no longer based upon engagement just with western nations, although this is still an important consideration. Instead, there now appears to be an increasing degree of intra-Asian regional integration (Kwan and Cheung, 2006; Wachter, 2007).[28]

In the software industry, in common with other IP-rich knowledge goods, the transformation of sales from a captive local community to wider national and global perspective can take place in a number of different ways, each of which can be usefully grouped into three main variants. Each one of these has different degrees of dependency on the structure and effectiveness of the IP regime in place within the respective target market, with each providing different transaction costs and

[28] For example, China has now become a highly favoured off-shoring location for technology and software service businesses in Japan and Korea, in a similar way that India is seen as currently being the destination of choice for United States enterprises. Recent estimates have Japanese and Korean markets representing "nearly 60%" of China's US$1.4 billion offshore software business. These perspectives would seem to confirm the author's own experience and dialogue with Chinese offshore specialists in meetings and interviews. See the chapter on China for further details.

benefit externalities for the exporting and importing organisation concerned (Lippoldt, 2006).

First, the captured subsidiary model. Transnational corporations can establish wholly-owned subsidiary enterprises within the local economy that operate as predominantly sales and marketing centres. These offices act as a base for penetrating the domestic market by distributing directly to consumers those goods or services that encapsulate the IP owned by the parent company. Typically, local subsidiaries will sell finished goods imported from the company's home market and will often be staffed with a mix of local and third-country employees. This route involves the least risk of IP theft for the product owner as local control remains tied to the parent corporation, but it also incurs the most effort and highest initial costs and is therefore often only available to substantial-sized organisations (and even then only if local laws permit this).[29]

However, this option presents the least benefit to the host country's economy as knowledge of embedded IP is retained within the parent company, with both products delivered and services transmitted vertically between headquarters and local office, with little or no opportunity for seepage, thus constraining learning spillovers for other domestic firms. The establishment and promotion by state institutions in host countries of technology clusters that mix domestic and foreign firms within a tight-knit locale, with close commercial and human contact between workers, can mitigate this tendency, but only if elements of embedded IP and product development knowledge are to be transferred to the local office in the first place, and such a decision would have to include a risk assessment of the host country's IP regulatory strength. If the local office remains simply a sales and marketing function, domestic learning opportunities are minimised.

The early exploitation of IT markets in both India and China exhibited these tendencies as major overseas corporations had little confidence in local IP policies and it was understood that engagement in even arm's length trade could result in IP violations. But first mover advantage within less developed local markets coupled with the size of the opportunity can make the risks worthwhile especially for large corporations that can perhaps better absorb the potential costs of piracy.[30]

[29] China has only recently permitted wholly foreign owned enterprises to operate in many of its domestic economic sectors, with continuing constraints in some.

[30] This can be characterised as the "capture and lock-in" approach to sales.

This therefore allows technology leaders such as Texas Instruments in India and Microsoft in China to pioneer engagement through local offices and product distribution centres even despite weak regime characteristics.

Second, the licensed distribution model. A company can place products into overseas consumer and commercial markets via local retailers and distribution centres through the use of licenses that permit use of the technology under an IP-controlled contract. Clearly, if local IP laws have not yet developed to the point where licensing arrangements of this kind are legally viable and commercially sensible then there is a strong risk of direct appropriation of any specialised knowledge encapsulated in the product or service if it is of a type that can either be easily copied or where its underlying know-how can be easily determined.

The main concerns of overseas firms in this kind of relationship are trademark infringements that can harm customer confidence and corporate reputation. To some extent, risks can be mitigated by ensuring that supplies arrive for sale as finished goods, wherein the critical elements of value-added know-how necessary for their design and any related internal product secrets thus vested, are retained within the originating company's home nation and protected under a stronger IP regime. This strategy can be used by both large and small organisations but is most suitable to the types of goods which are difficult to pirate or counterfeit. A particularly successful user of this approach is the Coca-Cola Company which depends totally on trade secrecy laws and trademark assertion rather than patent control of its flavourings.[31]

Knowledge spillovers for local firms will vary under this model based on the precise commercial arrangements put in place by each agreement but they will likely rest mainly with softer mechanisms of knowledge gathering, such as skills learning through employee exchanges between the cooperating companies concerned. This is a process that is often required during the early stages of even a simple agreement in order to bring the local distributor's knowledge of the product up to the level required to support a distinct customer base. It promotes more limited learning potential, largely centred on sales and

[31] The coca-cola secret syrup recipe is one of the most successful trade secrets in modern business and is alleged to be known by only a handful of staff at the company's US headquarters.

marketing skills rather than that possible through the formal exchange of technology and application-specific intellectual property that can happen between enterprises enjoying a closer working relationship.

Third, the joint-venture or partnership model. Foreign firms can establish partnerships for product development or specialised contracts for advanced services delivery under a variety of different legal relationships with local operators. This engagement can range across a spectrum. For example, typical arrangements with Indian knowledge sector firms can include offshore and outsourced services, such as development of software products and high level joint research activities. Many of these are designed to be re-exported back to the commissioning customer's country.

In China, by contrast, in high technology and software sectors in particular, there appears to have been a greater propensity to create closely intertwined joint ventures for domestic market distribution and product branding, whereby the partner acts as a value-added reseller as well as product distributor, often undertaking important localisation work on an international version of a product (such as software screen dialogue translations for non-Roman language markets). There is still, undoubtedly, an important element of computer and electronics hardware manufacturing that are produced just for export, given China's status as the world's leading exporter in this sector. However, it can be argued that the importance of China's large domestic market in decision-making about joint venture engagement by overseas firms is significant given the popularity that ventures of this kind continue to have, even despite the easing of rules over the creation of Wholly Foreign Owned Enterprises (WFOE). It can be further argued that in areas such as lower-level manufacturing, an assembly-for-export model, has retained greatest visibility.

This type of undertaking particularly characterises firm strategies where the local market is significant enough to warrant the effort required to establish trust between partners and where an understanding of cultural sensitivities is essential for success. It is also important to see that the popularity of such joint arrangements may persist even after local legal changes have made the creation of wholly foreign-owned enterprises easier.[32]

[32] Note as an example of this, the failure of eBay to understand and successfully exploit the local Chinese internet marketplace, requiring a recent realignment from a

This third level of engagement engenders the greatest risk to an overseas company's IP because elements of encapsulated knowledge must be transferred to the local partner and there is a risk that unscrupulous piracy will help create competitors much sooner than would be the case under conventional market mediated exchanges and legitimate competitor product development. In order to be attractive for the overseas party, therefore, this type of engagement with local firms is more likely to take place in an environment where IP regime sophistication has evolved to the point that both the legal system and the enforcement regime can provide at least a reasonable chance of protection for commercial entities. Such an assessment will be one of the factors to consider when evaluating the commercial rationale for such a relationship, as will the domestic market potential of the engagement.

The benefits, however, can be significant for all parties. First, the commissioning enterprise gains a local lead into new markets; second, the local partner learns much about the latest technology through creating value-added extensions for markets it knows best; and third, the host country's knowledge industry gains in the longer term as new skills are acquired that help engender local innovating enterprises.

The corollary of this type of relationship is a regime that enables foreign firm partnerships to thrive and increases the trade in and distribution of knowledge goods around the world. It is also one that facilitates the emergence and growth of locally nurtured technology innovators whose interests in securing IP protection begin to coincide with their overseas counterparts. Leading local firms may subsequently develop the objective of undertaking international market penetration themselves using the security of their home base as a platform for export-led growth (Wachter, 2007).

4.5 *Intellectual Property Regulations and Market Engagement*

Of course, intellectual property regulation is not the only determinant of whether foreign knowledge-based enterprises will seek to engage with a developing country's economy and a number of scholars have pointed to other factors that are also influential (Maskus and Reichman, 2005).

---

wholly owned approach to one that involved a joint venture with a Hong Kong based internet portal. *Financial Times* 25th January 2007 Asia Edition.

In this context, it is important to differentiate between foreign direct investment that is market seeking with that which is resource seeking. In China, the size and increasing sophistication in consumption preferences of the local market presents an especially attractive proposition for overseas enterprises and is now likely to be overtaking resource-based incentives in manufacturing as a motivator for FDI engagement with the country. This may also explain why China continues to be attractive as a recipient of FDI even despite the economic slowdown that has afflicted both international and domestic Chinese firms, as growth sectors still exist, such as high technology, and national government stimulus continues to persist in these industries as part of new policy-setting priorities.

In India, by contrast, it can be seen that much of the foreign investment has been oriented towards meeting resource needs of overseas high technology firms based on the country's available pool of English-speaking high technology engineers. However, it may be that during the next few years, in concert with India's domestic market expansion, an increased level of market seeking investment may take place indicating that perhaps, further convergence between the characteristics of these two countries may accelerate.

Dynamics such as these may help to explain the increased visibility of China and India, both as destinations of interest for FDI and as targets for broader commercial engagement, illustrating that perhaps their relative attractiveness may be independent of their respective IP regime strengths.

Further factors that may influence FDI decision-making include the effectiveness of a country's physical and communications infrastructure.[33] These can be seen as conditions where China would currently appear to possess a clear lead over India. However, in respect to elements of education and aspects of workforce skills development, India could be seen to hold more assets through both its English language skills and its broader framework of problem solving abilities, as opposed to the rote-learning training curricula often found in mainland China.

Issues of cultural significance also determine the efficacy of a country's IP regime. Regulatory characteristics need to be assessed within a broader framework of governance and institutional competence, which can include aspects of legal transparency and attitudes to public sector

[33] For broad based discussion of other factors, see <http://spicyipindia.blogspot.com/2007/08/novartis-patent-dispute-of-spins-and.html>.

rent-seeking. India's perceived advantages[34] under its recognised common law legal system stand in contrast to China's sometimes opaque legal instrumentalism and its ongoing, though often provincial level, corruption.[35]

IP regulations do not therefore operate alone but they work within a mix of regulations that draw influence from both external factors and internal motivators that help to shape their character.

4.6 *Conclusion*

This chapter has outlined the different factors that can influence both the pace and legal structure of national IP regime adoption. It has presented a number of examples of Asian legal system development at different historical points in time to show that the legal enhancements and social attitude adjustments that appear to be taking place in China and India are not of themselves unique events but form part of a regime evolutionary process across the region.

These developments would seem to have been influenced by a combination of endogenous factors including domestic policy priorities such as the engagement of export-led growth strategies and the prioritisation of local technology industries, as well as exogenous pressures such as from policy actions by the United States as a hegemonic power and from the norm-setting trends emanating from systemic evolution under the influence of international institutions. Perhaps the most striking feature of regional regime progress in Asia is that it can be closely identified with domestic technological development and growing economic confidence within the region's principal economies. To this extent, external factors alone do not seem to have been able to engender meaningful change to a state's domestic IP regime. Such characteristics are to be found in particular in the positions currently being adopted by the Chinese and Indian political and commercial elite.

---

[34] There are some counter arguments to this perspective that focus on ongoing inefficiencies within the Indian legal system.

[35] This may help to explain the rigour with which China's national politicians have been seeking to curb illegal activities of even very senior provincial officials, recently highlighted by the arrest and detention of Shanghai's mayor.

CHAPTER FIVE

STATE SPONSORED INITIATIVES IN CHINA

This chapter argues that the evolution of the country's intellectual property (IP) regulations is now characterised by a noticeable move towards a more sophisticated regime whose maturity runs in concert with the nation's economic, technological and social development. This progress is part of a wider transition of China's legal system from one that accepted the traditional hierarchical values of "rule of man" to one that exhibits key principles of the "rule of law" that are more typically found in the western legal tradition.[1] A legal system based on the "rule of law" certainly provides access to a more reliable due process, offers a greater level of judicial independence and sustains a normative acceptance of statutory superiority by all agents of the domestic elite.

This evolution captures four main principles (Alford, 1995:1): first, that the long-held premise that "[i]ntellectual property law, and in particular copyright, has never taken hold in China"[2] needs a timely re-evaluation in the context of contemporary Chinese society. Second, that this evolution in attitudes and actions in respect of IP law stems not just from external and international influences but also from internal factors that have emerged in the last decade, including the changing domestic dynamics of growing knowledge industry sectors such as software development, outsourcing and research and the importance of export markets to high technology hardware and electronics sectors. Third, that in China, actors within the national state machine have

[1] The changing nature of China's legal system from one based on *renzhi* (rule of man) to *fazhi* (rule of law) has long interested international scholars. See especially (Peerenboom, 2002). But see also an earlier discourse on legal corporatism within China in contrast to Rule of Law principles in a research article by (Dowdle, 1999).

[2] This book is one of the seminal works on intellectual property law's historical development in China and takes a culturally sympathetic but broadly pessimistic stance on IPR assimilation in the People's Republic. However, the final chapter, entitled 'As Pirates Become Proprietors', lends a hint to a potential change based on increases in future technological *ownership* in contrast to just technological *consumption* and uses Taiwan as a then timely illustrator of this trend.

taken the lead role in promoting and embedding the assimilation of new thinking within the country, in concert with leading academic thinkers, returning diaspora and western educated elites. Fourth that the recent improvements in enforcement of IP laws across all regions of the country, whilst still exhibiting ongoing difficulties and therefore remaining a cause for concern internationally, illustrate a resurgence of central power over the provinces as key political figures in Beijing see IP system development as part of the national policy for further economic growth and international respectability.

5.1 *Examining Historical Contingencies of the Chinese IP Regime*

Analyses of China's contemporary adoption of a modern legal system cannot be made in isolation from the past and must include the events and social premises that have helped to shape present policies and give character to past principles. It is a widely held perception that an understanding of yesterday's China is pivotal in coming to terms with today's China (Alford, 1995)[3] and it can be argued that this is particularly appropriate when addressing the characteristics of intellectual property law. In maintaining that modern China is changing in its attitudes and its behaviour, especially in respect to intellectual property, an explanation needs to be provided as to why the many previous attempts over the last 100 years to create a protective climate for knowledge goods have failed to take hold and why no such indigenous protection existed at all in earlier imperial times.

A number of explanations have been presented by scholars for these conditions that are still important to current debates. First, it has been argued that the instrumentalist[4] and paternalist nature of the traditional Chinese socio-legal system did not sit well with an overtly adjudicative western approach to creating concrete legal texts and formal

[3] Chapter 2 is actually entitled 'Don't Stop Thinking About Yesterday'. This part of the book reinforces how historical attitudes in China over many hundreds of years have shaped contemporary behaviour in regard to IPRs, at least up to the middle 1990's.

[4] This is a specialist term highlighting that Chinese law has been, and some would argue continues to be, used as a direct "instrument" in wider social and political policymaking, largely at the whim of political leaders, as opposed to the impartial nature of western "rule of law" systems. In this sense, an instrumentalist legal system imposes few if any restraints on the senior political actors that represent the ruling elite.

dispute resolution mechanisms. Second, the enlightened notion that emerged in 17th and 18th Century Europe[5] that authors and inventors could hold a private property and defend their interests against those (including the state) who sought to exploit that property "had no counterpart in imperial Chinese history" (Alford, 1995:18).[6] Third, early 20th Century attempts by the new Chinese republican administration to introduce western norms of knowledge protection should perhaps be better seen as a bargaining counter with the western powers, as much designed to seek an end to extraterritoriality in key Concession cities as any genuine embrace of the new philosophies. Finally, it can be argued that intellectual property norms did not take hold successfully in the past because it was simply not in China's interests for them to do so. Until the turn of the millennium and the country's subsequent membership of the WTO, it had been a predominant consumer rather than producer of knowledge goods and had appeared to focus far more on consumption and manufacturing than it had on innovation.

The deep-seated concept that in China "law is an instrument of policy" (Ostry, 2003:35) has heavily influenced China's international relations over many years. The notion long predates the accession to power of the Chinese Communist Party in 1949 (CCP) and is conceptually premised on the belief that the needs of the state must be prioritised over those of the individual, and that the primary function of the law is to serve the state and to facilitate the implementation of state policy. Chinese instrumentalism was linked to the principle that the role of the state was to maintain harmony and re-establish the same when the chaos of disputes arose, regardless of actual blame and irrespective of the principles of fairness that might prevail in any individual case at hand (Alford, 1995).

---

[5] For a useful summary history of intellectual property law over the centuries, see: Granstrand, The Economics and Management of Intellectual Property, especially pp. 28–29. Patent ordinances in England can be traced to the Statute of Monopolies granted in 1623 to codify long-held practice, whilst legal protection for English authors first appeared in 1709, taking a further 30 years before being then adopted on the continent of Europe in 1741 (by Denmark).

[6] Indeed, during the Maoist period of Communist rule it became an all but extinguished privilege.

This philosophy has been characterised as "parental disciplinary" in nature[7] where the normative response was "submission and obedience to the authority of status superiors in the hierarchy" and where "the elements of contract and many other legal relations in Western jurisprudence...were not within the horizons of thought of any Chinese administrative official". Critical concepts such as "rules" and "contract" differ in their meaning and impact under a disciplinary based tradition, with the former capable of being interpreted as "formalized instructions of superior authority, capable of being superseded in any particular case by other instructions" whilst the latter could be better understood by the word "agreement", with an emphasis on agreeing "statements of present intention" with the implication being that these, too, could simply be superseded and ignored when no longer relevant to one party's current intention (Stephens, 1992:10–30).

These cultural conditions were compounded by limited corporate structures and an ongoing lack of literacy, especially outside the cities (Alford, 1995),[8] such that mutual trust and interdependence actually stemmed hierarchically from relationships between acknowledged individuals, under the concept of *guanxi*,[9] in what could be interpreted as more of an extended family bond rather than a reliance on a judicial process for settling disagreements. Issues of familial networking and interdependence as a business model permeate the economic history of Asia, with scholars noting that within "societies where men cannot rely on strangers to give faithful service, the family may be the most appropriate unit for large-scale enterprise" (Lewis, 1955:115).[10]

These historical characteristics of the Chinese legal environment have generated ongoing tension and misunderstanding between China and its principle economic partners over many decades and across many policy areas, not the least of which has been in the area of intellectual property regulation. In particular, *guanxi* corporatism and conflict

[7] It is believed that this dates directly from Confucian teaching under the principles of *fajia*, meaning a "model of obedience".

[8] Prof. Alford maintains that literacy levels in China in the early 20th Century could have been as low as 20%.

[9] A Mandarin Chinese term literally meaning "connections" and often used to illustrate how the social and business culture even today remains embedded in issues of relationship building and trust formation at an individual level set in a complex network.

[10] The role of the extended family as an important productive institution in emerging economies has been much discussed. See also Alford, To Steal a Book, pp. 20–24.

avoidance principles may have hindered the assimilation of new legal approaches based on western judicial methods and may have proved difficult for some to reconcile with the adjudicative nature of the legal minimums with which they were increasingly being required to absorb through both bilateral and multilateral international arrangements. But China has sought to adhere to those international arrangements as the modern era developed.

Prior to the 19th Century, it has been argued that the Chinese legal landscape had been devoid of anything even remotely corresponding to a western interpretation of IP controls, although this is not to say that there were no controls over publishing and reproduction, but that none of them resembled the IP principles of the western world. For example, control edicts on publication and reproduction of written material proliferated across the imperial dynasties but were introduced with the intention of restricting the flow of information to ordinary people about subject matters seen as the preserve of the emperor (such as calendars, the mathematics of the stars and other matters central to maintaining the prestige of the "Son of Heaven")[11] rather than a concern about the piracy of materials for their own sake. These imperial era controls would therefore seem to have been far more about power than copyright and to have centred on the restriction of knowledge rather than the protection of valuable inventions. Given these conditions, they cannot reasonably be described as forerunners of coherent IP regulation.[12]

Progress in the regulatory environment of IP during the late 19th and early to mid 20th Centuries was hindered by domestic disturbances and foreign interventions, but such advances that were made were characterised by the desire of key members of the domestic elite to modernise China's development.[13] At the same time, attempts were also made to reduce international involvement in the country's internal affairs by exhibiting a propensity towards adopting western style IP principles to try to stem emerging piracy problems (Stephens, 1992).

---

[11] A term frequently used to refer to the Emperor of China, indicative of his separation from his subjects.

[12] Alford dates the first record of any control imposed on the unauthorised reproduction of texts in China back to Emperor Zhou in 1122 B.C. but also contends that the first real *codified* edict came in A.D. 835 under the Tang dynasty.

[13] This was known as the Westernisation Movement.

During the final years of the Qing Dynasty (1644–1911), two initiatives were promulgated: first, a ten-year protection was announced on certain scientific and mechanised processing techniques, alongside of which, for the first time, the administration also introduced the idea of rewards for inventing technologies useful for society—an idea later copied by the Chinese Communist Party (CCP). Second, a Copyright Law was enacted in 1910 that sought to regulate the behaviour of the growing number of independent publishing houses emerging at that time. In each case (Yang, 2003:17–36; Stephens, 1992), however, the initiatives largely failed to achieve their objectives as "there were no driving forces from the top that would lead to decisive steps towards IPP [intellectual property protection] [sic]", and a legally based IP system did not properly emerge in China until the republican Nationalist government under the Kuomintang (KMT) finally established a semblance of order during the mid 1920's.[14]

Under the KMT, in the period prior to World War II, the country saw some successful urban industrial development within the mainland and a consequent desire for imports that had an impact on the IP regime, as both foreign and domestic products, "from textbooks to tobacco", began to be supplied in counterfeit form to an expanding middle class urban elite who had emerged as a consumer market for these types of goods[15] (Alford, 1995:43–45). Inevitably, this led to pressures from Treaty powers for a vigorous domestic response adding to the stresses of the KMT as it sought to find ways to end extraterritorial control of the court system within the Treaty Ports. These influences led to successive legislative activity from which emerged both a copyright law and a trademark law, each within two years of the other, in 1928 and 1930 respectively, along with a patent law that arrived on the statute books in 1944.[16]

---

[14] This was following a long period of internal strife that dated from the fall of the last Qing Emperor in 1911, during which time the Chinese legal landscape was dominated by both extraterritorial foreigners who controlled areas in Shanghai and presided over the Shanghai Mixed Court, and extraterritorial Chinese, such as Marshall Sun Chuafang, who controlled the area of non-Concession Shanghai and surrounding provinces.

[15] Alford illustrates this point by describing the experience of Chinese author Xu Zhenya (famous for his spiritually uplifting book "Yuli hun", lit. "Jade Garden Spirit") who was so blighted by piracy of his work that he resorted to giving away original copies as a defence.

[16] Unfortunately, this law came into force just in time to be rescinded by the victorious CCP at the end of the Civil War in 1949.

None of these IP initiatives by the KMT, however, appeared to have any perceivable effect on local behaviour, and largely failed to stem the tide of fake products that by then were circulating within the domestic market as they "presumed…a legal consciousness that did not then exist in China" (ibid.:49–52). They were also coupled to structural problems throughout this pre-Communist period in respect of the training, quality and ability of local judges and other officials tasked with enforcing the new laws such that both the late imperial and nationalist eras appeared to make no substantive difference to Chinese domestic attitudes to, and cultural affinity for, intellectual property regulation.

The CCP's victory in the civil war in 1949 swept away all existing domestic statutes and all remaining vestiges of foreign-dominated lawmaking, "which spelled the end of all pretense [sic] to the reception of Western jurisprudence in China" and led to a distinctly different approach to all kinds of property ownership (Stephens, 1992:120). Throughout the 1950's and until the commencement of the Cultural Revolution[17] in 1966, the CCP followed a progressive strategy of political centralisation, national unification and ideological transformation across the country that had impact within all major social and legal areas, including intellectual property legislation (Teiwes, 1997).

The Soviet model became the framework within which new laws were shaped and the overarching IP philosophy became one of public ownership of inventions, of ideas and of all written work, underpinning the "Yan'an principles of self-sacrifice" in the wider interests of society (Keith and Lin, 2001:7). However, as part of nationwide reconstruction after the ravages left by foreign invasion and civil war, the leadership sought to ensure that sufficient stimulus was provided for new technology inventions by creating 'Provisional Regulations' in 1950 that provided for both a monetary award and public recognition for initiatives deemed to be suitable and useful to the nation, without there being generated any semblance of a "marketplace of ideas" in the modern sense but, rather, the creation of exhortations towards a common Chinese inheritance.[18] In fact, these measures did at least acknowledge that reward-oriented regulations could generate

[17] Its full name was the Great Proletarian Cultural Revolution.

[18] In this sense, there can be seen to have existed some ongoing tensions between communist philosophy and the need to promote national reconstruction.

outcomes that might be in China's own interests as it sought to modernise its society. This contrasted with legislative activity in an IP context undertaken by previous generations, where past foreign interference has been characterised by scholars as representing the view that "what was good for each treaty power was deemed... perforce, to be good for China" (Alford, 1995:49–64).

These minimal steps introduced in the early phases of socialism to both regulate the ownership of, and nurture the development of, knowledge-based outputs abruptly ceased during the social chaos and near disintegration of the legal system during the Cultural Revolution.[19] It was not until Deng Xiaoping rose to power in the late 1970's and wholesale reform took place of China's political and economic landscape that further progress towards a more sympathetic IP regulatory framework could begin again.

5.2 *Building a new IP regime in the Reform Era*

The economic development in China of the last 25 years has produced huge changes in the way that business and society are regulated and this has been reflected by considerable improvements in the legal protections and enforcement capabilities afforded to both domestic and overseas owners of intellectual property.

The strengthening of the IP regime began almost immediately after the decision was made by the Chinese leadership to re-engage with the outside world and introduce radical economic reforms in 1978/9. Some scholars have described the early reform era as a "dualist trade regime", combining export promotion in areas such as manufacturing and technology with commensurate liberalisation of foreign exchange, whilst continuing to maintain an import substitution strategy in other areas (Naughton, 2007:382). Over time, the export-promoting regime grew rapidly and became the model for further reform. Many commentators also see these developments as part of a need to promote spillovers to backward domestic processes by attracting critical foreign-owned technology into the country under the protection of

[19] The Ministry of Justice was actually abolished in 1959 and was not recreated until 1979.

legislative IP concepts more compatible with international norms (Yang, 2003).

To this effect, China joined the World Intellectual Property Organisation (WIPO) in 1980 which led, in rapid succession, to a Trademark Law in 1982 followed by a Patent Law in 1984. China acceded to the Paris Convention in 1985. This was followed by the introduction of the first Copyright Law of the modern era in 1990, which was immediately followed by consolidated Software Regulations in 1991 (largely to correct numerous inconsistencies and deficiencies in respect of computer software protection left wanting by the Copyright enactment). Accession to the Berne Convention came in 1992, followed by membership of the Patent Cooperation Treaty in 1994, with the country becoming a signatory to the UPOV Convention on Plant Varieties in 1999. China became a party to the TRIPS agreement of the WTO in 2001, which led to modification of all existing IP regulations to bring them in line with new requirements.

Scholars now argue that the nature and extent of these legal reforms, at least as they exist on paper, have in fact surpassed the country's obligations and that "China's legal system exceeds [that of] TRIPS standards" (Taubman, 2003:351; Kong, 2002:270). Others maintain that "purely in terms of lawmaking, China is no longer a serious concern in the eyes of its IP negotiating counterparts" (Yuan, 2006:57).

IP system development during the first two decades of reform, however, should not be seen as a smooth continuum but rather a series of movements led by circumstance and opportunity, where the leadership's strategic planning had to contend with the realities of domestic tensions. Progress was exacerbated by difficulties in trying to simultaneously appease diverging local interests and increasingly vociferous international stakeholders in regime development, all participating within what rapidly became a multi-level game where contrasting concerns at home had to be juggled with tightening obligations abroad (Putnam, 1988; Lisowski, 2003).

5.3 *Influences in China's Acquisition of IP Principles*

China introduces further complexities into an analysis of such developments as it also has such sharply diverging domestic interests, some of which reject IP controls altogether, under the justification of maximised self-interest, whilst others, particularly those already engaged in high technology-oriented corporate expansion, actively promote them as defenders of knowledge-industry growth.[20]

Recent research has highlighted the ongoing and important role that the Chinese academic community has had in this area, both in framing the debate about IP regulation within the political leadership and in influencing policy outcomes across the different positions taken by state entities. In this way, they appear to be performing a similar role to that played by western business lobby groups, with perceived diminished visibility for traditional business sectors in China perhaps stemming from their relative immaturity in cultivating an understanding of IP issues as part of their commercial operations (Yuan, 2006).

Chinese sources have also pointed to the historical significance of a series of educational lectures given to the top leadership over ten years ago on intellectual property, trade and economic law, designed by the academic community and led by Li Buyun, a senior specialist at the Chinese Academy of Social Sciences (CASS). These lectures were hosted by the then two most senior members of the communist hierarchy, Jiang Zemin and Li Peng, inside their own private compound of Zhongnanhai in central Beijing and shows both the commitment of the leadership to absorb new concepts and the influence of—and trust placed in—key academics during this learning process (Keith and Lin, 2001).

These study sessions ran at regular points between December 1994 and December 1997, and focused on the increasing internationalisation of trade related legal systems and the impact that such concepts would have in relation to China's developing economy into the future. It would appear to be increasingly clear that the national leadership had come, even by then, to regard the protection of IP rights as a matter of "urgency" (ibid.:32–34). This attitude of the elite might have been especially sharpened by the establishment on 1st January 1995 of the WTO and its remit in IP standard setting through the TRIPS agreement, given China's objectives of future membership.[21]

---

[20] This is especially the case in the software industry as a new generation of innovators have had to compete with an ongoing climate of piracy.

[21] The model that emerged under these tensions took its character from both the priorities of the domestic leadership as they sought to advance the pace of change and the concerted pressure of key actors within the international arena in tandem with emerging multilateral norms that further sharpened the focus on deficiencies in China's adolescent regime. Such progress was, therefore, neither uniformly successful

These competing pressures manifested themselves in a number of ways. First, the Chinese leadership held a strong ongoing desire throughout this time to join the international trading community as a full independent member (rather than having to renegotiate annually with the United States its Most Favoured Nation status) which sharply increased the impact of multilateral IP agreements (such as TRIPS) on the learning consciousness of the national leadership and this should not be underestimated in its influence in shaping regime development (La Croix and Konan, 2002).

Second, China was facing demands for its implementation of recognised IP norms through intense international pressure, with particular tension arising from trading relationships with the United States. During the first half of the 1990's, for example, the two countries came close to a full-scale trade war over the weakness of China's IP regulatory enforcement in respect to the piracy of American goods. Using the special executive powers granted under Section 301 of the US Trade Act, and after frequently including China in its annual report of "Priority Watch" countries, the US threatened to impose punitive tariffs and other sanctions on goods imported from China into the US unless an immediate improvement was made to internal policing mechanisms to control IP infringements, especially in respect to software and motion pictures (ibid.).

These disputes led to the signing of two Memoranda of Understanding in respect to intellectual property characteristics and enforcement between the US and China. Negotiations may have been made particularly tense as the American government was itself coming under domestic pressure from its own industry lobby groups who were looking for a decisive lead to curb the rising cost of counterfeits and unlicensed copies that were circulating around China at that time, which were likely to have been undermining export-based sales from US commercial interests (United States Trade Representative, 2006b).[22]

Third, the regime's very shape and existence had to be determined under the scrutiny of competing internal ideological and policy tensions within the CCP itself, especially in respect of the growth and development priorities across different sectors of the economy and

in convincing trading partners of its merits nor universally welcomed by all domestic actors.

[22] Also other years by the United States Trade Representative "maintaining China on the Priority Watch List".

in the extent to which the state's primary interests of control could be preserved. For instance, those who sought to introduce the Patent Law had to struggle for supremacy with those in the conservative wing of the party who argued against the very concept of patents as being fundamentally "un-socialist", whilst the first efforts at copyright and software protection were as much about controlling the spread of written "heterodox" ideas as any true embrace of emerging software technologies, which helps to explain their perceived weaknesses and inconsistencies (Alford, 1995:69–72).

Finally, the Chinese government has also had to contend with a growing struggle between the priorities of domestic sectors for which stronger IP laws were becoming an increasing necessity, such as software development companies and private-sector publishers, and those organisations whose operations centred on counterfeiting and pirating as a matter of routine economic endeavour. Indeed, as recently as 2004, Chinese policymakers expressed concern that problems combating the local incentives available to IP violators in Guangdong Province were still as problematical as they had been back in 1995 (Yuan, 2006).[23]

Not all these IP violations are in high technology areas. Trademark infringements, for example, are typically associated with low technology products such as apparel, luggage and watches, but still generate considerable friction between overseas interests and the central Chinese administration, especially from the Europeans. This can create additional tensions within the political structure as authorities in Beijing strive to promote domestic technological progress and a positive view of innovation to overseas observers, whilst provincial level actors may be frequently more concerned about maintaining economic rents from pirate operations.

Given these competing influences on Chinese authorities, it is perhaps not surprising that legal processes designed to strengthen IP controls continued to draw criticism from different sources. However, it can be strongly argued that such progress which has been made over the last ten years has likely been due in no small part to the national leadership's pragmatism in attempting to internalise the spirit of new IP measures and improve the enforcement of IP laws, whilst at the

---

[23] Outlining on Chinese political meetings at the APEC 2004 Conference, which she attended as an observer.

same time trying to appease both major international and key domestic actors.

This sea-change in attitude has been accelerating recently as the strategic appreciation of intellectual property protection has grown at the highest levels of government.[24] Moreover, some Chinese government ministries are known to be taking the lead in putting IP protection at the forefront of their own policy agenda as it is seen to be in their interests to do so. In particular, for example, the Ministry of Commerce believes that "stronger IP protection will generate more exports" and thus benefit the economy as a whole in the longer term (Yuan, 2006:71). It would therefore appear to be too simplistic to describe the country as simply a safe-haven for pirates, at least in respect to high technology, despite some ongoing problems.

In tandem with this change in mindset by elements in the administrative leadership, there has been a rise in economic importance of high-value knowledge sectors, such as domestic software product development, small and medium sized enterprises and export-oriented software service outsourcing, that now appear to compete with the traditional manufacturing staples of the past as platforms for economic growth into the future. In this context, rampant piracy is increasingly being understood as a disincentive for technology firms not just for foreigners keen to develop their products for the Chinese market, but also as an expensive barrier to entry for domestic enterprises. This is especially felt in an industry like software, where typical costs of entry are far lower than that required for hardware production or manufacturing. The impact of IP violations is also exacerbated, as smaller software enterprises often lack the financial power to absorb losses from industrial-scale piracy in ways that larger organisations can, especially when knowledge-based outputs can be copied so easily and so quickly by those within the black market.

Emerging sectors such as software, within the wider high technology industry, can offer a useful litmus test for the leadership's true commitments to knowledge-industry development and IP protection. A more accurate reflection of China's current and future IP trajectory may thus be made by tracing linkages between the country's legislative

[24] Op. cit. author's interview at China's Mission to the WTO, Geneva, May 2005. See also, a speech by Chinese President Hu Jintao on the importance of IP regulatory issues by the Xinhua news agency on the eve of Hu's official visit to the United States (Xinhua News Agency 27th May 2006).

progress on its IP framework commitments on the one hand, and the government's determination to nurture high technology sectors of the economy as growth priorities in the national interest, on the other.

5.4 *State Leadership in High Technology Development*

The Chinese state has long taken a lead in promoting high technology industries as a way of generating economic growth, from the earliest initiatives in the 1980's to the very latest 11th Five-Year Plan. In March 1986, Deng Xiaoping "personally approved the National High-tech R&D Program, namely the 863 Program"[25] which led to the investment of billions of yuan[26] to nurture specific projects in high tech/high growth sectors and helped to shape the financial, political and regulatory support that such sectors have enjoyed in China since that time. In the early 1990's, a National Compendium was created that attempted to lay out a "grand blueprint" to focus the country on high technology development into the 21st Century, illustrated by the creation of the Ministry of Information Industry in 1998, merging a number of administrative responsibilities with control of operational standards overseeing R&D initiatives (Pecht et al., 1999:67).

Linkages between the national government and highly successful organisations have traditionally been a strong and recurring feature of China's industrial development, sometimes through the personal *guanxi* of the founders, such as with Legend Computer Group (now Lenovo), which was created as an entrepreneurial venture from the computing branch of the Chinese Academy of Sciences, and with Huawei, a company that in recent years has become "a major manufacturer of wireless phone and networking equipment" (Newsweek Print Edition, 16th January 2006:31), whose founder was a former officer in the People's Liberation Army (PLA). There are also more formal mechanisms of interconnection such as the outright state ownership of conglomerates such as the Great Wall Trading Group that produces everything from microcomputers to grape wine.

---

[25] See the special programmes section of Chinese Ministry of Science and Technology (MOST) at http://www.most.gov.cn/eng/programmes/programmes1.htm last referenced 5th August 2006.

[26] The Chinese currency is formally termed the Renminbi (RMB) or People's Money but is more conversationally known as the "yuan".

In some areas over the last two decades, growth in production volumes by some of these organisations has been remarkable: for example, the output of manufactured microcomputers by China had reached over 45 million units for the year 2004, up from just over 70,000 units produced in 1989, whilst production of integrated circuits rose from 131 million in 1989 to an astonishing 21 billion for 2004.[27] Moreover, high technology product exports from China across different sectors grew by over 43% during the lifetime of the 10th Five-Year Plan between 2001 and 2005 (China Daily Online, 2006a), and China is now regarded as a major actor within advanced technology unit and component manufacturing and in consumer electronics, with the combined export value for the "Electrical and Mechanical Products" category of the Chinese Customs Bureau reaching a total of over US$323 billion for 2004.[28]

These absolute figures highlight the strategic challenges that have had to be overcome as domestic organisations have striven to upgrade the skills base of China's technological capability. In the early stages of economic growth, much of the manufacturing output was effectively nothing more than a low-skilled, assembly line process meaning that knowledge spillovers in the underlying technologies being assembled were weak in a social improvement sense, in that the IP-rich content of such outputs were simply imported from abroad and effectively "burnt-in" to the product[29] to be included within the assembly lines as required. It can be argued from this that the primary objective of the early Open Cities and Special Economic Zones were in fact to "promote [the] acquisition of and domestic capability in advanced technology" (Pecht et al., 1999:30). In this context, IP regulations were at this point provided only to a sufficient level to attract this much needed foreign know-how, but that, in the early stages of the development cycle, the real objective is more acquisitive rather than creative

[27] See National Bureau of Statistics of China, 'Output of Major Industrial Products 1978–2004', *China Statistical Yearbook 2005*, <http://www.stats.gov.cn/tjsj/ndsj/2005/indexeh.htm>, accessed 7th August 2006.

[28] China Statistical Yearbook 2005, <http://www.stats.gov.cn/tjsj/ndsj/2005/indexeh.htm>, accessed 9th August 2006.

[29] Computer chip microcode, often called firmware, is actually highly advanced software instructions that form the basis for making the brain of the computer function correctly. Such instructions are physically hardcoded into the circuitry when the chip is built and is the product's real 'value added intelligence'.

and it is important to put IP enforcement weaknesses into this wider economic picture.

China first introduced Special Economic Zones in the early 1980's around Shenzhen near Hong Kong and then along other parts of its eastern coastline and these parks have long been the home of many different types of assembly and manufacturing, including high technology hardware using imported intermediate goods from other parts of East Asia. However, recent initiatives would appear to have centred on creating higher-level skill centres of excellence, where both western and local specialists may work together and exchange valuable knowledge as equal partners.

Increasingly, this new focus is including software development, localised R&D and specialist language support services, with both Chinese and international firms active in this trend. For example, Oracle Corporation, the US software and database giant, opened a new R&D centre a few years ago near Shenzhen (followed by a later one near Beijing, specialising in government contract work) to both increase the company's visibility in the mainland and to enable a concentration on business solutions that better serve the distinct and specific Chinese market demand (Oracle Corporation, 2005; China Information Online, 2002).[30] Huawei, also headquartered in Shenzhen, is seen as an emerging force in telecom related software development and has both an R&D centre and a skills "university" to foster professional career development.[31] These initiatives would appear to represent a major step forward in the drive to cultivate China as more than simply a low cost assembly-line hub.

A particularly notable illustration of this advanced development park theme can now be found just outside Shanghai at the Suzhou Science Park, where an entire new community has been created over the recent few years (J.S. China Network Online, 2006).[32]

---

[30] These announcements actually caused some concern in India, where the company's Bangalore research centre had, until then, been seen as the company's main Asia centric high value business hub.

[31] Author's interviews with a Chinese senior technology consultant. Beijing, January and June 2005. Update interview in Shenzhen, January 2008.

[32] This promotes a real incubator feel for newer companies which, together with high quality business services and matching infrastructure of high speed cable and excellent housing standards, all help to attract and retain larger and well established organisations with both domestic and international staff. Even the overnight express trains between Shanghai and Beijing now make an additional scheduled stop, morning and night, at the new Science Park station to both pickup and set down business

Nor are these developments just limited to the special zones of the main metropolitan areas of Beijing, Shanghai and Shenzhen, as a notable example of software clustering has emerged over the years in the provincial town of Hangzhou, the lakeside capital of Zhejiang Province in Eastern China. The explosion of activity around this city may have been particularly spurred by the decision of Alibaba, the highly successful Chinese language internet and software service portal, to host its development headquarters in the city (Hangzhou Municipal Government).[33]

One of the primary aims of Chinese leaders throughout recent Five-Year Plans has been to provide stimulus to the nation's R&D capacity and its high technology output, to boost socio-economic development, reduce national inequalities (People's Daily Online, 2006a), and to achieve breakthroughs in the latest scientific techniques (Ministry of Science and Technology, 2006).[34] These strategies have led to annual growth rates in R&D expenditure of over 21% year-on-year between 1998 and 2004,[35] with much of this focused on advanced telecommunications and related electronics research that, in 2004, totalled over RMB18.8 billion (about US$2.3 billion).[36] This philosophy has been taken forward to the next stage by the country's *National Program for Medium and Long-Term Scientific and Technological Development 2006–20* (hereinafter Science and Technology Strategy), providing significant state-backed investment to put China at the leading edge of R&D intensive nations (State Council, Government of China 2006). Three main themes that have emerged as priorities from this initiative have been to promote original scientific discovery, to better integrate related technologies into new products and services, and to

passengers, who are now able to make direct trips to attend meetings at locations in the Park from their offices in city centres, rather than having to connect on to a local service from Shanghai Central train station on a separate journey.

[33] This has led to an explosion of complementary service providers locating there and the upgrading of rail, road and housing services to create a genuine software hub atmosphere. See details of Alibaba's strategic partnership with Yahoo, signed in the last business quarter of 2005, (Newswire Today Online 8th December 2005).

[34] See the information statement released by the Ministry of Science and Technology in the summer of 2006 about progress in a Nano-Biotechnology programme funded through Project 863.

[35] See Statistical Yearbook Online 2005, 'Expenditure on Research and Development', <http://www.stats.gov.cn/tjsj/ndsj/2005/html/B0203E.HTM>, accessed 5th August 2006.

[36] See online Ministry of Science and Technology, <http://www.most.gov.cn/eng/statistics/2005/t20060317_29724.htm>, accessed 5th August 2006.

ensure that China absorbs knowledge from best-of-breed technologies available internationally. Specific objectives included raising China's R&D intensity ratio[37] from 1.43% in 2006 to an ambitious 3% by 2020, whilst also providing much improved and much needed support to innovating technology-driven SMEs, particularly through the expansion of clusters and incubators across the country (OECD, 2008).

This progress reveals a number of important interconnections. First, it shows that a strategy of technology-driven prioritisation can work in China and can reap tangible benefits. Second, it brings intellectual property protection into greater salience as a way to safeguard the fruits of this high-value knowledge for the benefits of the Chinese themselves. Third, it can act as a springboard for further development in emerging technology sectors, such as software. Finally, it may help IP evangelists from academia, politics and business to convince sceptics of the necessity of continuing on the course of regulatory reform and effective IP enforcement into the future in order to sustain this success.

There may also be other factors determining the importance of high technology growth that can be seen to be taking place in locales such as Suzhou and Hangzhou, in that it may help to mitigate the potential risks posed to economic and social stability by the economic recession that struck the export-focused manufacturing sector in China during late 2008 and into 2009. The national leadership may be considering that undue dependence on overseas consumption of low-tech commodity products creates too high an exposure to international demand variations, and that domestically driven, technology-led growth through innovation can help provide an important balance within the wider Chinese economy. This may help to explain why high technology and scientific innovation have been slated as sectors likely to benefit from the stimulus package announced by the Chinese authorities in November 2008, and reiterated by Chinese Premier Wen Jiabao in a number of speeches made during his visit to Europe in February 2009.[38]

---

[37] R&D intensity refers to the gross expenditure of research and development investment from government and non-government sources expressed as a percentage of GDP per annum.

[38] For a transcript of one of Premier Wen's keynote speeches during his visit to the United Kingdom, made at Cambridge University (the author attended this speech in person), see China's official news agency, Xinhua, at <http://news.xinhuanet.com/english/2009-02/03/content_10753336_2.htm>, accessed 5th February 2009.

5.5 *The Development of the Software Industry in China*

One of the greatest beneficiaries of this drive to create higher value outputs and improved IP conditions has been the nation's growing software industry.

Software in China emerged from the shadow of the hardware market during the decades after the Cultural Revolution, largely due to deliberate encouragement and planning by senior leadership within government departments that oversaw technology industries, such as the Ministry of Science and Technology (MOST) and the Ministry of Information Industry (MII). Of particular significance was the declaration in 2000 that software sector growth was a national goal and that software should become an official "encouraged industry" under the "National Torch Project"[39] with specific subsidies available in tax, investment and earnings distribution, which effectively launched the next phase of development for the sector (State Council of P. R. China, 14th July 2000).[40] Before then, and for some time, software was in fact regarded as simply a mechanism for making high technology hardware function effectively, rather than as a value-added product in its own right, in contrast to attitudes in the United States and India.

Some of the earliest achievements in software development were actually solutions that supported the creation of the first Chinese word processing machines and for some time afterwards the nature of Chinese society viewed employment in software firms as second class to that in hardware and engineering ventures, which limited the attractiveness of employment in this sector for the elite of the country's technical schools (Pecht et al., 1999). The problem that software engineering had at that time was that outputs had no physical presence and most software companies were small and thus failed to provide sufficient "face" to top graduates in their everyday social interactions.

However, attitudes have now evolved as a new generation of entrepreneurs has now grown up who have been driven by the pursuit of wealth and who have enjoyed more engagement with western attitudes (Fortune Magazine, 2004). Returning members of the country's diaspora have also influenced decision-makers, as an increasing number of

---

39 See details of funding for high technology firms under the Project, accessed 20th March 2007 at http://www.innofund.gov.cn/english/index.htm.

40 This helped to set in motion ongoing double-digit growth.

Chinese professionals who chose to go abroad for both education and work experience are now taking the chance to lead the next generation of high tech entrepreneurs at home (Bell, 2007).[41] Not only do these overseas Chinese bring back much needed skills in sales and management techniques but they also help to imbue local colleagues with the attitudes and priorities that will be encountered when dealing with western counterparts.

Businessmen closely involved with technology companies have emphasised the point that, having spent time abroad, they were particularly sensitive to the importance attached by foreign clients to the protection of their company's intellectual property as a function of doing business with a Chinese service supplier or through a Chinese distribution contract.[42] This knowledge has enabled them to tune domestic attitudes and construct corporate policies that could reassure potential western clients and partners.

The opportunities available in this sector are by no means inconsequential. According to official statistics, staff numbers employed in technology, computer services and software across the country reached over 1.1 million by the end of 2004, a rise of over 6% on the previous year (China Statistics Yearbook, 2005). Moreover, average annual earnings for the same year in private sector computing and software companies in the large cities of Beijing and Shanghai (under what the statistical authorities still term as "other ownership units", meaning non-collective based and not state-owned) reached a very respectable RMB61,000 and RMB57,000 respectively (around US$8,000), compared to a national average of RMB44,000 for technology workers in general and RMB14,500 as a national average of those employed in manufacturing operations (ibid.). Competition for staff has in fact been increasing, with some specialist skills in programming and project management commanding particularly high premiums in Beijing.[43]

---

[41] The importance of overseas educated returnees—the *haigui* [lit. sea turtles]—has been recognised recently by the establishment of a RMB2.5 billion finance scheme by China Development Bank to support returnees setting up domestic ventures.

[42] Author's interviews in Beijing, January 2005, with i) Senior VP and Co-Founder of an outsourcing and software development company based in Beijing, who had previously worked overseas for a "top 5" consulting firm and ii) a Chinese executive who was educated in the US but who returned to China as a technology consultant.

[43] Interestingly, the software development industry appears to be one of the few sectors in which Beijing outpaces Shanghai for reward opportunities, likely to be due

These developments in terms of both available reward and societal standing for the software sector have diluted old prejudices which, coupled with increasing domestic demand for software outputs and international interest in software outsourcing, have enabled the industry to grow steadily over the last few years, with local enterprises gaining increasing visibility within high technology clusters through brand development, internet advertising and initiatives that have begun to include foreign market penetration (Lu, 2000).[44]

The software industry is now "the fastest growth sector in the [Chinese] electronic information industry" (China Daily Online, 2006a), expanding at a rate of over 40% in terms of sales revenues in 2005 compared to the previous year. Foreign software firms, however, were reported to have accounted for around 65% of the software revenues for 2004, according to the United States Department of Commerce.[45] Although domestic firms continue to make inroads into this imbalance, it does indicate the continued dominance of innovating American organisations in the international software market and may also help to explain the significance of China's domestic IP regulations in US commercial and political consciousness.

In terms of its actual size, China's software industry presents some challenges to be able to create an accurate assessment. Its exact size is open to dispute: according to the OECD, "[f]igures on Chinese software industry revenue (both exports and domestic products) and exports vary widely, seem high or are not available from official sources" (OECD, 2006:157). As a result of some of these issues, it may be most appropriate to use the various sources and figures in order to derive trends rather than focus on exact statistical values. Some of the difficulties may originate from the extent to which the value of hardware and software package combinations have been combined together in revenue estimates. Unlike India, there would appear to be

in large part to the long-standing clustering success of the Haidian district and the increasing number of smaller and medium sized software service and export oriented ventures that have arisen in and around that area. Author's update interview with vice president of a Beijing based outsourcing services company whilst visiting UK customers, in Cambridge, November 2006.

[44] Dr. Lu describes of the rise of the Haidian district of Beijing and the Zhongguancun cluster therein. See also the Beijing Science and Technology Commission and its support for local organisations at http://www.bjkw.gov.cn/English/ last referenced August 2006.

[45] See US Dept of Commerce *BuyUSA Service* <http://www.buyusa.gov/china/en/computers.html#section_2> last accessed 23rd November 2006.

less emphasis on software enabled services revenues, with perhaps a greater focus on combinations of integrated software and hardware system sales. Software product consumption is also likely to grow as Chinese companies upgrade their financial management accountabilities and customer service systems as part of the trends towards greater business sector sophistication as China approaches the second decade of the 21st Century.

According to official Chinese figures, accumulated revenues across the country for all types of software enterprise reached RMB390 billion (approximately US$48 billion) in 2005 (People's Daily Online, 2006b), of which just over US$3.6 billion was exported—a remarkable achievement on figures for 2000, which were respectively, RMB59.3 billion (about US$6.9 billion) and US$250 million.[46] The trends in export value seem to have been increasing markedly over recent years, in line with the country's national objectives, but they still appear to illustrate a marked difference in balance with the Indian software industry, which is far more export-dependent, and is estimated to have exported US$18.2 billion of its software and enabled services outputs, representing about 60% of total revenues of its IT industry in 2005 (NASSCOM, 2006). This could give the Chinese IT services sector a vital platform of solid domestic demand from which to weather the economic slowdown in western IT markets predicted to take place until early 2010, as OECD economies grapple with global recession.

There is, however, some confusion in regards to the overall figures for the industry quoted by the Chinese government. The OECD recently counselled that the Chinese industry's total revenue levels "must be used with care" when set against the posted worldwide revenues of leading international software companies, which it estimates as having been US$84 billion for the same period in 2005 (OECD, 2006:157).

For example, the US Department of Commerce estimated the size of the Chinese software industry for 2004 at US$25.4 billion, with a growth rate of 28% over revenue values of the previous year.[47] Extrapolating a similar growth figure for 2004, US assessments would seem

[46] See the China Software Industry Association at http://www.csia.org.cn/chinese_en/index/index.htm for an overview of the industry and growth trends since 2000. See also technology newswire at (Silicon Newswire Online).

[47] See China Survey within 'US Commercial Service of the Department of Commerce' *Buy USA Service* <http://www.buyusa.gov/china/en/computers.html#section_2>, accessed 20th November 2006.

to value the Chinese software industry at around US$32 billion for 2005. These estimates also maintained that the country's software firms accounted for only 2.6% of the global software market, and it is important to keep in mind that China is still a relative minnow in international terms, at least for the time being.

Nevertheless, despite these valuation discrepancies and difficulties, there is evidence of export services growth by China in software coding outsourcing over the last few years.[48] One software outsourcing company executive based in Beijing commented that his company had experienced significant growth in European customers, which now accounted for half of his firm's revenues (with the United States being a significant 'other'), and that this expansion was centred especially within northern EU states such as the UK, the Netherlands and Finland.[49] These trends would appear to be supported by the perspectives of other executives in similar software service sectors.[50]

There is also now a noticeable trend towards the creation of full-function overseas development centres for propriety software building, moving beyond their use by predominantly Japanese corporations, which have been the traditional user of Chinese services due to cultural and language familiarity. Chinese service providers now appear to be securing new customers from Western Europe and America as well.[51] Even UK start-ups have begun to contract out discrete devel-

---

[48] Author's interview with the COO of a London headquartered software company, February 2005. In conversation, this executive indicated that a key variable in the final decision to approve overseas development was that the supplying company already had two UK reference sites of customers that had used their services before, one of them having done so for over a year.

[49] As a consequence, this company had more than doubled in size over the a two-year time frame and was now far more focused on the Microsoft and the proprietary internet-enabled solutions market that appealed particularly to his new customer base, with his Microsoft teams now being three times the size of his Linux and Java software groups. Author's update interview with visiting vice president of a Beijing based mid-sized software outsourcing. Cambridge, November 2006.

[50] Author's interviews with both two senior executives of a tier 1, Beijing based, software product company that had diversified in 2006 into outsourced software services as part of a broader international strategic focus, conducted whilst attending India's Annual NASSCOM Conference in February 2006 in Mumbai, where both executives were intent on raising the visibility of Chinese software service providers in general, and their own firm in particular.

[51] By the end of 2005, one London based software firm whose executives worked with the author on exploring China as an outsourcing destination, had established an overseas development centre that comprised Chinese programming professionals and a local project manager, all based in Beijing. See also discussion of China as a location for software outsourcing in the NASSCOM, Strategic Review 2006, pp. 136–139.

opment projects, following a trend first begun by Silicon Valley SMEs with encouragement from their venture capital investors, where both the skills mix available in China and the price point offered for these services made a good match with a typical start-up's requirement to quickly create solutions and bring them to market ahead of the competition.

In a recent report to members, the UK's Institute of Directors (a lobby group for smaller and medium sized British enterprises) characterised in positive terms the country's attractiveness in terms of its available scale and market potential, for both ITO services supply and technology product market entry—even for smaller ventures to exploit—in addition to the pace of change that is affecting the way that business is now carried out in urban centres (Institute of Directors, 2006).

These developments may help to account for the rise in *both* export and domestic revenues for China's software product and service industry, and would appear to be a result of formal support by government, in terms of the sector's status as a 'Golden Project' within the country's 'Torch Program', by its visibility within the 2006–2020 Science and Technology Strategy, and by the state's own procurement policy that "channels a portion of its software purchasing to domestic companies to support the domestic industry" (International Finance Corporation, 2005). In fact, the Chinese government agreed to "delay" the introduction of an overtly discriminatory 'Software Government Procurement Regulation' that would have forbade foreign software companies from even bidding for government procured contracts. This decision came after intense negotiations with the US government in July 2005, when the Chinese agreed to make revisions.[52] Significantly, China has not yet acceded to the WTO's Agreement on Government Procurement (GPA), which, observers acknowledge, "would be a major step in the evolution of China's procurement system" (WTO Trade Review China, 2006:98).

---

[52] See news report on US-China high level contact talks in Beijing on 11th July 2005, at <http://www.hktdc.com/info/mi/a/baus/en/1X00DWVH/1/Business-Alert-%E2%80%93-US/US-China-Achieve-Concrete-Results-at-JCCT-Talks.htm>, last accessed 3rd July 2009.

5.6 *Challenges and Tensions in China's Software Sector*

However, the domestic corporations within the Chinese software industry are still relatively immature, in terms of both their technical capability and their organisational sophistication. Under the Capability Maturity Model (CMM),[53] which is an internationally recognised benchmark for assessing a firm's software development abilities, China has only a small handful of companies that have reached CMM Level 5 (the top level), most of which are foreign managed outsourcing specialists,[54] compared to India which is estimated to have over 90 organisations having reached that level of certification, with many of them home grown (NASSCOM, 2006).

The domestic software industry in terms of both product and services sub-sectors could also be characterised as immature in terms of its structure, with the number of software and service enterprises put at around 10,000 "of which only half are capable of developing their products independently" (Kumar et al., 2005:238). Many of them are small scale privately funded ventures with less than 50 staff. Furthermore, the national business group for the industry, the CSIA, appears to be predominantly a vehicle used by the government to channel information and regulations in a classical top-down strategy of state centric direction rather than the industry-led initiatives more common in India.[55]

This more detailed picture of the Chinese software industry is illustrative of the ongoing problems that the country faces as it continues to industrialise and expand its high technology sectors and perhaps shows that strengthened IP regulations are only part of the required solution. According to IFC research, during the decade since 2000,

[53] The CMM was developed out of the Software Engineering Institute of Carnegie Mellon University with independent appraisers trained and authorised by the SEI making inspection assessments of application companies, similar to the way that Quality Management kitemarks are assessed in the UK. There is, however, some debate about the usefulness of these assessments as they focus only on processes rather than products and project outcomes, but for now at least, Level 5 remains the target.

[54] For corporate examples see: Bleum Software of Shanghai, <http://www.bleum.com/news/news_22.htm> and FreeBorders Outsourcing, <http://www.freeborders.com/news/press20060208_b.html>, accessed August 2006. Neusoft Corporation was the first Chinese company to be granted Level 5 status, in 2002.

[55] A brief look over their respective websites gives more than enough evidence of this perspective, with NASSCOM having far more sophistication in its services, function and operational feel. The Chinese version of CSIA's website is also largely 'informative' and exhortatory than the more service oriented Indian version.

only five Chinese corporations have emerged with any ability to challenge established international vendors in product specialities and of these, only two have held continuous market share in the top ten of China's software vendors since 2000, with the market continuing to be dominated by western multinational corporations (IFC, 2005).

Respectively, these five major corporations are: Kingdee in enterprise resource management (ERM) software; UFSoft (now renamed UFIDA as a specific part of its international branding strategy) in accounting and asset management solutions; Neusoft in CT scanner software and related medical services; Huawei in telecom support software; and finally, the China National Computer Software and Service Corporation (CS&S, now called ChinaSoft), a part state-owned organisation with interests across IT products and services.

Scholars have outlined a number of causes to help explain these problems. First, China has had to face the tasks of skills enhancement for its people, gradual market opening of key sectors and the modernisation of its industrial base whilst being in the full glare of international competition, where trade flows and technology ownership trends have already been well established across the world and where the United States has such a totally dominant position. These circumstances contrast sharply to those that existed when "new tiger" nations, such as Korea and Taiwan, and the powerhouse of Japan before them, were undergoing their own period of industrialisation and technology driven economic growth and it is now much more difficult for a domestic venture in high technology to grow beyond a niche market in terms of size, sales and supply (Nolan, 2004).

Second, some have argued (Keane, 2004:14) that, in China, "much innovation lacks core creativity" and that there has been an absence of what could be described as a true culture of innovation, even whilst the country has been trying to develop pioneering companies within its high technology industries. This could have been caused predominantly by the traditional nature of Chinese education that puts a premium on rote learning and memorizing what is the "right" answer to a series of questions rather than on permitting young minds to flourish by sustaining inventiveness, supporting innovative enquiry and teaching problem solving techniques.[56] Especially in the English-speaking

---

[56] It is important that this issue is put into perspective, as China has achieved considerable success in combating illiteracy across its vast country and in reducing levels of absolute poverty.

world of international software services, some scholars maintain that the country continues to face challenges in equipping its new executives with an appropriate arsenal of softer skills such as team building, problem solving and project management (Li and Gao, 2003).

The educational issue is one that the government, in its capacity as strategy leader, has recognised as important but agreeing national curricula changes in the context of cultural sensitivities would appear to have made for rather limited progress since the China's Education Ministry introduced its "Guidelines for Curriculum Reform of Basic Education" in 2001, urging schools to put "an end to overemphasis on imparting of book knowledge [sic]" (People's Daily Online, 2005b; China Education and Research Network, 2001). Some observers point to the responses by the private sector across China whose fee-paying parents have actively sought out establishments that base their teaching on imported methods from either the international models of America and Britain or the regional variants of those models present in Singapore and Hong Kong (Cheng and DeLany, 1999).

However, they also believe that modifications need to be made to both teaching techniques and examination systems in concert with each other, to provide consistency between what is taught and how abilities can be evaluated to remain fair to a child's chances of exam success. This is especially the case in respect of the national university entrance test (known as the *Gao Kao*), which continues to be modelled on traditional lines of rote learning, and it can be argued that this type of approach does not combine well when coupled to an innovation-oriented learning regime that some provinces have experimentally adopted in their schools (Economist Online Edition, 2003).[57] In keeping with the manner in which change can now be initiated in China, much of this progress has been left to individualistic educational pioneers, largely operating in the private sector with new commercial education ventures, to make attempts to reverse this trend.[58] These issues in particular can help to explain why returning entrepreneurs with overseas experience have become especially important to the growth objectives for companies in the Chinese software industry.

---

[57] This disconnection has caused strains in some cases as parents believe their children may have been disadvantaged when tested under exam conditions.

[58] For example, in the field on English language learning especially, some independent educationalists have adopted a different approach to knowledge acquisition, suitable for both students and young professionals alike, using western techniques such as subject context setting and conversational confidence building.

Conditions such as these may also partly explain the current weakness in respect to innovative product development by Chinese software enterprises. The reality would seem to be that these companies typically provide their customers with scarcely more than a domestically created and procedurally sympathetic version of a software concept that has already been pioneered by existing western competitors (Hu, 2006).[59] This implies that, unless greater levels of genuinely innovative products can be created and successfully delivered to market, the aspirations of leading domestic enterprises such as Kingsoft, Kingdee and UFIDA may have to centre on regional dominance at best (Nolan, 2001).[60]

5.7 *The Improving Climate of China's IP Regime*

Chinese commentators maintain that it has been widely accepted by the national elite that intellectual property protection and effective enforcement together have a vital role to play in engendering the conditions in which such success can thrive and therefore continued to be a key strategic goal of the Chinese government's 11th Five-Year Plan.[61] Problems of counterfeit and piracy can also be seen to have become an issue for Chinese technology producers as well as overseas corporations, which may be connected to their increased engagement in overseas trade in line with their strategies to further penetrate domestic markets (Li & Gao, 2003). In response to this, there has been a marked increase over recent years in the propensity of Chinese claimants to turn to IP courts and administrative agencies to seek redress, whether as a corporate or as an individual claimant (Rouse & Co., 2005).[62]

---

[59] Kingsoft, for example, is a successful domestic word processing provider to mainly private and retail markets in China rather than the business and corporate focus of other companies herein discussed, although in mid year 2006 it did announce a change of strategy in a bid to win enterprise share from competitors, which it rightly sees as mainly coming from Microsoft.

[60] Oracle PeopleSoft Corp. dominate the market in respect of both UFIDA's accounting products and Kingdee's ERM resource management solutions.

[61] Op. cit. author's interview at China's Mission to the WTO, Geneva, May 2005, where the official emphasised that the symbiosis between encouragement for high tech centres and the strength of IP regulations had been understood by [the Chinese] government.

[62] A particularly interesting example of this trend took place in May 2005, where former executives of Huawei were successfully sued for breaching the confidentiality

Three significant developments during 2005–2006 helped to show the importance attached to improving China's IP regulatory environment and indicated that there appeared to be genuine causes for optimism.

First, in early 2005, the Chinese National IP Strategy Formulating Working Group was established, chaired by then Vice Premier Wu Yi, with the responsibility, in her own words, to "positively meet the challenge of the rapidly changing international IP trends and to protect the national interests and economic security [and] to accelerate the establishment of a sound and fair market environment and to improve innovation capability...for our country [sic]" (State Intellectual Property Office, 2005).[63] This has been seen by many as a forum that is more than just a talking shop[64] and the committee's creation has been publicly supported even by the United States, whose official trade representative and whose lobby groups such as the International Intellectual Property Alliance (IIPA) and the Business Software Alliance (BSA) have frequently lambasted China for making exhortations and gestures instead of real progress.[65]

In response to Madame Wu's appointment and subsequent work to coordinate more effective responses on IP, the US government announced that it "recognizes and appreciates the efforts of the many officials in China...who continue to give voice to China's commitment to protecting intellectual property rights and work hard to make it a

---

and trade secret portions of their employment contract after they resigned from Huawei and directly contacted former clients on behalf of their new employer. Huawei's claim against them was successfully upheld in Shenzhen's Intermediate Court.

[63] Speech by Vice Minister Wu Yi to the inaugural meeting of the IP Strategy Working Group, 30th June 2005, and referenced in full on SIPO's website in a page created 9th May 2006 at <http://www.sipo.gov.cn/sipo_English/laws/whitepapers/200804/t20080416_380356.html>, accessed 27th July 2009.

[64] SIPO held a conference in July 2006 to which foreign and international participants were invited to comment and critique developments and a website exists to provide further information to the general public at <http://www.nipso.cn/> though not yet with an English translation.

[65] Contrast the positive statements in the 2006 reports with those included in previous USTR and IIPA reports especially during the trade disputes with China over IP protection during the mid 1990's.

reality".[66] Clearly, Madam Wu's approach would seem to have been viewed by American negotiators as a positive development.[67]

Second, in March 2006, the government announced the creation of a national Judicial Court of Intellectual Property as part of the civil court system under the country's Supreme People's Court (China Daily Online, 2006b). The aim of its creation would appear to be to centralise the quality and reliability of IP civil adjudications, especially in light of concerns in respect of local collusion and potential corruption and is separate to the administrative enforcement channels that have typically been used by many foreign litigants in the past (Hitchcock, 2006). The timing of the announcement of the court's creation may very well have been linked to President Hu Jintao's impending meeting with US President George Bush later that year, where it was expected that IP rights violations were to be discussed.

Third, in April 2006, a few days prior to Hu's arrival in America, the Chinese government announced that it would in future require all computers that were to be assembled in China to have pre-installed licensed versions of operating system software and that government agencies would be restricted to only buying computers where such pre-installation had taken place (SIPO Review, 2005).[68] This latter point is particularly important as government buying preferences can act as a benchmark for private sector behaviour in the future. In addition to domestic considerations, it may be that this announcement illustrated that China was moving to legitimise overseas IP vested in China's high technology exports, from companies such as Lenovo, in ways that would be consistent with the central government's attempts to project a responsible attitude towards IP internationally.

---

[66] Priority Watch List Report for China, US Trade Representative's Special 301 Report 2006, page 16. This attitude was also reflected in an TV interview with Franklin L. Lavin, US Under Secretary for International Trade, given on Chinese state TV's *Dialogue* programme on CCTV-9, broadcast at 07:30 Beijing time 2nd August 2006, where Mr. Levin emphasised that "progress was being made" across a number of trading issues with the US, "including IPR".

[67] In particular, they may have seen her as "someone with whom [we] could do business". This phrase was most famously used by Prime Minister Margaret Thatcher on her first meeting with the then newly appointed Soviet leader Mikhail Gorbachev in December 1984 and has since been seen to have marked a sea-change in attitudes towards constructive engagement between the Western and Eastern blocs at that time. It is not unreasonable to see Madame Wu's appointment to publicly lead China's fight against IP violations, and the US reaction to it, in a similar way. (Thatcher 1993:463)

[68] See also see BBC News at http://news.bbc.co.uk/2/hi/technology/4902976.stm last accessed August 2006.

It remains unclear whether the Chinese saw this pledge as a *de facto* victory for Microsoft Windows in its increasing dominance of the computer market or as a possible stimulus for domestic open source software vendors such as Red Flag Linux.[69] The latter company's software offerings could just as easily be installed into Chinese made hardware, and would, by definition, be legal under the concept of the General Public License (GPL) that is central to the Open Source approach.[70]

This policy's potential to influence the local retail market is, as yet, unproven. This part of the economy has been typically less responsive to government edicts about piracy, as price-points for individual copies of software can be more significant to private purchasers than to corporations.[71] Indeed, in many illicit trading markets across the eastern provinces, piracy can still be seen to be a continuing problem, led largely by price differences that make illegal products so much more attractive to ordinary Chinese buyers, whose gross monthly income is unlikely to be much more RMB1,400, even in a prosperous urban area, from which food, commuting and living costs must be regularly deducted.[72] In relation to these income levels, a pirate copy of either Microsoft Word or Kingsoft's WPS2002 may be had for as little as RMB10 (about US$1.50) which compares far more favourably with the legitimate cost of WPS at around RMB100 and nearly RMB1,500

[69] Born out of the Chinese Academy of Sciences (CAS) in August 1998, Red Flag is a leading vendor of open source solutions in mainland China. Open source solutions have been gaining popularity over the years, especially in government as a means of combating what is seen as the dominance of America's Microsoft, but face a challenge to dislodge the market penetration and ease-of-use offered by rival propriety software.

[70] This states that software covered by its protection may be freely shared, altered and enhanced provided that such changes are also made publicly available for use by others in the open source community. There are, however, current problems over the next steps for open source licensing internationally based on disagreements about what should be the characteristics of the next version of the GPL. These have dogged the industry for some time, but the concept still retains many advocates, not least from hardware vendors Sun Microsystems and Hewlett Packard, and probably represents the main serious global rival to Microsoft's operating system dominance.

[71] Trade discounts are typically available for volume purchases under large-scale corporate licenses.

[72] China National Bureau of Statistics shows annual income for Beijing in 2004 at just over RMB17,000 whilst the overall national average was just over RMB10,000. However, if only rural households are included this figure drops to just over RMB2,290. See op. cit. China Statistical Yearbook 2005, <http://www.stats.gov.cn/tjsj/ndsj/2005/indexeh.htm>, accessed 5th August 2006.

(about US$220) for a legitimate full-function copy of Microsoft Office Suite (Yang, Ghuari, and Sonmez, 2005).[73]

Some international vendors are using the operating system software itself to take the initiative away from the pirates. For example, Microsoft announced in 2006 that stringent technology-based anti-piracy controls would be "deeply integrated" into a "Software Protection Platform" that would form a key part of the company's worldwide Genuine Software Initiative for new product releases (Microsoft Corporation, 2006e). Such developments, although independent of an individual state's regulatory regime, were designed to target two main areas of concern to vendors in particular. First, the industrial-scale illegal copying of operating system software by unscrupulous hardware retailers on to clean machines prior to sale has been a special problem in China and formed part of the Beijing government's incentive for promulgating its regulation about legitimate installs in the first place. Second, the unlicensed installation of software on to multiple machines by private users, and their communities, in the retail market.[74] This could bring into sharper relief any government's failure to combat illegal software piracy and make it more difficult for officials to hide inconsistent actions behind salutary statements.

Nevertheless, the publicly announced undertakings by the Chinese government to enforce legitimate software purchases and to galvanise legislative co-ordination at the highest levels through a high-level committee should still be considered to be a major step forward for business software regulation. It would appear to confirm the importance attached by those in the leadership of raising the consciousness of IP best practice across different branches of the administration.[75]

Piracy levels across a range of products and sectors have actually been reducing over the last few years (for business software as well as

---

[73] The author's personal experience is relevant: working in Beijing as a client to export oriented Chinese outsourcing companies it could be observed that, whilst some Chinese organisations make particular efforts to keep within all copyright rules and show an exemplary level of staff monitoring, it is at the point of individual purchases in domestic retail markets that many problems still persist.

[74] It remains to be seen whether this policy of technical software-level enforcement of IP controls will be ultimately successful and how quickly workarounds to the controls will be discovered. However, it is possible that its reach could in future apply to all Microsoft layered product and utility software implemented on to a user's computer even after the operating system is installed, such as with office staples like word processing, spreadsheet management and anti-virus software.

[75] Op. cit. author's interview at China's Mission to the WTO, Geneva, May 2005.

for records and music), even if only slightly and from very high starting points. Figures from the IIPA in 2006 show that levels reduced from 92% to 88% for software between 2001 and 2005,[76] which is much in line with the focus of government efforts at prompting a change of attitudes across the population at large in these vertical sectors.[77]

The domestic knowledge industries do seem to have responded to this state stimulus, evidenced by sharp increases in patent and trademark applications across industrial sectors over the last few years. According to the State Council's Information Office, it took from 1985 to 2000 for China's totality of patent applications to reach one million, but only from 2000 to 2004 for that total to double to two million, with 82% of this total being from domestic applications (Information Office of the State Council, 2005).[78] Furthermore, according to official figures, patent applications by all applicants have increased by an annual rate of over 20% during the years 2000–2005, and most tellingly for local policymakers, "the annual increase rate of domestic applications was 13% higher than that of foreign applications" (SIPO, 2005:2) with enterprises making 80% of applications, after which came universities, research funds and even ministries being included in the breakdown (People's Republic of China Government Statement, 2006).

This lends authority to the priority placed by China's policymakers in increasing levels of industrial and technological innovation within their Science and Technology Strategy (OECD, 2008; Irwin Crookes, 2009). In this context, China appears to be showing serious intent to challenge the current leadership of the United States, Japan and the European Union as centres of innovation excellence, and it is perhaps not surprising that upgrading its domestic intellectual property legal

---

[76] See IIPA Special 301 Report for China on "Levels of Piracy", issued 13th February 2006, page 112.

[77] Many such programmes against piracy take place in China each year and, in typical exhortatory style, are often accompanied by banners and rallies and are usually covered by national TV as well, giving them a penetration beyond the city suburbs into the countryside. One example was the "Special Campaign for IP Protection" initiated in August 2004 by the State Intellectual Property Office. See SIPO website. Others have been initiated by the National People's Congress.

[78] Note that "domestic" means an ordinarily resident or domiciled individual or company, so it is likely that foreign organisations with Chinese operations have been included in this figure, but that aside, it is still a remarkable achievement. Similar ratios to those mentioned also pertain to patent approvals during the same period (see page 9).

system is seen by both China's political and corporate leadership as a key ingredient in this process.[79]

In terms of corporations themselves, Huawei is perhaps best recognised as the benchmark for innovating domestic enterprises. The company was reported to have submitted the largest number of domestic filings in 2005 (Xinhua News Agency, 2006b). This indicates the important advances in telecommunications, communications software and related research fields that the Chinese government has been heavily promoting over the last few years. The only US firm in the top ten for Chinese patent applications in 2005 was IBM, whilst the largest number of foreign filings came from Samsung of Korea.[80]

In respect of accepted trademark registration applications for 2005, covering both goods and services, a rise of just over 10% was achieved over the previous year. Perhaps most interestingly, in the special category of "well-known trademarks", over 90% of the 177 total were "attained by Chinese enterprises" which would seem to illustrate a growing recognition of the importance of IP to business expansion strategies (SIPO, 2005:3). There has also been a healthy growth in both the number and visibility of software and outsourcing companies in the eastern hubs of Beijing and Shanghai, with a number of these companies developing an increasingly international and outward-looking strategy.[81]

These developments can help to explain how national policies and economic priorities in unison with international pressure may be able to change internal behaviour in respect of attitudes to intellectual property regulation in ways that external action alone has, in the past, found more difficult.

---

[79] In 2006 alone, OECD estimates have China spending upwards of US$86 billion on gross R&D expenditure, in purchase power parity terms (PPP). See also Irwin Crookes, 'Maintaining Europe's Innovative Advantage', page 14.

[80] The example of South Korea is a particularly interesting example of a nation whose principles and priorities have undergone profound change: the country was once regarded, during much of the last two decades, as a central figure in East Asia for piracy and counterfeit infringements and as a major producer of "imitative products". Dedrick and Kraemer, Asia's Computer Challenge, page 132.

[81] At the annual NASSCOM 2006 technology conference in India, the author noted the increased number of *Chinese* software outsourcing firms competing for international attention along with the traditionally strong Indian presence. Conversations with Chinese executives present at the conference whose offices were based in the Haidian District of Beijing. Mumbai, 15th February 2006.

5.8 *Structural and Political Challenges for Regime Enforcement*

There remain, however, a number of key structural problems within the domestic IP regulatory system in China that appear to be regarded as continuing causes for concern internationally.

One of the principal criticisms often used against China's approach at combating IP violations is the emphasis that the current model makes on the use of administrative resolution.[82] Under this administratively sponsored arrangement, the state initiates action on the request of a plaintiff and conducts its own investigation as to the merits of the case. The state administers disputes involving IP violations through the auspices of a number of government bodies, including the State Administration for Industry and Commerce (SAIC) in conjunction with the Chinese Trademark Office (TMO), the National Copyright Administration of China for copyright infringements (NCAC) and the State Intellectual Property Office (SIPO) for patent license violations (SIPO 2005). The SAIC also has responsibility for administrative enforcement of regulations under China's Unfair Competition Law.

During this process of administrative resolution, the appropriate body (SAIC, NCAC or SIPO) gathers evidence and investigates the claims of both sides whilst seeking to arbitrate and conciliate between the parties. Sometimes, where necessary, the authorities will initiate a raid on the offending party's premises, often accompanied by police and television coverage, which can have a special impact on persuading the violating party to reach a settlement. However, many commentators have pointed out that the decision on whether to bring a subsequent criminal prosecution is often more one of the perceived degree of loss suffered by the plaintiff and even the extent of embarrassment caused to the nation by the defendant's behaviour and the final decision is often "up to the official making the distinction" (Menon, 2005:21701–22602).

An alternative approach, though sometimes more complex, is a pure civil court action where the state behaves as a western style adjudicator between plaintiff and defendant and where damages may be recovered. This approach lacks the strength of the state's proactive tendency under its administrative powers, but such a process can sometimes be

[82] This is separate from either a plaintiff-initiated civil action or state-initiated criminal proceeding.

used as a means of persuading the appropriate administrative body of the merits of a case prior to further action.[83]

Guidelines have been created for Chinese judges that have attempted to define threshold levels of the financial gain that an accused party may have derived from their illegal sales and IP violations (Schlesinger and Smith, 1999). This is especially important in terms of criminal law as it assists in the evaluation of whether a criminal prosecution should follow for the offenders. Such assessments, however, are often made based on the value of the counterfeit product rather than the actual loss that might have been suffered at the genuine article's price, which, at least in the case of software in particular, is rarely a fair reflection of the investment effort required to produce the original.[84] These monetary levels have been lowered within the last 18 months by the state authorities, meaning that it is now purportedly easier to show a level of unlawful gain from illicit IP activity that would warrant a criminal prosecution (currently triggered when illegal gains exceed just over US$6,000).[85] But such changes need to be monitored within the context of the state's willingness to bring criminal sanctions to bear upon IP transgressors at all.

Furthermore, the all-powerful Adjudication Committee oversees cases of a sensitive nature typically involving foreign high profile parties, and can by itself decide that a criminal prosecution is warranted (Menon, 2005). This potential myriad of different pathways and organisations involved in enforcement exercises can create both uncertainty

---

[83] See 'Intellectual Property Protection in China. Civil Law Protection' last referenced 20th February 2007 at http://english.ipr.gov.cn/en/remedy_4.shtml. This very distinctive "dual system" resonates with the past of imperial times, where disputes were solved with dialogue and compromise by the principals, outside the full glare of court proceedings. Whilst the announcement of the creation in March 2006 of a national Judicial Court of Intellectual Property may make civil court action more attractive in the future, use of the administrative route is still likely to remain a prominent feature of the Chinese enforcement regime.

[84] Some argue, however, that this might not be so unreasonable a position. There is certainly much debate in business circles about whether, for example, the billions of dollars lost to piracy and counterfeit claimed by bodies such as the BSA and IIPA are in reality accurate, as they presuppose that a legitimate sale would have taken place if the violating product had not existed, whereas, some argue, cost differences often mean that sales only take place because cheaper counterfeits are available.

[85] See Jiang Zhipei, Supreme People's Court, P. R. China, <http://www.chinaiprlaw.com/english/news/news39.htm>, accessed 5th August 2006.

and delay especially for foreign firms, and continues to give IP holders of all nationalities cause for concern.[86]

Further problems appear to manifest themselves in respect of IP enforcement in the current political, economic and administrative framework of the People's Republic. Often seen by casual observers to be the very definition of a centrist state, China after Deng's reforms actually became remarkably devolved in nature in order to stimulate more radically inclined reformist provinces to make progress, released from many of the strictures of what was then (in the late 1970's) a predominantly conservative Beijing (Rudman, 2006:40).[87] Many commentators have pointed out that it is important to realise that genuine power is held at the local and provincial levels across the country as well as in the national capital.[88]

This diffusion of power introduces a number of tensions. First, some provinces have highly active counterfeiting and copyright piracy ventures as central to their local economy as opposed to other localities where genuine high value outputs are produced. Such conflicts can even occur in different parts of the same province, as with Guangdong, for instance, which is at the same time a centre of pioneering R&D (especially around Shenzhen) whilst being pivotal to many organised criminal counterfeit syndicates (Rudman, 2006). This would suggest a problem whereby the spillovers gained from new research and product development lead not just into groundbreaking ventures but also into an expansion of illegal piracy. Some observers claim that even within the same factory, shifts can change from legitimate to illegal output operations as a matter of routine planning.[89] In circumstances like this, it is particularly difficult for patent, brand and copyright owners (domestic or international) to seek redress when such local economic

---

[86] Interview with CEO of a London based software company, where he affirmed that he was extremely concerned about his company's IP being exported to China and that outsourcing evangelists in his firm "had a lot of convincing to do" before he was satisfied that it was safe. March 2005, London.

[87] Some scholars have described Deng's move as the 'Balkanization' of China.

[88] Much useful information on this area was given to the author by Dr Jianbo Lou, both in his fourth lecture during Autumn 2004 at Cambridge University entitled 'Lawmaking in the PRC' and in subsequent private conversations with the author both in the UK and China. See also op. cit. Deborah Cass, China and Trade Law Constitutionalism, page 30.

[89] Author's discussion with a director of a London based business strategy firm, who worked as an interim manager with a western law firm in China during 2005, and encountered just such problems as these. Cambridge, November 2006.

interests are at stake as provincial officials may not recognise the merits of such cases where special interests interact in this way (Chow, 2003).

Second, some Chinese observers point to what is believed to be persistent and endemic collusion between some local enterprises and political figures within provincial authorities, which often involves financial corruption. This frequently enables counterfeiting organisations to avoid detection or minimise the impact of infringement raids through advance notice by provincial administrative organs, meaning that the bulk of illegal products disappear before the raid commences (Yuan, 2006).

Third, relationships between provincial and national levels of the same organisation can have a negative impact on justifiable pursuit across provincial boundaries. For example, some scholars maintain that it is not unusual for there to be little or no cooperation and coordination work between the State AIC in Beijing and any of its provincial or local counterparts, which substantially reduces the strength of enforcement rights granted to litigants by the law. This has led to some cases becoming dominated not by legal argument but by jurisdictional disputes and assertions of power plays between central and national levels of government (Ostry, 2003).

Moreover, China has a poor standing within the international Corruption Perception Index maintained by Transparency International.[90]

All of these characteristics may inhibit some companies from entering into business contracts within China. At the very least, they can raise transaction costs of contract management as they create additional complexities in negotiations and increase management time required for oversight and verification of service delivery standards (Qu and Brocklehurst, 2003).

In light of some of the difficulties inherent in building a reliable business relationship across China, a range of responses have been evident by both domestic and international actors in an IP context. First,

[90] The country holds a rating of between 2.9 to 3.5 on a scale of 0–10 for a variety of different indicators, based on feedback from business and political actors on national practices, where 10 is least corrupt and 0 is most corrupt. This ranks the country at 78 equal out of 158 places for the year 2005 (interestingly, India ranks lower at 88th equal). See Transparency International, 'Survey Indices 2005', <http://www.transparency.org/policy_research/surveys_indices/cpi/2005/>, accessed 5th August 2006.

some of the very newest Chinese software companies, especially those influenced by returning members of the country's diaspora and who are focused on export-oriented growth business models, have taken responsibility themselves by creating their own controls and procedures. They have mandated strict contractual codes of behaviour on staff and have combined these with physical access constraints within the office.[91]

Second, many western IP holders seek to protect their intangible assets through contractual obligations placed on the Chinese service provider or partner distributor. These ensure that safeguards are in place and that they are adhered to by staff, coupled with careful control of what exact product mix and program source definitions are exported to China in the first place.[92]

Third, western lawyers familiar with the enforcement situation in China typically advise their clients to include an element of binding arbitration within business contracts to try and fill the remaining gaps in the regime's credibility in respect to enforcement. These objectives are made easier by use of the New York Convention, to which both China and the UK are signatories (Lo and Tian, 2005). Under this Convention each Contracting Party agrees to recognise and enforce cross-border arbitral awards made in another contracting state. There already exist recent case histories to indicate that the Chinese Supreme Court will honour and uphold such arbitration judgements when made in accordance with the treaty.[93]

---

[91] Author's observations and interviews, Beijing-based Chinese software outsourcing services company, Beijing, January–March 2005. For example, elements of particular high value in project assignments (such as core product source code) will often be made accessible only to those who are specifically assigned to a defined technical task—these controls can include techniques such as computers with limited or no hard and floppy drives (i.e. they effectively become terminals to the central server, much in the way that Defence contractors operate in western nations), the use of locked and key-coded access to development rooms and the requirement to use sign-in / sign-out regulations for handling finished deliverables.

[92] Interview with the COO of a London based UK software company, March 2005, where the importance was made clear of having such contractual controls agreed during the negotiations prior to establishing an overseas development centre in Beijing.

[93] For example, an arbitration award in favour of the London Sugar Association in 2001 brought against the China Sugar and Wine Group was upheld in the Supreme People's Court in Beijing in 2003 despite being rejected by lower Chinese authorities. The award was enforced under the auspices of China's recognition of the New York Convention that was made in 1995. See Judge Jiang Zhipei's website at <http://www.chinaiprlaw.com/english/default.htm>, last accessed 4th July 2009.

Finally, it is not unusual for contracts to include reference to preferred Chinese jurisdiction localities for settling disputes between the parties if and when conflict should occur, so as to ensure that dispute resolution takes place within sympathetic and sophisticated eastern judicial regions.[94]

Despite the difficulties that continue to exist, many western organisations espouse the view that creating development outsourcing and software distribution partnerships with China no longer represents a pioneering risk at the business frontier. Instead, some executives now view such moves as having become a reliable model with a recognisable process that, while still involving some risks, brings with it the advantages of first mover status[95] with considerable cost attractions over European and Indian skilled-labour charges.[96] It can therefore be argued that commercial and political interests in China have intersected over the need to work effectively to maximise IP protection, given the importance of stimulating high technology domestic expansion and increasing exports of both IP-rich products and services.[97]

China would appear to be particularly keen to attract these kinds of international high value contracts across a range of advanced technologies that can complement expansion in domestic knowledge-based industries. This can help put into context why the central government has therefore invested considerable effort to raise the standard of IP adjudication and enforcement across the country and has made increased endeavours to generate respect for its enforcement regime at both criminal and administrative levels.

These efforts seem to be showing some progress: statistics on IP enforcement investigation indicate an increasing tendency by authorities

---

94 The operation of the new national Judicial Court of Intellectual Property may reduce the need for this in future.

95 The CEO of a London based software company reaffirmed this apparent contradiction by describing how Chinese firms his company approached were able to offer the safety of UK based reference sites (who had already had a successful relationship) whilst also being willing to tailor their services to precisely the clients needs in a way very reminiscent of early stage business development. Interview, March 2005.

96 For example, fees charged by one Beijing software services supplier for a five year plus experienced graduate IT project manager with fluent English amounted to less than US$2,800 per month inclusive (around £1,500 as at March 2005), which is less than half that required to employ a similarly skilled professional in London. Interviews, Beijing, March 2005.

97 This is particularly illustrated by an increasing number of overseas companies engaging in software services partnerships in China as a part of their strategy to exploit the cost advantages of local Chinese firms.

to take matters of this kind seriously, whilst also illustrating the continuing scale of the problem. For example, in 2005, 49,412 trademark violations were completed by various levels of AIC bodies, with an increasing number of these compared to 2004 (up by 23% at 6,770) being foreign-related mark disputes (SIPO, 2005). Under national copyright controls for 2005, "more than 107 million pieces of different kinds of pirated products were confiscated", of which 13% were electronic publications and just over 7% were pirated software disks, with the vast majority of the remainder being pirated DVDs and VCDs (ibid.:3).

Within the judiciary itself, there are high profile individuals who would appear to have been encouraged to take a more public stance in the argument and to consistently push the case for wider and deeper appreciation of IP issues at all levels of the court system. One notable example of an IP evangelist who carries much weight within the domestic legal and political system is Supreme Court Judge Jiang (Jiang Zhipei), who is the Chief Justice of the Intellectual Property Rights Tribunal of the Supreme People's Court in Beijing and was recently quoted urging western companies to "take their complaints [about IP violations] to court".[98] Since 1998, the Public Security Bureau (national police force) has coordinated criminal level investigations through a specially created department that, between 2000 and 2004, "cracked 5,305 cases of criminal infringement on IPR, which involved nearly RMB2.2 billion, and arrested 7,100 suspects" (Information Office of the State Council, China, 2005:29).

In order to increase the breadth of specialist IP divisions at various higher levels of the national court system, highly focused training programmes for IP judges have been introduced, sometimes taken overseas to gain the experience and the cultural sympathy required for this work and, in tandem with this, efforts have been made to widen the reach of specialist IP adjudication divisions across the country.[99]

---

[98] Judge Jiang Zhipei, <http://www.chinaiprlaw.com/english/forum/forum76.htm>, accessed 9th August 2006.

[99] Judge Jiang Zhipei, 'Recent Developments in China's Judicial Protection of Intellectual Property Rights', 18th August 2003 <http://www.chinaiprlaw.com/english/forum/forum43.htm>, accessed 20th March 2007.

5.9 *Conclusion*

It can be argued that China has been grappling with a number of key issues in its IP regime development over recent years and has been, in the tradition of all states, seeking solutions that most favour its own position. A regime that was too strong and too early could have given power to external forces without enabling and nurturing nascent domestic development. Now, however, too weak a regime would be likely to inhibit the growth of locally established high tech businesses, undermine export growth and could, in fact, ensure that the primary economic winners would be foreign-owned organisations large enough to absorb IP infringement costs within the Chinese market whilst able to locate their own R&D elsewhere.

In the early years of the 21st Century, therefore, China appears to have recognised that the needs of the country are evolving and that complex parts of its legal system, such as IP regulation, need to evolve at the same pace. The central planners of the communist era have been successfully replaced by technocratic strategists of the market era who would find no great difficulty in agreeing with a comment by a senior Chinese diplomat: "respect for IP rights is a function of economic development of [the] population".[100] China's increased economic power now appears to be operating in concert with advanced levels of technological sophistication and an increasing level of high value exports. It can be argued that these factors are now acting together to help make reliable IP regulations and effective IP enforcement a growing reality across the country.

[100] Op. cit. author's interview at China's Mission to the WTO, Geneva, May 2005.

CHAPTER SIX

MARKET DRIVEN DEVELOPMENT IN INDIA

This chapter will examine the connection between the strength and development of India's intellectual property regime and the nation's sustained success in the international market for software services, off-shore outsourcing and pharmaceutical manufacturing. The regulatory framework for knowledge protection in India has been characterised by a number of key factors that provide both contrast and similarity with China, the country's principal rival to developing nation leadership in Asia.

Analysis has shown that India has been able to exploit a number of natural advantages it enjoys over its Asian neighbour. First, India inherited the full panoply of IP legal arrangements, including a patent office, under the common law principles derived from British imperial times rather than them having to be consciously created and culturally absorbed from scratch.

Second, Indian nationals have benefited from specific domestic factors that have been pivotal in fostering the skills necessary for knowledge sector success, such as a natural speaking ability in the English language that for many in the professional classes begins even before school takes a hold of a person's education, as well as an innate tendency to thrive in numerical and problem-solving tasks that are at the core of high value sector outputs, especially in respect to software solution building.

Third, the country's development of its IP regulatory framework has been based around a successful partnership between state and corporate actors whereby key characteristics of India's modern regime have often come from strategic guidelines initiated by industry leaders themselves during proactive dialogue with government leaders. This has helped to make reforms especially relevant to domestic market needs at different points in time and it is by way of this formal symbiosis between evangelising individuals, leading organisations, powerful lobby groups and different levels of government that the Indian dimension distinguishes itself from that of its more centrally orchestrated top-down Chinese competitor.

Yet there also exist some uncanny similarities that can be observed in the Indian experience with those of China's development. First, with the increasing internationalisation of knowledge goods production, it is clear that the Indian government has come under similar pressure to China to adjust key features of its IP protection policies to bring them into line with current international norms, particularly from state actors within the United States and European Union, operating both unilaterally and through multilateral frameworks. Second, the popular but somewhat simplistic perspective that the Indian government supported some of its knowledge sectors simply through benign neglect is not evident from research, as there have, across the years, been highly focused state-sponsored initiatives to nurture and develop knowledge sector product industries.[1]

The characteristics of these state-sponsored actions have been remarkably similar to those chosen by China: the creation of tax incentives to stimulate sector development; the building of science parks to promote clustering; and the encouragement of an education and training agenda that has attempted to feed these sectors with appropriately skilled resources. It is true, however, that the Indian software industry in particular has benefited greatly from a climate that has been devoid of the regulatory levels of control endured by many other economic sectors.[2]

However, some complexities in the Indian dimension become apparent when seeking to evaluate the details of the Indian government's support for the development and expansion of its knowledge industry sectors. These relate primarily to distinctions in attitude towards software technology and pharmaceutical manufacture. While the former was encouraged to focus on export-led expansion from an early stage in its evolution, the latter had been heavily protected by high

---

[1] Indeed, even those scholars who perhaps more favoured the characterisation of "benign neglect" and have downplayed the Indian government's supportive role, have come to view state actions as being more "inconsistent and ineffective" rather than plain neglectful. See works of Ashish Arora for more on "benign neglect" theory, and especially 'The Indian Software Industry And Its Prospects', a research paper published by The Heinz School of Public Policy and Management, Carnegie Mellon University at page 18, for analysis of why "neglect" may not be a sufficient explanation. Available online at <http://www.heinz.cmu.edu/research/302full.pdf>, last accessed 3rd April 2009.

[2] After Independence but before the economic reforms of early 1990's, India followed a largely Soviet style model replete with quotas, permits and licenses that became colloquially known as the "License Raj".

tariffs, price controls and regulatory support consistent with import substitution industrialisation but which is now moving to embrace export-oriented opportunities. This disparity can help to explain the continuing tensions that can be seen to exist which particularly characterise the Indian dimension, both between the two industries and within pharmaceuticals itself, in the context of the country's IP regime development.

6.1 *Reconciling Historical Legacies with Contemporary Priorities*

The concepts of industrial property protection and the wider IP rights to exploit the benefits from an individual's knowledge and inventions have long been part of India's legal landscape, though progress has not been without international controversy.

The country's first Patent Law was enacted in 1856 to protect domestic ideas and promote inventiveness, predating even the Paris Convention let alone many European nations. Indeed, the very first patent filing in India under the 1856 Act was carried out by a local inventor as early as September of that year (Malavika, 2006).[3] In a similar manner, the Indian Merchandise Act of 1889 created the ability for merchants to protect their marks and brands and laid the foundation for the current implementation of such controls under the Trade Marks Acts 1999.

In terms of copyright controls, legislative history predates even that of patents, with the first Copyright Law of India enacted by the British in 1847, followed by the direct incorporation of the 1911 English Copyright Act into Indian jurisdiction under the integral legal system that operated within the British Raj, with the nation joining the Berne Convention in 1928. It was not until 1957 that the country established its first post-independence Copyright Law, and, indeed, even that "borrowed extensively from the new Copyright Act of the United Kingdom of 1956" (India Copyright Office). The Act was subsequently modified and substantially strengthened to take account of the computer

[3] See the Hindu Times for an excellent introduction into the early years of IP activity in the country and an especially fascinating description of "An Efficient Punkah Pulling Machine", which was the subject of the first Indian patent. Indeed, after this successful filing, the inventor specialised in patent advisory work and established a law firm that is still active in this field across India.

software industry's already growing importance in 1994 and was further amended in 1999 to take account of India's obligations under the TRIPS agreement (along with some changes made to the Patent Act). India has had, therefore, a distinct platform of statutory recognition for many of the key principles of IP protection for over 150 years and illustrates a consciousness that is in marked contrast to the experience of their Chinese neighbours and it is one of which the Union government is proud (Indian Embassy to United States).

There are some important and positive aspects to this historical inheritance. Under the Common Law system established in India by the British and maintained largely intact by domestic authorities after independence in 1947, India has been able to absorb legal principles and policies that were not necessarily part of any specific national statute but were still capable of being used across the country through their creation under courts of the same or higher standing in complementary Common Law jurisdictions (such as the United Kingdom).[4]

A particularly important example of this concept that is highly relevant for IP control is the Anton Piller Order,[5] an instruction for the search and seizure of allegedly unlawful items produced in contravention of prevailing intellectual property laws.[6] It can be argued that Common Law has also provided intangible principles that have assisted India's developing IP protection regime, with perhaps the most significant being the concept of "natural justice" or "fair play in

[4] The legal concept of *stare decisis* is fundamental to the Common Law system of precedents that is in use by the Indian legal system.

[5] Now called the 'Search and Seizure Order'.

[6] The Order originated from a ruling in the UK's House of Lords in 1976 and was first used without additional legal procedures in India in 1979 and continues to be one of the more effective means to combat piracy and illegal production. The Order is typically granted *ex parte*, giving it particularly strength as this means that the defendant in the case is actually absent from the proceedings and thus the subsequent raid comes as a surprise. The first Indian use of an Anton Piller Order was made by Mr Pravin Anand (appearing for the plaintiff) who is the Senior Partner of a renowned Indian IP legal firm Anand and Anand. The case involved the HMV record company commencing legal proceedings against Super Cassette Industries who were allegedly creating unlawful copies of copyrighted musical material and the subsequent Anton Piller Order and product seizures led to a successful settlement of the matter before court appearances became necessary. Information provided by Mr Anand to the author in personal email dialogue in June and July 2003.

action" encapsulated in the traditional English legal process (Krishna Iyer, 2001).[7]

Legal scholars and Indian officials alike point proudly to the country's long-standing traditions in upholding these fundamentals, such that, "through a series of progressive rulings, India has acclimatized [sic] natural justice as a pervasive principle beyond defiance by the executive or other state edicts" (ibid.). This can be illustrated by a case in which a sculptor was able to exercise his moral rights against the Indian government itself, after serious damage was found to have been done to one of the plaintiff's works that had actually been purchased by the government (Managing Intellectual Property Online Edition, 2005a).[8] Nor is it just in direct individual interaction where such Common Law approaches impact on IP system refinement, as law to protect geographical indicators (especially for Scotch Whisky and Champagne) was first introduced across India in response to edicts from a Hyderabad court between 1986 and 1988.[9]

It would be a false analysis, however, to see India as necessarily a better keeper of IP principles simply because of imposed legislation from an imperial past, as it has relentlessly pursued its own priorities in legal system development where the Union government deemed it necessary and there had always been critics of imperial era legislation (Drahos with Braithwaite, 2002). As part of its national strategy for domestically nurtured industrialisation and import substitution for the benefit of local interests, new patent protection terms were set down by the Indian government in 1970 that were far more sympathetic to local inventors.

Nor has the Indian climate for IP protection been met with universal praise from the international community, with successive Union administrations in New Delhi being subject to disputes and threats along similar tramlines to those experienced by Beijing. The United States has been at the forefront of IP disputes with India over a wide range of infringements, from software and motion picture piracy

[7] This article in the Hindu Online Version quotes Indian legal author Tapash Gan Choudhury about these concepts. V. R. Krishna Iyer, 'Natural justice and law', *The Hindu Online*, (13th November 2001), <http://www.hinduonnet.com/thehindu/br/2001/11/13/stories/2001111300120300.htm>, accessed 30th August 2006.

[8] *Amer Nath Sehgal v Union of India*. For further details see It is truly difficult to imagine such a case ever being launched in the controlled climate of the People's Republic of China.

[9] Op. cit. author interview, Indian Mission to WTO, Geneva, July 2005.

through to objections over India's handling of pharmaceutical product patents and its lack of provision of mailbox facilities for patent owners under the TRIPS transitional arrangements for a new patent regime. American objectors have used both multilateral[10] and bilateral vehicles to exercise its distinctive economic and political power.[11]

As early as 1993, India joined a list of countries designated as "Priority Watch" under the special provisions of Section 301 of the US Trade Act, after having spent the previous two years in a higher category of risk by being designated as an identified "Priority Country" under the same monitoring provisions, particularly for its attitude on patent protection for pharmaceutical products (Embassy of India, Indian Embassy Factsheet).[12] Independent pressure groups have also been critical of India's stance on rights protection. For example, in its report of February 2006, the International Intellectual Property Alliance (IIPA) based in the US recommended that "India be retained on the Priority Watch List" for another year (International Intellectual Property Alliance, 2006:63). However, some specialists maintain that the US has, over recent times, reduced its use of Section 301 sanctions directly and instead, has begun to use their threat as part of more aggressive bilateral negotiations during the establishment of free trade agreements covering specific areas of concern.[13]

In similar terms to the priorities and approach adopted by China, a better understanding of the subtleties and underlying tensions of India's IP regime may be made by evaluating regulatory progress in the context of how government has supported the industries that it believes best serve the country's economic development, the often termed "sunrise" industries[14] of pharmaceuticals production and, in particular, the software development and IT enabled services sectors.

---

[10] See United States against India, World Trade Organisation, 'Dispute DS50', <http://www.wto.org/english/tratop_e/dispu_e/cases_e/ds50_e.htm> accessed 1st September 2006.

[11] Op. cit. author interview, Indian Mission to WTO, Geneva, July 2005.

[12] See historical trade issues with the United States at 'Indian Embassy Fact Sheet', <http://www.indianembassy.org/indusrel/trade.htm>, accessed 1st September 2006. Note that this is an archived web page maintained as accessible for historical reference.

[13] Op. cit. author interview, Indian Mission to WTO, Geneva, July 2005.

[14] A term frequently used in both media and business circles to differentiate these new sectors.

6.2 *IP Patent Regime and Support for India's Pharmaceutical Industry*

The government's philosophical belief in import substitution industrialisation, trade autarky and economic isolation that characterised India's industrial policy prior to the economic reforms of the early 1990's is usefully captured by the framework of the country's approach towards patent protection for pharmaceutical manufactures, encapsulated in its 1970 Patent Act administered by the Indian Patent Office under the supervision of the Controller General of Patents, Designs and Trademarks.

Yusuf Hamied, chief executive of Cipla, one of India's leading generic drug producers, in concert with the Indian Drug Manufacturers Association (IDMA), has now been widely recognised as having spearheaded the campaign to persuade then Prime Minister Indira Ghandi to change the country's patent law to create the new framework in 1970 (Lele, 2005; Bhandari, 2004). To some extent there may also have been elements of earlier regulatory capture by domestic drug producers, which may indicate that the country's stronger, pre-1970 imperial era IP regime, had, by that time, become increasingly disconnected with the objectives of both state and non-state domestic actors (Bate and Tren, 2006).[15]

Under the 1970 Act, product patents for pharmaceuticals were unenforceable save for the processes under which the various chemical reactions and resulting outputs were generated. This meant that separate and distinct processes could be legally used to create what were effectively the same resulting products that helped to spawn the generic drug manufacturing industry across India and brought tensions between local and international producers. During this time, India thus developed an IP regime for pharmaceutical patent protection that was specifically adapted to an import substitution growth model and that the 1970 Patent Act represented an encapsulation of this domestic policy.

There are various estimates of the overall size of India's pharmaceutical market, ranging from a value of US$6 billion in 2004 made

[15] The 1970 patent reforms were critical in helping establish generic based industrial strength, whilst high tariffs, despite some price controls, were also important in domestic market exploitation. For some perspectives on Indian high drug tariffs.

by western analysts (KPMG International, 2006), to US$8 billion in 2005 in an assessment made by the FICCI, an Indian business group (Federation of Indian Chambers of Commerce and Industry, 2005:2). According to the Organisation of Pharmaceutical Producers of India (OPPI), the country ranks 13th in the world by value of its industry and 4th by volume (India Pharmaceutical Industry Portal, 2005), with around 40% of production being exported (FICCI 2005). Within the country, Indian companies dominate over multinationals with local firms taking over three quarters of market share, with some observers seeing this as a direct result of the governments patent policy relaxations in 1970, in response to which foreign firms substantially reduced their corporate presence across India (ibid.).[16]

Whilst the attitudes of overseas manufacturers may have been hostile to India's process patent regime when it was introduced, limited leverage was available to them given India's largely closed economy prior to 1991. However, this antagonism became especially pronounced as India began to open up to the outside world after the start of economic reforms. There has been consistent growth in exports over the years since market opening, as Indian companies have made further penetration into overseas markets, particularly in terms of "pharmaceutical medicaments".[17] This sub-sector includes the classification of drugs that have been measured and packaged for retail sale abroad, a grouping in which India has particular strengths. Industry figures have shown annual export growth rates for pharmaceutical products in excess of 10% for each year from 1999 to 2004,[18] confirmed in broad terms by government assessments, even despite some aggregation issues (Reserve Bank of India, 2006; Government of India Archive).[19]

[16] This balance may switch in the future, given the IP regime modifications over recent years, which may prompt multinationals to re-engage with the country, either to use local firms for outsourced manufacturing of patented products or to reassert their own presence in the local market through captured subsidiaries, especially in the context of designing new active pharmaceutical ingredients (APIs).

[17] Standard International Trade Classification (SITC) 542.

[18] Note that this includes some wide variations across the years, with, for example, the year 2000 / 01 recording growth of over 20% but 2001 / 02 recording only 11%. Nevertheless, the trend of increased exports appears to be consistent across all years over the past decade. FICCI, page 3. See table 'Growth of Pharmaceutical Exports'.

[19] Note that Indian government figures for pharmaceutical export values appear to be aggregated with basic chemicals and cosmetics—see Table 136, page 208. Despite these issues, however, the figures show export growth over the last few years wholly consistent with commercial assessments.

The increase in pharmaceutical medicament exports to the developed markets, such as those of the United States and the United Kingdom (UK), also appears to have been especially noticeable over the last decade (Reserve Bank of India, 2006),[20] even despite the fact that around 50% of India's drug exports remain targeted towards other countries.[21] Import values of this class of product from India into these two economies would seem to support this perspective and can provide a useful and reliable proxy to India's own assessments. According to the US Department of Commerce, imports of medicaments from India increased from an almost insignificant US$1.1 million in 1995 to US$436.3 million in 2006 with a trade deficit of almost the same amount that year,[22] whilst UK figures from H.M. Revenue and Customs show similar trends, growing from GBP12.9 million in 2001 to GBP63.9 million by the end of calendar year 2006, again with a significant trade deficit in this sub-sector.[23]

The economic opening of the country in combination with an increasing export presence in medicaments may thus help to explain the collision of interests that took place between Indian and overseas pharmaceutical corporations. First, international product patent owners clashed with generic producers as the foreign companies tried once again to compete in the domestic Indian domain, after having reduced their focus on Indian opportunities in the years after the 1970 Patent Act was passed. Second, there was conflict in overseas markets with Indian firms that had begun to accelerate their engagement with

[20] See Table 140 'Exports of Selected Commodities to Principal Countries', page 223, that specifically includes *inter alia* the US, the UK, Germany, the Netherlands and Italy.

[21] Typically other developing countries. See section 'Others' in Table 140 referenced above.

[22] US Dept of Commerce 'Imports of SITC 542—Medicaments' from India 1995–2006. See online statistics database at http://tse.export.gov/ last accessed 20th March 2007. Total imports of SITC 542 for the US in 2006 were US$35 billion, mostly from Europe and Canada, with the US running a deficit of US$18 billion for this sub-sector, which perhaps helps to explain some of the sensitivity of US firms to India's previously relaxed patent regime in areas of high value drugs imitation. See 'Balance of SITC 542'.

[23] UK World Trade for 2001(earliest date available) and 2006—SITC 542. Database of trade statistics at H M Revenue and Customs http://customs.hmrc.gov.uk trade website http://www.uktradeinfo.com both last accessed 20th March 2007. Whilst the UK actually has an overall surplus in medicaments trade worldwide of around GBP3 billion, including GBP80 million with China, it runs a deficit of around GBP45 million with India for SITC 542.

the international trading system by selling their generically produced medicines abroad as part of a newly acquired export-led growth strategy. Indeed, some scholars maintain that it was this shift towards greater liberalisation combined with "India's continuing minimalist IPR regime" that "created a comfortable and stable economic climate where several of the larger firms...ventured out to acquire facilities in developed countries in the 1990's (for example, the USA) [sic]" (Gehl-Sampath, 2007:14).

Perhaps it is not, therefore, surprising that the years after 1991 coincided with an increasing number of disputes in an IP context both bilaterally with specific trading partners such as the US, and multilaterally at the WTO. A number of industrialised economies used WTO Dispute Settlement mechanisms to bring cases against the Indian government complaining about its patent laws,[24] whilst United States Trade Representatives used their annual reports to highlight India's legislative weaknesses.[25] American action in particular was of importance to India given the considerable significance of the US market to the Indian economy,[26] both in terms of exports generally but also as a market for generic manufactured drugs (Beningo and Sloboda, 2006; Chadha, 2005).[27]

All of these moves will have underlined to India the seriousness of intent of western powers to make the country comply with its international obligations. This may help to explain why India's Union government (newly elected in 1998) decided to make at least some modifications to domestic law to accommodate TRIPS patent application mailboxes and exclusive marketing requirements, and also to

---

[24] See WTO Dispute Settlement Procedures against Indian Patent Laws by the US and EU under DS50 and DS79 both in 1997 at http://www.wto.org/english/tratop_e/dispu_e/dispu_subjects_index_e.htm#patents accessed 20th March 2007.

[25] See Indian Embassy in Washington D.C. at http://www.indianembassy.org/indusrel/trade.htm and also United States Trade Representative 'Special 301 Reports' http://www.ustr.gov/Trade_Sectors/Intellectual_Property/Section_Index.html, accessed 20th March 2007. Note that online reports only date back to 2002.

[26] According to Reserve Bank of India provisional figures for Financial Year to April 2006, 16.75% of India's total exports by value were destined for the United States market (US$17.2 billion), making the country India's largest and most important export market. See RBI: 'India Handbook of Statistics Foreign Trade 2005–06' September 2006 last accessed 20th March 2007 at http://www.rbi.org.in/scripts/PublicationsView.aspx?id=8692. Note that US import figures *from* India put the figure for 2005 at US$18.8 billion and 2006 at US$21.8 billion, at http://tse.export.gov/.

[27] Research has estimated that the United States market accounted for 17% of all of India's pharmaceutical exports in the year 2002 / 03.

accede to both the Paris Convention and the Patent Cooperation Treaty, both of which India had hitherto declined to join (Remfrey & Sagar, 1998).[28]

Nevertheless, India was determined to use its full transition period as a developing country under TRIPS rules to enact regulations that would bring its IP protection for patents into full conformance with its obligations, perhaps indicating the domestic sensitivity that such changes would impact. The government passed further amendments to the 1970 Act in 2002 in addition to those of 1999, rather than introducing full new regulations immediately (Sreedharan, 2003).

The introduction of the new laws for pharmaceutical product patents in 2004 became the subject of national debate and considerable controversy, not least because the Bill went further than required to achieve TRIPS compliance. It introduced over 70 new clauses, including those designed to make product patent applications easier (for both domestic and multinational applicants) by simplifying patent grant and application procedures. Intense lobbying was carried out by different industry alliances across the Indian drugs industry.

The Indian pharmaceutical industry was effectively divided amongst itself in seeking to respond to these legislative initiatives, provoking sharp debate between domestic firms who opposed changes to the *status quo*, domestic firms that supported moves towards tighter patent standards as a stimulus to further innovation, and international firms with Indian subsidiaries that welcomed wholeheartedly the embrace of a TRIPS compliant framework. Such divisions are usefully captured by distinctive industry bodies in India, whose members spanned the spectrum of opinion towards the new laws.

There are at least three different lobby groups in the pharmaceutical sector, each with different perspectives: the Indian Drug Manufacturers Association (IDMA) which continues to lobby for the interests of generic producers; the Organisation of Pharmaceutical Producers of India (OPPI) which represents research-based and innovating multinational corporations, as well as local firms such as Ranbaxy and Nicholas Piramal, which are, to a lesser or greater extent, seen as outward looking and innovation driven Indian enterprises (although the extent

[28] See legal comment on what was termed at the time as a "radical change to the present government's approach to intellectual property protection" in October 1998. Note that prior to these legislative moves, TRIPS requirements had been introduced under Presidential Ordnance, which had since lapsed.

to which Ranbaxy can now still be considered as wholly *domestic* in its orientation, since its acquisition by Japanese drugs major Daiichi Sankyo, may be open to debate). Completing the main groupings is the Indian Pharmaceutical Alliance (IPA) which in broad terms supports a middle ground approach to IP regulation (Bhandari, 2004). Whilst the IDMA and IPA have acted in concert over matters of mutual concern in the past, such as over particular points of concern in respect to patent law reform, OPPI tends to pursue its own distinctive agenda.

By contrast, the country's software industry has only a single lobby group, which appears to exhibit a singular unity of purpose in its dealings with government.[29]

A Presidential Decree was actually required for the new law to be issued on 26th December 2004 so as to meet the WTO deadline of 1st January 2005 (Lele, 2005). The Act amending the 1970 legislation was finally passed by the Indian parliament in March 2005 (KPMG International, 2006). There still remain, however, some contentious elements of the new legislation, in that, now three categories of pharmaceutical products exist in India.

The first category consists of those pharmaceutical products that have been granted product patents after 2005 and for which generic production is now forbidden under the new regulations.

The second category relate to drugs that are now either off-patent internationally or comprise those that were granted a patent before 1995, and may still be subject to patent protection outside India. According to research produced on behalf of the UK government, "it is legal for generic companies [in India] to continue to market generic versions of the originator's products in India (or to introduce new generics) [sic]" (Grace, 2004:31). Estimates have been made indicating that this category represents "over 90% of the products on the market in India", which may imply the possibility for further patent disputes in this group before products lose patent protection (ibid.). However, the cost of legal action may make this less attractive.

The third category involves pharmaceuticals which were granted product patents outside India between 1995 and 2005, but which had been already subject to generic research and production within India prior to 1st January 2005, when the new Indian regime came into force. Commentators expect particular controversy over patent license

[29] Op. cit. author's interview with a NASSCOM vice president, February 2006.

management issues for drugs in this group (ibid.) as the new law provides for the ability to continue generic production on payment of a negotiated royalty that is reasonable" with the innovating IP owner (Multinational Monitor Online, 2006). However, no official guidelines appear to exist to determine what exactly constitutes a "reasonable" royalty and it may require litigation, or its threat, to determine further clarity in this context (ibid.).

A compulsory license waiver also exists in the legislation to enable local firms to apply for permission to export from India still-patented drugs to less developed countries in need.[30] Linked to this, it could be surmised that the WTO's decision to make permanent an export waiver that facilitates trade in such generics for countries unable to manufacture pharmaceutical products themselves will continue to be a driver for generic drug exports from India for products in this category (World Trade Organisation, 2005c). However, the recent withdrawal in September 2008 by Natco of its bid to export generic versions of anti-cancer products still under patent to Nepal, which marked the first use of these provisions in India's new law, may in fact indicate the difficulties and inhibitors prevalent in securing use of available flexibilities.[31]

Further potentially contentious areas also exist, such as sections of the Act designed to prevent extended patenting of existing drugs products known as the process of "ever-greening", and these have already been subject to judicial review in India's legal system and have caused great controversy (Hiddleston, 2007). For example, the rejection by the Madras High Court, under principles of questioning a new product's enhanced "efficacy" over a previous version of a 2007 bid by Novartis to enforce a patent application for their anti-cancer drug, prompted fierce debate from all sides of the argument about both the constitutionality and fairness of key sections of India's patent laws (Basheer and Reddy, 2008).

[30] This provision is encapsulated in Section 92A of India's Patent Law amendments.

[31] Natco had objected to the fact that India's High Court had granted a hearing for the patent holders to make a defence in both cases, but Natco failed to make its case that such a hearing was not legal under TRIPS or India's domestic law. See C. H. Unnikrishnan, 'Natco withdraws plea on making patented cancer drugs', *LiveMint Wall Street Journal*, 28th September 2008 at <http://www.livemint.com/2008/09/28214903/Natco-withdraws-plea-on-making.html>, last accessed 15th December 2008.

Despite these areas of potential dispute (Basheer, 2005; Bhandari, 2004), it can still be argued that the Indian patent protection regime has now fundamentally shifted, and that, whilst debates continue over the extent to which India's 2005 amendments make its IP legal regime fully TRIPS-compliant, India now appears focused on promoting an innovative and export-driven strategy through membership of the international trading system.[32] In this context, the 2005 patent protection regulations would seem to exemplify the country's move away from import substitution in the same way that the earlier 1970 Act had captured the spirit of its then inward looking policy approach.

These developments have brought into sharper relief those companies whose income streams were derived from creating variants from patented products which formed a significant part of the sector's annual revenues. In one sense, there is a challenge presented to them to move their business models away from imitation and into innovation. However, on the other hand, some commentators have pointed out that in fact, some of the world's most popular drugs have recently come off-patent which may mitigate potential losses due to the increased flexibility that off-patent status allows generic producers. For example, since the turn of the millennium, four of the top ten retail drugs, including Prozac and Claritin, have ceased to enjoy patent protection and it is estimated that over US$40 billion worth of drugs are set to come off-patent in the next few years, which could act as a major stimulus to the generics industry in India (Kopenski, 2002). Not only does this growth in out-of-patent popular drug compositions influence counter prices in international markets, it also could help to maintain market revenues for generic producers in India, even with new domestic legal constraints (Digital Vector, 2005).

It would, however, be overly simplistic to characterise the entire Indian pharmaceutical industry's response to government initiatives on IP system reform as wholly unwelcome, as the changes in patent protection that came into force in 2005 were in fact seen as distinctly positive by some parts of the Indian drugs production industry. Those involved in negotiations have pointed out that there had, in fact, been long running tensions within the sector itself for some years, between

---

[32] Based on a number of private, first-hand interviews with industry leaders and politicians in 2004, Bhandari posits that incentives behind India's IP realignment might have included securing improvements in India's bargaining position in international negotiations at the WTO by providing an "example of leadership".

generic producers on the one hand and those seeking to move up the value chain and create international alliances on the other.[33] These tensions were of a similar nature to the relationships facing generic producers with foreign multinational interests, whereby one group wished to maintain the flexible *status quo* under the original 1970 Act and the other promoting to government the need to strengthen the IP regime.

Innovation-oriented companies, such as Dr Reddy's and Ranbaxy, have looked upon improved IP protection enthusiastically. Distinctive perspectives on tightening the IP regime were put forward by innovating companies as compliance rules were being planned in that, they made clear their belief that a strengthened IP regime would enable them to infuse more funds into the development process and allow them to enhance their credibility with potential transnational partners, and that they viewed the new regulations as a functional response of doing good business.[34] Innovating Indian firms have even considered major acquisitions within the European pharmaceutical industry (Financial Times Asia Edition 13th March, 2007).[35]

Moreover, the OPPI had long made it clear that the organisation welcomed stronger patent laws and emphasised in its public comments on the debates that such initiatives "encourage, stimulate and sustain innovation in the field of pharmaceuticals" that could "lead to a more progressive healthcare system and availability of newer and better medicines [for India]" (Organisation of Pharmaceutical Producers of India, 2008).

Importantly, not everyone agrees with this perspective, particularly inside India, and debates continue amongst lobby groups, industry bodies, legal commentators and academics, and will likely do so for some time to come. One interesting angle to this mosaic were those who called into question the underlying relationships between types of pharmaceutical innovation and perceived necessities for product patent protection in developing countries such as India at all, citing

---

[33] Op. cit. author interview, official at the Indian Mission to the WTO, Geneva, July 2005.

[34] Ibid.

[35] It can be forcefully argued that such actions show Indian pharma is no longer an "infant industry" requiring special protection measures. The bid was subsequently withdrawn by Ranbaxy, which itself was later to become the subject of a successful takeover bid by a Japanese pharmaceutical firm, acting as a further illustration of the sector's international visibility.

limited evidence of benefits for emerging economies in embracing developed-country levels of IP compliance.[36] It is therefore important to recognise the depth of feelings that abound in respect to TRIPS compliance, the disagreements still ongoing about the current position of Indian firms on the innovative spectrum, and the potential future trajectory of the country's pharmaceutical industry as a whole.

In competitive terms, some Indian industry observers have pointed to China's potential as a centre of pharmaceutical development as one possible threat to the future development of India's industry, particularly given cheaper Chinese labour costs and the more flexible employment regulations that are in place in the People's Republic (Digital Vector, 2005). However, other research has highlighted weaknesses in the country's capabilities, pointing out China's lower levels of chemistry abilities, its own focus on traditional medicine as a competitor to western methods and its language barriers as disincentives for greater international engagement by pharmaceutical companies with mainland companies (Grace, 2004). Whilst China's IP strategies in patent enforcement remain a cause for concern amongst pharmaceutical industry managers, in keeping with many other industries (Ernst & Young, 2006), there have been some noticeable improvements in the country's approach to IP in general that has filtered through to the pharmaceutical industry.[37]

China has a markedly different export profile in medicaments to that of India, especially with major developed markets such as the US and UK.[38] Import values from China into these economies are far less than those from India, totalling just US$16 million and GBP6 million respectively for 2005. Indeed, both the US and UK run healthy

[36] This argument centres on assessments that there is limited R&D intensity carried out in new chemical entity (NCE) research in India, and that continuing development of successful generics manufacture does not require such forms of protection mandated by TRIPS. See Sudip Chaudhuri, 'Is Product Patent Protection Necessary in Developing Countries for Innovation: R&D by Indian Pharmaceutical Companies After TRIPS', Working Paper Series, Indian Institute of Management, No 614, 2007, Kolkata.

[37] See the discussion by Pantesco on the creation of China's new national Judicial Court of Intellectual Property, and also the successful resolution by of Pfizer's Viagra China Patent Infringement Case, June 2006, BBC News, <http://news.bbc.co.uk/2/hi/business/5047640.stm>, accessed 28th February 2007.

[38] China combines Medical and Pharmaceutical Products and includes Chinese Medicines and Pharma Goods—see op. cit. China Statistical Yearbook 2006, 'Main Export Commodities', Table 19–9, page 754.

trade surpluses with the People's Republic in pharmaceutical medicaments,[39] with China appearing to concentrate instead on bulk exports of vitamins, Chinese medicaments, medical products and ancillary medical materials.[40] This may help to explain different assessments of threat made by western companies about China versus India, and may be one of the reasons why it has been India at the centre of IP disputes in a pharmaceutical context over recent years. Nevertheless, whilst the Chinese drugs industry is perhaps less strategically significant than India's at present, this balance may change in the future as local innovative skills improve and further foreign engagement takes place (Grace, 2004).

It is not simply in matters of intellectual property that the Indian government has taken an active and interventionist role in the operation of the country's pharmaceutical industry. High external tariffs of up to 55% in combined duties and taxes[41] have made imported foreign drugs artificially high in the domestic arena that has, to some extent, had the effect of cushioning the local producers from international markets for some time (International Policy Network, 2004). To counter balance some of the negative impact on domestic availability of major drugs, tariffs have been combined with domestic price controls as a long-standing part of the Union's policies in the pharmaceutical sector, although originally with a very small set of products being subject to control. The Drug Price Control Order of 1995 and the related establishment of the National Pharmaceutical Pricing Authority in 1997 were introduced along with price control orders on the leading 74 consumer drugs within the domestic market "to ensure availability at reasonable prices of essential and lifesaving and prophylactic medicines of good quality" (Pharmaceutical and Drug Manufacturers).

Initiatives towards greater price control have, however, continued and widened under the Dr. Manmohan Singh's government, particularly after a recent order issued by the Supreme Court of India that reaffirmed the national government's duty to make essential medicines available to the public (Narrain, 2004). The political perspective may have been partly shaped by a widely held belief that many domestic manufacturers and retailers maintain artificially high drug prices for

[39] SITC 542. See previously footnoted trade data in this chapter.

[40] These definitions are taken from the US Dept of Commerce and the UK Revenue and Customs trade statistics databases.

[41] Compared to, for example, equivalent totals of 0.01% in Malaysia.

the local population, well beyond what many consider to be cost plus a reasonable mark-up, in order to sustain them with profit margins that help to make the exported generics that much more attractive. Some prices paid by consumers for common staples have been reported being up to 32 times what the National Pharmaceutical Pricing Authority considers as reasonable (British Medical Journal Online, 2004).

In November 2006, expected intervention by the government to fix trade margins on commonly used medicines led to voluntary price reductions on a number of different types of basic drugs despite ongoing disagreements within the industry as to whether retailers, generic producers or government licensing controls and taxes are to blame for the disconnection between local production costs and local prices (Hindu Business Line, 2006; Mukherjee, 2006). The generic producers would now appear to be in a position where their future strategy will be shaped by the country's new domestic and international legal environment, which they will need to accommodate in their development plans.

It is useful to contrast the regulatory battles involving tariffs, pricing control orders, patent protection and commercial exporting strategies that characterise the Indian drugs market with the relative disengagement from such principles exhibited in its dealings with the country's software industry. The dichotomy between these two sectors may stem from the fact that pharmaceuticals established itself first as a domestic industry operating under the protection of import substitution strategies from which it only latterly launched an export-led drive for growth, whereas the software sector "was export-oriented from the outset, recognizing [sic] the potential for software exports and the futility of import-substitution" (Sridharan, 2004:31–32).

6.3 *The Indian Software Industry, Copyright Controls and the State*

In India, the software industry and the related enabled services markets are protected by copyright, administered by the Ministry of Human Resource Development. The original 1957 Copyright Act has undergone considerable refinement and strengthening over the years in response to three main developments: the evolution of the industry domestically; the development of international norms; and the demands of the industry's corporations themselves. The current Indian copyright regime has been generally characterised as meeting international standards, even despite some sharp criticisms of enforcement practices from some quarters (Nollen, 2004:36).

The software sector has enjoyed long-standing support from the Union Government of India, with both structural and legislative encouragement over many years that have helped to sustain successful growth of the sector in both absolute terms of its revenue generation and in relative terms of its increasing significance as part of the wider Indian national economy. Revenue and growth estimates for the IT industry in India, published by NASSCOM for the financial year 2005/06, predict growth over the previous year of 28%, reaching revenues of US$36.3 billion for 2005 of which just over US$23 billion worth are expected to have been exported, with about two-thirds of these destined for the United States market. This accounts for almost 5% of the nation's GDP (NASSCOM, 2006).

Its significance as a national icon of success should not be underestimated and a number of scholars maintain that its predominantly export-oriented earnings bias has helped the country in a number of different ways (Balasubramanyam and Balasubramanyam, 1996a). First, the export focus has fostered international partnerships that have laid foundations for further technological investment between domestic and international firms. These have also led to socially useful spillovers in priority local sectors, such as the drive towards e-government (to help reduce corruption and speed up local decision-making) and the greater engagement of local people in economic development—for example, by helping to develop language independent software that is better able to adapt to the many different dialects across the nation (Bagga, Kenniston and Mathur, 2005).

Second, export facing markets promote knowledge acquisition through contact with foreign business practices, their strategic goals, and the processes used to achieve them, which facilitate much needed learning on next stage challenges as Indian companies grow within the international business sector. Finally, the foreign currency income assists with the nation's balance of payments schedules and helps to reduce the chance of crises such as that which overtook the economy in 1991 from being repeated (D'Costa, 2004a).

This support for the software sector should also be seen in the wider context of India's strategy for national economic and technological development. The distinctive and supporting measures from government enjoyed by this sector in its early years during the 1980's should not be interpreted as just an unexpected aberration from the previously rigid state planning of Prime Minister Jawaharlal Nehru's soviet-centric community. Rather, a number of scholars have maintained that instead, they should be seen more as an expression of disappointment in the quality of outputs from the central planning process, whereby the confidence India's national elite in the country's ability to find solutions to its ongoing development agenda had undergone "a severe trauma" (Bagga et al., 2005:26) in the years since Independence.

In this context (ibid.; Franda, 2002:27) it is appropriate to see Rajiv Ghandi's support for the fledgling software market in India as part of a wider exercise to re-orientate the administration to sustain "broad based development" as part of the Prime Minister's personal vision that "recognised the importance of information technology for future economic growth". The software market, especially, was a suitable target as it was then far less regulated as an entity in terms of quotas and licensing regulations that heavily blighted other industries (such as textiles, manufacturing and motor industry production), largely because the sector was a relatively new phenomenon in India at that time. Therefore, the supporting initiatives introduced by Ghandi at this pivotal moment in the sector's history should be seen as a way of recognising software as a distinct industry in its own right for the first time and one to which "major policy liberalisations" could thus be directed from scratch (Heeks, 1996:44).

The emergence and growth of the Indian software industry that has occurred over the last 20 years can be seen to have taken place in three distinct phases and the evolution of the country's IP regime can best be understood by tracing linkages with the characteristics of each of these development periods. In terms of its behaviour and priorities over this time, the industry moved from knowledge accumulation and initial market entry during the mid 1980's and early 1990's, through to full engagement, market consolidation and high growth from the mid 1990's until the turn of the millennium. It has now, over the last few years, started to concentrate on innovation in its third phase of growth, as part of a globally expansionist strategy for the modern era. Each phase can be seen to be associated with sympathetic government responses and initiatives that were designed to shape further success and provide routes to the next stage of development.[42]

---

[42] There are two particularly useful discussions that explore the theme of staged development of India's software sector from both industrial and governmental per-

6.4 *Knowledge Acquisition in India's Technology Growth*

The first phase can be termed the "knowledge accumulation" period for the industry where private sector actors learnt the principles of doing business in the sector, initiated market entry for their organisations and created pioneering business models to generate early profits. The "codified knowledge" (D'Costa, 2004a:1–26) that they created for themselves about markets, customers and delivery methods, was largely publicly available to all participants and relatively easy to acquire. During this period, many of the major names in Indian software first entered the market, such as Tata Group and Wipro, often moving into IT from less technological staples—perhaps driven by the incentives of first mover status into the relatively unregulated sector[43]—which were later joined by technology-specific ventures as the market grew. In this way, the structure of the early industry in India can be seen to have been characterised by a blend between traditional organisations that moved into the market after having established their credentials and financial soundness in other sectors, alongside genuine entrepreneurial start-ups such as Mastek and InfoSys, both of which were founded in the Indian IT sector from scratch during the 1980's.

All of these early pioneers created distinct business models that focused on arbitraging labour cost advantages of Indian technologists in onsite development projects for western clients under a technique known within the IT industry as "body-shopping", in a business framework that has been described as "the export of labour" (Heeks, 1998:15). In this period, entire project teams were often imported en-masse by western customers, along with their associated team leadership structures and programming specialisations, with only project managers, business analysts and specialist consultants being derived from the local client's workforce.[44]

---

spectives in some detail. First Sridharan: 'Evolving Towards Innovation', pp. 27–50. Second, a paper by Richard Heeks from 1998, in which he makes remarkably accurate analyses about India's future trajectory and export led priorities: 'The Uneven Profile of Indian Software Exports'.

[43] For instance, until it entered the IT marketplace, Wipro was better known as the Western India Vegetable Products Company whose main outputs were cooking oil, soap and related domestic products. For further details about the company's history, see their website http://www.wipro.com/ last referenced August 2006.

[44] During this time Mastek became a familiar name to many companies across the UK, with many drawing heavily on integrated Indian project development teams to

Government action during this first phase "carefully nurtured" (Bagga, 2005:29) the early years of the industry, with its Computer Policy of 1984 marking the formal beginnings of official support by the Government of India for the emerging software sector. This approach included a number of related liberalisations that were critical to building a platform for future expansion. First, access for market entry into software was completely de-licensed[45] and refocused away from supporting the operations of government-funded supercomputer project which greatly reduced timescales, paperwork and administrative burdens that had to be incurred by new start-ups keen to enter the market.

Second, regulations pertaining to quotas and permits on importing foreign computer hardware and international commodity software[46] were relaxed under the 1984 policy, and were further relaxed two years later under the country's Computer Software Export Development regulations within the New Software Policy of 1986. This later initiative enabled much needed physical high technology to be used by these new companies as India's own conventional hardware sector was largely non-existent at that time, which meant that the nascent domestic software sector had nothing similar to the product sophistication available to start-up firms in the United States.

Third, the use of operational satellite technology for private communications was permitted for use by software companies, which greatly facilitated private line communications with international clients. This development came after "Texas Instruments gifted the link to the government and began software export operations from Bangalore", even though the satellite link itself remained state controlled until 1992 when private satellites became possible and opened the market even further (Sridharan, 2004:32). An exemption for IT companies was promulgated that freed them from paying excise taxes on

---

achieve cost and time deadlines for major business system developments. Author's own experience.

[45] Prior to this, a great deal of software industry's focus had been on support for the government's own supercomputer production and specialist hardware export policy ("supercomputers" are computers with very high computational power used in defence services, code breaking and with algorithms connected to nuclear fission). Their design and production by India was a response to America's then ban on the export of such technology to places such as India and other potentially suspect localities.

[46] Typically word processing, spreadsheet management and multitasking operating system software.

required software imports, which helped to reduce the costs of obtaining operating system and development support platforms critical for the establishment of skills levels, internal training routines and professional familiarisation with the latest products that formed a vital input into the Indian software industry's service delivery model.

In response to these incentives, software service revenues between 1984 and 1986 jumped over 40% to US$38.9 million although, as a counterbalance, scholars point out that, under a labour exporting model, much of the advantages in business sales growth can be consumed by relatively high operating costs outside of the wage bill (Heeks, 1998). These were largely expressed in terms of travel costs, overseas work visa application fees, staff living expenses whilst abroad and the associated management costs of dealing with so many employees working around the world on different projects.[47]

This positive progress made by government in its business support initiatives contrasted markedly with the picture in respect of the country's IP regime development at this point in time. The 1984 Software Copyright Regulations, which had been designed to strengthen the original 1957 Copyright Act with additional rules more sympathetic to high technology had had little impact on the problem of software piracy that was emerging, especially in respect to the piracy of business software utilities by all types of Indian corporations (Heeks, 1996).

As a result of these negative developments, India's attitude towards copyright goods came into the radar of United States trade protection monitors under the USTR's Special 301 measures during the early 1990's, in addition to patent law deficiencies that were generating concerns in respect of pharmaceutical companies. Over this period, reports indicate that the country was also pressured in multilateral talks at GATT conferences by American officials (Raghavan, 1993).

It may be useful to consider why such limited progress was made in terms of the country's IP sophistication at this time and in its enforcement regime during this period, especially given the cultural and historical legacies enjoyed by India in this context. Two interrelated reasons appear salient and are directly linked to the emerging structure of the industry.

---

[47] Some estimates have put this cost figure as high as 40% of sales for overseas assignments, especially in areas of high daily living costs like London. For example, Heeks 1998, page 2.

First, most of the intellectual property value being created at that time by Indians was actually being built abroad under the full IP control of client companies and thus tight standards of domestic protection were not yet necessarily of direct interest to Indian software service companies and may not therefore have been on the critical path of the boardroom agenda. Indeed, the main asset being accumulated by staff at this time was knowledge and experience of advanced software development processes, practised, refined and accumulated overseas during international projects, sometimes even under the tutelage of their foreign hosts.[48] Thus, it can be argued that the predominant concern for Indian business leaders at that time would have been to repatriate and exploit that knowledge back home as part of moving from the first to second stage of industrial growth, rather than with a concern about domestic piracy.

Second, scholars have argued that higher levels of piracy can actually be expected during early business development stages. For example, the costs associated with installing fully licensed and supported software across multiple machines could place considerable burdens on new entrant companies (and not just those in the software industry itself). In circumstances such as these, it has been forcefully argued that piracy can actually help achieve business objectives by "providing a wide base of software skills [and by] providing Indian users with the latest technology...saving greatly on foreign exchange" and "one might therefore recommend it as a strategy for countries with immature industries" (Heeks, 1996:135).

Third, the copyright legislation that had been created by the Union government under the 1957 Act, despite some amendments in the 1980's and early 1990's, facilitated relatively weak copyright controls, including permitting the practice of reverse engineering strategies as part of flexible "fair use" definitions that enabled novice software engineers to observe how internal algorithms of market leading solution packages actually worked.[49] This upset elements in America especially

[48] Author's own experience, who, at that time, worked as part of a UK based consultancy supplying advisory and training services directly to European multinationals and regularly led training sessions of advanced programming and design techniques to groups of Indians who had been hired by a client but where certain specialist skills, such as databases, might be lacking.

[49] See specific criticisms of India's copyright implementation in respect to reverse engineering by the IIPA in their 2001 'Special 301 Report. India', page 393, claiming that some sections of the legislation still granted "an overbroad exception per-

which typically characterised behaviour of this kind as a form of legalised "free riding", not permitted under its own regulations,[50] a perspective that could be considered somewhat ironic given America's own lackadaisical attitude to foreign-owned copyright material during the 19th Century.[51] There was, however, some useful progress in IP developments towards the end of this first period of the industry's evolution when India passed substantial copyright reforms in 1994 which helped to move the country's legal framework towards a more internationally acceptable structure,[52] although even these efforts were not without their critics (Beherens and Levary, 2008).[53]

6.5 *IP Controls in the Expanding Indian Services Market*

The second phase of India's software and service sector development, from the middle of the 1990's to the turn of the millennium, could be termed a period of market engagement and organic growth for the

mitting the decompilation of computer programs". Even as late as 2008, the IIPA found India's proposed new copyright amendments to be providing "overly broad exceptions" in a number of respects, including copying. See International Intellectual Property Alliance, '2008 Special 301 Report' Submitted to the U.S. Trade Representative. Available online and last accessed 2nd April 2009 at <http://www.ustr.gov/assets/Trade_Sectors/Intellectual_Property/Special_301_Public_Submissions_2008/asset_upload_file141_14486.pdf>.

[50] For a discussion on American attitudes to "free-riding" see op. cit. Maskus, Intellectual Property Rights in the Global Economy, especially Chapter 3 'Globalisation and the Economics of Intellectual Property Rights', page 45.

[51] During the 19th Century, the works of European authors were routinely copied by American publishers. Commentators trace this approach to what has been termed the "antiproperty" rhetoric found in the judgement of Stowe vs Thomas, in the 1853 American Circuit Court of Appeals, where the court found in favour of a domestic defendant against a European (German) plaintiff who had been complaining about unauthorised translation and copying of his work. These attitudes were further extended during the "cheap books" movement of the 1890's.

[52] These reforms did much to assuage US attitudes over India's approach to intellectual property protection for software, whereby India's copyright protection mechanisms were now seen by US authorities as "on par with international standards", although concerns have persisted. See United States Trade Representative report from 1996 USTR Document Archive, '1996 National Trade Esimate-India' [sic], available online and last referenced 2nd April 2009 at <http://www.ustr.gov/Document_Library/Reports_Publications/1996/1996_National_Trade_Estimate/1996_National_Trade_Esimate-India.html?ht=>. See especially the section on "Copyrights".

[53] The issue of reverse engineering remains a highly controversial area of copyright and continues to be a source of potential confusion, tension and legal uncertainty across the industry. See also views of the IIPA.

industry. The most significant change in business model that evolved during this time was a move away from the export of labour towards the export of services—onshore to offshore from the customer's perspective—and the accumulation of what scholars have termed critically valuable "tacit knowledge" vested in increasingly vertical specialisations within key western business sectors (D'Costa, 2004a:56). These have included areas such as banking, insurance, logistics, general finance and healthcare, with much of the initial engagement having been begun in the earlier era of labour exporting of technology programmers, but where initial contacts and reputations already made were now directed towards exploiting a different value proposition: the overseas development centre.

It can be argued that the catalyst for this accelerated pace of expansion during the second half of the 1990's was a coincidence of two major projects emanating from the western world that were ideal candidates for an offshore delivery and solutions model: the millennium date change and the eurocurrency conversion. These two projects dominated the technology change management agendas of many international corporations[54] and during the four years from 1996, revenues for IT services by Indian companies more than doubled to over US$8 billion by the end of the decade with much work devoted across many projects to these important tasks (NASSCOM, 2006).

Whilst attempting to spread the project load and reduce dependence on pure code conversions, many organisations had up to 30% of their revenues devoted to this type of Year 2000 Conversion (Y2K) work. (D'Costa, 2004b). A particularly distinctive characteristic of much of the work at this time was that, unlike during earlier phases of the industry where work had been carried out on client sites, in this case, in order to execute the conversion tasks successfully, the designs from the client's original software innovations together with almost all of the original program coding and change specifications were now held in India. This meant that these collaterals became subject to Indian

[54] It is important to recognise that solutions to the two-digit year computerised date problem (the worrisome prediction of a time shift in the world's computers at the end of 1999 back to 1900 instead of on to 2000) did not just involve the repetitive tasks of updating variable lengths in old COBOL programs from two to four digits (although this was an important element of the service) but, often, actually included version upgrades of software systems and even complete platform migrations, where compatibility issues across different software layers needed to be handled. Not all of this was always billed directly to a Y2K project itself. [Author's personal experience as a senior consultant to a number of corporate Y2K readiness teams in 1996 to 1999].

corporate controls and government legislated regulation, with privacy and anti-piracy protection becoming the contracted responsibility of Indian supplier companies. During this time, the existence of a long-standing propensity towards effective IP controls within India (whether in fact a true reflection or not) also began to be used in the marketing and presentation material by Indian companies seeking to attract high value outsourcing contracts as part of an increased service-export expansion, first as a complement to, and second as a replacement for, their traditional labour exporting models.[55]

In terms of IP regime development during this second phase of the Indian software industry's evolution, much progress was made in terms of both legislative enactments and enforcement characteristics. Building on reforms to the Copyright Act that were made in 1994, further improvements were passed in 1999 which were particularly targeted at correcting software specific weaknesses of earlier amendments.[56] Pressure to secure these legislative developments could be explained by the increased visibility amongst senior executives about the importance of Indian legislative restraints in the area of intellectual property, along with the remedies and constraints available to them to enforce their international contract mandates. It can be argued that the commercial imperatives of this period thus helped to make government responses about IP protection part of the corporate agenda as well as the political one, for both domestic export-oriented suppliers and international customers seeking to use these services.

This may help to explain why the climate against IP infringement began to change during the second half of the 1990's within the industry itself. Developments of this kind were greatly facilitated by organisations such as NASSCOM, the Confederation of Indian Industry (CII) and the Computer Society of India (CSI) acting at the behest of their memberships, the majority of whom were drawn from private organisations with many being leaders in the IT and software services markets. Links between NASSCOM and the American Business Software

[55] Author's personal experience as a consultant working with clients using services from Mastek, London, 1993–1996. A similar mantra could be heard even more recently, where the author met individuals representing a number of outsourcing suppliers who promoted the business and legal culture of India as being one of the unique selling points (USPs) to both small and medium sized industries in western countries when compared with the alternatives [author's experience, Mumbai, February 2006].

[56] The "fair use" exceptions for software decompilation and program flow observation continue to be codified in specific subsections under Article 52 of the Copyright Act.

Alliance (BSA), which had been established during the early part of that decade, were also substantially strengthened during this period in order to help build behavioural norms for protection criteria and enforcement standards across India. In this way, it could be said that NASSCOM developed something of a dual role, on the one hand, transmitting international best-practice into India in co-operation with overseas corporations anxious about their own IP, whilst on the other, lobbying to secure commercial objectives from domestic enterprises about necessary IP policy changes to the Indian government.

This emerging attitude towards IP can be seen as an active policy-centric partnership, with the business world increasingly at the forefront of negotiations over the content and structure of actual policy developments.[57] Education to the wider national audience in the principles of IP and in its importance across the economy was a particular focus of these activities during the second half of the 1990's. One particularly important outcome from this relationship was the creation of a Certificate of Recognition that defined accepted corporate behaviour in matters relating to IP controls, effectively creating an anti-piracy kitemark that was offered to businesses across different sectors of the economy and into all types of corporations, which substantially expanded the scope of IP regulatory education than had previously been the case.

Indeed, NASSCOM's view is that, even today, this large-scale use of vertical market linkages across the panoply of user industries such as the motor trade and textiles on the one hand and specialist SMEs like architectural designers and accountancy firms on the other, continues to offer the best means of reducing piracy rates across the country.[58] Additionally, an anti-piracy hotline[59] was established in 1994 to persuade those observing software piracy to do something positive about it and this attitude was supplemented by billboards, brochures

[57] Op. cit. author's interview with a NASSCOM vice president, February 2006.

[58] Ibid. In particular, it was pointed out that non-software corporations were a particular focus of NASSCOM activity, with all manner of niche products such as computer aided design software and three dimensional modelling solutions being just as likely to be pirated as more conventional packages like Microsoft's Word and PowerPoint.

[59] Although it was admitted that this line and its outcomes had not been not a priority for police authorities, the number provided has the 1-600 free phone format to encourage use across the country. Each complaint is initially investigated by NASSCOM themselves before passing the details on to an appropriate authority for further enforcement action as required. See also the NASSCOM <http://www.nasscom.in/Nasscom/templates/NormalPage.aspx?id=6246>, accessed September 2006.

and other direct marketing tactics to try and embed a philosophical approach in the wider user community.

It was not just the user community that needed an educational centred approach. NASSCOM and the BSA have, over the last decade, spearheaded the training of police officers across the regions of the country so that they can better understand what exactly is software as a copyrightable material and how licensing (and thus infringement) works in practice in the corporate environment.[60] This has been far from a trivial undertaking, given that enforcement is the responsibility of state government in federal India and that each police authority will have its own priorities for manpower use and investigative agenda. In NASSCOM's view, this initiative represents a key ingredient to ensure greater understanding amongst the enforcement community[61] although by 1999, according to an official government study, only in seven states (of 30) did there exist a dedicated police unit that dealt specifically with copyright related crimes and that a number of states had officially admitted "that enforcement of copyright law in general [was] not satisfactory in India" (Government of India Ministry of Human Resource Development, 1999).

It can be argued that these initiatives had a beneficial effect on the levels of corporate software piracy and related attitudes. According to IIPA's own figures, piracy levels as a percentage of legitimate installed software programs fell from 78% in 1995 to 61% in 1999, although the absolute amounts involved increased in response to the growth of the software industry and the country's economy as a whole, rising from loses of US$114.6 million to US$160.2 million for the same period (IIPA Special 301 Report for India, 2001).

Union government support for this expansionary phase of growth was not just vested in a tightening of IP controls but instead encompassed both business support, manpower expansion and infrastructure development. First, a number of Software Technology Parks (STPs) were established, with the first ones being deliberately located close to the already bustling "electronic cities" of Pune and Bangalore, with

[60] The most recent example of this is the creation of the Mumbai Cyber Lab for Police training and cyber crime countermeasures.

[61] Op. cit. author's interview with a NASSCOM vice president, February 2006, who was especially emphatic that measures such as this had to be part of a long-term strategy that required perhaps a 10-year development timescale to achieve desirable results.

the latter in particular having long since been a centre of technology development with Prime Minister Nehru himself declaring it as the country's first "electric city" in the 1950's (Lateef, 1997).

These initiatives had the overall objective of relieving expansion pressure on the Mumbai technology hub of Nariman Point (Heeks, 1998). These new development environments were used to promote the benefits of clustered knowledge exchange as well as providing both infrastructure support and first stage incubation for smaller and second mover companies that could allow them to initiate their business models in a sympathetic environment. This was especially important as the ongoing deficiencies of infrastructure quality in the wider country meant that often, smaller organisations would have difficulties in securing even the most basic of telephony services, whereas the STPs took care of these issues (Government of India Ministry of Communications and Information Technology).

Second, the propensity towards clustering coincided with the arrival of the internet, which was to become a critical technological development for software service delivery during the second half of the 1990's as it moved communication options with international clients away from just a channel of dialogue to one that could encompass multiple media, including email for project communication and progress management, with associated jointly run online demonstrations of partly completed work. The internet could also facilitate the exchange and testing of discrete modules between supplier and customer during development, as well as introducing new forms of technology assisted project and business support services. It can be argued that such a radical development as this had the same kind of impact on smaller and medium sized service suppliers that the deregistration of private satellites had had on larger corporations a few years earlier, and enabled this sector of the market to grow and develop particularly well (Nambiar, 2006).[62]

Third, there was an increasing recognition amongst the professional community that manpower shortages of suitably skilled programming

[62] For the purpose of useful comparison, Avendus, an Indian investment bank and mergers and acquisitions specialist to the Indian IT services sector, segments the market into large, medium and small capitalised companies using the following structure: large-cap are those with capitalisation of more then US$1 billion; medium-cap are those with between US$100 million and US$1 billion; small-cap include those with market capitalisation less than US$100 million. Added to this last segment are the numerous small but high value private enterprises who have not yet issued their initial public offering (IPO) on a stock market.

staff were likely to emerge and that future market needs could not be satisfied solely by the graduate communities from the handful of elite Indian Institutes of Technology which were located around the country (Partasarathi and Joseph, 2004). It was realised that such shortfalls were likely to impact on the IT sector's ability to reach its ambitious growth targets into the future. In response, the new Union government in 1998 introduced a number of initiatives as part of an Information Technology Action Plan to promote IT across the country under a policy known as "Target ITEX-50", standing for "IT service exports to reach US$50 billion by 2008" (Government of India IT Task Force, ITEX-50). It had the personal backing of the new Prime Minister, Atal Bihari Vajpayee, who promoted IT as one of his government's top five priorities.[63] Significantly, scholars have pointed out that "the chief executives of leading private sector software companies [were] fully involved with these task forces" (Partasarathi and Joseph, 2004:89).

Under these schemes, the Union government supported the creation of private sector IT learning schools covering the full range of skills required for software production, including design, coding and testing. These schools were to be established through the mechanisms of both formal accreditation and policy liberalisations. In particular, the government mandated that technology education should be regarded as part of the less regulated "IT Services" sector. In order to provide incentives for the establishment of these independent IT schools, the policy authorised the creation of special IT education bonds to help Indian banks and other financial institutions raise capital to fund specialist lending which was then to be offered to appropriate organisations under specially low interest rates as part of the principles of treating human resource development as a "priority lending sector" (Government of India IT Task Force, Human Resource Development). In this way, by the end of 1999, "there were 1,832 private educational institutions that trained over 68,000 computer software professionals", which at least partially addressed the objective to relieve skills bottlenecks being experienced during the ongoing expansion in demand for all types of software specialist that was occurring at this time (Partasarathi and Joseph, 2004:90).

[63] This policy was first announced in a televised address in March of that year by the Prime Minister. Along with tangible help such as infrastructure and training assistance, the policy included a range of tax and customs relief incentives.

6.6 *Innovation and Global Expansion in the Indian Software Industry*

The Indian software industry entered its third stage of growth at the start of the new millennium and found itself presented with both challenges in a rapidly changing international market and opportunities available to exploit India's established leadership in offshore software and services provision. In response, the new decade has been characterised by an emphasis by Indian firms on moving up the value chain of product and service outputs, which has increased both the value and knowledge content of corporate products. From 2000 to 2005, the Indian IT Services and IT Enabled Services industry has seen a compound annual growth rate of 28%, which was a remarkable achievement in performance given the issues that were emerging by the turn of the millennium (NASSCOM, 2006). It can be argued that these trends also helped to reinforce the significance of IP regulations and the enforcement of knowledge goods protection as a central pillar of both corporate and government strategy.

The immediate challenges for the industry as the new century began crossed a number of dimensions. First, as part of the global technology slowdown that emerged between 2000 and 2001 and that originated with American shareholder pessimism about internet companies' future profitability, India suffered lost markets in its principle export partners especially within the United States.

Second, in India specifically, this international trend was combined with the cessation of the recurring revenue streams of the Year 2000 Conversion (Y2K) and the Euro Conversion projects, which had come to their natural conclusion by the end of 2001. It can be argued that this rapid collapse of two highly profitable parts of the software business in India may have been a driver in helping the domestic software market to refocus on seeking new opportunities to use the capacity that had become available within the industry. External events of this kind can have a considerable motivating effect to senior executives in their strategic planning objectives.[64]

---

[64] The author's own experience would suggest that at least some of the downturn in the international software market may have actually assisted Indian companies as their cost advantages for software development became very attractive to downsizing American and European firms keen to reduce staff costs but also needing to sustain

Third, the rise of China was already being observed within both the business and political communities. The leadership of the Union government and key Indian corporations combined in jointly exploring the relative opportunities and threats presented by this new strategic actor, whose workforce and cost bases directly challenged the Indian value proposition to western customers.

The China-focused initiatives included leadership visits by both countries' premiers to establish good working ground rules given the long-standing suspicion with which Chinese ambitions had been viewed in India, and vice versa in Beijing (Swamy, 2001). Additionally, there were corporate-centred explorations about horizontal linkages between technology firms, which included early negotiations for the establishment of Indian overseas development centres using Chinese technology hubs as a base of further penetration into China's corporate sector.[65] It can be seen as especially noteworthy that Prime Minister Vajpayee's 2003 delegation to the People's Republic included an "unprecedented large business delegation from the Federation of Chambers of Commerce and Industry and the Confederation of Indian Industries" (Mansingh, 2005).[66]

Meanwhile, China continues to present some of the most pressing questions for the next stage of India's corporate development. The 2006 release of the global location index for outsourcing preferences, compiled by international analysts A. T. Kearney, placed China second only to India in its overall ranking, (NASSCOM, 2006). In a further 2005 report by Indian IT industry analyst NeoIT, China's future attractiveness for IT services supply to international customers was rated as "High" (along with Malaysia, Poland and the Czech Republic as well as India itself). These indications can help to show just how timely and appropriate is India's strategy of upgrading the value of its outputs in the context of the country's export strategy and to a lesser

profits by tackling at least some new product development to maintain their own market share.

[65] This type of political engagement coexisted with business links between technology companies such as Tata Consultancy and InfoSys taking strategic interest in expanding their presence in China's high tech heartlands such as the Shanghai Software Park. Interview with the Business Manager, University of Science and Technology of China R&D Center, Shangua Pudong Software Park, March 2003.

[66] The visit of Indian Prime Minister Vajpayee in 2003 and the reciprocal meeting between Manmohan Singh and Wen Jiabao in 2005 represent a high watermark of official engagement between the two countries.

extent, its domestic market development, both seen as important parts of a wider response to this new competitive dimension from other regions (NeoIT, 2005).

Indian corporate responses during this time appear to have varied, based on company size and an organisation's established corporate strength, but, in general, local companies would seem to be emphasising a broadening of their vertical business specialisations such as within insurance or banking or healthcare. The objective appears to be to maximise income by refocusing on higher value service outputs that could exploit the sophisticated technology that has now become available, whilst also facilitating a differentiation in the international market between the maturity of India's business experience and its service reliability, with those of potential challengers. Whilst this group of competitor nations necessarily includes China, it now also encompasses new European Union nations offering a near-shore pricing model such as Hungary and the Czech Republic.

These developments can help to explain why this third and current phase of Indian software industry's development has involved a concerted effort to internalise IP within a company across a range of services and to create distinctive products in the market that merge software technology with networked service delivery. This momentum can be seen to have manifested itself across different sectors of India's IT services and software industry in a number of ways over the last few years.

First, medium scale businesses have been able to offer solutions to more complex projects than they have been able to do in the recent past by emphasising specific firm level abilities in vertical markets and by using specialised software modules developed in-house as part of a program to offer "service packages" to the international customers often combined with a fixed-price menu of service options. These packages are often linked to meeting a client's operational needs in human resource and financial planning departments, along with providing assistance with computer system integration issues that link software and business processes across different teams in an overseas company (typically in the past, the domain of larger service providers).[67]

---

[67] Author's interview with the Operations Director of a mid-sized Indian BPO firm, February, 2006 in the company's Indian headquarters, Mumbai.

Such solutions can also involve specialised data mining and discovery services for a particular group within an organisation, in a market often tackled by niche-skilled medium and smaller enterprises. For example, one mid-sized Indian service provider has evolved its strategy from an original market entry in 2000, with 50 staff focused on routine electronic form filling. The company now specialises in advanced electronic data discovery services based on highly sensitive document analysis for the US legal community that uses a combination of human skill and a custom-built document control and text recognition software product. It has grown to over 500 employees.[68]

Second, the larger and well established actors in the market have also diversified into new areas of higher level value outputs in software services including outsourced research and development activities, offshore software engineering services and even entire product development for international customers. This specialist service sector includes both non-IT business verticals and global software product makers, many of whom have been exploiting this approach through captive subsidiaries such as Microsoft and Oracle in software development and Ford and GM in motor car design (NASSCOM, 2006).

Over the last five years, industry surveys have also shown a growing trend by middle tier international companies lacking either the resources or the incentive to establish captive offices themselves to use Indian third party services under an offshore model which will often have come about through an ongoing relationship that has matured from a pure cost advantage under labour arbitrage to joint-vendor development initiatives. One Bangalore-based software supplier, for example, formed an engineering design and software development partnership with an international aerospace firm as part of a dedicated overseas centre that would tackle a range of requirements for US and UK-based offices (ibid.). According to NASSCOM, there are currently over 200 multinational organisations active in this field alone.

Moreover, senior industry executives have been highlighting the innovative service delivery methods which have begun to be created by Indian companies. For example, one announced in 2006 that their company is pioneering a remote R&D service for its large-scale international technology clients, and has developed its own IP in wireless communication for innovative service delivery options (Premji, 2006).

[68] Ibid.

Other technology leaders have reiterated the need for the country to move away from the low cost labour arbitraging that characterised earlier phases of India's industry growth. Indeed, it would appear that a number of industry leaders and entrepreneurs share the perspective that the country must nurture skills in early stage creativity to complement what is perceived to be India's established lead in high quality delivery.[69]

NASSCOM itself has also responded to these trends. In its latest Strategic Review for 2006 it has, for the first time, differentiated the revenue contributions made to the industry as a whole by the high value specialist segments that comprise R&D, design, software engineering and software product development. According to the latest figures, this sub-sector has grown significantly in the last five years and now represents 17% of total IT exports, with current revenues in excess of US$3 billion for the financial year to the end of 2004/05, compared with just over US$300 million in the financial year 2001/02 (NASSCOM, 2006).[70]

6.7 *The Challenge of Software Product Development in India*

Perhaps one of the most striking contradictions of the current Indian software market is just how small the sector is that involves independently created and domestically branded software products which are in fact most associated internationally with retained IP value by way of direct licensing income and partner resale revenues. This segment accounted for only just over one percent of the industry's overall income, with estimated revenues for the year ending 2006 of some US$400 million. It may be useful to try and seek explanations for what some scholars have termed India's decoupled IT growth trajectory (D'Costa, 2004b).[71]

---

[69] 'Innovation Conclave' and subsequent seminar discussion at the NASSCOM Annual Conference, 16th February 2006, Mumbai attended by the author.

[70] This change may have a wider significance to India's statistical gathering system, as NASSCOM provides IT industry figures direct to the Reserve Bank of India, which may mean that future national assessments of growth from government figures could begin to further differentiate this sub-sector.

[71] Prof. D'Costa points out the difficulties facing the current service firm leaders achieving global market presence and discusses a decoupling between existing actors and software products, hardware manufacturing and *domestic* consumption.

First, there is the problem of market scale and global penetration. The Indian commercial organisations that currently exist within this sub-sector do not yet appear to have penetrated the world market as meaningful suppliers of branded software products. These firms may be suffering from constraints that would seem similar to their Chinese counterparts in that multinational industry-leading competitors already exist, and dominating the sales and purchasing agendas of customer boardrooms, especially in respect to very high value enterprise level software product market such as financial front office support, risk management, customer relationship management and accounting services.[72] Whilst a number of Indian companies have become active in the pure product market, none appears to have yet achieved a position commensurate with their standing in the services domain (Krishnan and Prabhu, 2004).

One interpretation of this contradiction is that there could be an absence of incentives in the product market for Indian companies based on the risk of turning customers into competitors, which poses the question of whether it makes commercial sense for companies that are dependent on revenues from international software product companies to create competing products in those same markets.[73] For example, InfoSys, which has emerged over the last few years as one of the leading Indian providers of packaged software solutions, concentrates on the finance and banking sectors and offers its "Finacle" product for licensed sales. However, the company has only a small market presence in global terms and derives less than 5% of its income from this sphere of its activity.[74] It has limited visibility in international tier-one financial customers.[75] Yet in IT services and exported R&D facilities, InfoSys leads the Indian sector as an international giant with revenues touching US$2 billion for 2006 alone (InfoSys Corporation, 2006).

---

[72] Oracle and SAP are world leaders in these areas.

[73] This perspective was made by a number of executives during informal talks with the author at NASSCOM's Annual Conference.

[74] According to the company's annual accounts sales of software *products* represented only 3.95% of total software related revenues, representing 357crore rupees (or around US$77) million on total software revenues of 9,028 crore rupees.

[75] Its main European recognisable customers are Credit Suisse and ABN-Amro, but others include the less well-known National Commercial Bank of Jamaica and First Bank of Nigeria (no mean achievement indeed but equally not a roll call of tier one institutions). For more information on this program suite, see <http://www.infosys.com/finacle/customers.asp> last referenced September 2006.

Second, there appears to have been a limited domestic market base for technology consumption. This relative immaturity in India may have caused difficulties for software product development initiatives in the past as a nurturing local base would have been absent for Indian product vendors, which is especially important as a stimulus for early-stage software SMEs. This may help to explain why new entrants focused more on service-oriented export channels.

The domestic market does, however, show some potential for expansion. Local consumption of computer hardware and networking products across Indian industry in general, which clearly act as essential pre-requisites for successful product penetration, appears to be increasing, having reached spending of US$5.3 billion for the financial year to 2005, representing a growth of 20.6% from the previous year. Overall, the entire domestic market for IT and ITES (including hardware) has been valued by NASSCOM at US$12.4 billion for the financial year to 2006, but within this, software products and packaged software sub-sector in India reached revenues of only an estimated US$850 million for that year, which would seem to confirm some of the difficulties facing Indian product enterprises in their domestic growth strategies (NASSCOM, 2006).

Third, these domestic characteristics have an impact on Indian venture capital (VC) investment which has been described by observers as "small and immature by US standards" (D'Costa, 2004b:18). However, to be fair to Indian achievements, all VC markets across the world are relatively immature when reviewed against the standards of Silicon Valley fundraisers. Moreover, in certain centres of India, particularly Bangalore and Pune, there are incubation centres and funding opportunities that would appear to be well in advance of many competitor nations.

Nevertheless, capital raising weaknesses in the domestic market exacerbate the difficulties for new start-ups in creating compelling value propositions, as business growth models for software product companies that are based solely on an export-only approach introduce sales complexities and exchange rate risk that can raise transaction costs, increase customer capture complexities and reduce profit growth. All of these issues can act as inhibitors to creating high growth initiatives in software product sectors along the lines of incubation models prevalent in the United States. It can also be argued that the country's exceptional success in "exogenously driven" growth, dominated by a premier league of market leaders which dominate the market, may have made it particularly difficult for breakthrough to be achieved by smaller and medium sized businesses (ibid.:7–9).

A growing theme of debate amongst scholars, politicians and practitioners in India centres on how best to achieve more endogenously driven growth in the IT sector and especially one in which smaller and medium sized companies that currently comprise only 14% of the overall revenue of the IT services market can participate (Bakht, 2006). One approach that might achieve these objectives has been endorsed at the very highest levels of the national administration and involves greater focus on SME support by promoting a move towards closer firm integration through use of consortia (Kalam, 2006).[76] Under this approach vertical and horizontal relations are built between active firms in a market enabling a blend between large presence and small skill to be realised within a group firm culture.

Such arrangements are, however, more typically seen in East Asia rather than in India, where it can be argued that a more Anglo-American approach of entrepreneurial and independent enterprises has typically dominated. Prospects for Dr. Kalam's ideas remain unclear and it can be argued that some structural issues may need to be overcome if such a trend were to be able to achieve long-lasting success.

In this context, the progress of India's proposed "Innovation Act" will be watched with keen interest. The Bill appears to have been modelled on American initiatives to stimulate early growth in innovative enterprises that originated with the Bayh-Dole Act of 1980 which altered the way IP from federally funded research projects could be commercially exploited, whilst also resembling in spirit the America Competes Act of 2007 that promoted increased research investment, an expansion of science-based education which gave a boost to US innovation infrastructure development. India's legislative moves appear to be part of the emergence in policy circles of a discernable national innovation system, with a particular emphasis on promoting high technology SMEs. While perhaps lacking the scale of R&D expenditure and the vigour of China's policy endeavours, it clearly represents the next stage of India's national competence upgrading (Irwin Crookes, 2009).

[76] Then President of India, Dr Kalam urged further focus on small and medium sized businesses as part of the nation's technology growth strategy.

However, whilst it remains difficult for innovating SMEs that produce software product to become established and to grow successfully in India, there is evidence to suggest that IT start-ups can succeed. For example, NASSCOM awarded its "Innovation 2005" title to Bangalore-based Skelta Software Limited whose CEO Sanjay Shah was formerly a member of India's diaspora and had held a prominent position in the US software industry before returning to found the company in 2002.[77] The company's revenue model is primarily built on software product license sales, working in concert with business consulting and associated services but with the latter income sources operating as a follow-through from the former rather than services being a discrete operation in their own right.

Moreover, the company's primary strategy is based on increasing domestic sales under its own name, whilst the use of third-party resellers is to be reserved primarily for international markets (Shah, 2006).[78] Company executives appear to have confidence in the domestic Indian market's prospects for expansion, sharing the views of a number of commentators.[79]

---

[77] It is interesting to note that in keeping with its Chinese neighbour, India has over recent times been keen to attract back to the domestic market those who originally travelled overseas for educational and business development opportunities. The Indian government has recently introduced a new class of citizenship known as 'Overseas Citizen of India' (OCI) to try and resolve the problem that dual nationality as an Indian has never been permitted. The OCI status enables Indian born individuals with foreign passports to hold nearly all privileges, bar electoral rights, that are accorded to regular citizens whilst still allowing them to retain their 'foreign' nationality, which, given that this is typically encapsulated in a US or UK passport, enables the returnee to continue to have travel and working rights in critical overseas markets. It is perhaps noteworthy that as yet this approach has not been adopted by the People's Republic of China.

[78] The company's product suite is anchored on Microsoft technology (SharePoint Services) and uses some of the latest internet enabled component building techniques to provide customisable business workflow and document management across different types of organisation. For further information, see the company's website, at <http://www.skelta.com/company/about-skelta.aspx> last referenced September 2006.

[79] A number of recent studies by a range of organisations, such as McKinsey, NASSCOM itself and A. T. Kearney have all pointed to considerable, and as yet largely untapped, potential in the Indian domestic market for the consumption of high technology products, clearly stimulated by the overall growth experienced by the Indian economy as a whole over the last few years, which has grown at an annual rate of between 6% and 7% since 2002 and is expected to reach 8% for the financial year 2005/06.

6.8 *IP Strategy in Response to High Value Product and Service Growth*

In this third phase of value-added growth for the Indian software market, coupled with the need to stimulate more domestic innovation and product building, it may not be surprising that legislative initiatives sympathetic to new technologies, together with stronger IP enforcement channels, have been central to the dialogue between state institutions and the IT industry during this decade.

For this reason, NASSCOM has been improving its regular liaison with various government departments over recent years to create what has been described as an "inclusive approach"[80] to dialogue. This has brought together different parties in complementary lines of business, combining, for example, a number of legal service business process outsourcers together with document management software suppliers and license management specialists into meetings with ministers and senior officials in both the Ministry of Information Technology and the Ministry of Commerce and Industry.[81] This kind of inclusive approach would appear to characterise a unified attitude towards IP regime evolution within the software industry as a whole and can be usefully contrasted to the sectoral divisions that may be exacerbating tensions within the country's pharmaceutical industry.

At the national level, the Indian government's actions have been threefold. First, they have sought to regulate emerging technologies to enhance business opportunity; second, they have made efforts to tighten the IP enforcement approach in concert with international policy links in an attempt to combat criticisms of the national enforcement capabilities; lastly they have made clear their willingness to review existing laws as required for the benefit of the industry's future.

The first major piece of technology related legislation of the new millennium was the Information Technology Act 2000, which sought to legalise and codify much of the internet-driven business methods that were then emerging into common use. This Act, whilst not being directly focused on intellectual property issues, rationalised rules for dealing with e-commerce transactions and recognition of digital signatures for identity verification. The Act also introduced regulations

---

[80] Op. cit. author's interview with a NASSCOM vice president, February 2006.
[81] Ibid.

governing a growing trend towards internet-based database access and codified legal responses in the event of unlawful data extraction and digital copying. In so doing, it appears to have succeeded in creating a confidence level for organisations to exploit these technologies within their service delivery portfolios (Premji, 2006).

The government also took action to directly address growing criticisms about the realities of IP enforcement capabilities failing to meet the expectations promised under law, especially once it had emerged that piracy levels in business software had actually *risen* during the first four years of the new century and had reached 74% by 2004 (International Intellectual Property Alliance, 2006). The Union government was prompted to introduce a number of initiatives. The Copyright Enforcement Advisory Council (CEAC) that is linked to the Copyright Act was reconstituted in April 2006 for a further three-year term to provide an overview of progress in IP enforcement, bringing together industry and political leaders from both national and local levels (Government of India Ministry of Human Resource Development, 1999). Moreover, for the first time, the CEAC had a full Secretary of Education appointed as Chairman, instead of the previous lower rank of Additional Secretary who chaired previous meetings (Hindu Online, 2006).

Whilst this was indeed a useful starting point, India, like China, enforces copyright at the provincial (state) level and has thus had to implement national policy and international norms across distinctly different local conditions, which has often meant that both knowledge of copyright principles and training for police and other enforcement officials has been difficult to achieve in a uniform manner. Having sent circulars to each of India's state-level administrative centres, calling for the establishment of locally based specialist police enforcement teams in a classically exhortatory approach to policymaking, only 23 such IP police units had been set up by the end of 2002 (Indian Embassy to United States). However, it has been reported that these teams frequently lacked critical resources and that the training programmes envisaged had largely failed to improve conditions (IIPA Special 310 Report for India, 2001).

Leading international and domestic actors, such as the IIPA and Indian legal specialists, have commented that "there have been negligible criminal convictions for piracy in India since January 1, 2000" and that "the legal system is plagued by delays...where a [IP] criminal prosecution may take over 5 to 7 years and a civil case over 10 years for a decision" (ibid.:63; Lall, 2004).

To overcome some of these shortcomings, the Indian government appears to have been prepared, under special conditions, to supplement its own responses and resources through India's Central Bureau of Investigation (CBI) with bilateral specialist assistance, co-operating in respect to complex economic crimes such as particular cases of IP infringement, with the American Federal Bureau of Investigation (FBI). An example of such cooperative international measures became public in a high profile case in 2002 after the successful arrest of a dismissed Indian software specialist who had been attempting to illegally sell the source code of his former employer's software product to those whom he had thought represented competitor companies, but who in fact were CBI/FBI undercover operatives (ComputerWorld).

The central Government's support for the software industry has also included active legal reform of the IP regulatory landscape, as well as more general regulatory measures. Whilst the Patent Amendment Act of 2005 largely addressed issues of relevance to the pharmaceutical sector, a less well-recognised subsection sought to introduce a reform of potentially long term significance for the software industry. For the first time, the Government of India tried to create a framework within which patents could be granted for embedded software programs where such software is in concert with, and dependent upon, at least one hardware component for its operation (Managing Intellectual Property Online Edition, 2005a; 2005b).

Such an approach would be consistent with moves towards the "assetisation" of knowledge-based outputs through a patent model for software that originated in the United States. However, any move in this direction would, according to observers, need to be framed in the interests of the *Indian* software industry rather than on global practice or Treaty developments.[82] In this respect, India has traditionally never been a particularly strong proponent or practitioner of patenting rights for software, even where available such as within the American market. For example, Indian residents working for Indian technology companies have filed, and been assigned, only nine software related utility patents through the US Patent Office between January 2000 and the end of 2006.[83] These values may be usefully compared to total

---

[82] Author interview, Indian WTO Mission, Geneva, July 2005.

[83] These patent grants were defined as "utility type" (note this is different from a "utility *model*" patent, which the US does not provide). Using the USPTO advanced patent search engine at <http://patft.uspto.gov/netahtml/PTO/search-adv.htm>, with each application having had the keyword "software" in their invention abstract description,

figures for companies outside the software industry which show that Indian residents working for Indian registered corporations filed, and were assigned by the USPTO, a total of 1,218 utility-type patents for the same period, with the vast majority based within the biotechnology, chemical and pharmaceutical industries.

This reticence for creating software *product* assets may stem from two reasons: first, there may be reluctance to commit funds to the process because of the large costs involved in either filing US or PCT-based international applications.[84] Second, there may be a perception amongst Indian companies that patent protection in the US is of limited value for services-oriented organisations whose primary outputs are not software products, even despite evidence of growing patent portfolios by American-based technology services organisations (Nollen, 2004).

By contrast, according to the US Patent Office, utility-type patent grants of software related inventions by Indian residents working for non-Indian organisations (in fact, mostly American companies) numbered 65 for the six years to September 2006. This may be explained by a greater focus on patents that typically characterises American corporations and also, in passing, helps to indicate the value of individual Indian inventive knowledge to those organisations (USPTO Patent Search).

This issue of patent value may grow in significance as the domestic market for creating and consuming both services and, more importantly, domestically produced software *products*, expands across India in the future. Perhaps unsurprisingly, actors within the Open Source movement have vigorously opposed any trends toward the adoption of software patents in all jurisdictions including India.[85]

with inventor nationality set as "Indian" and filing company domicile set as "India", last accessed in September 2006. The majority of those filed were made by Tata Consultancy Group (TCS) of Mumbai.

[84] Estimates put a patent application costing around US$30,000 in various fees and direct filing costs, added to which must be put management time and procedure monitoring during the typical two to three year review process required.

[85] For example, see a speech given by Open Source evangelist Richard Stallman 24th July 2001, one of a number given over the years to various audiences along similar themes, at the Government Model Engineering College, India, an extract of which is published online by GNU, accessed 8th April 2009 at <http://www.gnu.org/philosophy/stallman-mec-india.html>. See also India's Open Source movement's perspectives here, available online and last accessed 8th April 2009 at <http://osindia.blogspot.com/2008/11/practical-problem-with-software-patents.html>.

The ongoing debate about patent reform and software's potential inclusion under a future protective patent framework has by no means yet been resolved, with the Indian Parliament actually striking down radical relaxations to software patent definitions proposed prior to the 2005 Amendments. Some industry commentators have emphasised that any future modifications to patent laws in respect to software inventions would need to be made on the basis of what was in the best interests for Indian companies, and would have been carried out in the context of recommendations and consultations between NASSCOM, industry corporations and relevant government departments.[86] Lively debate can be expected if and when this issue returns to the legislative agenda in the future.

6.9 *Future Trends and Objectives for Policymakers*

The Indian software sector is clearly strong and successful, employing over 1 million workers, and continues to enjoy an international standing amongst customer nations as a reliable and technically sophisticated service supplier. According to NASSCOM, over 90 firms hold the CMM kitemark at Level 5 for coding and product output complexity (its highest level), with almost 50 holding the more recent "six sigma" methodology rating for their business process quality. Indeed, it can be argued that a particularly attractive feature of Indian firms when compared with other Asian outsource locations is the predominance of recognisable international standards across the range of delivery and product development operations. For example, the ISO9001 international quality standard has been achieved by a growing number of Indian organisations in both its original and "2000" updated form (NASSCOM, 2006).[87]

A number of firms now hold the important BS7799 data security standard, indicating an acknowledged ability to maintain data, source code and related information securely and confidentially during all phases of an international business relationship (ibid.; Heeks et al., 2000). Factors such as these appear to have high visibility in determining customer contract outcomes and featured strongly in a 2006

[86] Op. cit. author's interview with a NASSCOM vice president, February 2006.

[87] NASSCOM lists over 336 firms, of both Indian and international origin, that had achieved at least one of these standards (ISO9001 or ISO9001:2000) by the end of 2005.

NASSCOM review of the requirements for success as an offshore location.[88] The Indian government appears to have also been sympathetic to demands by business groups to upgrade its own data protection standards to better coincide with those of the UK (NASSCOM, 2006), whose protection of both personal data and business trade secrets is recognised as a strong and effective benchmark from which India could craft its own common law based approach.[89] Such developments may best be seen as part of a strategy to counter what is regarded in some commercial circles as the potential for aggressive competition from the new accession states of the EU such as the Czech Republic.

Maintaining and improving the regulatory environment is not the only arena in which government has an important role to play. In recent industry surveys, the major threat to continued success within the Indian IT sector centred on ensuring "a continuous supply of skilled labour" (NeoIT, 2005:15).[90] This would seem to imply that further government action might be needed to ensure that the talent pool of technologists is regularly refreshed and that industry continues to be re-supplied with appropriate numbers of specialists to enable India to remain price competitive.

The process of software development, and in particular, product and package design, requires especially flexible mindsets with keen problem solving skills which have long been the traditional comparative advantage offered by Indian IT specialists against those of their East Asian neighbours (Balasubramanyam and Balasubramanyam, 1996b).[91] However, prior to recent recessionary influences that may have reduced traditionally high staff churn rates amongst IT firms in India, this advantage had become the subject of concern within the industry with dialogue centred on remedies to avoid what NASSCOM had described as "a talent crunch" in staffing and recruitment, with

---

[88] Particularly important determinates were seen as: cost advantage; talent availability; scalable infrastructure; operational capability and excellence; and a supportive business and regulatory environment.

[89] Interview with the Vice President of Operations at a mid-sized Indian BPO firm, Mumbai, February 2006.

[90] Of all government and industry challenges, skills availability was placed first for India in a review of opportunities and threats facing the leading IT outsource supplier nations.

[91] In their analysis, the authors of this work point out that abstract concepts such as software appeal to the Hindu mindset and that the Brahmin caste in particular has longstanding association with logic and numerical sciences (it is pointed out that Indians introduced the numeral "zero" to mathematics).

its consequent labour cost and business growth implications (NASSCOM, 2006:146).

A related issue for some in the industry appears to centre on the actual quality of the skills of those emerging from some of the newer technology schools and from universities in general across India. Some practitioners have highlighted what has been characterised as a change of style within the education system, away from traditional problem solving and softer skills towards a more mechanical emphasis based on multiple choice questions and answers, engendered as part of a "fast track learning method"[92] and being promoted, perhaps in order to combat the very problem of numerical shortages already highlighted. Industry executives have emphasised that care needs to be taken by government in this particular situation, as it is argued that qualitative shortcomings could have an especially detrimental and disrupting effect on expansion for organisations as they try to raise the value of their service and product outputs.[93]

The other main issue confronting political and business leaders is the question of how to respond to the rise of China, not only as a potential economic leader in the region but also as a direct competitor to a number of India's previously unique selling points: legal regime, cost advantage and technical capability. A report produced in 2005 for the American outsourcing market provides significant messages for the technology industry in India, and specifically highlights the dangers for them of being too complacent about maintaining the Indian advantage against rising competitors like China and counsels against an over confidence about Indian leadership in key business areas (NeoIT).[94] In particular, China's emerging software development and overseas coding centres were seen as examples where China's more limited advanced English skills were actually less critical to contract

[92] Interview with the Operations Director at a mid-sized Indian BPO firm, Mumbai, February 2006.

[93] Ibid.

[94] The author was particularly struck by the confidence expressed in meetings and seminars by a number of Indian businessmen about the leadership that India enjoyed over China and its likely continuance. For example, Atul Nishar, a former chairman of NASSCOM and currently running Hexaware Technologies in India, expressed the much held view that China lags behind India in skills, regulations and service sophistication by as much as 10 years. He also maintained that in his experience, even if costs in India were higher by as much as 25%, western corporate decision makers would still choose India over China as the destination of preference. Seminar discussion at NASSCOM Annual Conference Mumbai 17th February 2006.

decision-making by western companies than may at first have been realised (ibid.). It would appear that Indian software business groups and the national government have together already recognised this threat and have begun to convene regular meetings with key stakeholders to address specific areas of policy that may need either government or corporate action.[95]

The relationship with China can also be characterised within a geopolitical context, as it is important to recognise that there remains a traditional realist dimension to the engagement between these two states (Price and Wall, 2005; People's Daily Online, 2006c).[96] These aspects may have even greater implications in future due to a growing economic relationship that has seen trade between the two countries increase rapidly over recent years to an anticipated value of US$20 billion by the end of 2006 (India I.P. Wire Online, 2006; People's Republic of China Embassy to India, 2005).[97]

6.10 *Conclusion*

India in the 21st Century appears to have a determined strategy to exploit its advantages in high value industries, especially those of offshore software development and pharmaceuticals manufacturing. Its success has been built upon a platform of historical legacies: a respected legal system; innate communication skills in the English language; and naturally fostered numerical, scientific and problem solving skills, all of which have been strengthened by distinctive partnerships between industry lobby groups, key corporate leaders and government actors that are especially visible in the software industry, that also may help to account for the strategic evolution of pharmaceuticals.

---

[95] Op. cit. author's interview with a NASSCOM vice president, February 2006.

[96] Most recently, the high level dialogue between the two countries has sought to promote a message of "strategic partnership" rather than highlight continuing disputes over borders and the lingering memory of armed conflict.

[97] See bilateral trade estimates of US$20 billion for year 2006/07, discussed by the Union Minister of Commerce Kamal Nath. Note also that Chinese estimates of bilateral trade for 2004 quoted a figure of US$13.6 billion, which gives an indication of a rapidly accelerating trading relationship. Equally important, India's strengthening relationship with the United States would seem to have moved beyond the issues of visa policies and skills exchanges, to include areas of wider mutual interest such as nuclear technology exports, United Nations Security Council reforms, and India's place as a strategic partner for the US internationally.

The nation's intellectual property laws in particular act as a benchmark for this process in terms of both copyright and patent regulations, with policies being crafted by government to fit the development phase of the industry itself. The country's IP laws have been shown to have been relatively loose and flexible during the early stages of industry growth, to promote knowledge acquisition in the software sector and to foster generic drug production in pharmaceuticals. Regulations have become increasingly stronger and more sophisticated in concert with required international norms and the commercial development of higher value services in each of these two knowledge industries, illustrated by the emergence of genuine software products and highly advanced services solutions in software and the creation of export-led innovation in Indian drug production.

Notwithstanding the crisis of confidence in software services over the Satyam scandal in early 2009, or the mixed domestic response to news of Ranbaxy's acquisition by Japanese pharmaceutical giant Daiichi Sankyo in June 2008, both industries in India appear to be gaining strength, and leading elements within each are clearly moving outwards into new markets, using a strong IP framework as one of the driving forces with which to achieve success in this strategy (Kripalani, 2009; Chaudhuri, 2008). In the case of both pharmaceuticals and software, therefore, it has been argued that it has been the engagement with the international trading system that has helped to shape not only attitudes to specific IP regulations within each industry, but also their respective growth possibilities as they consolidate their market positions.

Each industry has evolved over different timelines and from different starting perspectives, with pharmaceuticals at first heavily protected under an import substitution model and only latterly engaging with innovation and export orientation, contrasting with the software sector that began as largely export-led from the outset, although with relatively unsophisticated value propositions, but which rapidly moved into high value relationships with overseas customers.

Deep divisions still seem to remain in pharmaceuticals, with the bifurcation anchored on the extent to which individual enterprises have embraced an innovation-based export-oriented strategy. This acts as a contrast to the uniformity of purpose that appears to characterise the software and services sector, even despite the potential challenges and new competitive dimensions that may be facing the industry's corporations in future.

This chapter has also presented evidence of both contrasts and similarities with its neighbour China. In India, there does appear to be a much greater level of partnership between business organisations and government institutions with an emphasis on upward sectoral pressure on state actors, especially in software. However, the policies of the Indian and Chinese administrations clearly appear to have coincided in some areas, such as in the promotion of science parks and clustered development hubs to facilitate software industry expansion and the nurturing of suitable technology skills and exploitation of foreign generated knowledge spillovers.

In reality, what perhaps may now be observable is that these two nations, regardless of their historical legacies or cultural differences, have recognised that economic success can be most effectively achieved through the promotion of knowledge industries. Both nations' governments appear to be tackling this challenge in a way that best suits their own local conditions and their attitude towards the evolution of their country's intellectual property regime would seem to have encapsulated a part of this wider development trajectory.

CHAPTER SEVEN

A CENTRAL ROLE FOR IP IN THE GLOBAL DOMAIN

This chapter focuses on the key observations in respect to the development of the international intellectual property regime. It puts forward argument showing that there is a clear trend towards the emergence of a global set of rules in IP regulation and that this convergence has been accelerating in recent years due to the increasing significance of knowledge industries economically and the growing complexity in how best to preserve ownership interest in new markets. It will also present a considered approach to a better understanding of the interconnections between different actors involved in norm setting and IP regime evolution, reiterating that there appears to be clear evidence of distinctive stages in national regulatory development and emphasising the variation in visibility and behaviour that state and non-state actors seem to exhibit during these different stages. Finally, it provides a functionally based interpretation that may help to put into sharper context the trajectory of regime evolution whilst providing a framework within which to better understand the required characteristics that appear to have determined a successful adoption of IP regulatory norms in China and India.

Trends towards the emergence of a global regime for intellectual property regulation can be captured through analysis of three developments that have characterised recent years. First, there has been a deepening of the scope of IP regulations that has penetrated vertically into new issue areas and deeply into domestic law. Second, there has been a marked horizontal widening of participation in regime building and norm setting that has encompassed the ideas and influence of actors well beyond the traditional formal institutions of the state, which has taken place in concert with an increasing level of sophistication in actor behaviour towards generating desired outcomes from regime development. Third, it can be argued that there has been a noticeable convergence in both the agreed norms and the appropriate structure for implementing each element of an IP-based regulatory framework. These issues range from successive drives towards a global patent law, increasing consistency in copyright protection within the internet era and a growing tendency for a number of key countries, in not only the industrialised sphere, such as the US and the EU, but also amongst leading developing countries, such as China and India, to reach a measure of consensus on accepting these norms, prompted by growing appreciation of regulatory outcomes that are in the best interests of domestic innovating enterprises.

7.1 *Deepening the Scope of IP Regulations*

The vertical deepening of the scope of IP regulations is particularly significant in this analysis, whereby there can be seen the emergence of a more complex regulatory framework for creating, managing and enforcing intellectual property internationally, beyond a purely territorial bias and reflecting especially the reality that "national regimes generally disregard cross-border externalities and the resulting need for policy coordination" (Maskus and Reichman, 2005:9).

New areas have also been introduced with both a speed and a significance that has challenged the previously existing regulatory norms encapsulated by the Great Conventions and that has required action by both state and non-state actors. In this regard, there has been particular concern about the way in which the internet plays a radically enlarged role, compared with traditional media, as a means of legal marketing and sales channel enlargement on the one hand and illegal distribution and associated piracy on the other. These trends have become particular concerns for those involved in the creation of electronically available knowledge goods such as software, video and music.

The dimensions of vertical regulatory deepening and the salience of new issues have encompassed a number of initiatives as the actors that participate in rule setting for the evolving global IP regime have sought an adequate response to these new challenges. Activities have been characterised by a blend of outcomes that have included new and refined agreements from multilateral negotiations, regional directives to promote greater harmonisation in areas such as the EU, as well as behind-the-border reforms spurred by bilateral treaties between trading partners, captured particularly by recent American-led Free Trade Agreements (FTAs).

Visibility for IP issues within multilateral forums primarily rests with WTO and WIPO. However, each institution has contributed to the international regulatory framework in a different way and there are a number of major distinctions between the character and operation of each organisation.

The WTO is focused on establishing the minimum framework required for the legal system of IP in member states and introduces issue linkages into the debate over IP regulation in the context of wider trade negotiations. Whilst there have been criticism of developing countries' constrained room for manoeuvre within the resulting multilateral bargaining positions within the organisation (Ostry, 2002; Narlikar, 2005; Busch and Reinhardt, 2002), especially in relation to the organisations dispute settlement mechanisms, developing countries can have important visibility at the WTO, reinforced by the openness of their markets and by alliances of mutual interest as much as by the specific levels of their GDP (Harvard Centre for International Development).[1]

WIPO, on the other hand, should best be seen as an institution that is more concerned with the technical nature of specific areas of IP protection policy, with its rule-making work on internet copyright issues and patent law procedure harmonisations being two cases in point. This may bring about a narrower focus to WIPO's activities and can reduce its scope for making connections between different subject areas in resolving problems and can limit the diplomatic levers that may be used to secure consensus. For example, although WIPO does have its own Development Agenda established in 2007, the "one nation, one vote" format of state-centric institutions such as WIPO

[1] In particular, China and India may now becoming increasingly important in their own right within trade negotiations due to their current progression towards full market opening and the potential of their domestic economies. It can be argued that such influences can become independent of any country alliances in which they may participate, and the recent meetings of the G20 Group of Nations in the light of economic strains in global growth, showed how prominent were the positions of China and India, in achieving consensus.

"Alliance diplomacy" at the WTO may have become more complex over recent years perhaps due to the "rejection of North versus South bloc diplomacy by many negotiators".

See also World Trade Organisation, 'Annex 1-ABC of WTO Global Coalition Groups', <http://www.wto.org/English/res_e/booksp_e/casestudies_e/case27_e.htm>, accessed 27th 20th March 2007.

See also op. cit. Narlikar, International Trade and Developing Countries, page 83.

contrasts with the consensus-building decision making that persists in the WTO, which may dilute developing country activism and which could help to explain the more limited visibility and progress of the organisation's endeavours despite the important subject matter (Yu, 2008; Weinstock Netanel, 2009).[2]

Furthermore, WIPO does not possess either an enforcement mechanism or a dispute resolution system for states to attempt to resolve disagreements in a way similar to that available at the WTO. Due to this, power dynamics at WIPO may sometimes appear quite confrontational at times, given the absence of deflecting negotiating avenues, and this is perhaps illustrated by some of the difficulties that have been encountered over substantive patent law harmonisation.

The development of the IP regime at the multilateral level would now seem to be based on a complement of negotiating outcomes between the two institutions. Historically, industrialised nations saw their agenda being captured at WIPO by developing country priorities, which may explain why the institution appears to have been somewhat marginalized during the 1980's. However, the creation and the significance of TRIPS under WTO auspices did not in fact eclipse WIPO in the way that might have been expected and WIPO re-emerged with a significant purpose through an expansion of its traditional role of looking at new areas of regulation (Cheek, 2000–01) and providing technical assistance with the regulatory implementation of TRIPS.[3]

WIPO's management decision to change the way that new issue areas were presented for discussion at diplomatic conferences may have helped to raise the organisation's profile again in IP framework evolution. Under the new rules introduced in 1996, IP strategy initiatives were no longer to be the exclusive preserve of WIPO's own International Bureau, but could instead be directly contributed by member state delegations. This change not only radically enhanced the organisation's capability to become a driver for new initiatives but scholars have suggested that it also substantially influenced its rehabilitation as a functional part of the international IP regime building network in the eyes of the principal industrialised countries, as it

---

[2] Both these works explore in particualr Chinese and Indian attitudes to access to medicines in general and WIPO's evolution in particular.

[3] World Trade Organisation, 'Agreement between the World Intellectual Property Organisation and World Trade Organisation', <http://www.wto.org/english/tratop_e/trips_e/intel3_e.htm>, accessed 20th January 2007.

enabled key issues of concern to their national constituents such as controlling the spread of illegal music piracy through the internet to be propelled directly by enterprises and industry groups through their government representatives into treaty-making negotiations (Cheek, 2000:313–14). Indeed, it has been argued that WIPO's traditional role as a "balanced agency" (Sell, 2003:20) has now been compromised, with its discussions increasingly being based around "the interests of the favoured factions of capital" (ibid.). Such a view, however, may not reflect the complexities now inherent in the rise of Chinese and Indian enterprises whose interests in a reliable, enforceable and consistent approach to IP regulation may be increasingly intersecting with those of their industrialised trading partners. Nevertheless, it would seem to be clear that there now exist two complementary multilateral venues concerned with IP related initiatives, heralding what some scholars have described as a "bimodal intellectual property regime within which the two organisations shared authority" (Helfer, 2004:25).

New issue areas have been a significant part of the emerging consensus on what is considered appropriate subject matter for IP-oriented regulation in a technologically globalised international economy. The rise of the internet as a means of generating product sales and trade in intangibles has meant that existing regulations have had to be reviewed in order to facilitate legitimate new operating channels and profitable business models, as well as better controlling illegal activity that might undermine right holders exploiting their creations. Led by the principles encapsulated in the international agreements of the WCT and the WPPT, substantial levels of behind-the-border controls on manufacture, distribution and sale of anti-circumvention measures and devices now operate in major trading areas of the world.

Moreover, the bilateral negotiating strength of the United States has also been a contributor of the growth in IP legislation that different nations have introduced within their own domestic regimes,[4] in response to preferential market access protocols to different US sectors under the umbrella of registered Free Trade Agreements permissible

[4] For example, the negotiations with Australia included elements of IP system reform as a mandatory part of concluding a successful treaty. Initiatives such as this typically introduce enhanced levers of control over and above existing requirements stipulated by TRIPS (under what has been termed "TRIPS-Plus") and often necessitating a major overhaul of key domestic copyright and patent laws.

under WTO rules.[5] American actions would seem to confirm that it regards access to the country's open market as very much dependent on reciprocal respect for its own IP exports.

In particular, US commercial interests appear to have been successful in propelling their position into treaty negotiations, whereby US officials would appear to be consistently emphasising conformity with domestic American legislation. These key elements include controversial copyright and internet distribution control measures that were framed within the DMCA, such as ISP criminal liability and the introduction of rigorous prohibitions on anti-circumvention measures for digital content.

However, it can be argued that it is too simplistic to see these trends as representing only American corporate perspectives being asserted, in isolation to the growing intersection of interests within the wider international knowledge-based industries.

7.2 *Widening Participation in IP Regulatory Development*

In concert with the deepening of regulatory activity and the extension of IP into new issue areas, it can be argued that there has been a noticeable horizontal widening in the number and nature of actor participants in regime building over the recent years. Scholars have asserted that there are now multiple "spaces" (Bowrey, 2005:55) within which IP law is framed, debated and created which extend participation beyond the conventional diplomatic and ministerial representation of government institutions.

Instead of a state centric dominance, broad communities of common interest have begun to create networks of communication that operate both formally and informally along fault lines quite distinct from national borders. New actors in regime building include multiple different groups: technical specialists who help to broaden understanding of new issue areas, such as the World Wide Web Consortium

[5] Members are required to notify the WTO of any regional FTAs agreements made. See <http://www.wto.org/english/tratop_e/region_e/regfac_e.htm>, accessed 12th January 2007. In this context, the US would seem to be operating as a self-appointed arbiter of international IP harmonisation, beyond the negotiating forums of both WIPO and the WTO, wherein the domestic law passed in these third countries becomes an effective mirror of the current regulatory structure of that which operates across the federal United States.

(W3C); proprietary corporations such as Microsoft, Lenovo, Sony and Huawei, which actually own IP assets; lobby groups and subject-issue associations such as the International Intellectual Property Alliance (IIPA) and the Business Software Alliance (BSA); and professional lawyers and economists working in global organisations such as the Internet Corporation for Assigned Names and Numbers (ICANN).

There are also subject experts involved in the secretariats of WIPO and the WTO, along with academic specialists whose research and advice can often help to shape the thinking of national politicians through both formal and informal channels. Examples of this phenomenon include panel membership of the UK government's Commission on Intellectual Property Rights which helped to underpin British political perspectives at the turn of the millennium,[6] and participation by leading domestic academics in private lectures given to the Chinese leadership during critical parts of the country's assimilation of IP norms more than ten years ago. It has been argued that these private lectures in particular helped to mould Chinese political opinion prior to its membership of the WTO and acted as a proxy for commercial pressure group influence which was then largely absent (Yuan, 2006).

Informal specialist networks operating within existing institutions can also help multilateral forums re-engage with emerging priorities within rapidly developing regulatory areas such as technology and intellectual property. The Stockholm Group at WIPO, for example, is an informal association that originally met to link key IP stakeholders including Sweden and Finland, where companies in these countries control a growing stock of IP assets to the emerging internet agenda for the 1996 WIPO Diplomatic Conference. The Group has, however, continued to meet since then and is considered an important forum where "policy makers from the industrialized countries [are] able to gain a better understanding of the problems and issues facing other states" (Cheek, 2000:313–15). Indeed, WIPO has since introduced its own formally sponsored regional groupings for pre-conference policy debate to mirror the Stockholm Group's success.[7]

"All of these groups are involved in changing the face of intellectual property in practice", although it must be remembered that such bodies will have its own precise agenda for different aspects of regulatory

[6] The Commission's Panel included a number of leading IP academic specialists.
[7] The "Asian Group" is one such example.

development and it is likely that each will expect to make alliances across other groups, with these associations perhaps shifting with the issues that are under review (Bowrey, 2005:56).

In this context, whilst the formal power over treaty making at WIPO and the WTO as well as domestic law making in national assemblies and parliaments still reside within the preserve of administration diplomats, government ministers and political legislators, the very agenda items and position papers brought to bear at these forums may now be structured as collaborative efforts, with new actors which would appear to be participating in peer-to-peer dialogue independent of national loyalties.

International debate about the next stage of IP regulations development encompasses a number of complex and often politically controversial issues that will very likely have to take into account differences in perspective amongst a wide collection of stakeholding groups including royalty-free advocates such as the W3C, open source supporters who want to shift debate towards global licensing arrangements and corporate boardroom perspectives that still maintain that there is a place for strong defensive patent portfolios as a function of wealth creating business models.[8]

Neither is this simply a phenomenon of widened participation from groups only from the industrialised world. NASSCOM, the Indian software services business lobby group, has created alliances with a large number of similar bodies and related organisations through a series of horizontal technical and policy exchanges.[9] This includes dialogue with entrepreneurial cross-sector business forums such the Indus Group (TiE) that hold special interest seminars on varied matters including licensing, intellectual property issues and the significance of China's technological development on the international IT industry.[10] Networks such as this often interact within what can be termed informal email communities to help set agenda priorities and

---

[8] See for example, World Intellectual Property Organisation, 'Current and Emerging Issues Relating to Patents', <http://www.wipo.int/patent/law/en/developments.html>, accessed 15th January 2007.

[9] See NASSCOM, <http://www.nasscom.in/Nasscom/templates/NormalPage.aspx?id=5386>, accessed 15th January 2007.

[10] TiE interest group website <http://www.tie.org/Home/Programs/TiE%20SIGs/index_html/view_document>, accessed 15th January 2007.

discuss relevant issues amongst participants which can include specialist practitioners, industry leaders and academics.[11]

NASSCOM also actively participates within more formal international agenda setting arrangements within the World Information Technology and Services Alliance (WITSA), a pan-industry consortium that although based in Virginia, USA takes membership from over 60 international IT lobby groups around the world and has the protection and promotion of intellectual property rights as one of its founding principles.[12] These functional links, while complementary, are independent of the group's domestically focused activities in its dialogue with the Union Government of India in connection with technology legislation and IP regulation at a national level.[13] This helps to illustrate how much more complex the global IP framework has become over recent times.

Individual firms can also engage with the wider IP regime, defending their commercial interests against counterfeit and piracy in the domestic courts of both their own state and those of their trading partners,[14] whilst also seeking to enforce contractual obligations through international arbitration forums more generally[15] or by using WIPO's mediation services directly if the dispute pertains to IP law.[16]

Linked to this phenomenon of expanded actor participation has been an increasing sophistication amongst both existing and new actors within the global intellectual property community, both in the extent to which they use network connections to expand issue areas

---

[11] Author's interview with a director of The Indus Group (TiE) in London, December 2006.

[12] See WITSA website at http://www.witsa.org/about/index.htm last referenced 15th January 2006.

[13] Op. cit. author's interview with a NASSCOM vice president, February 2006.

[14] Companies that believe counterfeit goods may be being imported into a particular national territory can seek to use customs and border control laws through the local courts to facilitate seizure of those goods. Organisations may wish to arrange seizures at points of destination rather than ports of origin where there may be localised collusion to redirect goods back into circulation. By arranging customs raids in destination countries, such as in the US or in EU member state ports, IP owners can help to ensure that the illegal goods are destroyed and thus unavailable for resale.

[15] This mechanism is facilitated by the New York Convention, a treaty that will be examined in more detail within the context of global regime convergence in a later section of this chapter.

[16] See World Intellectual Property Organisation, 'Arbitration and Mediation Center', <http://www.wipo.int/amc/en/center/background.html>, accessed 27th February 2007.

in their own interests and in the way that they can shift debate from one venue to another in order to secure the most appropriate forum for agreeing new agendas. Some scholars see this tendency towards what has been termed "regime shifting" (Helfer, 2004) and as part of a greater objective to create a "functionally efficient transnational system of innovation" (Maskus and Reichman, 2005:33) whereby regime participants have been involved in ongoing attempts to revise and reinterpret IP protection standards as a response to changing priorities of, and shifting power structures between, state and non-state actors in a number of different international forums. In this way, IP-focused actors, including industry organisations, issue-specific lobby groups, and broader based NGOs, "shift lawmaking initiatives from one international venue to another" to secure outcomes more in line with their own agenda priorities (Helfer, 2004:6).

For example, during the 1980's, a useful illustration of this behaviour occurred with the success of first world national governments, including the United States and the EU, operating under pressure from their own corporations and IP asset owners, to shift the competence for a new regulatory paradigm for IP regulation away from what was then seen as the consumer-friendly WIPO towards the more rigorous and producer-friendly venue offered by the GATT and its associated dispute handling mechanism. There was also an attraction in being able to combine issues on market access to first world economies by developing nations with the introduction of increased IP regulatory minimums, whilst also locating the significance of knowledge goods within the context of trading relationships and asset ownership rather than the principles of the global commons which it can be argued had encapsulated debate hitherto within WIPO. These moves can be seen as part of the raised visibility of trade issues in international relationships.

But regime shifting is not necessarily limited to just the very powerful actors of the international community. Some scholars have interpreted the WTO's Ministerial Declaration on TRIPS and Public Health in August 2003[17] as an illustration of NGO's success in shifting debate away from the issue of how best to fund expensive pharmaceutical research, which was of most concern to western patent holders and their networks, and towards the more emotive focus on human

[17] World Trade Organisation, 'WT/L/540', <http://www.wto.org/english/tratop_e/trips_e/implem_para6_e.htm>, accessed 16th January 2007.

rights to life and exclusion from access to medical care in third world communities (Maskus and Reichman, 2005:29–31). Conferences and seminars hosted by bodies such as Oxfam brought together academics, scientists and policymakers into new network groupings outside of the traditional multilateral negotiating rooms, whilst the related publications from these debates informed a wider opinion of their respective positions (Drahos and Mayne, 2002).[18]

It follows that there have been a number of important developments within the process of framing, creating and regulating the global IP regime that have focused especially on induced, "bottom-up" initiatives in policymaking which have both created new regulatory areas and introduced new norm-creating participants. The threads of this process point markedly towards the convergence of IP norms across the world and illustrate a more sophisticated balance in the power dynamics of rule setting between state and non-state actors.

7.3 *Convergence in Global Norms and Regime Structures*

A number of recent trends can be observed that would appear to show a convergence of issue areas amongst different types of actors involved in IP regime building. It can be argued that these issues fall into three broad areas: a convergence of commercial interests amongst international enterprises owning IP assets; convergence on an appropriate legal form for IP elements such as copyright, patents and trademarks along with a growth in international agreements to support these legal forms; and a growing convergence around instruments that support effective IP enforcement across borders.

It is important to recognise that a number of scholars have grave concerns about these perceived trends and reject the view that a commercially based perspective is appropriate as a means of evaluating the efficacy of IP regulations (Chang, 2004; Stiglitz and Charlton, 2005; Bhagwati, 2004). A number of scholars and practitioners have combined to express growing anxiety over the disruption of the supply of public goods below optimum levels by private right-holders seeking to exercise their exclusive rights, to the detriment of wider social outcomes. Some have even called for a "moratorium" on new IP laws

[18] This book was based on papers submitted at the 'Oxfam International Seminar on Intellectual Property and Development' in Brussels, 20th March 2001.

and regulations to assess their wider impact (Maskus and Reichman, 2005:40–44). Others have suggested a "Public Interest Test" prior to issuing protective grants, an idea put forward by members of the online community, the "Adelphi Charter", as part of a wider restriction on the proliferation of IP controls. All of these concerns and initiatives have been seeking to prevent what has been seen by some as the growth in potential constraints on opportunities for knowledge sharing and mutual learning from sources such as scientific research and traditional cultural resources.

Current developments are characterised as representing a departure from the traditional IP bargain that seeks to balance common good and public welfare with rights to profits and the protection of creators, with the consequence that that new IP norms may now be putting "private power over cultural output" (Porsdam, 2005:104). It is also argued that there has been an unbalanced focus on industrialised commercial priorities, illustrating that "the convergence of intellectual property rights is primarily a response by industrialised nations to the convergence of domestic industries" (Westkamp, 2005:110).

These negative perspectives on IP regime evolution do not appear to take account of a widening participation within international innovation industries that have promoted knowledge-based economic growth beyond the industrialised countries of the US and EU. Nor do they appear to fully recognise the investment required in the development and production of knowledge goods within the commercial sector and the importance of providing sufficient financial incentive and legal protection in the context of shortening product lifetimes and reducing first mover advantages, conditions which mean that IP protection is often required to make sure that knowledge-based product innovation takes place at all.[19] There also appears to be an underlying assumption in critiques of IP convergence that views such trends as being in the interests of only the corporations based in major industrialised powers.

In contrast, there would seem to be strong evidence to argue that there are now shared interests amongst the technology enterprises of both industrialised economies such as the US and the EU and developing

[19] This is especially true in industries such as software development where new products can be rapidly superseded but less so in sectors such as financial services and derivative instrument invention, where short term gains can be sufficiently large to offset short product lifetimes.

countries such as China, Korea and India. There also appear to be clear trends towards developing countries asserting their own rights under IP norms to protect and safeguard commercial exploitation of traditional indigenous knowledge.[20] It can be argued that these interests centre on exploiting open markets, embracing export-oriented growth strategies and controlling piracy and counterfeit to safeguard ongoing incentive in order to bring innovative products to market. This may be explained by the growing importance of IP assets and revenues to a country's economy.

It has been shown that, over the last few years, technology based knowledge goods have gained in economic and trading significance and there has been a marked shift towards protection and safeguarding corporate IP assets, whilst securing legitimate returns on the investment encapsulated in these outputs.[21] Some of the most valuable corporations on international stock markets today comprise organisations built almost entirely upon business models largely free of physical assets, such as Google and Microsoft, with their economic wealth centred squarely on intellectual property asset ownership.

The growth in export penetration of overseas markets in knowledge-based sectors by corporations from both industrialised and developing countries can be seen to have operated in concert with market opening strategies and innovation-oriented technological development in emerging economies such as those of India and China. This engagement has helped to give IP regulations in these developing nations greater salience internationally, whilst providing important incentives for domestic regulatory enhancement as enterprises seek to move up the value chain of IP-rich product development. These changes appear to have moved the debate in these countries beyond a purely domestic focus to one that has begun to recognise the importance of embracing global norms as part of a wider strategy to exploit and protect locally fostered innovation (Callan, 2007).[22]

---

[20] Op. cit. author interview, Indian Mission to WTO, Geneva, July 2005.

[21] For example, many current corporations have seen their market value increase substantially in relation to their underlying book (asset) value over the last thirty years, with the difference mainly accounted for through IP assets such as patent portfolios, trademarks and intangible goodwill.

[22] However, progress in combating illegal activity cannot be said to be uniform across these countries and some sectors, such as those in China, would appear to be exhibiting ongoing internal tensions between innovators and pirates.

There also appears to be evidence of a growing convergence amongst regulatory authorities over the norms and outcomes inherent in what should comprise a successful IP protection regime, although this progress has not been without difficulties and setbacks in some areas.

In copyright controls, there appear to have been visible trends towards the realisation of IP protection focused on safeguarding the entrepreneurial risk-takers who bear the economic cost of production and distribution in what many have described as a distinctly American view of IP principles. There is now significant similarity in context and practice between the EU's implementation of WIPO's Internet Treaties under its various Directives and the United States' DMCA (Grosheide, 2006).

The US approach to granting patent controls in addition to copyright protection for intangibles such as software and business processes can be seen to have influenced the current debate. It can be argued that it has created discussion amongst IP stakeholders in many countries, including the EU, China and India, about appropriate regulatory vehicles for protecting investments in the production of economic assets that, whilst nominally being intangible creations, are in fact capable of holding accountable value and of providing recurring revenues to corporations in ways that directly mirror tangible assets and industrial inventions.[23]

Patent harmonisation appears to have moved along similar trajectories to that of copyright with noticeable progress being made towards greater interconnection between patenting grant authorities across the world. Much of this progress has been achieved through WIPO's Patent Cooperation Treaty that has made a tangible difference to the ease with which applications may be posted to different countries whilst maintaining invention priority. The Patent Law Treaty (PLT), which seeks to create uniform and streamlined "formal procedures in respect of national and regional patent applications", has also recently come into force and may well accelerate these trends (World Intellectual Property Organisation).[24]

[23] The extent of debate on software patenting across commercial entities in both Europe and India would seem to support the importance of this topic to the future of the industry.

[24] The Patent Law Treaty came into force in April 2005, including the United Kingdom in March 2006.

Observers (Barton, 2005:618; Mossinghaf and Ku, 1998:549) also point to an increasing convergence across individual national authorities towards adherence to assessment criteria that match the current US style of "weak patentability standards and broad subject matter standards", even despite the filing differences of the US regime, which adopts "first-to-invent" filing priority.[25]

However, attempts at consolidation of underlying patent principles have been less successful and may show the limits of potential harmonisation within sensitive issue areas where states in particular feel that they have significant principles to protect. The Substantive Patent Law Treaty (SPLT), which seeks to move debate beyond procedures into the substance of grant approvals, has been characterised as the first steps towards a truly global patent. However, negotiations have progressed slowly within a context of considerable disagreement amongst participants.[26]

There has been ongoing disagreement over progress with the SPLT due primarily to a clash of principles between actors who see the world in different ways, especially over areas such as public interest flexibility, the transfer of technology and biodiversity controls. For example, at the Tenth Session of the Standing Committee on the Law of Patents (SCP) in May 2004, some participants presented joint proposals that focused on priority areas of patenting harmonisation such as a better understanding of what can be legitimate prior art, securing agreement to the principles of genuine novelty and in making effective assessments as to an applications inventiveness. However, led by Brazil as

[25] They maintain that there are in fact so minimal a number of disputes based on invention timelines that the US "now has a virtual first-to-file system". This may help to explain why the country's differences in respect of legal text have not, in reality, been a barrier to closer cooperation and further harmonisation with other authorities. In 1998, of 220,000 patent filings, less than 0.1% had disputes relating to differences between inventing and filing dates associated with them, and of these, less than one third were subsequently amended to favour the second filing party.

[26] First introduced in November 2000 to a general level of enthusiasm, it has subsequently encountered problems with progress. Under these negotiations, the USPTO, the EPO and the Japanese Patent Office (JPO) frequently present joint proposal documents under the auspices of their "Trilateral Offices" (a term used to describe the close cooperation between these three major patent offices) along with the "Group B" negotiating group of industrialised countries. For an overview of the SPLT and its connections with both the PLT and the PCT, see World Intellectual property Organisation, 'Report of the Standing Committee on the Law of Patents', 24th September 2001, <http://www.wipo.int/edocs/mdocs/scp/en/scp_6/scp_6_5.pdf>, accessed 20th January 2007.

leader of the Group of Friends of Development[27] and with support from India, where issues such as the protection of "traditional knowledge" have high political implications,[28] this developing country alliance opposed these further consolidations.

These initiatives show the challenges in creating international treaties in issue sensitive policy areas and may indicate limited prospects for further patent harmonisation success in respect to the SPLT (Gerhardsen, 2006).[29]

Nevertheless, enterprises that create IP-rich products continue to have particular incentives to promote further harmonisation in terms of achieving a truly global patent award, especially within industrialised and high technology-oriented economies, due to the significant costs associated in securing patent protection across different jurisdictions, unlike in the case of copyright where protection largely occurs automatically. These costs must be replicated under current international rules in each country or region where protection is sought, and some estimates have put minimum charges to secure worldwide patent protection at upwards of US$1 million even despite application streamlining and integration offered by the PCT (Mossinghaf and Ku, 1998:530). Clearly, transnational organisations that trade within a globalised marketplace in knowledge goods have real incentive to promote further integration along these lines and can be expected to pressure their respective national government offices accordingly.

Difficulties in regulatory convergence in patent law are not limited to multilateral treaties. In Europe, disagreements over patent

---

27 This group also includes countries such as Kenya, Cuba, Tanzania, Iran and Egypt amongst others.

28 The Indian government has take active steps to protect India's traditional knowledge. For example, see this article by the Science and Development Network, highlighting India's database of traditional knowledge resource to ensure protection for specialist products, available online and accessed 7th April 2009: Katie Mantell, 'India logs traditional knowledge', Science and Development Network, 23 April 2002, at <http://www.scidev.net/en/news/india-logs-traditional-knowledge.html>, as well as this article, discussing policy objectives for the database to protect the special properties of products such as tumeric, at public affairs and policy development journal India Together: Ramesh Menon, 'Intellectual Property. Traditional knowledge receives a boost', *India Together*, 13th January 2007. Available online and last accessed 7th April at <www.indiatogether.org/2007/jan/eco-tkdl.htm>.

29 This work comments on moves by India, supported by China and the UK, to break the deadlock introduced by linking Intergovernmental meetings on Biodiversity with Patent Harmonisation meetings as a way to prevent overlap and conflict at WIPO, last referenced 18th January 2007. See also See (New and Gerhardsen 2006)

strategies exist between some regime actors even within an otherwise relatively well integrated region. In this case, it concerns parallel initiatives towards the creation of the EU's "Community Patent" (Barton, 2005:620–27) and parallel initiatives by the EPO. This European problem is not simply a dispute about power and authority between institutions, as there in fact seems to be much accord between these two bodies in respect to achieving harmonisation in patent law at a European level (European Patent Office, 2006). Instead, it focuses on the legal foundations required to support the creation of a unitary patent grant across Europe in the context of the European Patent Litigation Agreement (EPLA).[30]

In international trademark regulations, there have also been recent trends towards regulatory convergence, greater application interconnection and procedural harmonisation, mainly through the Madrid Protocol[31] administered by WIPO, which has gained far wider acceptance and much greater visibility amongst leading industrialised nations and regions in the last few years, as trademarks have become more valuable assts on company balance sheets (World Intellectual Property Organisation, 2005). It has been shown that trademarks themselves have become significant objects of retained value for international enterprises and the rapid expansion of trade in goods across all parts of the globe promotes greater focus on trademark protection, brand recognition and the maintenance of consumer confidence.

---

[30] The EPO raises concerns about resolving the current contrasts in post grant litigation outcomes that continue to persist across the different national courts of EPO participants. These would, it maintains, continue to exist across the EU under a unitary patent unless moves were put in place to create a suitably empowered common European IP court with rights that would of necessity be above and beyond those that currently subsist within the existing pan European legal framework. These debates over further convergence are set to continue into the future.

[31] The Protocol introduced an extraterritorial dimension into the administration and granting of marks when compared to the older and less widely adopted Madrid Agreement of 1891, by enabling an international registration to take place in designated third countries based only on a national application of origin by a citizen or entity of a contracting party. Enforcement of trademark rights remains within the purview of national courts, although TRIPS ensures that minimum standards are maintained across its own membership and also enforces recognition for "well-known marks" under special arrangements within domestic law. See also international application procedures under WIPO authority, <http://www.wipo.int/madrid/en/forms/how_to.html>, accessed January 18th 2007 and op. cit. WTO TRIPS Agreement, 'Trademarks—Art 16.2', <http://www.wto.org/english/tratop_e/trips_e/intel2_e.htm>, accessed 20th January 2007.

The Madrid Protocol came into force in April 1996 but recent developments have raised its profile and importance within IP regulations. Most importantly, both the United States and the European Union have recently acceded to the Protocol in 2003 and 2004 respectively, actions which have boosted significantly the opportunities to achieve a truly global protection regime by incorporating not only the world's largest economy but also the integrated protection offered by the Europe's Community Trademark[32] that provides a unitary registration across EU member states, in addition to optional registration rights in each member individually.[33]

Some observers maintain that Madrid Protocol developments are a logical consequence of the notion that trademarks have always had a distinctive extraterritorial element to their enforcement, even despite the rejection of universality of trademarks under the Paris Convention. In the US in particular, it has been argued that the country's Supreme Court has on some occasions asserted jurisdiction in trademark cases when violations of US registered marks have been abused abroad, especially when such infringing products are then re-imported into US territory under the false mark.[34] Such direct judicial aggressive action does not take place within the realm of copyright or patent violations in the same way and some scholars have distinguished only trademarks as being subject to this very distinctive approach, although there would appear to be practical limits to this approach even for the United States (Bradley, 1997; Putnam, 2006).[35]

---

[32] The Community Trademark is administered by the Office of Harmonization for the Internal Market which became operational on 1st January 1996.

[33] See the official 'WIPO Magazine—Focus on Trademarks', March—April 2005, WIPO Publications Geneva, pp. 2–4.

[34] For example, in the case of counterfeit watch imports from Mexico, judgement was made in favour of the plaintiff even though no US company was actually involved in illegal acts, enabling the trademark holder to pursue the Mexican corporation through the US courts. See *Steele v Bulova Watch Company* Supreme Court 344 US 280 (1952).

[35] It has been pointed out that the American Justices' interpretation of their extraterritorial powers would be very likely to take into account the potential for international repercussions, and that this would include informal assessments of the relationships at stake as well as more formal considerations under the Doctrine of International Comity, whereby courts may impose upon themselves certain restraints in exercising jurisdiction based on damage to foreign relations or harm to US interests in multilateral forums such as the WTO. See Dr Putnam's paper at <http://www.lawandsocietysummerinstitutes.org/workshop06/participants/tonya.pdf>, accessed 18th January 2007.

Greater convergence can also be observed in the exercise of IP enforcement within the international regime, although it can be argued that less progress has been achieved in this area when compared to the foundation of general principles of IP law. On the positive side, domestic legal arrangements, international treaties and multilateral forums have combined to create a number of options for state and non-state actors to secure their enforcement objectives. However, enforcement realities often touch upon highly sensitive domestic cultural and legal arrangements, such that arguments over enforcement deficiencies can generate considerable tension between trading partners at both a state and non-state level.

Multilaterally, it is the WTO rather than WIPO that has been the locus of development in respect to IP enforcement as it mandates minimum acceptable procedures and provides a mechanism for conflict management through the Dispute Settlement Understanding (DSU).[36] However, there are still considerable differences in the ways that each nation addresses precise details of enforcement policy[37] and this vexing problem of diverging enforcement practicalities would seem to have become an increasingly visible theme in trading relationships. These wider aspects would appear to be especially relevant to interdependencies in the relationship between the United States and China, which usefully illustrates how tensions between commercial trading partners can escalate to have a wider international significance.

In April 2007, the US lodged a DSU complaint against China over the country's failure to provide adequate enforcement through criminal

---

[36] Some WTO members provide a communications vehicle within their own jurisdiction for channelling and initiating these complaints, such as the EU's Trade Barriers Regulation (TBR). This empowers the EU Commission to investigate and act on receipt of a complaint from an EU registered enterprise against trade practices of a non-EU country, whereby the European Commission may take the matter forward, for example to the WTO level, after reviewing the substance of the complaint. See European Commission, 'Trade Barriers Regulation', <http://ec.europa.eu/trade/issues/respectrules/tbr/index_en.htm>, accessed 20th February 2007.

[37] These variations are, in fact, perfectly legitimate and can be seen to run along similar tramlines to the differences in the political and legal framework of the membership as a whole. For example, China's civil law based system operates dual administrative and judicial remedies at both national and provincial level in keeping with its partial federal structure and history of instrumentalist administrative policymaking. India, by contrast, adopts a common law approach that, whilst sensitive to its federal political structure, is still rooted in its historical similarities with the Laws of England.

convictions of IP violations.[38] Some legal experts argued at the time that moves of this kind would present the United States with a number of legal and political difficulties, not least because "there is no precedent at the WTO for how to interpret these international treaty obligations to provide 'effective' enforcement procedures for intellectual property" (Hughes 2006).[39] Moreover, the burden of proof placed on the US authorities under such an action could prove problematic, especially as that small number of DSU cases which had been brought to date were all settled without recourse to Panel Adjudication or Appellate Body comment, making it difficult to gauge how such proof might be interpreted (ibid.).

However, it can be argued that this issue introduces wider dimensions to the US-China relationship. Bilateral trade is vital to both countries, with the United States accounting for just over 21% of China's exports in 2006, making the US a significant export partner (National Bureau of Statistics of China, 2006). Moreover, the relationship has global significance, indicated in some part by the stock market turmoil experienced at the end of February 2007 that some commentators saw as linked to concerns about China's growth prospects and their interconnection to American economic figures.[40] Whilst it is important to highlight that share market fluctuations should not be confused with a detailed review of underlying national fundamentals, such linkages may help explain the extent to which US administration officials have been counselled against actions that might disrupt this delicate balance (Mertha, 2006).

---

[38] They also filed a second claim concerning market access to foreign films and books into China's domestic markets. The first case in particular would appear to stem from perceived deficiencies in China's criminal enforcement regime, whereby fines rather then imprisonment have been the norm and any changes in this respect by Chinese authorities may require modifications to the country's criminal code. In the second dispute case, the issues are also likely to be considered as cultural and political by Chinese authorities as the country heavily controls the availability and distribution of foreign audio-visual and print materials, even in major cities (author's experience living in Beijing over a number of years). This case might be linked, however, to the widespread availability of pirate films of all kinds from street vendors, and may therefore be part of American attempts to connect market access with IP enforcement.

[39] See also a transcript of Prof. Hughes's testimony accessed July 2009 and available at <http://www.uscc.gov/hearings/2006hearings/written_testimonies/06_06_08wrts/06_06_7_8_hughes_justin.php>.

[40] See BBC News 'World Stock Slump hits second day' last accessed 28th February 2007 at http://news.bbc.co.uk/1/hi/business/6402915.stm.

Some scholars had indicated that too hard an attack on China's IP regulatory weaknesses by the US could have led the Chinese to "respond defensively", resulting in even slower progress on improvements to the enforcement regime (ibid.; McGregor, 2007).[41] Whilst this kind of response by China could have led to lost momentum towards improvement in the IP regime, this does not appear to have materialised, even after what American government officials have termed a judgement "victory" in the Panel Report announced in early 2009.[42] That the Chinese have continued to protest the validity of US claims is perhaps understandable, but that these disputes have not escalated is perhaps due to both an acknowledgement that "the majority of Beijing's elite decision makers genuinely believes [sic] in the importance of protecting intellectual property rights", and that China is willing to operate within the rules of international institutions to which it has acceded (Mertha, 2006:1). These disputes would also seem to confirm the continuing importance to American export-oriented enterprises of securing effective IP protection policies in the home territories of their overseas trading partners (Zwaniecki, 2006).

There are, however, areas of even clearer progress in the Chinese context of the international legal resources available to commercial IP owners seeking an effective enforcement outcome by securing recourse to international arbitration, illustrating that non-state actors are able to protect their IP product interests independent of inter-government negotiations.

The New York Convention on the Recognition of Foreign and Arbitral Awards is the international instrument that supports this approach (United Nations Commission on International Trade Law, 2006).[43] As at 2007, it had 142 Contracting States, and includes amongst its signatories all of the major industrialised powers, as well as China and India. The Convention facilitates an extraterritorial reach for arbitration judgements across member countries, whereby corporate negotiators

[41] It remains to be seen whether this response develops into further antagonism between the two countries.

[42] See DS362 Panel Report 26th January 2009, at <http://www.wto.org/english/news_e/news09_e/362r_e.htm> accessed 9th April 2009. Many independent commentators have seen this as a "score draw" rather than a victory for any one side, but the exact outcomes are likely to remain unclear until appeals and next stage processes have been concluded.

[43] The New York Convention was adopted at a diplomatic conference in 1958 and entered into force in June 1959.

can reduce the uncertainties and risks associated with contract violation in foreign jurisdictions by including reference to the Convention as a place of final dispute settlement between the parties.

Whilst capable of applying to many different areas of potential contract level disputes, it presents particular attractions in IP related matters as it smoothes over those inconsistencies between the legal framework and the enforcement realities that can be most troubling for companies seeking reliable contractual arrangements. Over recent years, the Convention has evolved to become a recognised means of asserting IP rights within a country that is independent of national legal systems (Briner, 1998).[44]

In China, in particular, enforcement credibility varies greatly by region, which can introduce uncertainties into contract negotiation. However, the country's legal system has already recognised its responsibilities to enforce arbitration awards brought by foreign firms under the Convention (Virtual Library Arbitration Database, 1999).[45]

Those engaged in trans-provincial trade within China, therefore, play close attention to including referral to arbitration under the Convention within their contractual obligations with Chinese partners, with executives considering it both a necessary safeguard and a sensible precaution.[46] Experts have maintained that "[b]y and large, the enforcement of awards is considerably easier than the enforcement of judgements rendered by national courts", and, although the actual nature of enforcement procedures across different countries is not uniform, which is seen as an ongoing weakness, specific national arbitration laws can act as a benchmark for others to follow (Briner, 1998:8).[47]

---

[44] It is based upon the principles of mutual recognition across contracting parties of dispute arbitration awards granted by authorised courts, such as those offered by the International Court of Arbitration of the International Chamber of Commerce or the London Court of International Arbitration. For a useful overview of the Convention's principles.

[45] Note, however, the concept of the "reciprocity reservation" that has been adopted by China. This enables states to limit recognition only to those other states that are also contracting parties to the Convention. There is also a "commercial reservation" to the Convention, which restricts recognition to areas considered wholly commercial under the domestic law of the state where the dispute exists.

[46] Author interview with the Finance Director at a London based software company. London, April 2005.

[47] The arbitration laws of India, for example, have been acknowledged as creating just such a standard, which may promote further convergence in international procedures at this level.

In concluding a discussion on the trends towards greater convergence within the international IP regulatory regime, it can be argued that in all of these different ways, through the influence of commercial imperatives, through the establishment of global norms for different kinds of IP and their integration into domestic legal systems, and through the recognition of international mechanisms to support more reliable enforcement dispute outcomes, the IP regime would seem to be evolving in complexity, as well as changing the relationship between state and non-state actors within the wider trading system.

These changes of relationship and the different types of actor interdependencies that they introduce have been shown to be connected to distinct stages of IP regime evolution that appear to characterise the process of adoption and absorption. Such a connection is especially sharpened as countries progress from relying on technology catch-up through closed import substituting industrialisation models to embracing technological development through more open and innovation driven export-oriented approaches. In particular, such a framework can be observed in the development of greater regulatory strength and enforcement capability of the IP regimes of China and India.

7.4 *Understanding Chinese and Indian IP Regulatory Development*

It can be argued that the balance between state and non-state actor participation in regime building alters in concert with the technological development of a country's domestic knowledge industries and the associated incentives that these industries have in accommodating wider IP norms. It has been argued that China and India's IP regime evolution usefully illustrates how different stages operate to bring about change in the relationship between state sector direction and private sector initiative, with changes in emphasis and behaviour between them linked to technological development and international market engagement.

In the first stage of technology acquisition and IP regime evolution, the state's role can be seen as typically one of mentor and guide, as it takes the lead in creating a climate for knowledge sector take-off. In this phase, the state's role appears focused on both active and benign collusion in ignoring IP norms or in encouraging just sufficient rigor to promote foreign investment and knowledge spillovers without the commensurate restraints on how that acquired knowledge was to be used by domestic market imitators. This may help to explain attitudes of American publishers in the late 19th Century and the controversial approaches to IP regulatory obedience adopted by Indian drug manufacturers and Chinese IT hardware manufacturers in the last quarter of the 20th Century.

Attitudes to IP regime adoption in this early phase can also be shaped by cultural distinctions, whereby firm level skills and knowledge in some East Asian nations can be additionally protected, not in this case by state edict or even by the presence of international IP regime norms, but instead by different disciplines that are especially distinct to the region. These distinctions include group-firm market arrangements, such as the *kieretsu* and *chaebol*, together with familial loyalties and extended networked relationships, all of which are characteristics of many East Asian markets and which can explicitly reduce transaction costs in the creation and expansion of knowledge-based outputs. These conditions can mitigate many of the risks of losing commercial advantages in the early stages of knowledge acquisition due to IP theft in ways that might not be the case in more westernised corporate arrangements.

During this stage of evolution in a country's approach to IP norms, a process of "socialization through external inducement" and "cooperation through coercion" can become more evident, as overseas rightsholders in more powerful and technologically more creative countries seek to limit the effects of free-riding through piracy and counterfeiting by local imitators as the country engages in a more export-oriented approach (Sell, 2003:137).

However, it can also be argued that the influence of such tactics may actually be less than they first might appear, in that the extent to which this coercion leads to any material change of attitude amongst the local polity is open to debate (Whitman, 2005:25–27).[48]

For example, it seems clear from the evidence that China's evolution in attitude to IP reform over the last decade or more has had as much

[48] There may also be an element of caution in this respect even by the hegemonic power as they have an interest in mitigating the risk of systemic breakdown. Too great a level of force, or of the threat of force, or the perception of too few outcome incentives for developing nations being obliged to modify their behaviour in line with the convergence in global norms could increase such a risk by prompting a dwindling of actor participation by these weaker nations within regime forums and a diminishing of interest amongst their decision makers in regulatory evolution. See See especially pp. 35–37.

to do with the country's own national leadership's belief in such a necessary step and in the converging values of local technology-based businesses, which saw the logic in adopting tighter regulations, as it ever did from America's threats of trade sanctions and the establishment of Memoranda of Understanding during the 1990's. Indeed, the latter agreements were distinguished largely by their short-term failure to achieve any material change in local behaviour.

In India also, supportive legislative and fiscal policies to nurture the development of its nascent software services industry and the continuing encouragement towards infringing international product patents within its pharmaceutical sector took place despite persistent criticism and the threat of action under trade sanctions from the United States. These pressures occurred bilaterally during the first half of the 1990's as India's economy was opening to reengage with the international trading system, facilitated by America's Section 301 trade policy, and multilaterally after the creation of the WTO under its Dispute Settlement mechanism, from the second half of that decade onwards.

Instead, it has been shown that changed attitudes will typically be based less on the exertions of external powers and more on the emergence of a stimulus that is sufficient to generate a domestic will, typically manifesting itself in a blend of imposed and induced behavioural changes, where state action operates in combination with interested parties within segments of the local economy, as these enterprises move up the value chain and seek to exploit more specific codified market intelligence within specific overseas industries. For example, in the context of the Indian software industry, the move away from export of labour business models with generalised market sector knowledge into more specialised services exports can be seen as a key turning point in both the industry's attitudes towards protecting their newly acquired tacit knowledge and the national leadership's sponsorship of more effective copyright IP regulation and enforcement mechanisms.

Induced and imposed behavioural changes can therefore combine with potentially different levels of emphasis based on national culture and political institutional behaviour. In the Chinese and Indian dimensions, China appears to exhibit power characteristics that are based far more on top-down state instrumentalism that the bottom-up capitalist pluralism that is more prevalent, at least for some sectors, in India. It can be argued, therefore, that such an evolution cannot be fully captured if analysed solely in the context of either the impact of hegemonic power or the influence of systemic norm-setting, but instead there must be included a significant element of domestic incentive for explanations to be complete.

This combination can be seen as critical to a successful transition to the second stage of domestic IP regulatory development. In this second phase of IP development, the state can be observed moving into a partner role by nurturing and sustaining the continuing success of the local markets' newly acquired technological prowess and by developing more sophisticated relationships with local technology corporations. It has been shown that during this stage, greater concern is taken in regard to international norms by both commercial and government actors, using them as a guide to local regime building as external markets become increasingly attractive and domestic actors begin to demand protection for their own goods both inside and outside the national territory. Two-way channels of communication between enterprises and the government departments that regulate IP policy may begin to be established, as some of the leading innovating companies seek to express their regulatory objectives to government decision-makers. At this point, also, business associations and lobby groups may start to appear and interact with state actors in the process of agenda setting in ways that are appropriate to political arrangements in the territory concerned.

For example, in India, the role of NASSCOM has expanded rapidly during last decade of the country's technological development such that it now works in close affinity with national political bodies, promoting and initiating legal policies with a sufficiently high level of credibility that makes it extremely unlikely that further IP regime evolution would take place at the Union level in India without its close involvement. In a similar vein, Taiwan's Institute for Information Industry as an independent non-profit organisation describes its role as "well-orchestrated collaboration between the government and private sectors" which "has supported Taiwan's ICT industry with advanced technologies and international links to strengthen its global competitiveness" (Institute for Information Industry, 2008).

In China, by contrast, the country's software lobby group behaves in ways that are both characteristic of the less assertive tradition for such groups in the mainland and of the cultural networking realities that may explain why the primary link between government and industry at present appears to be at the level of individual firms rather than sectoral organisation. Furthermore, advanced levels of innovation appear to be more singular in their location within the broader

Chinese technology market, and that it is the leaders of these innovating firms such as Huawei and Alibaba that have had higher visibility than the industry as a whole, and that it is therefore their corporate leaders who enjoy particular credibility in national political circles.[49]

It can be argued that it is this increased strengthening of the role of industry interest groups, enterprises and individuals in agenda setting that particularly distinguishes the transition to the third stage of national IP regime development.

This third phase can best be characterised as taking place when the driving force behind political agenda setting and the creation of issue framing detail shifts from the state itself to commercial entities and interest groups, all of whom develop increasingly sophisticated ways to conduct dialogue with both national state actors and like-minded groups based beyond a territory's borders. These organisations and individuals conduct business globally and see regime evolution as a necessity at the same global level and they can help to promote distinctive regime developments.[50] In this way, the behaviour of state actors may evolve to one that is more in keeping with that of an operational agent for these sophisticated domestic entities.

Clearly, such a point can only be reached in the most technologically mature economies or within specific sophisticated sectors in less developed economies, and must also be combined with a configuration of state power that enables private sector agendas to be successfully projected into the international regime framing forums. It can be argued that the United States is the leading example of a state whose relationships have reached this stage, evidenced by the way that the major knowledge sector corporations and their IP lobby groups interact with government departments, the US Trade Representative Office, and, when necessary, the national court system.

However, the Indian software industry would also appear to be exhibiting key characteristics of these trends at a sectoral level and would appear to have reached this phase of development within a wider economy that has still yet to do so. Such a transition would seem

[49] However, it may be that political influence will widen across the industry in the next few years, given the rapid nature of technological development in China and the emergence of increasingly innovative second tier software service companies in Beijing's Haidian district.

[50] The involvement of technology enterprises and industry experts in the evolution of the WCT and the WPPT have already been highlighted as examples of these sophisticated intersections.

to be confirmed by evidence of NASSCOM's involvement in WITSA and other associated interest groups, its proactive relationship with the Union Government of India on the one hand and with leading corporations on the other, together with engagement by Indian companies such as WIPRO in overseas market penetration and in pioneering innovative cross-border service delivery models.

The increasing complexities evident in the interrelationships between state and non-state actors that evolve during this third phase of IP regime development can help to explain why some scholars have emphasised the importance of distinguishing between the formal structure and arrangements of some state-centric multilateral institutions and the realities of their internal operation, replete with shifting alliances, empowered non-state groups and shared incentives. At this point, endeavours may become "geared towards the globalisation of regulation" as a means to "expand, co-ordinate and harmonise rules and regulatory mechanisms" upon which group success is based (Whitman, 2005:36–37).

The argument can therefore follow that membership delegations of China, India, Korea and Taiwan on the TRIPS Council may have begun to have as great an interest in securing a robust international IP regulatory framework as have those participants from the United States and the European Union.

7.5 *A Functional Approach to IP Regime Development*

In these different ways, it can be seen that in the context of IP regulatory development, states appear to have become increasingly constrained by a combination of obligations imposed upon them by treaties from a systemic perspective and interconnections with the objectives of non-state actors such as corporations, professional associations and individual experts. It has also been shown that these non-state participants are themselves building networks that are often independent of the national authorities from which they might originate as individuals.

However, whilst the state may no longer be the sole participant in building the evolving IP regime, its power would appear to remain significant. Power dynamics remain important in shaping the fundamentals of issue area definitions: what exactly comprises a patentable invention; to what extent will copyright materials be subject to internet download controls; in what countries will an international trademark registration be permitted. This involvement of the state in IP regime building would therefore seem to have moved towards a more subtle representation of a genuine attempt by layers of interested parties to secure some form of systemic stability and attitude convergence in which there could be seen to be considerable mutuality of interests amongst the different actors.

In particular, it can be argued that the scope and structure of the emerging IP regime may reflect a move towards an embrace of global governance, as distinct from extending national government to a global level. These developments can be seen as part of what some scholars have described as the "shifts of globalisation", moving from the idea of a unitary state operating through exclusive government action to what has been termed "the disaggregated state", wherein constituent actors operate within layers of governance "addressing the issues and resolving the problems that result from citizens going global" (Slaughter, 2004:12–16).

It would therefore appear relevant to make an assessment of the extent to which this increasingly complex and globally focused IP regime can be described as the development of a functional solution to an international problem.

Under a functional perspective, there is a connection between the traditions of functionalism and the role of the international organisations that have arisen to link the specific task of improving intellectual property rules beyond the confines and limitations of the boundaries of specific states into a multilateral institutional relationship. Indeed, the movement from a loose organisation of interested parties into a tight institution with decision-making capability captures the very essence of a functionalist approach to problem solving at the international level (Haas, 1964:94–95).

There are strongly held arguments (Sell, 2003; Abbott, 2002:334) that criticise both the WTO and WIPO for failing to strike the right balance between private interests and public access in international IP norms, and for acting as host to "one size fits-all" IP legal principles. Nevertheless, in their distinctive ways, these institutions do appear to be promoting useful levels of integration between the IP laws of different states that would be considerably more difficult, if not impossible, to achieve if either or both of them did not exist (Haas, 1964:12–15).[51]

[51] Although writing in 1964 well before the internet, Haas illustrates his thinking by looking at the International Office of Public Health and describes a pattern of

However, it has not been proved that these entities have somehow wholly replaced the unique position of the state, nor has there been evidence of the emergence that any one of them is somehow transcending either the state's operational activities in domestic day-to-day IP rule making or its special position in global norm setting at an international level, in a way that the functionalist paradigm would present (Mitrany, 1975). The state has not shown any inclination to "wither away"[52] under the influence of a technologically induced transfer of loyalty to these global international regime institutions.

Instead, it may be necessary to look beyond a purely theoretical interpretation of a functionalist evolution of these institutions to see that the characteristics of the intellectual property regime do indeed exhibit "a system of functional co-operation", but that they do this as part of what some scholars have observed as the rise in "passive functionalism", or "the maintenance of a universal code of commercial behaviour" in respect to the interactions of actor participants (Mayall, 1975:253–57).

In summary, an interpretation can be presented that suggests that there are now increasingly complex interconnections between different actors during the stages that characterise national IP regime evolution. Different influences, across multiple phases of development, have been shown to exist that link the cultural, social, technological and economic characteristics of a country's domestic structure on the one hand with the emergence of international institutional vehicles enabling issue convergence and norm setting on the other.

It would seem to follow that the establishment of a successful national level regime for the protection of intellectual property rights in China and India can be explained by the confluence of a number of factors. First, the technological sophistication now present within key sectors of both countries has changed attitudes. Second, the domestically promoted development and market opening strategies that have been adopted by the national leadership within target sectors of their respective economies has raised incentives for international convergence. Third, these domestic developments have been able to coincide

---

technical cooperation "relying on systemic forces and a learning process for eventually transcending rather than defeating the old order" (page 13).

[52] This phrase was first used by Friedrich Engels in his 19th Century writings describing how the state's function changes under various stages of socialism but has since become used by analysts who focus on a functional approach to state behaviour.

with the emergence of agreed global norms that has helped to frame the absorption patterns of both nations and where these norms have themselves been shaped by commercial priorities of those corporations operating at the leading edge of innovation, both in the established developed economies and in the strengthening sectors of China and India.

Seen in this way, it would seem clear that the position of China and India can now be characterised as one of genuine participation in regime building, with an increasingly active role to play in both developing reliable domestic IP regimes and in participating within international rule setting forums.

7.6 *Conclusion*

This chapter has explored the development of the intellectual property regime as it is currently evolving within the international system. It has made connections between the increasing complexity of regime norms and a widening of actor participation in that development, so as to give a better understanding of how intellectual property is regulated and how this regulation may progress in the future, both at a national and systemic level.

It has been argued that there has been increasing convergence on issue areas between actors at different levels of the regime-setting matrix towards a set of globally accepted IP norms and that these are becoming more widely adopted through a complex web of treaties, bilateral agreements and national legislative initiatives.

It has been further argued that the implementation and adoption of these norms within a state's specific legal regime is not simply a product of hegemonic power exercised either by the US government or by Microsoft Corporation, or of the authority of particular multilateral institutions such as the WTO and WIPO. Instead, evidence has been presented to show that it is just as much a product of national technological development and international engagement in trade, and of the perceived benefits that can thereby accrue. Finally, a framework has been presented that enable these conditions to be viewed in a functional perspective that can help facilitate the analysis of China and India's success in both absorbing IP principles and constructively participating in international regime norm setting.

CHAPTER EIGHT

CONCLUSION

This research has explored the relationships between the technological development of China and India and the evolution of their intellectual property (IP) regulatory policy and has connected a number of interrelated themes in order to answer the questions posed in the introduction.

First, an analysis has been made of the factors that have pushed China and India towards a more enthusiastic embrace of international IP norms. It has been shown that the extent of their technological development and the corporate success visible in both of these countries was not an accidental by-product of national advantage but has taken place as part of deliberate policy objectives of the respective national governments.

National elites in both countries have recognised that power within the trading system is as much about openness of markets as it is about realist political notions of defence and that both of these governments have instituted marked shifts from old ideological attitudes that focused on import substitutions strategies, protected industries and weak respect for IP norms. They have both engaged in an export-led technologically driven approach as part of their strategy of expansion, with evidence suggesting that this has led to changed attitudes towards both domestic and overseas intellectual property. This has uncovered an important message for research scholars that may help to move the IP debate forward through looking at export strategies and their influence on national IP policy: whilst their markets were closed, foreign owners of IP had less concern about their rates of piracy *per se* as legitimate and counterfeit products were not competing directly, but now that market opening has taken place, the IP policies of both China and India have become part of an inter-firm and an inter-government agenda.

In particular, this work has suggested explanations for the differences in attitude to IP regime engagement, both within India's pharmaceutical industry and between it and the country's software industry. It also shows how high value and advanced software enabled services have put effective IP regulations at the forefront of priorities for IT corporations. It has also presented reasons that may help to account for the Chinese leadership's determination to ensure that legitimate software is embedded in the country's technology hardware exports and that further improvements are made to the country's judicial enforcement regime, as well as linking increased levels of domestic IT innovation with calls for IP regulatory enhancements that have come from both Chinese and foreign-owned enterprises.

Moreover, it has been argued that the evolution of the IP regime in both countries has been closely connected to government support for domestic knowledge industries. It can be inferred from the evidence that IP regulations have a positive role to play in stimulating technology sector development, with overlaps being shown to exist in a number of countries between the IP legal system's evolution and the technology industry's development that must be seen as more than just coincidence. Software industries in particular encapsulate a litmus test of how IP rights drive growth in knowledge-based economies. Empirical feedback from practitioners has illustrated the significance of IP protection levels and their perceived reliability in an international context in choosing not just what parts of a program's design to offshore in the context of specific software development projects but also in terms of driving key decision-making over the embrace of business-centric strategies such as outsourcing to a particular overseas location.

Decision-making at commercial levels and policy design at political levels intersect to create push-pull factors that can help to shape and channel the evolution of a country's software and high technology industry. Examples given in this work have revealed just such intersections in the state-led policy actions taken by a number of Asian nations to promote high technology development and engender a respect for IP rights with the sustained growth of enterprises within that sector.

This interplay between national IP regimes and technological capability has been manifested in a number of ways. Research has uncovered a significant growth in patent activism across technology industries, whilst inter-firm ventures have also grown in number and complexity in these sectors, extending beyond borders to include increasingly sophisticated forms of horizontal networking and deepening inter-relationships. Moreover, the future success of high value industries in China and India in particular has been shown to rest as much on increased IP rights protection and effective regime enforcement as they do on other economic factors.

Second, it has been shown that both domestic and systemic influences have played a part in facilitating these changes.

Domestically, a convergence of interests and attitudes has emerged between state and non-state actors across both China and India in respect to the necessity and value of IP regime development. However, it has been argued that the transmission of messages between participating groups is fundamentally different in each country. India exhibits greater levels of corporate and interest group power being exerted in highly sophisticated networks to drive forward national policy objectives through upward pressure in concert with government level action. This sits in contrast to China, where a dynamic state leadership exerting top-down pressure can be seen as promoting its own perception of the prerequisites for national economic growth, in which the high technology sectors have been determined as playing a fundamental part and for which improved IP protection and legal enforcement policies have been deemed essential. The latest research has shown that the Chinese government has created a framework in which academic debates acts as a proxy for political disagreement and helps to channel feedback to national elites on the appropriate characteristics that should be implemented as part of the country's IP regime evolution (Yuan, 2006).

Systemically, national regime development in the context of IP has been shown to be taking place as part of a wider functional dynamic. Evidence presented suggests an emergence of a set of increasingly global IP norms along with a deepening penetration of IP rules into national legal frameworks. It has been argued that these harmonising tendencies have arisen from outcomes initiated through both multilateral institutional agreement and bilateral pressures and that technology corporations and their lobby groups have made key contributions within this dynamic. Together, these different types of actor now seem to be setting parameters of behaviour in ways that states may find increasingly difficult to ignore as they move towards the adoption and absorption of IP regulatory principles.

China and India are both learning to engage with this new dynamic because it is now in their own national interests to do so and these systemic priorities will likely determine the direction of each country's future regime characteristics.

Third, following on from the previous point, it has been argued that new complexities are now visible in the interaction between state and non-state actors in IP regime formation. Observations have identified the emergence of a three-level game that goes beyond the realist notions of state primacy and the neo-realist perceptions of multinational corporate engagement with states to include new kinds of communications between different levels of participation. In particular, it has been shown that companies of all sizes are driven by commercial imperatives to focus on unified issue areas with partners and other industry organisations in ways that cross national boundaries and that are complementary to traditional forms of state-centred bilateral and multilateral dialogue to an extent that something towards a new regime may be emerging.

8.1 *Areas for Future Research*

In the process of setting out to answer the questions posed earlier, new areas of potential research have been revealed.

In India, the detailed growth strategies and likely developments of newly innovating pharmaceutical companies may bear fruitful further investigation in the future. Legislative changes that now enable product patents to be enforced have only very recently become part of India's IP framework, but they would seem to exemplify the country's shift to embrace a forward-looking and export-oriented future. Currently, inferences and assessments on the impact of these new regulations have had to be made based on prevailing opinion and observed industry developments, but the full impact of these new legal conditions will only become apparent as the next few years unfold.

In China, rapid social and economic change is taking place across the country at a startling pace and it remains to be seen what will be the wider influence on the global economy of the expansion in innovative capacity that can be observed taking place within the Chinese high technology industries. It would also be particularly interesting to take forward research on decision-making influences within the Chinese elite and the extent to which non-state actors may have on political policy debates, whether these are academics, returning members of the diaspora or local technology enterprise leaders. Such research work may be especially relevant as a way to explain how China might move from its current political structure towards a more pluralist framework.

For both countries, it would be interesting to expand upon the importance of export-led growth strategies in the context of their broader technology policy, beyond the specific focus on intellectual property regulations.

8.2 *Concluding Remarks*

This research has made the link between the growing significance of trade in goods that have a high IP content with incentives for developing countries to stimulate their own knowledge industries, to open their economies and to engage more closely with an evolving international IP regime. Charting this trajectory within a distinct Asian dimension, the IP policy prescriptions of China and India have been given particularly detailed focus in the context of the international importance that these two countries hold as leading developing nations.

BIBLIOGRAPHY

Abbott, Frederic. 2002. The TRIPS-legality of measures taken to address public health crises: Responding to USTR-State-Industry positions that undermine the WTO. In *The Political Economy of International Trade Law. Essays in Honor of Robert E. Hudec*, edited by D. Kennedy and J. Southwick: Cambridge University Press.

Adelphi Charter, The. *Mapping the Issues: Current Problems Facing Creativity, Innovation and Intellectual Property* [cited 22nd February 2007]. Available from http://www.adelphicharter.org/mapping_the_issues.asp.

Adhikari, Ramesh, and Prema-chandra Athukorala. 2002. Developing countries in the world trading system: an overview. In *Developing Countries in the World Trading System. The Uruguay Round and Beyond*, edited by R. Adhikari and P.-C. Athukorala: Edward Elgar.

Ahya, Chetan, and Mihir Sheth. 2005. India Infrastructure. (Morgan Stanley Research 8th November 2005), http://www.morganstanley.com/views/gef/archive/2005/20051108-Tue.html#anchor4.

Akester, Particia. 2004. Implementation of the protection of technological measures of Article 6 of the InfoSoc Directive (2001/29/EC) in the UK. *Copyright Laws in Digital Europe* (May 2004), http://www.euro-copyrights.org/index/8/13.

Alford, William P. 1995. *To Steal a Book is an Elegant Offense. Intellectual Property Law in Chinese Civilisation*: Stanford University Press.

——. 1999. A Second Great Wall? China's Post Cultural Revolution Project of Legal Construction. *Cultural Dynamics* Vol. 11 (No. 2 July 1999): pp. 193–213.

Alikhan, Shahid. 2000. *The Socio-Economic Benefits of Intellectual Property Protection in Developing Countries*: WIPO.

Amazon. 1999. Method and System for Placing a Purchase Order via a Communications Network. In *US Patent No. 5, 960, 411 28th September 1999.*

Analysis International, Beijing. *China Software market sales reached RMB 32.4 billion in 2005* (13th March) 2006 [cited 9th August 2006]. Available from http://english.analysys.com.cn/industry_refer/industry_refer_index.php?name=report&daohang=Software.

Anand, Pravin. 2003. Email to Author: Overview of First use of Anton Piller Order in India in 1979, July 2003.

Andersen, Brigitte, and Sue Kanzelmann. 2006. The Productive Potential of Intellectual Property Rights: Governance and Value Creation Processes. In *New Directions in Copyright Law*, edited by F. Macmillan: Edward Elgar.

Anderson, Chris. 2004. The Long Tail. *Wired Magazine* (October 2004), http://www.wired.com/wired/archive/12.10/tail.html?pg=5&topic=tail&topic_set=.

Ataman, Dr. Muhittin. 2002. Three-Level Game or Ignored Actors of World Politics: Transnational Factors. Abant Izzet Baysal University, Turkey, July 2002.

Bagchi, Jayanta. 2000. *World Trade Organisation. An Indian Perspective*: Eastern Law House.

Bagga, R. K., Kenneth Kenniston, and Rohit Raj Mathur. 2005. The State, ICT and Development: The Indian Context. In *The State, IT and Development*, edited by R. K. Bagga, K. Kenniston and R. R. Mathur: Sage Publications New Delhi.

Bakht, Anil. 2006. Breakthrough Phase in SMEs based on Innovation. *Building an Ecosystem for IT Innovation in India* NASSCOM Publications, New Delhi: pp. 51–55.

Balasubramanyam, V. N., and A. Balasubramanyam 1996a. The Distribution of Gains Between the Investing and Borrowing Countries Revisited: The Case of the Emerging Indian Software Sector. *Department of Economics Management School, Lancaster University* EC5/96.

——. 1996b. Software in South India. *Department of Economics Management School, Lancaster University* EC9/96 1996.

Barboza, David. 2006. Labor Shortage in China May Lead to Trade Shift. *New York Times Online* (3rd April 2006), http://www.nytimes.com/2006/04/03/business/03labor.html?ex=1301716800&en=49c0d472886e1f39&ei=5088&partner=rssnyt&emc=rss.

Barroso, Luiz Andre. 2005. The Price of Performance. *Association of Computing Machinery Queue* (No. 7, 7th September 2005), http://acmqueue.com/modules.php?name=Content&pa=showpage&pid=330&page=1.

Barton, John. 2003. Integrating IPR Policies in Developing Strategies. In *Trading in Knowledge. Development Perspectives on TRIPS, Trade and Sustainability*, edited by C. Bellman, G. Dutfield and R. Melendez-Ortiz: Earthscan Publications.

Barton, John H. 2005. Issues Posed by a World Patent System. In *International Public Goods and Transfer of Knowledge. Under a Globalised Intellectual Property Regime*, edited by K. Maskus and J. Reichman: Cambridge University Press.

Basheer, Shamnad. 2005. India's Tryst with TRIPS: The Patents (Amendment) Act, 2005. *The Indian Journal of Law and Technology* Vol. 1.

Basheer, Shamnad, and Mrinalini Kochupillai. 2008. Exhausting Patent Rights in India: Parallel Imports and TRIPS Compliance. *Journal of Intellectual Property Rights* Vol. 13: pp. 486–497.

Basheer, Shamnad, and Annalisa Primi. 2009. The WIPO Development Agenda: Factoring in the "Technologically Proficient" Developing Countries. In *Implementing WIPO's Development Agenda*, edited by J. DeBeer: Wilfred Laurier University Press.

Basheer, Shamnad, and Preshan Reddy. 2008. The "Efficacy" of Indian Patent Law: Ironing Out the Creases in Section 3(d). *Scripted* Vol. 5 Issue 2, August 2008.

Bate, Roger, and Richard Tren. 2006. The WTO and Access to Essential Medicines. *Health Policy Outlook, American Enterprise Institute for Public Policy Research* (16th Febraury 2006), http://www.aei.org/publications/pubID.23900/pub_detail.asp.

BBC News. 2005. Software Patent Bill Thrown Out. (5th July 2005), http://news.bbc.co.uk/1/hi/technology/4655955.stm.

——. 2006. China to tackle software piracy (12th April 2006), http://news.bbc.co.uk/2/hi/technology/4902976.stm.

——. 2007. Dow gain bucks global stock slide. (28th February 2007), http://news.bbc.co.uk/1/hi/business/6402915.stm.

Beebe, Alan, Chee Hew, Feng Yueqi, and Professor Shi Dailun. 2006. Going Global. Prospects and Challenges for Chinese Companies on the World Stage. (4th April 2006), http://www-935.ibm.com/services/us/index.wss/ibvstudy/imc/a1024122?cntxt=a1000074 (also http://www-935.ibm.com/services/us/imc/pdf/g510-6269-going-global.pdf).

Beherens, Brian C., and Reuven R. Levary. 2008. Legal Aspects of Reverse Engineering. In *Reverse Engineering. An Industrial Perspective*, edited by V. Raja and K. J. Fernandes: Springer Series in Advanced Manufacturing.

Beijing Municipal Science and Technology Commission. *Introduction and Mission* [cited 9th August 2006]. Available from http://www.bjkw.gov.cn/English/.

Bell, Jonathan. 2007. China's New Mantra: Innovate not Imitate. *Far Eastern Economic Review* Vol. 170 (No. 2 March 2007): pp. 37–40.

Bender, Tobias. 2006. How to cope with China's (alleged) failure to implement the TRIPS obligations on enforcement. *Journal of World Intellectual Property* Vol. 9 (No. 2 March 2006): pp. 230–250.

Beningo, Steven, and Brian Sloboda. 2006. Trade and Transportation between the United States and China and between the United States and India. *Conference of the Society of Government Economists, Washington D.C.* (27th October 2006), http://www.sge-econ.org/conf/documents/Slodoba_Beningo.pdf.

Bentley, Lionel. 2004. *Intellectual Property Law*: Oxford University Press.

Bhagwati, Jagdish. 2002. *Free Trade Today*: Princeton University Press.

——. 2004. *In Defense of Globalization*: Oxford University Press.

Bhandari, Maya. 2004. Intellectual Property Rights in the International System: the case of India. Unpublished Master's Thesis, International Studies, University of Cambridge.

Bowrey, Kathy. 2005. Can We Afford to Think about Copyright in a Globalised Marketplace? In *New Directions in Copyright Law*, edited by F. Macmillan: Edward Elgar.

Boyle, James. 2003. The Second Enclosure Movement and the Construction of the Public Domain. *Law and Contemporary Problems* Vol. 66 (Nos. 1 & 2 Winter / Spring 2003): pp. 227–256. (Duke Law School).

Bradley, Curtis A. 1997. Territorial Intellectual Property Rights in an Age of Globalism. *Virginia Journal of International Law* Vol. 37 (No. 2 Winter 1997): pp. 505–586.

Briner, Robert. 1998. Philosophy and Objectives of the Convention. *UN Colloquium: Enforcing Arbitration Awards under the New York Convention: Experience and Prospects* (June 1998), http://www.uncitral.org/pdf/english/texts/arbitration/NY-conv/NYCDay-e.pdf.

British Computer Society. 2000. Intellectual Property Rights in Software. A Practical Guide for Professionals and Business Managers. *BCS Guide*.

British Medical Journal Online. 2004. India to Extend Price Controls on Drugs. *BMJ* (14th August 2004), http://www.bmj.com/cgi/content/full/329/7462/368-c.

Brown, Ian. Implementing the European Union Copyright Directive. *Foundation for Information Policy Research*, http://www.fipr.org/copyright/guide/.

Busch, Marc, and Eric Reinhardt. 2002. Testing international trade law: Emperical studies of GATT/WTO dispute settlement. In *The Political Economy of International Trade Law. Essays in Honor of Robert E. Hudec*, edited by D. Kennedy and J. Southwick: Cambridge University Press.

Business Software Alliance. 2005. Economic Impact Study—Piracy. US IT Industry, http://www.bsa.org/idcstudy/pdfs/United_States.pdf.

BusinessWeek (Online Edition) 2005. *Innovation Metrics. Survey of Global Brand Value* [cited 20th October 2006]. Available from http://bwnt.businessweek.com/brand/2005/.

BusinessWeek (Print Edition). 2005a. Asia is Stem Cell Central. *BusinessWeek*, 10th January 2005.

——. 2005b. Information Technology Software. Linux Inc. *BusinessWeek*, 31st January 2005, pp. 50–57.

Callan, Eoin. 2007. U.S. Files W.T.O. cases to stem China piracy. *Financial Times Online—Asia Pacific* (9th April 2007), http://www.ft.com/cms/s/ede7a8da-e6bf-11db-9034-000b5df10621.html.

Cass, Deborah. 2003. China and Trade Law Constitutionalism. In *China and the World Trading System. Entering the New Millennium*, edited by D. Cass, B. Williams and G. Barker: Cambridge University Press.

Chadha, Alka. 2005. Product Cycles, Innovation and Exports: A Study of Indian Pharmaceuticals. *National University of Singapore Dept of Economics Working Paper Series* (5th November 2005), http://nt2.fas.nus.edu.sg/ecs/pub/wp/wp0511.pdf.

Chaisse, Julian, and Debashis Chakraborty. 2006. Dispute Resolution in the WTO: The Experience of India. In *Beyond the transition phase of the WTO. An Indian Perspective on Emerging Issues.*, edited by D. Sangupta, D. Chakraborty and P. Banerjee: Academic Foundation New Delhi.

Chandrasekhar, C. P. 2005. Economic Perspectives. IT Services as Locomotives. *Frontline Magazine (The Hindu Online Edition)* (Vol. 22 / Issue 13, 18th June–1st July 2005), http://www.hinduonnet.com/fline/fl2213/stories/20050701004412000.htm.

Chang, Ha-Joon. 2007. *Bad Samaritans. Rich Nations, Poor Policies, and the Threat to the Developing World*: Random House.

Chang, Ha-Joon, and Ilene Grabel. 2004. *Reclaiming Development. An Alternative Economic Policy Manual*: Zed Books London.

Chaudhuri, Sudip. 2008. Ranbaxy Sell-out: Reversal of Fortunes. *Economic & Political Weekly* 19th July 2008.

Chaytor, Beatrice. 1998. Dispute Resolution Under the GATT/WTO: The Experience of Developing Countries. In *Dispute Resolution in the World Trade Organisation*, edited by J. Cameron and K. Campbell: Cameron May.

Cheek, Marney L. 2000–01. The Limits of Informal Regulatory Cooperation in International Affairs: A Review of the Global Intellectual Property Regime. *George Washington International Law Review* Vol. 33 2000–2001: pp. 277–324.

Cheng , Haojing, and Brian DeLany. 1999. Quality Education and Social Stratification: The Paradox of Private Schooling in China. *Current Issues in Comparative Education* Vol. 1 Issue 2 30th April 1999: pp. 48–56.

China Daily Online. 2005. China highlights commitment to promoting multilateral trade system. *China Daily* (12th July 2005), http://www.chinadaily.com.cn/china/2006-09/24/content_695552.htm.

——. 2006a. China high-tech export grows 43.5% in past five years. *China Daily* (29th January 2006), http://www.chinadaily.com.cn/english/doc/2006-01/29/content_516335.htm.

——. 2006b. China Created Court to Enforce IP Cases. *China Daily* (10th March 2006), http://www.chinadaily.com.cn/english/doc/2006-03/10/content_531992.htm.

——. 2006c. Anti Monopoly Push May Hit Microsoft. *China Daily* (24th September 2006), http://www.chinadaily.com.cn/china/2006-09/24/content_695552.htm.

——. 2006d. President Hu Jintao New Year Address. *China Daily* (31st December 2006), http://www.chinadaily.com.cn/china/2007-01/01/content_772952.htm.

China Education and Research Network. 31st August 2001. Curriculum Reform. *CERNET*, http://www.edu.cn/20010831/200906.shtml.

China Information Online. *Oracle to Set up New R&D Center in China* 12th June 2002 [cited 9th August 2006]. Available from http://www.china.org.cn/english/investment/34394.htm.

China Internet Network Information Center. *Statistical Report on the Internet Development in China*. CNNIC 2006, July [cited 21st November 2006]. Available from http://www.cnnic.net.cn/en/index/0O/index.htm.

China Software Industry Association. [cited]. Available from http://www.csia.org.cn/chinese_en/index/index.htm.

Chiou, Jing-Yuan. 2005. A Simple Theory of Defensive Patenting. *Grenoble Applied Economic Laboratory* (April 2005), http://www.grenoble.inra.fr/Site/Conf/pages/Selected/050515_jychio_Defensive.pdf.

Chow, Daniel. 2003. Organised crime, local protectionism and the trade in counterfeit goods in China. *China Economic Review* 14: pp. 473–484.

Chow, Gregory C. 2002. *China's Economic Transformation*: Blackwell Publishers.

Comey, James. *Remarks of Deputy Attorney General James B. Comey, Jr.* 2005 [cited 28th February 2007]. Available from http://www.cybercrime.gov/Comey Remarks020504.htm.

Commission on Intellectual Property Rights. 2002. Integrating Intellectual Property Rights and Development Policy. London: Department for International Development, United Kingdom Government.

ComputerWorld. [cited 25th August 2006]. Available from http://www.computerworld.com/action/article.do?command=viewArticleBasic&articleId=87367.

Cook, Trevor, and Sandrine Rambaud. 2006–07. Problems with copyright in the Information Society Directive. *Copyright World. (Informa Law)*. Dec. 06 / Jan. 07 (Issue 166).

Correa, Carlos. 2003. Formulating Effective Pro-development National Intellectual Property Policies. In *Trading in Knowledge. Development Perspectives on TRIPS, Trade and Sustainability*, edited by C. Bellman, G. Dutfield and R. Melendez-Ortiz: Earthscan Publications.

——. 2005. Can the TRIPS Agreement foster technology transfer to developing countries? In *International Public Goods and Transfer of Knowledge. Under a Globalised Intellectual Property Regime*, edited by K. Maskus and J. Reichman: Cambridge University Press.

Crossick, Stanley, Fraser Cameron, and Axel Berkofsky. 2005. EU-China Relations—Towards a Strategic Partnership. *European Policy Centre, EU and Asia* (July 2005).

Das, Dilip K. 2001. *Global Trading System at the Crossroads*: Routledge.

David, Paul A. 2005. Koyaanisqatsi in Cyberspace. In *International Public Goods and Transfer of Knowledge. Under a Globalised Intellectual Property Regime*, edited by K. Maskus and J. Reichman: Cambridge University Press.

Davis, Christina. 2006. Do WTO rules create a level playing field? Lessons from the experience of Peru and Vietnam. In *Negotiating Trade. Developing Countries in the WTO and NAFTA*, edited by J. S. Odell: Cambridge University Press 2006.

Day, Peter. 2006. Speech: Role of Intellectual Ventures Corp. Paper read at Cambridge University Entrepreneurs Forum, 24th October 2006.

D'Costa, Anthony P. 2004a. Export Growth and Path Dependence: the locking in of innovation in the software industry. In *India in the Global Software Industry. Innovation, Firm Strategies and Development*, edited by A. P. D'Costa and E. Sridharan: Macmillan.

——. 2004b. The Indian Software Industry in the Global Division of Labour. In *India in the Global Software Industry. Innovation, Firm Strategies and Development*, edited by A. P. D'Costa and E. Sridharan: Macmillan.

Deardorff, Alan. 2006. *Terms of Trade. Glossary of International Economics*: World Scientific Publishing.

Dedrick, Jason, and Kenneth Kraemar. 1998. *Asia's Computer Challenge*: Oxford University Press New York.

Dernbach, Peter. 2005. From 301 Watch List to Leading Light—Taiwan's Copyright Turnaround. *World Copyright Law Report* (8th December 2005), http://www.worldcopyrightlawreport.com/.

Dezan Shira and Associates. *Minimum Salaries Rise in Tight Labour Markets* October 2006 [cited 31st October 2006]. Available from http://www.dezshira.com.

Digital Vector. October 2005. Indian Pharmaceutical Industry: Issues and Opportunities. http://www.piribo.com/publications/country/indian_pharma_issues.html.

Dowdle, Michael W. November 1999. Heretical Laments: China and the Fallacies of "Rule of Law". *Cultural Dynamics* Vol. 11 (No. 3): pp. 287–314.

Drahos, Peter. 2005. Death of a Patent System. In *Death of Patents*, edited by P. Drahos: Lawtext Publishing.

——. 2005. The Regulation of Public Goods. In *International Public Goods and Transfer of Knowledge. Under a Globalised Intellectual Property Regime*, edited by K. Maskus and J. Reichman: Cambridge University Press.

Drahos, Peter, and Ruth Mayne, eds. 2002. *Global Intellectual Property Rights. Knowledge, Access and Development*: Oxfam Palgrave.

Drahos, Peter, and with Braithwaite John. 2002. *Information Feudalism. Who Owns the Knowledge Economy?* London: Earthscan Publications.

Dudas, Jon. *Patent Prosecution Highway Program between USPTO. and JPO* 2006 [cited 30th January 2007]. Available from http://www.jpo.go.jp/torikumi/t_torikumi/pdf/highway_pilot_program/03.pdf.

Dutfield, Graham. 2003. Intellectual Property, Trade and Sustainable Development: Mounting Controversy. In *Trading in Knowledge. Development Perspectives on TRIPS, Trade and Sustainability*, edited by C. Bellman, G. Dutfield and R. Melendez-Ortiz: Earthscan Publications.

——. 2005. Is the World Ready for Substantive Patent Law Harmonisation? A Lesson from History. In *Death of Patents*, edited by P. Drahos: Lawtext Publishing.

E.U. Chamber of Commerce I.P.R. Working Group. 2006–07. European Business in China Position Paper http://www.europeanchamber.com.cn/upload/wysiwyg/20061010162128.pdf.

Economic Times Online. 2007a. Cipla lends support to anti-patent drive. *The Economic Times of India* (Thursday, 15th February, 2007), http://economictimes.indiatimes.com/articleshow/1614625.cms.

——. 2007b. Copycat drug cos convert, back MNCs on patents. *The Economic Times of India* (Friday 23rd February 2007), http://economictimes.indiatimes.com.

——. 2007c. Madras HC to rule on Novartis' patent case. *The Economic Times of India* (Tuesday 6th March 2007), http://economictimes.indiatimes.com.

Economist Online Edition. 2003. Roll over, Confucius. *The Economist* (23rd January 2003), http://www.economist.com/displaystory.cfm?story_id=1548706.

Economist Print Edition. 2004. A Survey of Outsourcing. *The Economist* (13th November 2004).

——. 2005a. Outsourcing and IT in India—Special Report. *The Economist* (23rd April 2005).

——. 2005b. Prescription for Change. A Survey of Pharmaceuticals. *The Economist* (18th June 2005).

——. 2005c. A Bad Week for Pirates. *The Economist* (2nd July 2005).

——. 2005d. A survey of patents and technology—Special Report. *The Economist* (22nd October 2005).

——. 2006. A survey of Business in India. *The Economist* (3rd June 2006).

Einhorn, Bruce. 2003. China Learns to Say "Stop, Thief". *BusinessWeek Online* (10th February 2003), http://www.businessweek.com/technology/content/feb2003/tc20030210_2338_tc058.htm

Empolis Company (Bertelsmann AG). *The PatAnalyst Patent Management Software Program* [cited 20th March 2007]. Available from http://www.patanalyst.com/.

Ernst & Young. 2006. Rising Confidence: Multinational Pharmaceutical Companies in India and China. *Progressions 2006*, http://www.ey.com/global/content.nsf/International/Pharmaceuticals_Library_Progressions_2006.

EUR-Lex. *European Union Law: Directive 2006/116/EC. Term of Protection of Copyright* 2006 [cited 20th February 2007]. Available from http://eur-lex.europa.eu/LexUriServ/LexUriServ.do?uri=CELEX:32006L0116:EN:NOT.

European Commission. *Trade Barriers Regulation* [cited 20th February 2007]. Available from http://ec.europa.eu/trade/issues/respectrules/tbr/index_en.htm.

——. 1995. 1307 Consultation on the Green Paper on the Protection of Utility Models in the Single Market SEC(2001) (COM(95)370). (July 1995), http://ec.europa.eu/internal_market/indprop/docs/model/consultation_en.pdf.

European Information Observatory. 2006. Worldwide IT Market Annual Growth 2005–2007. *EITO Market Report 2006*, http://www.eito.com/tables.HTML

European Parliament Observatory. 2002. Patentability of Computer Implemented Inventions. (COD/2002/0047), http://www.europarl.europa.eu/oeil/FindByProcnum.do?lang=en&procnum=CNS/2002/0047.

European Patent Office, The. 2006. The EPO's reply to the Commission's questionnaire on the patent system in Europe *EPO Press Releases* (12th July 2006), http://www.european-patent-office.org/news/pressrel/2006_07_12_reply_e.htm.

Evans, Gail. 2000. *Lawmaking under the Trade Constitution. A study in legislating by the World Trade Organisation*: Kluwer Law International.

Federation of Indian Chambers of Commerce and Industry. 2005. Competitiveness of the Indian Pharmaceutical Industry in the New Product Patent Regime *FICCI* (March 2005), http://www.ficci.com/studies/pharma.pdf.

Financial Times Asia Edition. 2007. Ranbaxy launches bid for Merck unit. *FT Online* (13th March 2007), http://www.ft.com.

Fitzgerald, Michael 2003. At risk offshore. *Computerworld Online: Management Section* (20th November 2003), http://www.computerworld.com/action/article.do?command=viewArticleBasic&articleId=87367.

Foese, Marc D. 2006. Contingent Protection Measures and the Management of the Softwood Lumber Trade in North America. *Estey Centre Journal of International Law and Trade Policy* (Vol. 7 / No. 2), http://www.esteycentre.ca/journal/j_pdfs/froese7-2.pdf.

Fortune Magazine (Print Edition). 2004. Inside the New China. *Fortune* Vol. 150 (No. 7, October 2004).

Franda, Marcus. 2002. *China and India Online: IT Politics and Diplomacy*: Rowman Publishers New York.

Fung, K. C., Lawrence J. Lau, and Yanyan Xiong. 2006. Adjusted Estimates of United States-China Bilateral Trade Balances: An Update. *Pacific Economic Review* Vol. 11 (No. 3): 299–314.

Galler, Bernard. 1995. *Software and Intellectual Property Protection: Copyright and Patent Issues for Computer and Legal Professionals*: Quorum.

Gehl-Sampath, Padmashree. 2007. Indian Pharma Within Global Reach? *Journal of Technology Analysis and Strategic Management* (September 2007), http://www.merit.unu.edu/publications/wppdf/2006/wp2006-031.pdf.

Gerhardsen, Tove Iren S. 2006. India Proposes Combined WIPO Meetings On Biodiversity, Patent Harmonisation. *Intellectual Property Watch Online* (10th April 2006), http://www.ip-watch.org/weblog/index.php?p=264&res=1024&print=0.

Govaere, Inge, and Paul Demaret. 2001. The TRIPS Agreement: A Response to Global Regulatory Competition of an Exercise in Global Regulatory Coercion? In *Regulatory Competition and Economic Integration: Comparative Perspectives*, edited by D. Esty and D. Geradin: Oxford University Press.

Government of Australia, Department of Foreign Affairs and Trade. Chapter Seventeen—Intellectual Property Rights. *Australia-United States Free Trade Agreement*, http://www.dfat.gov.au/trade/negotiations/us_fta/final-text/chapter_17.html.

Government of India Archive. *Pharmaceuticals Factsheet 2000* 2000 [cited 24th February 2007]. Available from http://pib.nic.in/archieve/factsheet/fs2000/pharmaceutical.html.

Government of India, Central Bureau of Investigation. *Overview of Interpol India Framework: Economic Offence Unit* [cited 25th August 2006]. Available from http://cbi.nic.in/.

Government of India IT Task Force. *Human Resource Development Initiatives* [cited 25th August 2006]. Available from http://www.it-taskforce.nic.in/actplan3/chap3.htm.

——. *ITEX 50* [cited 25th August 2006]. Available from http://www.it-taskforce.nic.in/itex50.htm.

Government of India Ministry of Communications and Information Technology. *Software Technology Parks of India* [cited 25th September 2006]. Available from http://www.stpi.in.

Government of India Ministry of Human Resource Development. *Overview of Copyright* [cited 18th September 2006]. Available from http://www.education.nic.in/copyright.asp.

——. 1999. Enforcement and Public Awareness of Copyright. *Study on Copyright Privacy in India*, http://www.education.nic.in/cr_piracy_study/cpr8.asp.

Government of Maharastra, India. 2003. IT and ITES Policy *ITES Policy Print Edition.*

Gowers, Andrew. 2006. The Gowers Review of Intellectual Property: HM Treasury, United Kingdom Government.

Grace, Cheri. 2004. The Effect of Changing Intellectual Property on Pharmaceutical Industry Prospects in India and China. In *Issues Paper—Access to Medicines*: DFID Health and Systems Resource Centre, June 2004.

Granstrand, Ove. 1999. *The Economics and Management of Intellectual Property. Towards Intellectual Capitalism*: Edward Elgar.

Grimmett, Jean. 2007. WTO Decisions and their Effect in US Law. *CRS Report for Congress RS22154* (30th January 2007), http://www.nationalaglawcenter.org/assets/crs/RS22154.pdf.

Grosheide, F. William. 2006. Globalisation, Convergence and Divergence in International Copyright Law: A Question of Expediency or of Right. In *New Directions in Copyright Law*, edited by F. Macmillan: Edward Elgar.

Guibault, L., and O. van Daaten. 2006. *Unravelling the Myth around Open Source Licenses. An Analysis from a Dutch and European Law Perspective*: TMC Asser Press.

Haas, Ernst B. 1964. *Beyond the Nation-State. Functionalism and International Organisation*: Stanford University Press.

Hammarlund, Per. 2005. *Liberal Internationalism and the Decline of the State. The Thought of Richard Cobden, David Mitrany and Kenichi Ohmae*: Palgrave Macmillan.

Hangzhou Municipal Government, P. R. China. *Science and Technology* [cited 9th August 2006]. Available from http://english.hangzhou.gov.cn/english/stin/node286/node289/userobject1ai945.html.

Harvard Centre for International Development. *India Summary* [cited 27th February 2007]. Available from http://www.cid.harvard.edu/cidtrade/gov/indiagov.html.

Heeks, Richard. 1996. *India's Software Industry. State Policy, Liberalisation and Industrial Development*: Sage Publications India.

——. 1998. The Uneven Profile of Indian Software Exports. *Development Informatics Working Paper Series, Institute for Development Policy and Management* (University of Manchester 1998).

Heeks, Richard, S. Krishna, Brian Nicholson, and Sundeep Sahay. 2000. Synching or Swimming: Trajectories and Strategies in Global Software Outsourcing Relationships. *Development Informatics Working Paper Series, Institute for Development Policy and Management*: University of Manchester.

Heiman, Richard V., and Anthony C. Picardi. 2006. Worldwide Software 2006–2010 Forecast Summary. (August 2006), http://www.idc.com/getdoc.jsp?containerId=203224.

Helfer, Lawrence R. 2004. Regime Shifting: The TRIPs Agreement and New Dynamics of International Intellectual Property Lawmaking. *The Yale Law Journal of International Law* Vol. 29 (No. 1 Winter 2004).

Hicks, Matthew. 2004. Software Licensing Moving Towards Utility Models. *eWeek Magazine* (20th October 2004), http://www.eweek.com/article2/0,1895,1680207,00.asp.

Hiddleston, Sarah. 2007. No need to patent small changes. *Frontline Magazine (The Hindu Online Edition)* (10th–23rd March 2007), http://www.hinduonnet.com/fline/fl2405/stories/20070323001604800.htm.

Hindu Business Line, The. 2006. 886 Drugs to be cheaper from Tomorrow. *The Hindu Online* (1st November 2006), http://www.blonnet.com/2006/11/01/stories/2006110102461000.htm.

Hindu Online, The 2006. Centre serious about copyright enforcement, says official. *The Hindu Online* (12 April 2006), http://www.hindu.com/2006/04/12/stories/2006041209370500.htm.

Hitchcock, Julian. 2006. China's New IP Action Plan. *Mills & Reeve Legal Comment* (May 2006), http://www.mills-reeve.com/article.asp?id=521.
Hoekman, Bernard, and Michael Kostecki. 2001. *The Political Economy of the World Trading System*: Oxford University Press.
Hu, Hongjun. 2006. Chinese office software maker eyes enterprise users. *China Economic Net* (8th June 2006), http://en.ce.cn/Insight/200606/08/t20060608_7259454.shtml.
Hufbauer, Gary. 2001. Trends and Prospects in the Global Economy. In *China, the United States and the Global Economy*, edited by S. Chen and C. Wolf Jr.: RAND.
Hughes, Prof. Justin. 2006. IP Enforcement in China, a potential WTO case, and US-China relations. *United States Congress, US-China Economic and Security Review Commission* (8th June 2006), http://www.uscc.gov/hearings/2006hearings/transcripts/june7_8/hughes_final_footnote.pdf.
Humphrey, John, and Dirk Messner. 2006. China and its Impact on Global and Regional Governance. *Institute of Development Studies* (DFID China Office, April 2006), http://www.ids.ac.uk/ids/global/AsianDriverpdfs/DfidAgendaPaper07.pdf.
IDC. 2006a. Worldwide Server Market Slows in Fourth Quarter. *IDC Market Analysis* (22nd February 2006), http://www.idc.com/getdoc.jsp?containerId=prUS20074406 (accessed 22nd November 2006).
——. 2006b. Intense Linux Competition in China, Market Landscape will Remain Unclear till Next Year. *IDC Market Analysis* (6th April 2006), http://www.idc.com/getdoc.jsp?containerId=prCN20118306 (22nd November 2006).
Idris, Kamil. 2003. *Intellectual Property. A Power Tool for Economic Growth*: WIPO.
Immigration Information Online. *The Overseas Citizenship of India* [cited 9th March 2007]. Available from http://www.immigrationboards.com/viewtopic.php?t=4779.
India Copyright Office. [cited 29th August 2006]. Available from http://copyright.gov.in/mainhome.asp.
India I.P. Wire Online. 2006. India, China set to achieve $ 20 billion trade by 2007. *India IP Wire* (17th March 2006), http://www.indiaprwire.com/pressrelease/other/20060317136.htm.
India Pharmaceutical Industry Portal. 2005. New Patent Law opens up vast business opportunities for Indian cos. *Pharmabiz* (2nd March 2005), http://www.pharmabiz.com/article/detnews.asp?articleid=26475&sectionid=42.
Indian Budget Office. 2006. India Economic Survey 2005–2006: Telecommunications. http://indiabudget.nic.in/es2005-06/chapt2006/chap94.pdf.
Indian Embassy to United States. *Policy Statement on Intellectual Property Rights and Enforcement of Copyright Law* [cited 24th September 2006]. Available from http://www.indianembassy.org/newsite/policystatements.asp.
——. *Special IP Section* [cited 2nd September 2006]. Available from http://www.indianembassy.org/special/ipr/ipr.htm.
——, *Indian Embassy Fact Sheet*, <http://www.indianembassy.org/indusrel/trade.htm>, [cited 1st September 2006] (archived record for historical access only).
Indian Journal of Traditional Knowledge. http://www.niscair.res.in/ScienceCommunication/ResearchJournals/rejour/ijtk/ijtk0.asp.
Information Office of the State Council, P. R. China. 2005. New Progress in China's Protection of Intellectual Property Rights: The State Council of P. R. China.
InfoSys Corporation. *Investors Annual Report 2006* 2006 [cited 25th September 2006]. Available from http://www.infosys.com/investor/reports/annual/Infosys_AR06.pdf.
Institute for Information Industry, Taiwan. 2008. *Introduction* [cited 4th July 2009]. Available from http://www.iii.org.tw/english/introduction.asp.
Institute of Directors. *The Benefits of Outsourcing* [cited 14th November 2006]. Available from http://www.iod.com.
——. 2006. Reflections on Doing Business in China. Summer 2006.

Intellectual Property Watch Online. 2006. India Proposes Combined WIPO Meetings On Biodiversity, Patent Harmonisation. *IP Watch* (10th April 2006).

Intellectual Ventures (Corporate Website). [cited 1st November 2006]. Available from http://www.intellectualventures.com/.

International Finance Corporation. 2005. The ICT Landscape in the PRC Market Trends and Investment Opportunities. (March 2005), www.ifc.org/ifcext/eastasia.nsf/AttachmentsByTitle/IFCReport_Chinese/$FILE/Report+V.2.0.pdf.

International Intellectual Property Alliance. 2001. Special 301 Report for India. *IIPA*, http://www.iipa.com/rbc/2001/2001SPEC301INDIA.pdf.

——. 2006. Consolidated Asia Pacific Report. *IIPA*, http://www.iipa.com/statistics.html.

——. *Special 301 Report—Submitted to the U.S. Trade Representative* 2008 [cited 2nd April 2009]. Available from http://www.ustr.gov/assets/Trade_Sectors/Intellectual_Property/Special_301_Public_Submissions_2008/asset_upload_file141_14486.pdf.

International Policy Network. 2004. Taxes and Tariffs deny patients access to medicines, says new study. *International Policy Network* (14th July 2004), http://www.policynetwork.net/main/press_release.php?pr_id=49.

Irwin Crookes, Paul. 2009. Maintaining Europe's Innovative Advantage: EU Policy Responses to the Asian Challenge in Pharmaceutics and Software. (Centre for European Studies, Brussels. 8th April 2009), http://www.thinkingeurope.eu/content.php?hmID=20&smID=34&ssmID=118.

Islam, Iyanatul, and Anis Chowdhury. 1997. *Asia-Pacific Economies. A Survey*: Routledge.

J.S. China Network Online. 2006. Suzhou Industrial Park-International Sci-Tech Park. (7th June 2006), http://english.jschina.com.cn/gb/jschina/english/biz/bizevents/userobject1ai1267748.shtml.

Japanese Patent Office. *History of Industrial Property Rights* [cited 22nd February 2007]. Available from http://www.jpo.go.jp/seido_e/.

Jiang Zhipei. *Judicial Protection for Copyright in Internet Environment by the People's Court* [cited 31st October 2006]. Available from http://www.chinaiprlaw.com/english/forum/forum50.htm.

——. *The questions about arbitration in China and the reply of Judge Jiang and Zhang* [cited 9th August 2006]. Available from http://www.chinaiprlaw.com/english/answers/answer27.htm.

Joyner, Christopher C. 1986. Legal Implications of the Concept of the Common Heritage of Mankind. *International and Comparative Law Quarterly* Vol. 35 (No. 1, January 1986): pp.190–199 (Oxford Journals).

Kalam, Dr. Abdul. 2006. Keynote Speech. Paper read at NASSCOM Annual Conference, at Mumbai, 17th February 2006.

Kamperman Sanders, Anselm. 2001. Legal Protection of Data and Databases. In *Intellectual Property in the Digital Age: The Challenges for Asia*, edited by C. Heath and A. Kamperman Sanders: Kluwer Law International.

Kasper, Alan. 2006. Corporate America's Slow Boat to China. *Managing Intellectual Property Print Edition—China IP Focus Special Supplement*: pp. 85–88.

Keane, Michael. Innovation and creativity in digital content industries in Australia and China: policy and practice. Paper read at International Cultural Industries Conference Proceedings, September 2004, at Taiyan, China.

Keith, Ronald, and Zhiqui Lin. 2001. *Law and Justice in China's New Marketplace*: Palgrave.

Keohane, Robert. 1993. The Analysis of International Regimes: Towards a European-American Research Progamme. In *Regime Theory and International Relations*, edited by V. Rittberger and P. Mayer: Oxford University Press.

——. 2005. Commentary on the Drahos Chapter. In *International Public Goods and Transfer of Knowledge. Under a Globalised Intellectual Property Regime*, edited by K. Maskus and J. Reichman: Cambridge University Press.

Knowledge@Wharton. 2008. Will India Become the New Vanguard of the Open Source Movement? (10th January 2008), http://knowledge.wharton.upenn.edu/india/article.cfm?articleid=4250.

Kong, Qingjiang. 2002. *China and the World Trading System: A Legal Perspective*: World Scientific Singapore.

Kopenski, Frank. 2002. A Closer Look: The Impact of Prescription Drugs Coming Off-Patent. *Millman Associates*, http://www.milliman.com/pubs/Healthcare/content/consultants_corner/Prescription-Drug-Patents-Expire-CC.pdf.

Korean Patent Office. *Annual Report 2005* [cited 1st February 2007]. Available from http://www.kipo.go.kr/kpo2/user.tdf?a=user.english.html.HtmlApp&c=60101&catmenu=ek60101.

KPMG International. 2006. Pharmaceuticals. The Indian Pharmaceutical Industry. http://www.kpmg.de/library/pdf/060618_KPMG_IndiaPharma_en.pdf.

Kretschmer, Martin. 2007. Is Copy Control Dead? *Copyright World. (Informa Law)*. Dec. 06 / Jan. 07 (Issue 166).

Kripalani, Manjeet. 2009. India's Madoff? Satyam Scandal Rocks Outsourcing Industry. *BusinessWeek Online* (7th January 2009), http://www.businessweek.com/globalbiz/content/jan2009/gb2009017_807784.htm.

Krishna Iyer, V. R. 2001. Natural justice and law. *The Hindu Online* (13th November 2001), http://www.hinduonnet.com/thehindu/br/2001/11/13/stories/2001111300120300.htm.

Krishnan, Rishikesha, and Ganesh Prabhu. 2004. Software Product Development in India: Lessons from Six Cases. In *India in the Global Software Industry. Innovation, Firm Strategies and Development*, edited by A. P. D'Costa and E. Sridharan: Macmillan.

Kumar, Sameer, Jamieson Jacky, and Sweetman Mathew. 2005. Software industry in the fastest growing market: challenges and opportunities. *International Journal of Technology Management* Vol. 29 Nos. 3/4: pp. 231–262.

Kwan , Nicholas, and Frances Cheung 2006. Asia Focus: Intra-Asia trade leads growth. *Hong Kong Trade Development Council (online)* (19th April 2006), http://international.tdctrade.com.

La Croix, Sumner, and Denise Eby Konan. 2002. Intellectual Property Rights in China: The Changing political Economy of China—American Interests. In *Department of Economics, University of Hawaii & Blackwell Publishers.*

Lacy, Sarah. 2006. Open Warfare in Open Source. *BusinessWeek Online* (21st August 2006), http://www.businessweek.com/technology/content/aug2006/tc20060818_977941.htm?campaign_id=techn_Aug21&link_position=link20.

Ladas & Parry Patent Attorneys. *US / Taiwan Memorandum of Understanding on Patents* [cited 2nd November 2006]. Available from http://www.ladas.com/Patents/patintl.html.

Lall, Chander M. 2004. Civil vs Criminal Remedies. *IndiaIP Online* (19th February 2004), http://www.indiaip.com/india/newsletters/civil_vs_criminal.htm.

Lamy, Pascal. 2004. Trade-Related Aspects of Intellectual Property Rights—Ten Years Later. *Journal of World Trade* Vol. 38 (No. 6).

Larkin, Adrian. 2007. Apple and EMI Deal. Songs Free of DRM. *BBC Music News Online* (2nd April 2007), http://www.bbc.co.uk/6music/news/20070402_apple.shtml.

Lateef, Asma. 1997. Linking up with the Global Economy: A Case Study of the Bangalore Software Industry. *International Institute for Labour Studies* (DP/96/1997), http://www.ilo.org/public/english/bureau/inst/papers/1997/dp96/index.htm.

Lavin, Franklin L. (US Under Secretary for International Trade). 2006. Interview on CCTV-9 "Dialogue" 07:30 Beijing Time. 2nd August 2006.

Lawsky, David, and Sabina Zawadzki. 2006. Microsoft to face challenge over Linux licenses. *Reuters News Agency* (21st November 2006), http://uk.reuters.com/article/ousiv/idUKL2059796120061121.

Lele, R. D. 2005. Impact of India's New Patents Law 2005: A Physician's Perspective. *Journal of The Association of Physicians of India* Vol. 53 (August 2005): pp. 871–875.

Levine, Robert. 2006. Geek Breaks iPod Code. *The Sunday Times*, 29th October 2006.

Lewis, W. Arthur. 1955. *The Theory of Economic Growth*: George Allen & Unwin.

Li, Mingzhi, and Ming Gao. 2003. Strategies for Developing China's Software Industry. *MIT Research Reports* Vol. 1 (No. 1, Fall 2003): pp. 61–73.

Lippoldt, Douglas. 2006. Can Stronger Intellectual Property Rights boost Trade, Foreign Direct Investment and Licensing in Developing Countries? In *The Intellectual Property Debate. Perspectives from Law, Economics and Political Economy*, edited by M. P. Pugatch: Edward Elgar.

Lisowski, Michael. 2003. A Three-Level Game Analysis of the International Climate Change Negotiations 2000/2001. Unpublished PhD Thesis, International Studies, University of Cambridge.

Lo, Vai Io, and Xiaowen Tian. 2005. *Law and Investment in China. The Legal and Business Environment after W.T.O. Accession*: Routledge Curzon.

Lou, Dr Jianbou. 2004. Lectures on Chinese Legal Reform: Lawmaking in the PRC. University of Cambridge Department of Law, Michaelmas Term, October / November 2004.

Lowe, Prof. John. 2006. Speech: Value of Patents to Smart Holograms Ltd. Paper read at Cambridge University Entrepreneurs Forum, 24th October 2006.

Lu, Qiwen. 2000. *China's Leap into the Information Age*: Oxford University Press.

Malavika, T. V. 2006. Intellectual property? Right! *The Hindu Online* (9th April 2006), http://www.thehindu.com/mag/2006/04/09/stories/2006040900150200.htm.

Managing Intellectual Property Online Edition. 2004. Interview with Samsung's IP Strategy Manager Kab-tae Han. Managing IP Online. Korean Special Supplement, http://www.managingip.com/?ISS=12728&PUBID=199&Page=17&SID=473483&SM=&SearchStr=.

——. 2005a. India takes a step forward in IP protection. *Managing IP Special Supplement—India IP Focus*, http://www.managingip.com/?Page=17&ISS=21608&SID=622159.

——. 2005b. India's biotech and software renaissance. *Managing IP Special Supplement—India IP Focus*, http://www.managingip.com/?Page=17&ISS=17631&SID=524406.

——. 2006a. Intellectual Property in 2005. The Starbucks Case in China. *Managing IP Online Supplement—China IP Focus*, http://www.managingip.com/?Page=17&ISS=21608&SID=622159.

——. 2006b. Microsoft Scores Chinese Software Victory. *Managing IP Weekly News* (7th April 2006), http://www.managingip.com/default.asp?Page=9&PUBID=198&SID=624434&ISS=21649.

Mann, Catherine. 2000. *Electronic Commerce in Developing Countries. Issues of Domestic Policy and W.T.O. Negotiations*: Institute for International Economics.

Mansfield, Edwin. 1986. Patents and Innovation: An Empirical Study. *Management Science* Vol. 32 (No. 2, February 1986).

Mansingh, Dr Surjit. 2005. India—China Relations in the Context of Vajpayee's 2003 Visit. *Sigur Center Asia, George Washington University* No. 21.

Mantell, Katie. 2002. India logs traditional knowledge. *Science and Development Network* (23 April), http://www.scidev.net/en/news/india-logs-traditional-knowledge.html.

Marsh, Peter. A New Twist to India IT Outsourcing. *Financial Times*, 31st January 2006.

Maskus, Keith. 2000. *Intellectual Property Rights in the Global Economy*. Washington D.C.: Institute for International Economics.

Maskus, Keith, and Jerome Reichman. 2005. The globalisation of private knowledge goods and the privatisation of global public goods. In *International Public Goods and Transfer of Knowledge. Under a Globalised Intellectual Property Regime*, edited by K. Maskus and J. Reichman: Cambridge University Press.

Mayall, James. 1975. Functionalism and International Economic Relations. In *Functionalism. Theory and Practice in International Relations*, edited by A. J. R. Groom and P. Taylor: University of London Press.

McGregor, Richard. 2007. China slams US over new WTO complaints. *Financial Times Online—Asia Pacific* (10th April 2007), http://www.ft.com/cms/s/79c28df2-e751-11db-8098-000b5df10621.html.

McKinnon, Robert, Ken Worzel, Greg Rotz, and Harriet Williams. 2004. Crisis. What Crisis? A Fresh Diagnosis of Big Pharma's R&D Productivity Crunch. (Marakon Associates 4th November 2004), http://www.marakon.com/ideas_pdf/id_041104_mckinnon.pdf.

McKinsey & Co. 2005. McKinsey Quarterly 2005. *McKinsey Quarterly* (Number 1), http://www.mckinseyquarterly.com/article_page.aspx?ar=1556&L2=4&L3=115&srid=7&gp=1.

——. 2006. The Value of China's Emerging Middle Class. *McKinsey Quarterly 2006-Special Edition*.

Menon, Deborah, ed. 2005. *China Intellectual Property Law Guide*: Kluwer Law International.

Menon, Ramesh. *Intellectual Property. Traditional knowledge receives a boost', India Together* (13th January) 2007 [cited 7th April 2009]. Available from www.indiatogether.org/2007/jan/eco-tkdl.htm.

Merges, Robert. 1996. Property Rights and the Software Industry. In *The International Computer Software Industry*, edited by D. Mowery. New York: Oxford University Press.

Mertha, Andrew. 2006. Testimony to the US-China Economic and Security Review Commission. *United States Congress, US-China Economic and Security Review Commission* (8th June 2006), http://www.uscc.gov/hearings/2006hearings/written_testimonies/06_06_08wrts/06_06_7_8_mertha_andrew.php.

Michalopoulos, Constantine. 2001. *Developing Countries in the WTO*: Palgrave.

Microsoft Corporation. 2006a. Lenovo and Microsoft Reaffirm Global Agreement. (17th April 2006), http://www.microsoft.com/presspass/press/2006/apr06/04–17LenovoPR.mspx.

——. 2006b. President Hu Jintao and Bill Gates to Discuss Microsoft's Commitment to the Chinese Software Industry. (18th April 2006), http://www.microsoft.com/presspass/press/2006/apr06/04–18ChinesePresidentPR.mspx.

——. *Annual Accounts for Financial Year to June 2006* 2006c [cited 10th November 2006]. Available from http://www.microsoft.com/msft/reports/ar06/flashversion/10k_fh_fin.html.

——. *Windows Vista Volume Activation* 2006d [cited 14th November 2006]. Available from http://www.microsoft.com/technet/windowsvista/plan/volact1.mspx.

——. 2006e. Microsoft Product Protection Platform. (4th October 2006), http://www.microsoft.com/presspass/features/2006/oct06/10–04SoftwareProtection.mspx.

Ministry of Information Industry, P. R. China. *Electronic Information Industry. Completion of Key Indicators* 2005 [cited 24th November 2006]. Available from http://www.mii.gov.cn.

Ministry of Science and Technology, P. R. China. *Ministry Press Room* [cited 5th August 2006]. Available from http://www.most.gov.cn/eng/pressroom/.

——. *Special Programmes: Project 863* [cited 5th August 2006]. Available from http://www.most.gov.cn/eng/programmes/programmes1.htm.

Mitrany, David. 1975. *The Functional Theory of Politics*: Martin Roberston Publishers.
Moffat, Mike. *Softwood Lumber Dispute Resource Center* [cited 22nd February 2007]. Available from http://economics.about.com/cs/agriculture/a/softwooddispute.htm.
Montgomery, Dr. Lucy. 2007. China's Film and Music Industries: Copyright, Business Models and Lessons. In *Defining the Field: Themes in Contemporary China Studies*. CRASSH Cambridge University.
Mossinghaf, Gerald, and Vivian Ku. 1998. World Patent System Circa 20XX, AD. *IDEA Journal of Law and Technology, Franklin Pierce Law Center* Vol. 38 1998.
Mukherjee, Ambarish 2006. Drug Companies Oppose Cost Based Pricing. *The Hindu Online* (6th October 2006), http://www.blonnet.com/2006/10/06/stories/2006100604770100.htm.
Multinational Monitor Online. 2006. Interview with Dr Hameid of Cipla: The Tamiflu Manufacturing Controversy. (Vol. 27 No. 2, Mar/Apr 2006), http://www.multinationalmonitor.org/mm2006/032006/interview-hamied.html.
Nambiar, Lakshmi. 2006. Sector report. IT Services Mid-Caps: The Untold Story: Avendus Ltd. India, February 2006.
Narlikar, Amrita. 2003. *International Trade and Developing Countries. Bargaining coalitions in the GATT and WTO, Studies in Global Political Economy*: Routledge.
——. 2005. *The World Trade Organization. A Very Short Introduction*: Oxford University Press.
——. 2007. Presentation of Unpublished Research on India, 14th February 2007: Centre of International Studies, University of Cambridge.
Narrain, Siddarth 2004. A life-saving order. *Frontline Magazine (The Hindu Online Edition)* (17th–30th July 2004), http://www.hinduonnet.com/fline/fl2115/stories/20040730004110300.htm.
Nath, Kamil. 2006. Keynote Speech. Paper read at NASSCOM Annual Conference, at Mumbai, 16th February 2006.
National Association of Software Service Companies. 2006. *Strategic Review 2006*: NASSCOM Publishing India.
——. (NASSCOM India). *Key Highlights of IT-ITES Sector Performance* [cited 10th November 2006]. Available from http://www.nasscom.in/Nasscom/templates/NormalPage.aspx?id=28485.
——. (NASSCOM India). *Mumbai cyber-lab for Police training and cyber-crime countermeasures* [cited 10th September 2006]. Available from http://www.nasscom.in/Nasscom/templates/NormalPage.aspx?id=6246.
——. (NASSCOM India). *NASSCOM Innovation Forum* [cited 31st October 2006]. Available from http://www.nasscom.in/Nasscom/templates/LandingPage.aspx?id=5721.
National Bureau of Statistics of China. 2005. China Statistical Yearbook 2005: Government of China.
——. 2006. China Statistical Yearbook 2006: Government of China.
National Science Foundation. 2006. Industry, Technology and the Global Marketplace. *Science and Engineering Indicators* (National Science Board, February 2006), http://www.nsf.gov/statistics/seind06/c6/c6h.htm.
National Torch Project of PRC China. *Innovation Fund for Technology Based Firms* [cited 20th March 2007]. Available from http://www.innofund.gov.cn/english/index.htm.
Naughton, Barry. 2007. *The Chinese Economy. Transitions and Growth*: MIT Press.
NeoIT Research. 2005. The China Reality Check. *Mapping Offshore Markets Update 2005* (Vol. 3/Issue 6, June 2005), http://www.neoit.com/gen/knowledgecenter/whitepapers.html.
Netcraft Web Statistics Review. [cited 21st November 2006]. Available from http://news.netcraft.com/.
——. [cited 21st November 2006]. Available from http://news.netcraft.com.

New, William. 2006. WIPO Broadcasting Treaty Advanced Past Disagreements *Intellectual Property Watch Online* (14th September 2006), http://www.ip-watch.org/weblog/index.php?p=395&res=1024&print=0.

New, William, and Tove Iren S. Gerhardsen. 2006. Group B+ Draft Patent Harmonisation Treaty Emerges. *Intellectual Property Watch Online* (7th November 2006), http://www.ip-watch.org/weblog/index.php?p=448&res=1024&print=0.

Newsweek (Print Edition). 2006. The Huawei Way. *Newsweek* (16th January 2006).

Newswire Today Online. 2005. Yahoo! Teams Up with China's Leading e-Commerce Company Alibaba.com. *Newswire Today* (8th December 2005), http://www.newswiretoday.com/news/1242/.

Nolan, Peter. 2001. *China and the Global Economy*: Palgrave.

——. *China at the Crossroads*: Polity Press.

Nollen, Stanley. 2004. Intellectual Property in the Indian Software Industry: Past Role and Future Need. *International Intellectual Property Institute, Washington D.C.* (June 2004).

Noronha, Frederick. India: Influential Voices Back "IP-Unencumbered" Software; Copyright Debate Heats up. *Intellectual Property Watch Online*, http://www.ip-watch.org/weblog/index.php?p=391&res=1024&print=0.

Noto, Aldo, Ami Shah, and John Harrop. 1999. The United States International Trade Court Commission and the Federal Court System as Fora for Challenging Unfair Chinese Intellectual Property Trade Activities. In *Chinese Intellectual Property Law and Practice*, edited by M. Cohen, E. Bang and S. Mitchell: Kluwer Law International.

O'Rourke, Prof. Maureen. 2006. The Story of Diamond v Diehr: Towards Patenting Software. In *Intellectual Property Stories*, edited by J. Ginburg and R. Cooper Dreyfuss: Foundation Press.

O Riain, Sean. 2004. *The Politics of High-Tech Growth. Developmental Network States in the Global Economy*: Cambridge University Press.

Oracle Corporation. *Oracle China Development Center* 2005 [cited 9th August 2006]. Available from http://www.pincn.com/clientpages/2005/oracle/youroracle/ocdc.htm.

Organisation for Economic Co-operation and Development. *Information and Communications Policy*. OECD 2006 [cited 9th November 2006]. Available from http://213.253.134.29/oecd/pdfs/browseit/9306051E.PDF.

——. 2008. *Review of Innovation Policy. China*: OECD.

Organisation for Economic Co-operation and Development Directorate for Science Technology and Industry. 1998. Measuring Electronic Commerce: International Trade in Software. (30th April 1998), http://www.oecd.org/dataoecd/32/52/2094340.pdf.

Organisation of Pharmaceutical Producers of India. 2008. *Position on IPR and Indian Patent Act 2005* [cited 3rd July 2009]. Available from http://www.indiaoppi.com/OPPIPositiononIPR.pdf.

Ostry, Sylvia. 1997. *The Post-Cold War Trading System. Who's On First?*: University of Chicago Press.

——. 2002a. The Uruguary Round North-South Grand Bairgain: Implications for future negotiations. In *The Political Economy of International Trade Law. Essays in Honor of Robert E. Hudec*, edited by D. Kennedy and J. Southwick: Cambridge University Press.

——. 2002b. The WTO Post Seattle and Chinese Accession. In *China and the Long March to Global Trade*, edited by S. Ostry, A. Alexandroff and R. Gomez: Routledge Curzon.

——. 2003. WTO Membership for China: To be and Not to be. In *China and the World Trading System. Entering the New Millennium*, edited by D. Cass, B. Williams and G. Barker: Cambridge University Press.

Oxfam. *Patent Rights and the US / Andean Free Trade Agreement* [cited 20th October 2006]. Available from http://www.oxfam.org.uk/what_we_do/issues/trade/bp90_andeanftas.htm.

Page Hargreave. *Overview of Utility Models* [cited 2nd November 2006]. Available from http://www.pagehargrave.co.uk/services/utility_models.html.

Pai, Yogesh Anand. 2007. Patent Protection for Computer Programs in India: Need for a Coherent Approach. *The Journal of World Intellectual Property* Vol. 10 (5): pp. 315–364.

Panagariya, Arvind. 2000. *E-commerce, WTO and Developing Countries, Policy Issues in International Trade Series 2*: United Nations.

Pantesco, Joshua 2006. China creates special intellectual property court. *Jurist Online Research, University of Pittsburgh School of Law* (10th March 2006), http://jurist.law.pitt.edu/paperchase/2006/03/china-creates-special-intellectual.php.

Partasarathi, Ashok, and K. J. Joseph. 2004. Innovation under Export Orientation. In *India in the Global Software Industry. Innovation, Firm Strategies and Development*, edited by A. P. D'Costa and E. Sridharan: Macmillan.

Pecht, Michael, Chung-Shing Lee, Zong Xiang Fu Jiang Lu, and Wang Yong Wen. 1999. *The Chinese Electronics Industry*: CRC Press New York.

Peerenboom, Randall. 2002. *China's Long March Toward Rule of Law*: Cambridge University Press.

People's Daily Online. *Comments of Chinese Minister of Commerce* (12th July 2005) 2005a [cited 24th February 2007]. Available from http://english.people.com.cn/200507/12/eng20050712_195513.html/.

——. 2005b. China Accelerates Curriculum Reform of Elementary Education. *People's Daily* (6th October 2005), http://english.people.com.cn/200510/06/eng20051006_212654.html.

——. 2006a. Ten features in China's 11th five-year plan *People's Daily* (8th March 2006), http://english.people.com.cn/200603/08/eng20060308_248947.html.

——. 2006b. Software Industry Posts 40% Revenue Growth *People's Daily* (17th March 2006), http://english.people.com.cn/200603/17/eng20060317_251505.html.

——. 2006c. China-India bilateral ties get a push *People's Daily* (21st November 2006), http://english.people.com.cn/200611/20/eng20061120_323530.html.

——. Statistical Difference in Sino-U.S. Trade Balance *People's Daily*, http://english.peopledaily.com.cn/whitepaper/16.html.

People's Republic of China Embassy to India. 2005. Bilateral economy and trade between China and India (30th April 2005), http://in.china-embassy.org/eng/jjmy/t193966.htm.

People's Republic of China Government Statement. *China Releases Revised 2004 GDP Figure* 2005 [cited 20th February 2007]. Available from http://english.gov.cn/2005-12/20/content_131956.htm.

——. *Patent application situation, statistics in 2005* 2006 [cited 25th August 2006]. Available from http://www.gov.cn/english/2006-02/15/content_187155.htm.

Pharmaceutical and Drug Manufacturers. *Drug Price Control Orders* [cited 25th November 2006]. Available from http://www.pharmaceutical-drug-manufacturers.com/pharmaceutical-policies/drugs-price-control-order.html.

PINR Internet News Portal. *Legal Framework of the Softwood Lumber Dispute* [cited 22nd February 2007]. Available from http://www.pinr.com/report.php?ac=view_report&report_id=361&language_id=1.

Poore, Alasdair. 2006. University Inventions—Lessons from Cambridge. (14th September 2006), http://pharmalicensing.com/articles/disp/1158246495_4509705f6bb6d.

Porsdam, Helle. 2005. From Pax Americana to Lex Americana: American Legal and Cultural Hegemony. In *New Directions in Copyright Law*, edited by F. Macmillan: Edward Elgar.

Porter, Michael. 1998. *The Competitive Advantage of Nations*: Macmillan Press.

Premji, Azim. 2006. Keynote Speech. Paper read at NASSCOM Annual Conference at Mumbai, 16th February 2006.
Price, Gareth, and David Wall. 2005. Friend and Foe. China, India and Japan. *The World Today. Chatham House.* Vol. 61 (No. 5, 2005).
Primo Braga, Carlos, Garston Fink, and Claudia Paz Sepulveda. 2000. Intellectual Property Rights and Economic Development. Washington D. C.: World Bank.
Pugatch, Meir Perez. 2004. *The International Political Economy of Intellectual Property Rights*: Edward Elgar.
Putnam, Dr. Tonya. 2006. Courts Without Borders: The Domestic Sources of US Extraterritorial Regulation. In *Wits Summer Institute.* University of Witwatersrand, July 2006.
Putnam, Robert. 1988. Diplomacy and Domestic Politics: The Logic of Two-Level Games. *International Organisation* Vol. 42 (Issue 3, Summer 1988): pp. 427–460.
Qu, Zhonghua, and Michael Brocklehurst. 2003. What will it take for China to become a competitive force in offshore outsourcing? An analysis of the role of transaction costs in supplier selection. *Journal of Information Technology* 18: pp. 53–67.
Raghavan, Chakravarthi *South North Monitor Service: GATT/WTO Negotiations* 1993 [cited 25th September 2006]. Available from http://www.sunsonline.org/trade/process/during/05130193.htm.
Ramanna, Anitha. 2005. Shifts in India's Policy on Intellectual Property. In *Death of Patents*, edited by P. Drahos: Lawtext Publishing.
Ramcharan, Robin. 2006. Singapore's Emerging Knowledge Economy: Role of Intellectual Property and its Possible Implications for Singaporean Society. *Journal of World Intellectual Property* Vol. 9 (No. 3, May 2006): pp. 316–343.
Red Flag Linux. *Red Flag China Joins OSDL* (7th January) 2005 [cited 22nd November 2006]. Available from http://www.redflag-linux.com/jujiao/enews_view.php?id=1000000031.
Redhat Linux Solutions. *Red Hat Announces Open Source Assurance to Safeguard Customer Investment* (20th January) 2004 [cited 22nd November 2006]. Available from http://www.redhat.com/about/presscenter/2004/press_OS_assurance.html.
Remfrey & Sagar. *Issue 7: Indian Government Approach to Intellectual Property Protection* [cited 10th September 2006]. Available from http://www.remfry.com/issue7.htm.
Reserve Bank of India. 2001. Handbook of Statistics on Indian Economy 2001: Reserve Bank of India.
——. 2006. Handbook of Statistics on Indian Economy 2006: Reserve Bank of India.
Rittberger, Volker. 1993. Research on International Regimes in Germany. In *Regime Theory and International Relations*, edited by V. Rittberger and P. Mayer: Oxford University Press.
Robat, Cornelius. *The History of Computing Project* [cited 18th November 2006]. Available from http://www.thocp.net.
Rodrigo, G. Chris. 2001. *Technology, Economic Growth and Crises in East Asia*: Edward Elgar.
Rooney, Paula. *Microsoft to Enforce Volume License Compliance* (26th June) 2006 [cited 14th November 2006]. Available from http://www.crn.com/sections/breakingnews/breakingnews.jhtml?articleId=189601573.
Rosamond, Ben. 2000. *Theories of European Integration*: Palgrave.
Rouse & Co. International Beijing. 2005. Intellectual Property Newsletter. (No. 255, 1st June 2005), http://www.iprights.com/publications/chinaipexpress/ciex_255.asp.
Rudman, Stephen Todd. 2006. *The Multinational Corporation in China*: Blackwell Publishing.
Sampath, Padmashree Gehl. 2006. India's Product Patent Protection Regime: Less or More of "Pills for the Poor"? *Journal of World Intellectual Property* Vol. 9 (No. 6, November 2006): pp. 694–726.

Schacht, Wendy. Patent Reform: Issues in Biomedical and Software Industries. *US Congressional Research Service*, http://www.fas.org/sgp/crs/misc/RL33367.pdf.

Schlesinger, Michael N., and Eric H. Smith. 1999. Crimes of Copyright Infringement Explained: The Prospect for Strong Judicial Enforcement Against Copyright Infringement. In *Chinese Intellectual Property Law and Practice*, edited by M. Cohen, E. Bang and S. Mitchell: Kluwer Law International.

Science Magazine (Online Edition). 2006. South Korean Team's Remaining Human Stem Cell Claim Demolished. *Science* (10th January 2006), http://sciencenow.sciencemag.org/cgi/content/full/2006/110/1.

Sell, Susan. 2004. Intellectual Property Protection and Anti Trust in the Developing World. Crisis, Coercion and Choice. (International Organisation 49 2 1995). In *Global Governance. Critical Concepts in Political Science*, edited by T. Sinclair.

——. 2003. *Private Power, Public Law. The Globalization of Intellectual Property Rights*: Cambridge University Press.

Shaffer, Gregory. 2005. Power, governance and the WTO: a comparative institutional approach, edited by M. Barnett and R. Duvall: Cambridge University Press.

Shah, Sanjay. 2006. Innovation Conclave and Seminar. Paper read at NASSCOM Annual Conference at Mumbai, 16th February 2006.

Shankland, Stephen. 2006. Windows Bumps Unix as Top Server OS. *CNet Online News* (21st February 2006), http://news.com.com/2100-1016_3-6041804.html.

Sherriff, Lucy. 2005. Vendors warn Euro patents bill wont add up. *The Register* (5th July 2005), http://www.theregister.co.uk/2005/07/05/patent_directive/.

Shi, Guangsheng. 2001. Deepening Co-operation and Achieving Common Prosperity. In *Recreating Asia: Visions for a New Century*, edited by F. J. Richter and P. Mar: John Wiley Asia, World Economic Forum 2001.

ShineTech Corporation, Beijing. *Company Overview: Team Skills and Costs* [cited 25th August 2006]. Available from http://www.shintechchina.com.

Sideri, Katerina. 2005. The Regulation of Peer-to-Peer File Sharing Networks. In *New Directions in Copyright Law*, edited by F. Macmillan: Edward Elgar.

Silicon Newswire Online. *Inside China Special Report* [cited 9th August 2006]. Available from http://www.silicon.com/research/specialreports/china/0,3800011742,39160774,00.htm.

Sivaprakasam, Dr. Kannan. *Commentary on Pharmacology Research* [cited 25th November 2006]. Available from http://www.boloji.com/health/articles/01036.htm.

Slaughter, Anne-Marie. 2004. *A New World Order*: Princeton University Press.

Software Information Industry Association / MacroVision. 2004. Key Trends in Software Pricing and Licensing. (October 2004), http://www.spa.org/software/pubs/SW_Pricing_Licensing_Report.pdf.

Sreedharan, Sunita (Anand & Anand Advocates). 2003. Intellectual property Rights in the Pharma Sector—Indian Initiatives. http://www.touchbriefings.com/download.cfm?fileID=488.

Sridharan, Eswaran. 2004. Evolving towards Innovation? The Recent Revolution and Future Trajectory of the Indian Software Industry. In *India in the Global Software Industry. Innovation, Firm Strategies and Development*, edited by A. P. D'Costa and E. Sridharan: Macmillan.

Srinivasan, T. N. 2002a. Emerging Issues in the World Trading System. In *Developing Countries in the World Trading System. The Uruguay Round and Beyond*, edited by R. Adhikari and P.-C. Athukorala: Edward Elgar.

——. 2002b. The TRIPS Agreement—Comment. In *The Political Economy of International Trade Law. Essays in Honor of Robert E. Hudec*, edited by D. Kennedy and J. Southwick: Cambridge University Press.

State Council, Government of China. 2006. Science & Technology Guidelines. Place Published. http://www.gov.cn/english/2006-02/09/content_183426.htm (accessed 25th February 2008).

State Council of P. R. China. *Policies for Encouraging The Development of Software Industry and Integrated Circuit Industry (Document No. 18)* (14th July) 2000 [cited 5th August 2006]. Available from http://www.csia.org.cn/chinese_en/index/No18.Document.html.

State Intellectual Property Office, P. R. China. 2005. China's Intellectual Property Protection 2005. *SIPO* (9th May 2006). http://www.sipo.gov.cn/sipo_English/laws/whitepapers/200804/t20080416_380356.html.

Stephens, Thomas B. 1992. *Order and Discipline in China. The Shanghai Mixed Court 1911–27*: University of Washington Press.

Sterkx, Sigrid. 2005. The Ethics of Patenting—Uneasy Justifications. In *Death of Patents*, edited by P. Drahos: Lawtext Publishing.

Stiglitz, Joseph. 2006. Scrooge and Intellectual Property Rights. *BMJ* (23 December 2006), http://www.bmj.com/cgi/content/full/333/7582/1279.

Stiglitz, Joseph, and Andrew Charlton. 2005. *Fair Trade for All. How Trade can Promote Development*: Oxford University Press.

Sun, Andy. 1998. From Pirate King to Jungle King: Transformation of Taiwan's Intellectual Protection. *Fordham Intellectual Property Media and Entertainment Law Journal* (Vol. IX/Book 1, Autumn 1998), http://law.fordham.edu/publications/index.ihtml?pubid=200.

Swamy, Subramanian 2001. *India's China Perspective*: Konark Publishers New Delhi.

Taft, Darryl. 2005. China's Red Flag sees Desktop as Linux battlefield. *eWeek Magazine* (13th December 2005), http://www.eweek.com/article2/0,1895,1900214,00.asp.

Taplin, Prof. Ruth. *Japanese Measures against IP infringement in China South Korea and Taiwan* (August) 2005 [cited 23rd January 2007]. Available from http://scientific.thomson.com/news/newsletter/2005-08/8283393/.

Taube, Florian 2002. Structural Change and Economic Development in India: The Impact of Culture on the Indian Software Industry. *Johann Wolfgang Goethe-University Research Papers, Frankfurt*, http://www.thinkcycle.org/tc-filesystem/?folder_id=37505 (download centre).

Taubman, Anthony. 2003. TRIPS Goes East: China's interests and international trade in itellectual property. In *China and the World Trading System. Entering the New Millennium*, edited by D. Cass, B. Williams and G. Barker: Cambridge University Press.

Teiwes, Frederick C. 1997. The Establishment and Consolidation of the new regime, 1949–57. In *The Politics of China. The Eras of Deng and Mao*, edited by R. MacFarquar: Cambridge University Press.

Thatcher, Margaret. 1993. *The Downing Street Years*: Harper Collins.

The Indus Group (TiE). [cited 15th January 2007]. Available from http://www.tie.org/Home/Programs/TiE%20SIGs/index_html/view_document.

Thurrott, Paul. *Windows Details Vista Anti Piracy* [cited 14th November 2006]. Available from http://www.windowsitpro.com/Article/ArticleID/93756/93756.html?Ad=1.

Transparency International. [cited 9th August 2006]. Available from http://www.transparency.org/policy_research/surveys_indices/cpi/2005.

Trebilcock, Michael, and Robert Howse. 1999. *The Regulation of International Trade*: Routledge.

Trefler, Daniel. 2005. Offshoring: Threat and Opportunities. *Brookings Trade Forum* (May 2005), http://muse.jhu.edu/cgi-bin/access.cgi?uri=/journals/brookings_trade_forum/v2005/2005.1trefler.html.

Tsigarides, Jody. *Samsung Set to Enforce Patent* (15th December) 2005 [cited 23rd January 2007]. Available from http://www.lawdit.co.uk/reading_room/room/view_category.asp?catcode=33.

United Kingdom Copyright Service. *Copyright Fact Sheet* [cited 20th February 2007]. Available from http://www.copyrightservice.co.uk/copyright/p01_uk_copyright_law.

United Kingdom Department of Health. *UK Stem Cell Initiative* [cited 31st October 2006]. Available from http://www.advisorybodies.doh.gov.uk/uksci/global/china.htm.

United Kingdom Government Revenue & Customs. 2006. UK World Trade 2001–2006 SITC 542: Medicaments for China, India, USA. http://www.uktradeinfo.com.

United Kingdom Patent Office. *Overview of Petty Patents* [cited 2nd November 2006]. Available from http://www.patent.gov.uk/policy/policy-issues/policy-issues-patents/policy-issues-patents-utility.htm.

United Nations Commission on International Trade Law. 2006. 1958-Convention on the Recognition and Enforcement of Foreign Arbitral Awards—the "New York" Convention. http://www.uncitral.org/uncitral/en/uncitral_texts/arbitration/NYConvention.html.

United Nations Conference on Trade and Development. *Transnational Corporations Statistics* [cited 22nd February 2007]. Available from http://www.unctad.org/templates/Page.asp?intItemID=3159&lang=1.

United States Archives. *The United States Constitution* [cited 20th March 2007]. Available from http://www.archives.gov/national-archives-experience/charters/constitution_transcript.html.

United States Association of Research Libraries. History of Copyright in the United States. *ARL*, http://www.arl.org/info/frn/copy/timeline.html.

United States Congress, Committee on the Judiciary. 1996. Congressional Report on the Copyright Term Extension Act July 1996. http://frwebgate.access.gpo.gov/cgi-bin/getdoc.cgi?dbname=104_cong_reports&docid=f:sr315.104.pdf.

United States Congress Office of Technology Assessment. 1990. Computer Software and Intellectual Property Background Paper OTA-BP-CIT-61: United States Congress.

United States Copyright Office. *Overview of Copyright* [cited 20th February 2007]. Available from http://www.copyright.gov/circs/circ1.html.

——. *Public Law 105th Congress—Copyright* [cited 20th February 2007]. Available from http://www.copyright.gov/legislation/pl105–298.pdf.

United States Department of Commerce. *Buy USA Information Service* [cited 23rd November 2006]. Available from http://www.buyusa.gov/china/en/computers.html#section_2.

——. 2006. Import, Exports, Balance of SITC 542–Medicaments. http://tse.export.gov.

——. 2006. Statistical Abstract of the United States: United States Government.

United States Department of Commerce, Commissioner of Patents and Trademarks Bruce A. Lehman. Right of Priority in Patent and Trademark Applications Available in Taiwan (30th April 1996). http://www.uspto.gov/go/og/con/files/cons086.htm.

United States Embassy to P.R. China. *The IPR Toolkit*. United States Government [cited 20th February 2007]. Available from http://beijing.usembassy-china.org.cn/protecting_ipr.html.

United States Federal Trade Commission. 2003. To Promote Innovation. The Proper Balance of Competition and Patent Law and Policy. (October 2003), http://www.ftc.gov/os/2003/10/innovationrpt.pdf.

United States Patent & Trademark Office. *Patent Search* [cited 20th September 2006]. Available from http://patft.uspto.gov/netahtml/PTO/search-adv.htm.

——. *Website* [cited 20th February 2007]. Available from http://www.uspto.gov.

——. 2005. Patent Law Harmonization Talks Stall; Brazil, Argentina, India Oppose Compromise. (14th June 2005), http://www.uspto.gov/main/homepagenews/bak2005jun14.htm.

United States Supreme Court. 1952. Steele v Bulova Watch Company Supreme Court 344 US 280.

——. 1981. Diamond versus Diehr US 175.

——. 2005. MGM Studios Inc. et al versus Grokster Limited et al. No. 04–480.

United States Trade Commission. *About the Commission* [cited 22nd February 2007]. Available from http://www.usitc.gov/ext_relations/about_itc/index.htm.

United States Trade Representative. *Exchange of Letters on Implementation of the U.S.-Australia Free Trade Agreement* [cited 22nd January 2007]. Available from http://www.ustr.gov/Trade_Agreements/Bilateral/Australia_FTA/Implementation/Section_Index.html.

——. 2002. India: Foreign Trade Barriers. *Trade Review Library Reports*, [cited 10th November 2006]. Available from http://www.ustr.gov/assets/Document_Library/Reports_Publications/2002/2002_NTE_Report/asset_upload_file830_6410.pdf.

——. 2006a. The Priority Watch List. *Special 301 Report*, http://www.ustr.gov/Document_Library/Reports_Publications/2006/2006_Special_301_Review/Section_Index.html.

——. 2006b. US—China Trade Relations: Entering a New Phase of Greater Accountability and Enforcement. *USTR Special Report*, http://www.ustr.gov/assets/Document_Library/Reports_Publications/2006/asset_upload_file921_8938.pdf.

——. 2004. US and Australia Address F.T.A. Implementation Issues *USTR Press Release* (17th November 2004), http://www.ustr.gov/assets/Document_Library/Press_Releases/2004/November/asset_upload_file236_6752.pdf.

United States Trade Representative, Document Archive. *1996 National Trade Esimate-India' [sic]* 1996 [cited 2nd April 2009]. Available from http://www.ustr.gov/Document_Library/Reports_Publications/1996/1996_National_Trade_Estimate/1996_National_Trade_Esimate-India.html?ht=.

University of Cambridge. *Intellectual Property Policy* [cited 1st November 2006]. Available from http://www.rsd.cam.ac.uk/about/policies/ip/ApprovedRegs.pdf.

Unnikrishnan, C. H. 2008. Natco withdraws plea on making patented cancer drugs. *LiveMint Wall Street Journal* (28th September), http://www.livemint.com/2008/09/28214903/Natco-withdraws-plea-on-making.html.

van Lam, Ngo, and Thitapha Wattanapruttipaisan. 2005. From Grain-Sized Innovations to Triple-Test Patents in Asean: Patterns, Issues and Implications in Development and Competitiveness. *ASEAN Economic Bulletin* Vol. 22 (No. 2).

van Wendel de Joode, R., J. A. De Bruijn, and M. J. G. van Eeten. 2003. *Protecting the Virtual Commons. Self-organising open source and free software communities and innovative intellectual property regimes*: TMC Asser Press.

Virtual Library Arbitration Database. 1999. Reservations: Convention on the Recognition and Enforcement of Foreign Arbitral Awards. Done at New York on 10 June 1958. *Interarb*, http://interarb.com/nyc/reservations.

VISA Asia. *VISA Asia Factsheet on China Market Activity* 2005 [cited 14th November 2006]. Available from http://www.visa-asia.com/ap/sea/mediacenter/factsheets/markets.shtml.

Wachter, Patrick. 2007. Project Watch—Chinese outsourcing on the rise. *Computer Business Review Online Edition* (2nd April 2007), http://www.cbronline.com/article_cbr.asp?guid=ED23811B-B0B2-465B-BD99-78AD9C0A889E.

Wade, Robert. 2004. *Governing the Market: economic theory and the role of government in East Asian industrialization*. Second Paperback Edition [Original 1990] ed: Princeton University Press. Original edition, Princeton University Press 1990.

Wang, Carol. 2006. Keeping Up. Regulations and Case Law during 2006. China. *Copyright World. (Informa Law)*. Dec. 06 / Jan. 07 (Issue 166).

Wang, Hui. 2001. US-China: Bonds and Tensions. In *China, the United States and the Global Economy*, edited by S. Chen and C. Wolf Jr.: RAND.

Watt, Richard. 2000. *Copyright and Economic Theory. Friends or Foes?*: Edward Elgar.

Weinstock Netanel, Neil, ed. 2008. *The Development Agenda. Global Intellectual Property and Developing Countries*: Oxford University Press.

Westkamp, Guido. 2005. Convergence of Intellectual Property Rights and the Establishment of 'Hybrid' Protection under TRIPS. In *New Directions in Copyright Law*, edited by F. Macmillan: Edward Elgar.

Whitman, Jim. 2005. *The Limits of Global Governance*: Routledge.

Wilkinson, Rordon. 2000. *Multilateralism and the World Trade Organisation. The Architecture and Extension of International Trade Regulation*: Routledge.

Wolfe, Robert. 1999. From War to Working Peace: the Functional Approach to the Management of Trade Conflict. In *New Perspectives on International Functionalism*, edited by L. Ashworth and D. Long: International Political Economy Press.

World Bank. 2002. Intellectual Property. Balancing Incentives with Competitive Access. In *Global Economic Prospects and the Developing Countries.* Washington D.C.

World Information Technology and Services Alliance. *What is WITSA?* [cited 15th January 2007]. Available from http://www.witsa.org/about/index.htm.

World Intellectual Property Organisation. 1996 Reprinted 2002. *Implications of the TRIPS Agreement on Treaties Administered by WIPO*: WIPO Publication No. 464E, Geneva.

——. *International Treaties and Conventions on Intellectual Property* [cited 20th October 2006]. Available from http://www.wipo.int/about-ip/en/iprm/pdf/ch5.pdf.

——. *Observer Rules* [cited 31st October 2006]. Available from http://www.wipo.int/members/en/organizations.jsp?type=NGO_NAT.

——. *The Patent Cooperation Treaty* [cited 2nd November 2006]. Available from http://www.wipo.int/treaties/en/registration/pct/.

——. 2004a. Submission to SCP by the Trilateral Offices. (May 2004), http://www.wipo.int/edocs/mdocs/scp/en/scp_10/scp_10_9.pdf.

——. 2004b. Patent Harmonisation. (May 2004), http://www.wipo.int/patent/law/en/harmonization.htm.

——. 2005. Focus on Trademarks. *WIPO Magazine* (WIPO Publications, Geneva. March–April 2005), http://www.wipo.int/edocs/mdocs/scp/en/scp_11/scp_11_4.pdf.

——. 2006a *WIPO Patent Report 2006* [cited 20th January 2007]. Available from http://www.wipo.int/ipstats/en/statistics/patents/pdf/patent_report_2006.pdf.

World Intellectual Property Organisation. 2006b *WIPO Patent Bulletin 2006* [cited 20th October 2006]. Available from http://www.wipo.int/portal/en/news/2006/article_0010.html.

——. 2006c *Standing Committee on Copyright and Related Rights Fifteenth Session* (19th July) [cited 2nd November 2006]. Available from http://www.wipo.int/edocs/mdocs/mdocs/en/sccr_15/sccr_15_14.pdf.

——. *The Patent Law Treaty* [cited 17th January 2007]. Available from http://www.wipo.int/treaties/en/ip/plt/summary_plt.html.

——. *Protocol Relating to the Madrid Agreement Concerning the International Registration of Marks* [cited 18th January 2007]. Available from http://www.wipo.int/madrid/en/pub_418/intro.htm.

——. *Report on worldwide patenting* [cited 20th October 2006]. Available from http://www.wipo.int/portal/en/news/2006/article_0010.html.

——. Submission by Brazil to Standing Committee on Patents. http://www.wipo.int/edocs/mdocs/scp/en/scp_11/scp_11_4.pdf.

——. *Summaries of Conventions, Treaties and Agreements Administered by WIPO*: WIPO Publication No. 442E, Geneva.

——. *WIPO Arbitration and Mediation Center* [cited 27th February 2007]. Available from http://www.wipo.int/amc/en/center/background.html.

World Trade Organisation. *Document Query Homepage* [cited 28th February 2007]. Available from http://www.wto.org/english/tratop_e/dispu_e/find_dispu_documents_e.htm.

——. *Index of Dispute Issues—TRIPS* [cited 12th January 2007]. Available from http://www.wto.org/english/tratop_e/dispu_e/dispu_subjects_index_e.htm#trips.

——. 2005a. Offshoring Services. *WTO Trade Report 2005*.

——. *Ministerial Declaration 18th December 2005: E-Commerce Section* 2005b [cited 18th November 2006]. Available from http://www.wto.org/English/thewto_e/minist_e/min05_e/final_text_e.htm#ecom.

——. 2005c. Members OK amendment to make health flexibility permanent. *WTO Trade Press Release* (6th December 2005), http://www.wto.org/english/news_e/pres05_e/pr426_e.htm.

——. 2006a. *Role of Experts and Advisors within the DSU* [cited 31st October World Trade Organisation. Recent Trade Developments: International Payments and Receipts of Royalties and License Fees 1995–2004]. *WTO Trade Report 2006*. 2006. Available from http://www.wto.org/english/thewto_e/whatis_e/tif_e/disp1_e.htm.

——. 2006b. World Trade 2005. Prospects for 2006. *WTO Trade Press Release 437* (11th April 2006).

——. 2006c *Trade Review for China 2006* [cited 18th November 2006]. Available from http://www.wto.org/english/tratop_e/tpr_e/s161-3_e.doc.

——. *The TRIPS Agreement: Legal Text* [cited 12th January 2007]. Available from http://www.wto.org/english/docs_e/legal_e/27-trips_01_e.htm.

Wunsch-Vincent, Sacha. 2005. *WTO, E-commerce and Information technologies. A Report to the UNICT Task Force*. Edited by J. McIntosh: United Nations.

——. 2006. *The WTO, the Internet and Trade in Digital Products. EC-US Perspectives*: Oxford.

Xinhua News Agency. 2006a. Chinese president calls for improvement of IPR system. *Xinhua* (27th May 2006), http://news.xinhuanet.com/english/2006-05/27/content_4609911.htm.

——. 2006b. IPR push sees patent applications rise. *Xinhua* (31st May 2006), http://news.xinhuanet.com/english/2006-05/31/content_4627632.htm.

Yang, Deli. 2003. *Intellectual Property and Doing Business in China*: Pergamon.

——, Pervez Ghuari, and Mahmut Sonmez. 2005. Competitive Analysis of the Software Industry in China. *International Journal of Technology Management* Vol. 29 (Nos. 1 & 2): pp. 64–91.

Yu, Peter K. 2008. Access to Medicines, BRICS Alliances, and Collective Action. *American Journal of Law & Medicine* Vol. 34: pp. 345–394.

Yuan, Yuan. 2006. Intellectual property Policy. Domestic Constraints on the International Negotiating Positions. Unpublished Master's Thesis, International Studies, University of Cambridge.

Zujic, Kosta. 2005. Memorandum on Chinese Law Ref KZ/25766.6. *Goodman Derrick Solicitors London* (29th March 2005).

Zwaniecki, Andrzej. 2006. Treasury Chief Urged To Promote Shift in China's Economic Strategy. *International Information Programs, US Department of State* (12 December 2006), http://london.usembassy.gov/china189.html.

INDEX

Social Sciences in Asia

1. Thang, L.L. and W.-H. Yu (eds.). *Old Challenges, New Strategies.* Women, Work and Family in Contemporary Asia. 2004. ISBN 90 04 13732 7
2. Lyons, L. *State of Ambivalence.* The Feminist Movement in Singapore. 2005. ISBN 90 04 13139 6
3. Hassan, R. (ed.). *Local and Global: Social Transformation in Southeast Asia.* Essays in Honour of Professor Syed Hussein Alatas. 2005. ISBN 90 04 14158 8
4. Ho, E.P. *Times of Change.* A Memoir of Hong Kong's Governance 1950-1991. 2005. ISBN 90 04 14047 6
5. Baber, Z. (ed.). *CyberAsia.* The Internet and Society in Asia. 2006. ISBN 90 04 14625 3
6. Abdul Rahman, N.A. *Colonial Image of Malay Adat Laws.* A Critical Appraisal of Studies on Adat Laws in the Malay Peninsula during the Colonial Era and Some Continuities. 2006. ISBN 90 04 15056 0
7. Lian, K.F. (ed.). *Race, Ethnicity, and the State in Malaysia and Singapore.* 2006. ISBN 90 04 15096 X
8. Therborn, G. and Habibul Haque Khondker (eds.). *Asia and Europe in Globalization.* Continents, Regions and Nations. 2006. ISBN-13 978 90 04 15350 9, ISBN-10 90 04 15350 0
9. Dake, A.C.A. *The Sukarno File, 1965-1967.* Chronology of a Defeat. 2006. ISBN-13 978 90 04 15382 0, ISBN-10 90 04 15382 9
10. Mizukami, T. *The Sojourner Community.* Japanese migration and residency in Australia. 2006. ISBN-13 978 90 04 15479 7, ISBN-10 90 04 15479 5
11. Chan, K.B. *Work Stress and Coping Among Professionals.* 2006. ISBN-13 978 90 04 15480 3, ISBN-10 90 04 15480 9
12. Koning, J. and Frans Hüsken (eds.). *Ropewalking and Safety Nets.* Local Ways of Managing Insecurities in Indonesia. 2006. ISBN-13 978 90 04 15487 2, ISBN-10 90 04 15487 6
13. Tong, Chee-Kiong. *Rationalizing Religion.* Religious Conversion, Revivalism and Competition in Singapore Society. 2007. ISBN 978 90 04 15694 4
14. Washburn, D. and A.K. Reinhart (eds.). *Converting Cultures.* Religion, Ideology and Transformations of Modernity. 2007. ISBN 978 90 04 15822 1
15. Kim, Kyong-Dong and Lim, Hyun-Chin (eds.). *East Meets West.* Civilizational Encounters and the Spirit of Capitalism in East Asia. 2007. ISBN 978 90 04 16021 7
16. Tan, K.P. *Cinema and Television in Singapore.* Resistance in One Dimension. 2008. ISBN 978 90 04 16643 1
17. Lian, Kwen Fee and Tong, Chee-Kiong (eds.). *Social Policy in Post-Industrial Singapore.* 2008. ISBN 978 90 04 16642 4
18. Sinha, J.N. *Science, War and Imperialism.* India in the Second World War. 2008. ISBN 978 90 04 16645 5
19. Lim, D.C.L. (ed.). *Overcoming Passion for Race in Malaysia Cultural Studies.* 2008. ISBN 978 90 04 16815 2

20. Lim, F. Khek Gee. *Imagining the Good Life*. Negotiating Culture and Development in Nepal Himalaya. 2008. ISBN 978 90 04 16787 2
21. Yahya, F. *New "Temples" of India*. Singapore and India Collaboration in Information Technology Parks. 2008. ISBN 978 90 04 17064 3
22. Narayanan, G. *Policing Marital Violence in Singapore*. 2008. ISBN 978 90 04 17131 2
23. Straughan, P.T. *Marriage Dissolution in Singapore*. Revisiting Family Values and Ideology in Marriage. 2009. ISBN 978 90 04 17161 9
24. Kudaisya, M. and Ng Chin-keong (eds.). *Chinese and Indian Business*. Historical Antecedents. 2009. ISBN 978 90 04 17279 1
25. Pirbhai, M.R. *Reconsidering Islam in a South Asian Context*. 2009. ISBN 978 90 04 17758 1
26. Lim, F. Khek Gee (ed.). *Mediating Piety*. Technology and Religion in Contemporary Asia. 2009. ISBN 978 90 04 17839 7
27. Irwin Crookes, P.C. *Intellectual Property Regime Evolution in China and India*. Technological, Political and Social Drivers of Change. 2010. ISBN 978 90 04 17975 2

ISSN 1567-2794

www.ingramcontent.com/pod-product-compliance
Lightning Source LLC
La Vergne TN
LVHW080644011026
849160LV00014B/1320